The Abbasid Calipha

The period of the Abbasid caliphate (750–1258) has long been recognized as the formative period of Islamic civilization with its various achievements in the areas of science, literature, and culture. This history of the Abbasid caliphate from its foundation in 750 and golden age under Harun al-Rashid to the conquest of Baghdad by the Mongols in 1258 examines the caliphate as an empire and institution, and probes its influence over Islamic culture and society. Ranging widely to survey the entire five-century history of the Abbasid dynasty, Tayeb El-Hibri examines the resilience of the caliphate as an institution, as a focal point of religious definitions, and as a source of legitimacy to various contemporary Islamic monarchies. The study revisits ideas of 'golden age' and 'decline' with a new reading, tries to separate Abbasid history from the myths of the Arabian Nights, and shows how the legacy of the caliphs continues to resonate in the modern world in direct and indirect ways.

TAYEB EL-HIBRI is Professor of Near Eastern Studies at the University of Massachusetts, Amherst. He is the author of *Parable and Politics in Early Islamic History: The Rashidun Caliphs* (2010) and *Reinterpreting Islamic Historiography: Harun al-Rashid and the Narrative of the Abbasid Caliphate* (1999), which won the Albert Hourani Award Honorable Mention at the Middle East Studies Association Convention in 2000. He has published articles on the Abbasids in journals including *Arabica, Der Islam, International Journal of Middle East Studies, Journal of the American Oriental Society,* and *Journal of the Economic and Social History of the Orient.*

The Abbasid Caliphate

A History

TAYEB EL-HIBRI
University of Massachusetts, Amherst

CAMBRIDGE
UNIVERSITY PRESS

CAMBRIDGE
UNIVERSITY PRESS

University Printing House, Cambridge CB2 8BS, United Kingdom

One Liberty Plaza, 20th Floor, New York, NY 10006, USA

477 Williamstown Road, Port Melbourne, VIC 3207, Australia

314–321, 3rd Floor, Plot 3, Splendor Forum, Jasola District Centre, New Delhi – 110025, India

79 Anson Road, #06–04/06, Singapore 079906

Cambridge University Press is part of the University of Cambridge.

It furthers the University's mission by disseminating knowledge in the pursuit of education, learning, and research at the highest international levels of excellence.

www.cambridge.org
Information on this title: www.cambridge.org/9781107183247
DOI: 10.1017/9781316869567

First published 2021

Printed in the United Kingdom by TJ Books Limited, Padstow Cornwall

A catalogue record for this publication is available from the British Library.

Library of Congress Cataloging-in-Publication Data
Names: El-Hibri, Tayeb, author.
Title: The Abbasid Caliphate : a history / Tayeb El-Hibri.
Description: Cambridge, United Kingdom ; New York : Cambridge University Press, 2021. | Includes bibliographical references and index.
Identifiers: LCCN 2020035181 (print) | LCCN 2020035182 (ebook) | ISBN 9781107183247 (hardback) | ISBN 9781316634394 (paperback) | ISBN 9781316869567 (ebook)
Subjects: LCSH: Abbasids – History. | Islamic Empire – History – 750–1258.
Classification: LCC DS38.6 .E45 2021 (print) | LCC DS38.6 (ebook) | DDC 909/ .0982201–dc23
LC record available at https://lccn.loc.gov/2020035181
LC ebook record available at https://lccn.loc.gov/2020035182

ISBN 978-1-107-18324-7 Hardback
ISBN 978-1-316-63439-4 Paperback

To my mother,
Salma Sibai

Contents

The plate section can be found between pp 192 and 193.

Figures

Plates

Black and White Figures and Coins

Maps

Acknowledgments

In the Western world, Islamic history is a field of many camps of scholars and many gaps of knowledge. I have eschewed its camps but have been interested in filling its gaps, and one of these is the glaring absence of a book on the Abbasid caliphate from its rise in 750 to its conquest in 1258. A root for this book grew out of a course that I taught on the Abbasids during a two-year stint as the visiting Alfred Howell Chair in the History Department at the American University of Beirut in 2014–2016. The variety of junctures often suggested for the end of Abbasid influence, whether in 861, 945, or 1055 CE, always seemed to be followed by resilience that required an explanation, and eventually it seemed that the story had to be traced for the entirety of a five-century period.

I would like to thank Maria Marsh, Middle Eastern Studies editor at Cambridge University Press, for identifying Abbasid history as a topic for a book survey, and for following the progress of the manuscript through its various stages. I also thank Dan Brown, Middle East editor at Cambridge as well, for keeping up with the review process, and Atifa Jiwa, assistant to the editors at the Press, for keeping the dots connected at various points. At the production stage, Stephanie Taylor was very helpful in making the book project advance with all the necessary supplements, while Mary Starkey applied her treasured copyediting skills to make the text flow with greater readability. On the illustrations front, I thank my colleague and Islamic art history expert, Professor Walter Denny, for his steady availability for consultancy, and am grateful to Islamic numismatist Dr. Michael Bates, of the American Numismatic Society, for generously helping in locating suitable Abbasid coins. The various staff at the Freer Gallery of Art and Arthur M. Sackler Gallery at the Smithsonian Museums in Washington, DC, the Ashmolean Museum at Oxford University, and Columbia University's Avery Architectural and Fine Arts Library, where the Frank Lloyd Wright Foundation Archives are housed, were all greatly helpful in making a variety of images available, and equally appreciated are the efforts of my departmental office manager, Rachel Diana, for helping in lining up the images and transforming them into manageable files.

The Talisman Gate image of "dragons and caliph" (ca. 1221), in the collection of the Metropolitan Museum of Art, remained elusive in circumstances of storage worthy of magic lamps, but thanks are still due to those who tried to retrieve it. To many students, the Abbasids have often been caught up in "Aladdin and Arabian Nights" types of tales relating to the caliph Harun al-Rashid, shady court ministers, flying carpets, and a Baghdad of glitz and splendor. I hope this book brings the topic closer to the reality of history, and helps to disentangle the term "caliphate" from modern myths and political exuberance. The question of why the Abbasids matter today is probably part of why we study history at all, but with a more particular answer – and an increasingly crucial one for today's world. Finally, and in a transition from my previous work on historiography, I wish to dedicate this book to my mother, Salma Sibai, who, I think, is more partial to history than historiography.

Note on Transliteration

The transliteration system used in the book follows the conventions of the *International Journal of Middle East Studies*, but goes further in simplifying the diacritical marks. Frequently used words and names, such as Abbasid, sharia, Abdallah, Umar, Uthman, Ali, and Aisha have been freed from the Ayn and Hamza markings, given their relative familiarity to Western readers. Less familiar names have kept the transliteration, but to a minimum. Although written the same in modern English transliteration, the name of the fifth caliph, Harun al-Rashid (pronounced "al-Rasheed"), needs to be distinguished from that of the later medieval brief rule of al-Rashid (pronounced "al-Raashid"). All references to the *Encyclopedia of Islam* refer to its second edition (dubbed "New Edition" when it was published). Dates are usually given in both the Islamic calendar of the *hijra* (AH), which begins in 622 CE, and in Common Era, except for regnal dates of rulers, which are given in the latter only.

Chronology

570–632	Lifespan of the Prophet Muhammad.
622	Beginning of the hijri Islamic calendar.
632–661	The rightly guided (Rashidun) caliphs: Abu Bakr (r. 632–634); Umar b. al-Khattab (r. 634–644); Uthman (r. 644–656); and Ali b. Abi Talib (r. 656–661).
661–680	Reign of Mu'awiya, who establishes the Umayyad dynasty, with Damascus as its capital.
685–705	Abd al-Malik b. Marwan reconsolidates Umayyad rule, mints the first fully Arabic and Islamic coinage, and builds the Dome of the Rock in 691.
705–715	The reign of al-Walid b. Abd al-Malik marks the Arab conquest of Spain, Transoxiana, and the Indus river region.
724–743	The reign of Hisham b. Abd al-Malik marks the height of Umayyad expansion. An Arab army is defeated at the battle of Poitiers by Charles Martel, while a Pyrrhic victory is achieved against the Turkic khanate in central Asia. Shi'i revolts by Zayd b. Ali (in Iraq) and his son Yahya (in Khurasan), and limitations surface on further conquests.
ca. 750	Religious scholars flourish: the jurist Abu Hanifa (d. 767); Ibn Ishaq (d. 768) compiles the Prophet's *Sira*; Ja'far al-Sadiq (d. 765) is the Sixth Imam of Twelver Shi'ism; and Malik b. Anas (d. 795) compiles the traditions (*sunna*) of Medina in the *Muwatta*.
743–744	The Abbasids begin their political call (*da'wa*). Abu Muslim makes the *da'wa* in Khurasan on behalf of the Abbasid Ibrahim al-Imam (based in Jordan).
749	The Abbasid forces conquer Kufa, and defeat the last Umayyad caliph, Marwan II, in northern Iraq at the battle of Zab.

750–1258	The Abbasid caliphate (reigning caliphs in bold).
750–754	Abu'l-Abbas **al-Saffah.**
754–775	Abu Ja'far **al-Mansur.**
756	Abd al-Rahman b. Mu'awiya b. Hisham b. al-Malik escapes to North Africa, and founds the Umayyad emirate of Spain.
762	The revolt of the Alid Muhammad al-Nafs al-Zakiyya in Medina.
762–763	al-Mansur founds Baghdad as the Abbasid capital.
772	al-Mansur constructs the city of al-Rafiqa near Raqqa.
775–785	**al-Mahdi.**
778	The building of the Palace of Ukhaydir
783	al-Mahdi's son, Harun, leads an army against the Byzantine empress Irene, reaches the Bosporus.
785–786	**al-Hadi.**
786–809	**Harun al-Rashid.**
786	Construction of the Great Mosque of Cordoba.
789–926	The Idrisids take control of the Maghreb.
797	al-Rashid sends gifts to Charlemagne.
798	The Abbasids and the Khazars reach a truce.
800–812	Ibrahim b. al-Aghlab, governor in North Africa, establishes the Aghlabid emirate that rules until 909.
802	al-Rashid establishes a covenant of succession between al-Amin and al-Ma'mun in Mecca.
803	The downfall of the Barmakids.
800	Charlemagne crowned emperor of the Franks.
808	The city of Fez founded by the Idrisids.
809–813	**al-Amin.**
811–813	The war of succession between al-Amin and al-Ma'mun.
813–833	**al-Ma'mun.**
813–819	al-Ma'mun rules the caliphate from Marw.
816–837	Revolt of Babak al-Khurrami.
817	al-Ma'mun designates Ali b. Musa al-Rida as successor.
821–873	The Tahirids are autonomous governors of Khurasan.
827	The Aghlabids begin conquest of Sicily (Palermo taken in 831, and Syracuse in 878). Crete is conquered separately.
831	al-Ma'mun's patronage of the Mu'tazila school of speculative theology (*kalam*) accelerates.

833	The caliph imposes the Mihna ("trial") against hadith scholars.
833–842	**al-Muʿtasim.**
836	al-Muʿtasim founds the city of Samarra as the new Abbasid capital.
842–847	**al-Wathiq.**
844	The Vikings raid Seville through the Guadalquivir river.
847–861	**al-Mutawakkil.**
848–852	The construction of the Great Mosque of Samarra.
850	al-Mutawakkil drafts succession plans amongst his children, al-Muntasir, al-Muʿtazz, and al-Muʾayyad.
848	al-Mutawakkil ends the Mihna program, and accepts the views of Ahmad b. Hanbal's followers as the new orthodoxy.
855	Abbasid expedition captures the African king of al-Bujja.
861	al-Mutawakkil constructs the Nilometer on Roda isle in Egypt, and the Madinat al-Mutawakiliyya near Samarra.
861–862	**al-Muntasir.**
862–866	**al-Mustaʿin.**
863	The Byzantines win a victory over the Arabs in Asia Minor.
865	The Bulgarian ruler Boris converts to Christianity.
866	Vikings establish kingdom in England; Alfred the Great rules Wessex, 871–899.
866–869	**al-Muʿtazz.**
868	Ibn Tulun governs Egypt independently of the Abbasids.
869–883	The Zanj rebellion in southern Iraq.
869–870	**al-Muhtadi.**
870–892	**al-Muʿtamid.**
885	Ibn Khurdadhbih completes his geographical work *al-Masalik wa'l-Mamalik*.
874	Hasan al-Askari, the Eleventh Shiʿi Imam, dies in Samarra; disappearance (occultation) of his child, Muhammad, the Twelfth Imam.
874–928	The Qaramita movement in southern Iraq; later it spreads to eastern Arabia.
876	al-Muwaffaq defeats the Saffarid Yaʿqub b. al-Layth.
877	Ibn Tulun takes control of Syria.

892–902	**al-Muʿtadid.**
	Baghdad reinstated as the Abbasid capital.
895	al-Muʿtadid changes the Nawruz date from 11 April to 17 June.
897	A Zaydi state is established in Yemen.
902–908	**al-Muktafi.**
905	The Abbasids regain control over Egypt.
907	Oleg of Kiev, leader of the Rus, attacks Constantinople.
908–932	**al-Muqtadir.**
908	Ibn al-Muʿtazz is caliph for one day
924	The Abbasid minister Ibn al-Furat is sacked.
909	The Shiʿi Ismaʿili Fatimids seize power in Tunisia, and expand to Egypt.
914	al-Tabari's *History of Prophets and Kings* concludes with events that year.
917	Byzantine embassy famously received in Baghdad.
929	al-Muqtadir is briefly deposed in favor of al-Qahir.
930	The Qaramita raid Mecca, remove the Black Stone, and return it in 951 after the Abbasids pay a ransom.
929	The Umayyads of al-Andalus proclaim themselves caliphs.
932–934	**al-Qahir.**
934–940	**al-Radi.**
935–937	Ibn Raʾiq appointed *amir al-umaraʾ*.
936–961	The Umayyads construct Madinat al-Zahra near Cordoba.
940–944	**al-Muttaqi.**
944	The Abbasids give up the Mandylion relic of Edessa, purported to have an image of Christ, to the Byzantines.
944–946	**al-Mustakfi.**
946	Buyid takeover of Baghdad.
945–967	The Hamdanid Sayf al-Dawla rules over Aleppo.
946–974	**al-Mutiʿ.**
949–983	Reign of the Buyid ʿAdud al-Dawla (from 977 in Iraq).
949	Embassy of Liutprand of Cremona, envoy of Otto I, to Constantine VII.
960	The conversion of "200,000 tents of Turks" (Qarluqs and Qarakhanids) to Islam in Kashgar.

961	The Byzantine Nicephorus Phocas captures Crete from the Arabs, and Cyprus in 965.
969	Cairo is founded by the Fatimids.
972–1152	The Zirids rule in Tunisia and eastern Algeria (vassals of the Fatimids till 1049).
974–991	**al-Ta'i'.**
985	The traveler and geographer al-Muqaddasi completes his survey of Islamic lands, *The Best Divisions for the Knowledge of the Regions.*
989	Vladimir the Great, leader of the Rus, converts to Christianity.
1004	al-Biruni composes *Chronology of Ancient Nations.*
1009	Church of the Holy Sepulchre destroyed by the Fatimid al-Hakim.
1014	Basil II of Byzantium destroys Bulgarian army.
991–1031	**al-Qadir.**
999	The Qarakhanids from Kashgar conquer the Samanids.
1010	Firdawsi completes writing the *Shahnameh.*
1012–1018	Avicenna composes the *The Canon of Medicine.*
1023–1079	The Mirdasids rule over Aleppo.
1031–1075	**al-Qa'im.**
1029	Mahmud of Ghazna captures Rayy and al-Jibal.
1030	al-Biruni completes his book survey of India.
1031	The end of Umayyad rule in Spain; start of the "Party Kings" of al-Andalus.
1036	The Abbasid caliph forbids transactions involving Fatimid dinars.
1040	The Seljuks defeat the Ghaznavids at the battle of Dandanqan.
1043	The Seljuk Tughril declares himself "Protector of the Commander of the Faithful."
1045	Movable type first invented in China.
1055	The Seljuk takeover of Baghdad under the leadership of Tughril Beg (r. 1038–1063)
1061–1091	The Norman Roger Guiscard captures Sicily from the Arabs.
1062–1067	The "great famine" in Egypt.

1065	Nizam al-Mulk, vizir of the Seljuks, founds the Nizamiyya of Baghdad, prototype of the Islamic madrasa.
1061–1106	The Almoravids under Yusuf b. Tashfin found Marrakesh in 1062 and win the key battle of Zallaqa in Spain in 1086.
1063–1072	Reign of the Seljuk sultan Alp Arslan.
1065–1092	Nizam al-Mulk presides over key period of Seljuk prosperity.
1066	The battle of Hastings and the Norman conquest of England.
1071	Alp Arslan defeats the Byzantine Romanus IV Diogenes at the battle of Manzikert.
1072–1092	Reign of the Seljuk sultan Malikshah.
1075–1094	**al-Muqtadi.**
1076	The Seljuks seize Damascus from the Fatimids.
1076	The end of Fatimid rule in Syria.
1076	Ghana empire converts to Islam.
1075–1122	Investiture controversy between emperor and Pope.
1077	Penitence of Henry IV at Canossa by Pope Gregory VII.
1081	Beginning of the Rum Seljuk state in Asia Minor.
1092	Nizam al-Mulk is murdered by Isma'ili Assassins.
1094	A split follows the death of the Fatimid caliph al-Mustansir between the Nizari Isma'ilis, who remove to the southwest Caspian region, and the followers of al-Musta'li, who continue to rule in Egypt.
1094–1118	**al-Mustazhir.**
1105–1118	Reunification of the western Seljuk realm under Muhammad b. Malikshah; divided again after Muhammad's death.
1118–1157	Sanjar rules over the Seljuk east from Marw.
1095	New wall built around east Baghdad.
1095	Council of Clermont, where Pope Urban II calls for a Crusade to Jerusalem
1097	The Anatolian Seljuks are defeated by the Crusaders under Godfrey de Bouillon.
1099	The First Crusade captures Jerusalem.
1118–1135	**al-Mustarshid.**
1118	The Seljuk empire breaks up into principalities.

1125	Start of Guelf–Ghibelline conflict.
1128–1256	The Khawarzm shah 'Ala al-Din Atsiz rules autonomously from the Seljuks in Gurganj (starting in 1141).
1135–1136	**al-Rashid.**
1136–1160	**al-Muqtafi.**
1137	Start of the Qara Khitay Khanate.
1137–1175	The Atabeg of the Seljuk sultans of Baghdad, Shams al-Din Eldiguz, establishes an independent state in Azerbayjan (until 1225).
1141	The Qara Khitay defeat the Seljuks at Samarqand.
1142	Peter the Venerable commissions the first Latin translation of the Qur'an.
1156–1192	Qilij Arslan II edges out the Danishmends from central Anatolia.
ca.1156	Yoruba states flourish in West Africa.
1157	Baghdad is besieged by the Seljuk sultan Muhammad.
1161	The Ghurids capture Ghazna, restricting the Ghaznavids to the Punjab and Lahore (till 1186).
1146	The Almohads take control of al-Andalus. King Roger II of Sicily mints the first European coins that use the Arabic numeral system, and invites Idrisi (d. 1163) to create a map of the world in 1138, which is completed in 1154.
1171	The Almohads build the Mosque of Seville with its La Giralda Minaret (converted to a church in 1248).
1175	Gerard of Cremona completes a translation from the Arabic of Ptolemy's *Almagest* (and Ibn Sina's *Canon* in 1180).
1160–1170	**al-Mustanjid.**
1169	Benjamin of Tudela visits Baghdad.
1169	Qilij Arslan II takes Ankara.
1170–1180	**al-Mustadi'.**
1171	al-Mustadi' grants Saladin the sultanate of Egypt, Palestine, and Syria; the Friday *khutba* in Egypt made in the name of the Abbasid caliph.
1175	The Ghurid Muhammad b. Sam invades India.
1176	The Seljuks of Rum defeat the Byzantines led by Manuel I Comnenos at the battle of Myriocephalon, near Konya.
1180–1225	**al-Nasir.**

1185	The Andalusian Ibn Jubayr visits Baghdad.
1187	Saladin defeats the Crusaders at Hittin and conquers Jerusalem.
1221	The walls of Baghdad are restored and the Talisman Gate is built.
1186	The Ghurids end Ghaznavid rule in the Punjab and eastern Afghanistan. The expansion led by Ghiyath al-Din Muhammad in Ghur (1163–1203) conquers Khurasan, and his brother Mu'izz al-Din Muhammad in Ghazna (1173–1206) conquers northern India.
1192	The Ghurids conquer Delhi.
1194	The Khwarazm shah Tekish defeats the last of the Seljuks in Persia.
1200–1220	Reign of the Khwarazm shah 'Ala al-Din Muhammad, famous for provoking Genghis Khan to invade Transoxiana in 1219.
1206	Genghis Khan recognized as Great Khan over the Mongolian peoples; rules till 1227.
1208	The Khwarazm shahs seize the Ghurid capital, Herat, and end Ghurid rule in 1215.
1194–1260	Building of Chartres Cathedral begins.
1204	The Fourth Crusade captures Constantinople; held by the Latins and backed by the Venetians till 1260.
1209	Francis of Assisi founds the Franciscan order.
1215	The Magna Carta drafted.
1215	The Mongols capture Beijing.
1219	Genghis Khan begins his invasion of Transoxiana.
1219–1237	The reign of 'Ala al-Din Kayqubad I; Konya flourishes as capital of Rum Seljuks.
1221	al-Nasir orders the construction in east Baghdad of Bab al-Wastani, whose Talisman Gate was blown up in 1918.
1225–1226	**al-Zahir.**
1227	Death of Genghis Khan, and the partition of his empire: Batu (r. 1227–1255) of the Golden Horde ruling in southern Russia and Khwarazmia; Ogedei (r. 1227–1241) ruling in northern China; Chagatai (r. 1229–1241) ruling in Transoxiana; and Tolui in Mongolia.
1228–1574	The Hafsids succeed the Almohads in Tunisia and eastern Algeria.

1229	Ogedei is recognized as Great Khan over the whole Mongol empire.
1229–1244	Jerusalem given by al-Kamil of Egypt to Frederick II.
1226–1242	**al-Mustansir.**
1220–1231	The last of the Khwarazm shahs, Jalal al-Din, resists the Mongols.
1231	The Chronicle of Ibn al-Athir concludes with events in that year.
1232	Muhammad I b. Yusuf b. al-Ahmar establishes the Nasrid kingdom of Granada.
1232	Construction of the Harba bridge on the Tigris, south of Samarra.
1233	The founding of al-Madrasa al-Mustansiriyya in Baghdad.
1235	Rise of the Mali empire.
1236	The Muslim city of Cordoba falls to Christian Castile.
1238	Batu of the Golden Horde Mongols destroys Moscow.
1241	The Golden Horde expands into Poland and Hungary.
1242–1258	**al-Musta'sim.**
1243	The Mongols defeat the Anatolian Seljuks (of Rum) at the battle of Kosedag near Sivas.
1248	The Seventh Crusade led by Louis IX invades Egypt.
1248	Seville is captured by the forces of Castile.
1253	The beginning of the Mongol invasion led by Hulegu.
1257–1266	The reign of Berke, first Muslim Khan of the Golden Horde.
1258	The Mongol sack of Baghdad.
1258	Qubilai Khan invades south China and Korea.
1260	Qubilai elected Great Khan.
1260	The Mamluks defeat the Mongols at the battle of Ayn Jalut, and again in 1277 at the battle of Elbistan.
1924	Atatürk abolishes the Ottoman caliphate.

Abbreviations

BSOAS	Bulletin of the School of Oriental and African Studies
CHIran	Cambridge History of Iran
EI²	Encyclopedia of Islam (2nd edition, 1960–2009)
IJMES	International Journal of Middle East Studies
JAOS	Journal of the American Oriental Society
JESHO	Journal of the Economic and Social History of the Orient
JRAS	Journal of the Royal Asiatic Society
NCHI	New Cambridge History of Islam

Genealogical Chart of the Caliphs

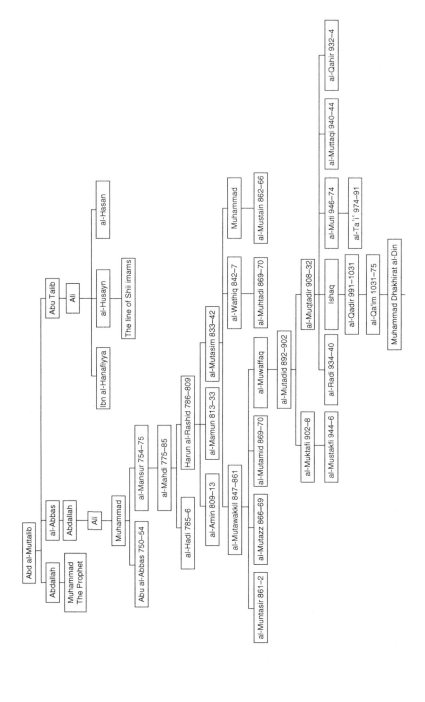

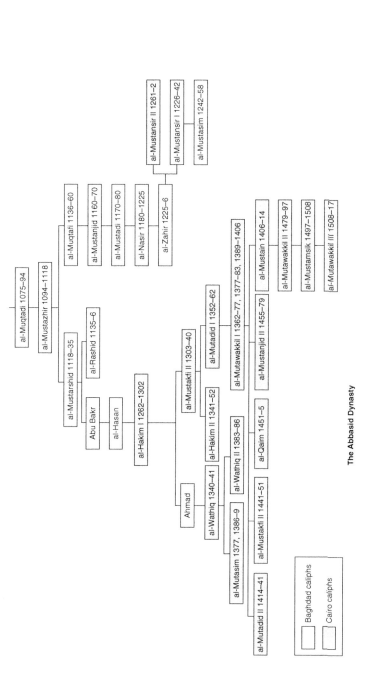

The Abbasid Dynasty

al-Muqtadi 1075–94

al-Mustazhir 1094–1118

al-Mustarshid 1118–35

al-Rashid 1135–6

Abu Bakr

al-Hasan

al-Hakim I 1262–1302

Ahmad

al-Wathiq 1340–41

al-Mustasim 1377, 1386–9

al-Mutadid II 1414–41

al-Mustakfi II 1441–51

al-Mustakfi II 1303–40

al-Hakim II 1341–52

al-Wathiq II 1383–86

al-Qaim 1451–5

al-Mutadid I 1352–62

al-Mutawakkil I 1362–77, 1377–83, 1389–1406

al-Mustanjid II 1455–79

al-Mustain 1406–14

al-Mutawakkil II 1479–97

al-Mustamsik 1497–1508

al-Mutawakkil III 1508–17

al-Muqtafi 1136–60

al-Mustanjid 1160–70

al-Mustadi 1170–80

al-Nasir 1180–1225

al-Zahir 1225–6

al-Mustansir II 1261–2

al-Mustansir I 1226–42

al-Mustasim 1242–58

Baghdad caliphs

Cairo caliphs

The Abbasid Caliphate
The Byzantine Empire
The Carolingian Empire
The Carolingian Empire (gains)
The Umayyad Andalus
Aghlabids
Idrisids

1. Map of the wider Abbasid empire

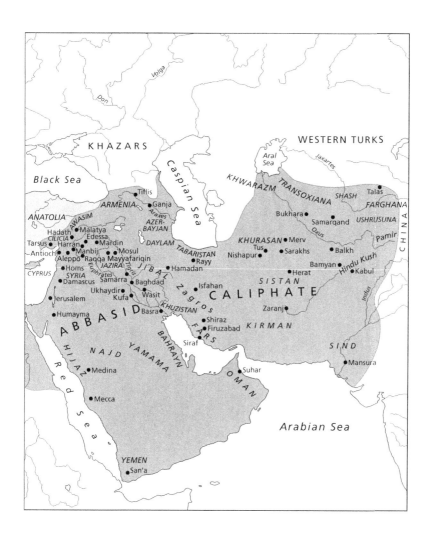

KHAZARS

Black Sea

Caspian Sea

WESTERN TURKS

Aral Sea

Volga

Don

Jaxartes

KHWARAZM

TRANSOXIANA

SHASH

Talas

FARGHANA

ANATOLIA

ARMENIA

Tiflis

Ganja

AWASIM

AZER-BAYJAN

USHRUSUNA

Bukhara

Samarqand

Pamir

Hadath

Malatya

Edessa

Araxes

DAYLAM

TABARISTAN

KHURASAN

Merv

Oxus

CHINA

Tarsus

CILICIA

Harran

Mardin

Mosul

Tus

Sarakhs

Balkh

Antioch

Manbij

Rayy

Nishapur

Bamyan

Hindu Kush

Aleppo

Raqqa

Mayyafariqin

JAZIRA

Euphrates

Tigris

JIBAL

Hamadan

Herat

Kabul

Homs

SYRIA

CYPRUS

Damascus

Samarra

Zagros

SISTAN

CALIPHATE

Jerusalem

Kufa

Ukhaydir

Baghdad

Wasit

Isfahan

Humayma

Basra

KHUZISTAN

Zaranj

KIRMAN

HIJAZ

NAJD

YAMAMA

BAHRAYN

Shiraz

Firuzabad

FARS

Siraf

SIND

Mansura

OMAN

Suhar

Medina

Red Sea

Mecca

Arabian Sea

YEMEN

San'a

ABBASID

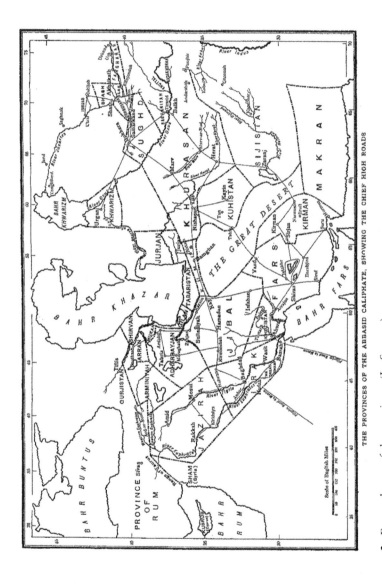

THE PROVINCES OF THE ABBASID CALIPHATE, SHOWING THE CHIEF HIGH ROADS

2. Focused map of the provinces (Le Strange)

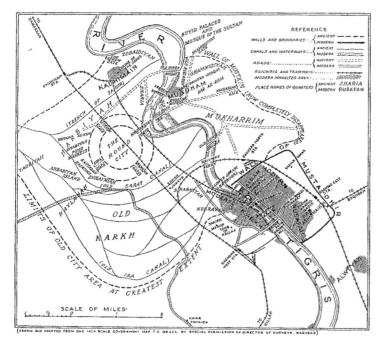

3. Focused map of Baghdad (Coke)

1 | Introduction

Why the Study of the Abbasids Matters Today

The modern world owes a great debt to medieval Islamic civilization generally, and to the Abbasid caliphate (750–1258), more particularly. In recent years a variety of popular surveys have described the critical scientific and intellectual achievements that took place in the golden age of the Abbasid capital, Baghdad, during the ninth century. The "House of Wisdom" movement patronized by the caliph al-Ma'mun (r. 813–833) promoted the revival of Classical Greek philosophy and science, long before these attracted attention in Europe in the later phases of the scientific revolution and the Enlightenment. To many readers, the names al-Razi, al-Khwarazmi, and al-Kindi are today as familiar as those of Aristotle, Ptolemy, Euclid, and Hippocrates, with both providing the two streams (ancient and medieval) that contributed to the stimulation of the Western Renaissance.[1]

Islamic history was still relatively young, less than a century and a half old, when the Abbasids came on the scene in 750, after the momentous events that spanned the era of the Prophet (610–632), the reigns of his Companion successors (the Rashidun caliphs, 632–661), and the period of Islamic conquests with the Umayyad dynasty (661–750). But the Islamic empire comprised a diversity of more ancient communities (Arabs, Persians, Jews, Christians, Zoroastrians, Manicheans, and Buddhists), all of whom partook in energizing the transition from the

---

[1] Jonathan Lyons, *The House of Wisdom: How the Arabs Transformed Western Civilization* (London, 2009); John Freely, *Light From the East: How the Science of Medieval Islam Helped to Shape the Western World* (London, 2011); Hans Belting, *Florence and Baghdad: Renaissance Art and Arab Science*, trans. Deborah Lucas Schneider (Cambridge, MA, 2011); Salim T. S. al-Hassani, ed., *1001 Inventions: The Enduring Legacy of Muslim Civilization* (Washington, DC, 2012).

divided world of Late Antiquity between the Roman (Byzantine) and Persian (Sasanid) empires straddling a border along the Euphrates river to a unified world of cultural and economic synthesis under the caliphate.

It is tempting to study the achievements of Islamic science and culture without attention to their context in political history, but this legacy would not have gone very far without the initial guidance and resources provided by a series of Abbasid caliphs, such as al-Mansur, al-Rashid, al-Ma'mun, and al-Mu'tasim, who were keen patrons of scientific discovery and professional thought. These caliphs were also famous for their patronage of literary and religious debate, and their reigns witnessed the rise of other Arabic classics that continue to resonate in the legal practice and cultural life of Islamic society today. The *Sira* (or saga) of the Prophet Muhammad was compiled in the mid-eighth century by Ibn Ishaq, and a little later jurists such as Abu Hanifa, Malik, and al-Shafi'i contributed the ideas and texts that provided the foundations for Islamic legal thinking for centuries to come. The Abbasid court became a magnet for pioneering linguists, such as al-Khalil and Sibawayh, who laid out the rules of Arabic grammar and the correct style of expression; for poets, such as Abu Tammam and al-Buhturi; and for belles-lettrists such as Ibn al-Muqaffa', famous for his book of animal fables, *Kalila wa Dimna*, and al-Jahiz, a prolific essayist.

In spite of these legacies, the attention of modern historians to the Abbasids has been slim and uneven, with as yet no full survey available for the entirety of the history of the Abbasid caliphate. Abbasid history has often tended to be caught up in wider surveys of medieval Islamic history, which mostly tell the story of the Prophet and the rise of Islam, later conquests under the Umayyads, and then provide a sketchy look at the caliphs of Baghdad. Coverage of the Abbasids has tended to focus excessively on the reign of Harun al-Rashid, and mostly for a fairy-tale image colored more by *The Thousand and One Nights* than actual history. The focus on a period considered a golden age of the caliphate has made the first century of Abbasid rule, with names such as al-Mansur and al-Ma'mun, well known, but those of other caliphs from later centuries, such as al-Mu'tadid (r. 892–902), al-Qa'im (r. 1031–1075), al-Mustadi' (r. 1170–1180), and al-Mustansir (r. 1226–1242), remain obscure to the general reader. As the central control of the Abbasids gives way to more assertive provincial dynasties or "successor states" such as the Tahirids, Samanids, and Buyids in tenth-century Iran, or to the Isma'ili Fatimids of Egypt; and as the Turkic sultanates of the Ghaznavids and Seljuks emerge in the eleventh and twelfth centuries, the Abbasid caliphate becomes lost in a forest of political changes.

This study aims to provide a survey of the Abbasid caliphate – mostly as a political history, but with digressions on the social and cultural developments that accompanied the five-century period of Abbasid history. An important part of this corrective in ranging beyond the first century of the Abbasids is to appreciate the caliphate not simply in terms of its early military and territorial hegemony but as a political office that remained a central symbol of historical continuity in Islamic society and a source of legitimation to various dynasts around the Islamic world. Caliphs such as al-Mansur and al-Rashid in the eighth and ninth centuries may have held great military and territorial reach, but what later caliphs lost in military power in the tenth and eleventh centuries they were able to make up for in the reigns of al-Qadir, al-Qa'im, al-Nasir, and al-Mustansir with an increase in their religious authority as a source of legitimacy for newly emerging dynasts. Various rulers, such as the Ghaznavids, Seljuks, Ayyubids, Ghurids, and the Delhi sultans could only project their new status as "sultans" upon receiving an edict of "blessing" from the caliph in Baghdad, who wielded a leverage similar to that of a medieval Pope in giving greater legitimacy to some rulers over others, and as such influenced the political geography of the Islamic world. To always measure the Abbasid caliphate by its military strength and territorial control in the early period overlooks the transformation of the caliphate over the centuries, and its ability to redefine its credibility and leverage in different phases of Islamic history.

A Survey of the Caliphate

To Western readers the term "caliph" remains enigmatic, and less recognizable in meaning than the terms "Caesar" or "Pope." And even for Muslims the term can be elusive, since the "caliphate" is not an institution enshrined in Qur'anic injunctions or recommended by the Prophet, but is more an accident of history. It was a makeshift political office hastily crafted by the Companions of Muhammad to help fill the leadership vacuum left after his death in 632. The Arabic word itself, meaning "deputy" or "successor," remained ambiguous, blurring the boundary between political and religious authority, and it remained unclear whether the term "caliph" meant "deputy of the

Prophet" or "the representative of God on earth." The religious and political dimensions of the leadership vacuum left by Muhammad were so strongly felt that when his Companions argued over the question they reportedly often referred to this leadership and succession challenge as "this matter" (*hadha al-amr*), not knowing what to call it, or whether the caliph was a religious or political leader. It took a relatively oppressive dynasty, the Umayyads (661–750), to establish the caliphate as a hereditary monarchal institution, but the full implications of the caliphal office did not crystallize until the Abbasids came to power. The Umayyads tried briefly to project a meaning of "caliph" as "deputy of God" rather than "deputy of the Prophet" during the reign of Abd al-Malik, but the experiment clearly failed, since the title was soon removed from coinage. Challenged by the family of the Prophet, Kharijites, and intertribal rivalry, the Umayyads found their only safety in projecting brute imperial force. Waves of conquest on different frontiers became a necessary distraction from internal questions of religious and political legitimacy.

The task of communicating both a political and religious meaning for the caliphal leadership, however, was far more successfully accomplished by the Abbasids, after the revolution that brought them to power in 750. As members of the Prophet's Hashimite family, and descendants of his uncle, al-Abbas, they held a special mystique. In the last years of Umayyad rule they had joined with the Alids, descendants of the Prophet's cousin Ali, in a revolutionary movement that was launched in Khurasan to overthrow the Umayyad dynasty, viewed by their opposition as usurpers of the greater, kin-based legitimate right of the Prophet's family to rule. Khurasan, with further cultural influences from neighboring Transoxiana and Central Asia, also infused Abbasid caliphal pretensions with additional dimensions of charismatic authority, based on notions of messianic renewal and divine election, to make the Abbasid political office a highly religious one. The new, post-revolutionary state was referred to as *dawla*, a term that carries connotations of a new order, and the new caliphs assumed titles that reflected their roots in Prophetic heritage and divine support, such as al-Mansur (the Victorious), al-Mahdi (the Guided), al-Rashid (the Wise), and al-Ma'mun (the Well-Entrusted). Later court writers, such as Baladhuri and Qudama b. Ja'far, would refer to the dynasty as "the blessed dynasty" (*al-dawla al-mubaraka*).

In social terms, the Abbasid state brought radical change after the Umayyad period in the way it opened up the Islamic empire, transitioning from the "Arab" kingdom of the Umayyads, which had relied on government by an Arab tribal confederacy and discouraged conversion to Islam. The Abbasid state instead opened up access to circles of power to new converts to Islam, promising an equality of sorts between the Arabs and non-Arabs, the former *mawali* (clients) of the Umayyad period. This trend toward Perso-Arab integration was perhaps best reflected in the office of the vizierate, which was dominated by the Iranian family of the Barmakids for many years between the reigns of al-Mahdi and Harun al-Rashid. The experiment opened the way for a stronger integration in the reign of al-Ma'mun, and the later emergence of provincial dynasties, such as those of the Tahirids and the Samanids. The Abbasids were not only aware of the social and religious diversity their empire spanned, but hammered out a legal system – in the Hanafi mold initially and with digressions to other trends later on – that ensured an attitude of flexibility in dealing with issues and groups. The institutions they put in place would later function as foundations of the great empires of Islam up until that of the Ottomans, which ended after World War I.

More than anything the name of the Abbasids has been associated with the city of Baghdad, which they founded in 762 as their new capital on the Tigris river. Baghdad grew rapidly to become the largest urban center of the medieval world – perhaps only matched in size by Constantinople – and it grew into an economic and intellectual powerhouse. The city comprised a learned society benefiting from numerous bookshops and public libraries, and became a hub for students traveling in search of knowledge.[2] The eleventh-century Khatib al-Baghdadi best described the sense of wonder surrounding Baghdad, when he said: "In the entire world, there has not been a city which could compare with Baghdad in size and splendor, or in the number of scholars and great personalities ... Consider the numerous roads, markets, lanes, mosques, bathhouses, and shops – all these distinguish the city from all others."[3] As for its reputation as a center of commerce, Baghdad was famous even earlier; a late eighth-century Chinese traveler, Du Huan,

---

[2] Olga Pinto, "The Libraries of the Arabs During the Time of the Abbassides," *Islamic Culture* 3 (1929), 214; Ibn Abd Rabbih, *al-'Iqd al-Farid*, ed. Ahmad Amin et al. (Cairo, 1940–1953), 2:223; Ruth Mackensen, "Four Great Libraries of Medieval Baghdad," *Library Quarterly* 2 (1932), 281.

[3] Khatib al-Baghdadi, *Tarikh Baghdad* (Cairo, 1931), 1:108–109, trans. Francoise Micheau as "Baghdad in the Abbasid Era: A Cosmopolitan and Multi-Confessional Capital," in *The City in the Islamic World* (Leiden, 2008), ed. Renata Holod et al., 1:244.

stated: "Everything produced from the earth is available there ...
Brocade, embroidered silks, pearls, and other gems are displayed all
over markets and street shops."[4]

The founding of Baghdad as the new capital of the Abbasid empire
on the Tigris signaled not just a political shift from the Umayyad capital
Damascus but a cultural and economic one as well. The Abbasids
recognized their debt to the Iranian east that had brought them to
power, and became strongly attached to the strategic location of
Baghdad in the richest agricultural heartland of Mesopotamia, which
was helped by the easy river transport that the Tigris and Euphrates
provided. With the proximity of the ruins of the Sasanid capital
Ctesiphon – famous for its Arch of Khusraw – and the vivid archaeological record elsewhere in Iraq of Assyrian and Babylonian ruins, the
founder of Baghdad, al-Mansur, was making a statement of final
imperial inheritance of ancient Near Eastern empires.[5] He was helped
in this by a diversity of communities that placed hopes on better times
under the Abbasids: Nestorian Christians who were deeply at odds
with the Church of Constantinople; Zoroastrians who yearned for an
ally against Manicheans and Mazdakites; Jews who still remembered
the harsh days of Byzantine rule under Heraclius; and Shi'i Muslims
who considered the Abbasids, as Hashimites, closer to the principle of
rule by the family of the Prophet than the Umayyads. And these were
still different from the hopes of the provinces, such as Khurasan, which
wanted to be in the driving seat of the empire; Armenia, which sought
a measure of self-rule; and the Hijaz, which looked for better integration with a caliphate always based in the north. In the inaugural age of
the Abbasid dynasty it seemed that everyone wanted this state to
succeed. The caliph was not viewed as a foreign leader but as
a promising ally, and generally as the enabler of political stability,
social order, and economic prosperity. Al-Mansur was in many ways
Persia's Cyrus in Arabic garb.

The general outline of Abbasid history defies a simple model of rise,
prosperity, and decline. There was more than one moment of decline,
and more than one of surprising recovery. This was noticed already in
the tenth century by writers in the Abbasid chancery, such as Ibrahim

---

[4] Xinru Liu, *The Silk Road in World History* (Oxford, 2010), 101.
[5] J. Lassner, *The Topography of Baghdad in the Early Middle Ages* (Detroit,
     1970), 162, 232 no. 6.

b. Hilal al-Sabi' (d. 384/994), who wrote in one letter on behalf of the caliph to the Buyid king Bakhtiyar, that "you and others have seen how [over the years] the Abbasid state (*al-dawla al-'abbasiyya*) weakens at times, and revives at others ... and yet in all conditions it has firm roots." Al-Sabi' explains that turmoil when it happens "[is] by way of divine instruction for the subjects and admonishment to them ... to a duration that God has preordained," and that it has also been a pattern that when God again decrees the restoration (of the caliphate), he does so by sending someone who is loyal to its cause, and that no sooner does this happen than we find the state becoming "young again, renewed in vigor, and sturdy as before."[6] Although al-Sabi''s reasoning for these ups and downs is religious, it is interesting nevertheless that he and his administrative cohorts held a historical view based on cycles in the fortunes of the Abbasid state.

The reign of Harun al-Rashid was undoubtedly a peak in Abbasid power. When it was followed by the succession crisis and civil war between his children, al-Amin and al-Ma'mun, and the rise of the first provincial dynasty of the Iranian Tahirids in the east, it may well seem like the end of the caliphate's story for traditional historians. Anyone trying to tell al-Mu'tasim, al-Ma'mun's successor, that he ruled over a period of decline might well have received the answer he allegedly once gave the Byzantine emperor: "The least of the territories ruled by the least of my subjects provides a revenue larger than your whole dominion."[7] Al-Mu'tasim built the new city of Samarra, some 60 miles up the Tigris from Baghdad, which for about half a century was the new Abbasid capital, filled with palatial mansions, military cantonments, athletic and hunting grounds. The frenzy of luxury and palace building at Samarra reached its peak with al-Mutawakkil, who built his own city of al-Mutawakiliyya in what reflected the revived ability of the state to spend, an ability to exercise central control over land-tax revenue collection, and a state treasury awash with funds.

After the assassination of al-Mutawakkil in the mid-ninth century the Abbasid state, which then had a string of short-lived, beleaguered caliphs, could have been written off, but toward the end of that century

---

[6] al-Sabi', *al-Mukhtar min Rasa'il Abu Ishaq Ibrahim b. Hilal al-Sabi'*, ed. Shakib Arslan (Beirut, n.d.), 316–318.

[7] al-Muqaddasi, *Ahsan al-Taqasim fi Marifat al-Aqalim* (Leiden, 1906), 64; trans. Basil Collins as *The Best Divisions for Knowledge of the Regions* (Reading, 2001), 60.

al-Mu'tadid brought about a military revival, and the Abbasid state went on to garner wealth from tax revenues that supported a glamorous court in the early tenth century. Ibn Khaldun, famous for his theory of how urban culture dilutes the ties of tribal and family solidarity, and how luxury breeds political feebleness, could find proof for his theories in history during this period, as the Abbasids were overwhelmed by the hardy Buyid mountain-dwellers from the Caspian region. If there was a time when the Abbasid state seemed on the verge of oblivion, it was with the era of Buyid domination over the regions of Iraq and Iran (945–1055). Caliphs lost all territorial control, and they became no more than emblems of the past in the Islamic world, reduced to having only their names included on coinage and invoked for blessing in the sermon (*khutba*) of the Friday prayer. Buyid adherence to Shi'i Islam (in its Zaydi and Twelver forms) added more pressure on the Sunni Abbasid caliphate.

But then historical circumstances turned against the Buyids with the rise of new Turkic dynasties, the Ghaznavids and the Seljuks, who espoused Sunni Islam and indirectly revived the importance of the Abbasid caliphal institution by aiming to act as its protectors against the Buyids and the rising Fatimids in Egypt. This coincided with a time when two Abbasid caliphs, al-Qadir, followed by al-Qa'im, were actively working on reviving in a new way the religious authority of the office. They had cultivated strong ties with the religious class of the 'ulama, postured as guardians of orthodox Islamic belief in an age of great schism between Sunni Islam and Isma'ili Shi'ism, and even set about articulating, in almost ideological terms, an official religious testament – the famous Qadiri Creed or *al-'aqida al-qadiriyya*, first made public in 409/1018. The main challenge in this conflict was no longer the Buyids, but the Isma'ili Fatimids in Egypt, who for a while seemed on the verge of overrunning the entire Middle East and ending the Abbasid caliphate.

During the Seljuk sultanate the Abbasid caliphs did not wield political control over territory any more than they had under the Buyids, but the relationship between caliph and sultan was markedly improved since both the Abbasids and Seljuks were Sunni, and their relationship found its best moment of equilibrium during the vizierate of Nizam al-Mulk, the Seljuks' famous Iranian chief minister and ideological architect of the Islamic educational institution known as the madrasa. Helped by their unusually long reigns, the Abbasid caliphs al-Qadir

(r. 991–1031) and al-Qa'im (r. 1031–1075) were able to revive the position of the Abbasids as a focus of Islamic and historical loyalty, and were aided in this effort by prolific jurists, such as al-Mawardi, who helped them articulate their authority as "Imams," as he laid out the political theory in his famous treatise *al-Ahkam al-Sultaniyya*, the first succinct theory of government from an Islamic juristic point of view. In Baghdad, the Abbasids and Seljuks each had their own palace as a base, with Dar al-Khilafa for the caliphs, and Dar al-Mamlaka (later Dar al-Saltana) for the sultans. This situation remained stable until the caliph tried to assert a claim for more control in the Iraq region. This was bound to happen given the distant anchor of the Seljuk empire in eastern Iran at Marw, and the Abbasid memory of their once wider scope of territorial sovereignty.

An attempt to assert renewed military power was put forward by the caliph al-Mustarshid (r. 1118–1135), and although he was defeated, his attempted move to empower the caliphate in Iraq seems to have galvanized later Abbasids into persisting with the project of trying to shake off Seljuk hegemony and revive their real political authority. Al-Mustarshid's successor, al-Muqtafi, gradually pieced together control over Baghdad, and extended it over southern Iraq. With an economic and political base in the Iraq region, a new caliphal state became a cohesive entity from Baghdad to Basra, and in the twelfth century the caliphs found new allies in place of the Seljuks with the rise of the Zangids, Ayyubids, and Rum Seljuks in Syria and Asia Minor. The background of war against the Western Crusades indirectly strengthened the position of the caliph as a central religious symbol for Islam. A diploma of investiture from the caliph to a Rum Seljuk or Ayyubid prince, usually accompanied by a robe of honor, a standard, a ring, and a sword, functioned like a coronation as well as religious blessing. Al-Mustadi''s designation of the Rum Seljuk prince Qilij Arslan II (r. 1156–1192) as "sultan" therefore raised the latter's profile in Asia Minor above that of other neighboring principalities, such those of the Artuqids and Danishmends, and similarly gave the Ayyubid sultan Saladin much-needed legitimacy, after once having served merely as vassal of the Zangids of Aleppo.[8]

---

[8] Songül Mecit, "Kingship and Ideology under the Rum Seljuqs," in *The Seljuqs: Politics, Society and Culture*, ed. Christian Lange and Songül Mecit (Edinburgh, 2011), 68.

The climax of Abbasid efforts at revival finally culminated with the near half-century reign of al-Nasir (r. 1180–1225), the longest-reigning Abbasid caliph, who was able to exercise political authority in Iraq without any outside influence. Al-Nasir's success was greatly helped by his crafting of a religious policy that attracted both Sunni and Shi'i loyalty, and later by his addition of a new dimension of Sufism. The twelfth century was a time of rising Sufi piety, especially with the saintly figure Abd al-Qadir al-Jilani (d. 561/1166), whose shrine in Baghdad became a place of pilgrimage that rivaled the shrines of Abu Hanifa and the Shi'i Imams. Al-Nasir joined Sufism through its Suhrawardi movement in 1207, and appointed as his key advisor the leader of this movement, Shihab al-Din al-Suhrawardi, who acted as his envoy on many official diplomatic missions. The caliph cultivated a chivalric order, known as Futuwwa, that centered on loyalty to his leadership and on practicing a set of virtues that was considered embodied in the heroic career of the caliph Ali. The caliph encouraged various leaders, including princes of the Ayyubids (1169–1260), Rum Seljuks (1077–1307), Ghurids (1000–1215), and others, to join this movement, envisioning the Abbasid caliph as a Grand Master within the frame of this chivalric order. Al-Nasir's long reign lent stability to his rule, and he was greatly aided by the help of a capable minister from Shiraz, Ibn al-Qassab, who helped expand Abbasid control over Khuzistan, Isfahan, Qazwin, and Rayy (modern Tehran). But above all, the Abbasid caliphate was helped in this twilight phase by foreign developments, namely the rise of new dynasts in the east, such as the Ghurids in India, who were bitter rivals to al-Nasir's enemies the Khwarazm shahs (1077–1231), and helped distract the latter, although the end of the Khwarazm shahs actually came with the invasion of Genghis Khan.

Abbasid Baghdad continued to progress during the reign of the caliph al-Mustansir, who built the famous madrasa of al-Mustansiriyya, an architectural and artistic wonder of its time, which was also the first to harbor an ecumenical tendency by including academic training in all four schools of Sunni jurisprudence, rather than only one, as was the case with previous madrasas. Al-Mustansir maintained an efficient army that on more than one occasion fended off Mongol attacks in areas adjacent to Baghdad. In order for the caliphate to survive at that critical juncture in its history it needed a vigilant and steady leader skilled at diplomacy and maintaining the social and religious unity of Baghdad in an hour of crisis. Al-Mustansir's successor, al-Musta'sim, was hardly the capable personality necessary for dealing with internal Sunni–Shi'i stresses and the imminent Mongol threat. His court was notorious for being manipulated by his treacherous minister Ibn al-'Alqami and for the rivalry amongst its officials. This seemed all too reminiscent of earlier reigns when a caliph withdrew into the background while ministers manipulated the state, but with the added calamities of natural disasters such as flooding in Baghdad, and rising religious tensions between Sunnis and Shi'a in Iraq. It was within this atmosphere that the final cataclysm came in 1258, with Hulegu's invasion of Baghdad and his destruction of the Abbasid caliphate.

Perceptions of the Abbasid Caliphate

Christian Views (Latin and Byzantine)

By its sheer longevity – five centuries – the Abbasid caliphate built up an image of antiquity in Islamic culture and took on the semblance of an indispensable political model in the Islamic world. This durability turned Abbasid caliphal legitimacy into something quite separate from the original circumstances that brought them to overthrow the Umayyads in 750. Foreign leaders in the Christian West always remained intrigued by the caliphate, and tried to establish some form of relations with it. Charlemagne famously sent more than one embassy to Baghdad in the reign of Harun al-Rashid in the late eighth century to establish an alliance against the Umayyads of Spain and acquire some access to Jerusalem and the Holy Land, and in 906 a Frankish princess, named Bertha, in northern Italy sent an embassy in the reign of al-Muktafi, also seeking diplomatic relations, and proposing marriage.

Medieval Western sources often referred to the caliph using a corrupted spelling of the caliph's other title, Commander of the Faithful (*amir al-mu'minin*), in distorted expressions, such as "Elmiram mommini," "Miralomin," or "Amir munmilin."[9] Carolingian sources, such as Einhard, referred to Harun al-Rashid as "king of the Persians," still categorizing the nations of the world under ancient labels, and in spite of Latin ignorance regarding Islam, an even later chronicler, William of Tyre (d. 1185), cast a favorable image of the Abbasids when it came to

---

[9] Thomas Arnold, *The Caliphate* (Oxford, 1924), 32–33; Norman Daniel, *The Arabs and Medieval Europe* (London, 1975), 50–51.

comparing their treatment of Christians, which he contrasted with the situation under the Fatimids and the Seljuks.[10] The existence of Islam as a religion was tied by some medieval writers to the very existence of the Abbasid caliphate, as they latched optimistically onto the pro-Abbasid legend that the caliphs would last until they handed over the leadership in apocalyptic terms to Jesus on his Second Coming, which, the Latin West believed, spelled the coming conversion of all Muslims to Christianity.[11]

On the Byzantine side, attitudes were more realistic. A history of conflict with the Abbasids was interspersed with many phases of cultural exchange and a perception of the caliph as an equal and rival to the emperor. Writing from Constantinople to the Abbasid caliph al-Muqtadir (r. 908–932) to ask him to improve the conditions of the populace in Cyprus, Patriarch Nicholas Mysticus (901–907, 912–925), who was regent for the young emperor Constantine VII, struck a warm diplomatic tone. In the format of missives usually sent to the Islamic ruler, with a double text, one in Greek written in gold letters and a parallel Arabic text written in silver, on purple parchment, the patriarch stated: "There are two lordships, that of the Saracens and that of the Romans, which stand above all lordship on earth, shining out like the two mighty beacons in the firmament."[12] In spite of the rivalry, the Byzantines viewed the Abbasids, as they had the Sasanids before, as an equal power and an anchor of organized statehood and society.

In the eleventh century the historian Ibn al-Athir depicted another moment in this mutual recognition following the Byzantine defeat by the Seljuks at the battle of Manzikert in 1071. After paying a staggering ransom to the Seljuk sultan Alp Arslan for freedom from captivity, the Byzantine emperor Romanus Diogenes reportedly asked, before he set out on his return journey across Asia Minor back to Constantinople,

[10] Margaret Meserve, *Empires of Islam in Renaissance Historical Thought* (Cambridge, MA, 2008), 156–161.

[11] R. W. Southern, *Western Views of Islam in the Middle Ages* (Cambridge, MA, 1962), 62.

[12] Jonathan Shepard, "Equilibrium to Expansion, 886–1025," in *The Cambridge History of the Byzantine Empire c. 500–1492*, ed. Jonathan Shepard (Cambridge, 2008), 496. Also, on the letter formats, Ann Christys, "The Queen of the Franks Offers Gifts to the Caliph al-Muktafi," in *The Languages of Gift in the Middle Ages*, ed. Wendy Davies and Paul Fouracre (Cambridge, 2013), 157; Romilly Jenkins, *Byzantium: The Imperial Centuries, AD 610–1071* (London, 1966), 266.

where the caliph was (i.e. the direction of Baghdad), and when this was indicated, he turned to that direction and bowed, as if in military salute to the higher authority in the Islamic world that had defeated him.[13]

Less typical perhaps was the reaction of the more secular-minded emperor Frederick of Hohenstaufen when he came to Jerusalem in 1229 to take over the city in an arrangement he had made with the Ayyubid al-Kamil of Egypt. While touring the religious sites of Jerusalem, he is reported to have asked his guide, Fakhr al-Din, about the caliph, who he was and what his office meant. "He is the cousin of our Prophet," Fakhr al-Din said, "and the caliphate continues in the Prophetic house, from father to son, in succession." At this Frederick reportedly marveled, and scoffed at the process of selecting leaders in the West, most likely in reference to the papacy, with which he was at odds (he had been excommunicated by Pope Gregory IX). Frederick replied: "This is indeed a sound principle, but that rabble [i.e. the Franks] take someone from the dumpster, an ignoramus, who has no connection to Jesus whatsoever and they put him in charge, standing in as deputy of Jesus."[14]

Frederick's attempt to compare the caliph with the Pope was not merely the gripe of a Western monarch involved in a fight with the head of the Christian Church. There was a growing tendency in the Middle East in the eleventh and twelfth centuries to compare the situations of Islam and Christianity. Muslim chroniclers often took the bold step during this period of comparing the positions of caliph and Pope by stating that the latter held the position of "caliph of the Franks" (*khalifat al-firanj*). If this merely sounded as if the Pope was a Christian "Commander of the Faithful," Ibn Wasil goes farther by trying to explain the comparison in pointed terms, stating that the Pope is "the caliph of Jesus (*khalifat al-masih*) among them, and the one standing in for him" (*al-qa'im maqamahu*), and to him belongs "the authority to permit and forbid, and he is the one who crowns the kings with their crowns, and installs them in office."[15] The comparison established by Ibn Wasil would enjoy wide circulation in Islamic writing over the next two centuries, featuring in the encyclopedic

---

[13] Ibn al-Athir, *al-Kamil fi'l-Tarikh*, ed. C. J. Tornberg (Beirut, 1965–1967), 10:67.

[14] Ibn Wasil, *Mufarrij al-Kurub fi Akhbar Bani Ayyub*, ed. Sa'id 'Abd al-Fattah 'Ashur et al. (Cairo, 1972–1977), 4:251.

[15] Ibn Wasil, *Mufarrij*, 1:248–249.

work of Qalqashandi, and a mirror for princes by a descendant of the Abbasids.[16]

Islamic Views (from Egypt to India)

In spite of its ups and downs, the Abbasid caliphate remained an enduring institution that cast a spell of perennial acceptance over the Islamic world. The fourteenth-century Ibn al-Tiqtaqa, author of *al-Fakhri*, a treatise on government, best summarized the view amongst Muslims:

> Know that this dynasty was one of the greatest dynasties. It administered the world by an administration combining religion with the state ... The caliphate and the sovereignty remained in it for the space of 600 (Hijri) years, then dynasties attacked it, such as the Buyid dynasty, which included a hero such Adud al-Dawla; the Seljuk dynasty, which included Tughrilbeg; the Khwarazm shah dynasty which included Ala al-Din, whose army comprised 400,000 troops; and the Fatimids ... All that, yet their rule was continuous, nor was any dynasty strong enough to strip them of their power, nor to efface their traces. Nay rather, one of these above mentioned rulers used to collect, muster, and lead great armies till he arrived at Baghdad, and when he arrived, he would seek an audience of the Caliph, and, when he was given it, would kiss the ground before him, and the utmost favor he sought from him was that the Caliph would "present" him with a standard and robe of honor.[17]

Although lacking military power, the caliphate stood as a vital institution of legitimation to various dynasts. The fifteenth-century Ibn Shahin al-Zahiri (d. 873/1469) states that no prince could aspire to the rank of "sultan" without first having a diploma for this from the caliph.[18] The acquisition of this honorific from Baghdad was not something just filed away in archives, but was announced in public declarations, and commemorated on coins and in architectural inscriptions. The Rum Seljuk sultans included mention of their alliance with

---

[16] al-Qalqashandi, *Ma'athir al-Inafa fi Ma'alim al-Khilafa*, ed. 'Abd al-Sattar Ahmad Farraj (Beirut, 2006), 5:443; al-Abbasi, *Athar al-Uwal fi Tartib al-Duwal*, ed. Abd al-Rahman Umayra (Beirut, 1989), 101.

[17] Ibn al-Tiqtaqa, *al-Fakhri* (Beirut, 1966), 140–141; trans. C. E. J. Whitting as *al-Fakhri: On the Systems of Government and the Moslem Dynasties* (London, 1947), 134.

[18] Ibn Shahin al-Zahiri, *Zubdat Kashf al-Mamalik*, ed. P. Ravaisse (Paris, 1894), 89. Arnold, *The Caliphate*, 101–102.

the caliph in inscriptions on their monuments, such as with Kay Kawus I (r. 1211–1219) who referred to himself as "Proof (*burhan*) of Commander of the Faithful" in the *fath-nama* inscribed on the walls of Antalya after its conquest, and his successor, Kay Qubad I (r. 1219–1237), used the same title in inscriptions on his architectural projects.[19] The Ghurid sultan Ghiyath al-Din Muhammad b. Sam (r. 1163–1203), who ruled over a territory roughly equivalent to that of modern-day Afghanistan, included mention of his monarchal titles (*al-sultan al-mu'azzam* and *al-shahanshah al-a'zam*) along with his newly acquired title from the caliph as Qasim Amir al-Mu'minin ("partner of the Commander of the Faithful") on the famous minaret of Jam – the tallest in Islam up until that time – which he constructed in 570/1174, probably specifically to commemorate his newly acquired honors.[20] The arrival of a caliphal endorsement was usually celebrated with processions and great fanfare. The ceremony of the investiture of the Ayyubid al-Malik al-'Adil in 604/1207 provides a representative snapshot of this, and similar events are attested for Nur al-Din and Saladin earlier.

Ibn Wasil states that when Shihab al-Din al-Suhrawardi, al-Nasir's emissary, approached Damascus, carrying the investiture honorific (*al-tashrif al-imami*), al-'Adil, together with his sons, al-Ashraf and al-Mu'azzam, and a formation of troops, met the emissary outside the city, and all the public turned out for the occasion. Al-'Adil held an official reception in the citadel, where he sat and accepted the honors. The caliph's emissaries then invested him with a black cloak and turban embroidered with gold, placed a heavy, jewel-studded gold necklace around his neck, and girded him with a sword whose scabbard glittered with gold. While this was happening, a banner was unfurled over his head, with all the titles of the caliph inscribed in white on the black cloth of the banner. Special commemorative (donative) gold coins were then showered on him, while the emissary handed other robes of honor to al-'Adil's sons, and his minister, Ibn Shukr. A proclamation was then read that described the investiture, and listed the new titles bestowed by

---

[19] Mecit, "Kingship," 70–71; Richard McClary, *Architecture of the Rum Seljuqs* (Edinburgh, 2017), 179. Kay Khusraw (r. 1237–1246) used the title "Partner of the Commander of the Faithful" over the portal of the Karatay Khan in 638/1241: Ahmet Ertug, *The Seljuks* (Istanbul, 1991), 93.

[20] C. E. Bosworth, "The Ghurids in Khurasan," in *Medieval Central Asia and the Persianate World*, ed. D. G. Tor and A. C. S. Peacock (London, 2015), 210–213.

the caliph on al-ʿAdil, "*shahanshah*, king of kings, friend of the Commander of the Faithful (*shahanshah, malik al-muluk, khalil amir al-muʾminin*)." After the ceremony al-ʿAdil mounted a white horse, rode outside the citadel for a distance, and then reentered through the gate of victory.[21]

The description of this ceremony was something that was repeated from Cairo to Konya, and from Yemen to Delhi. The titles, symbols, and political language surrounding the event linked a myriad of kingdoms and principalities in a federative loyalty to the Abbasid caliphate. The Abbasid court in Baghdad also provided to rising dynasties the model for building courtly institutions and the diplomatic language associated with it.[22]

Baghdad stood as a model of reference not simply due to the Abbasid caliphate but also as an intellectual and cultural center of the Islamic world. Prior to the rise of Egypt's al-Azhar as a center of Sunnism in the Mamluk period, the Islamic world looked to Baghdad for the best colleges – particularly the Nizamiyya founded in 457/1065 by Nizam al-Mulk – which graduated the brightest scholars on Islam and trained the gifted in the Arabic literary craft. The list of these luminaries includes such names as the philologist Ibn al-Anbari, who stayed on as professor in the Nizamiyya; the Andalusian jurist Abu Bakr b. al-Arabi, who reportedly took much new learning back to Seville; the historian Ibn Asakir; the biographer of Saladin, al-ʿImad al-Isfahani; and the Iranian poet Saʿdi of Shiraz. A student of al-Ghazali, al-Mahdi b. Tumart, who came from North Africa, took not only debating skills and the latest ideas on Islamic interpretation from his stint in Baghdad but also a recipe for regime change, as he cultivated the *daʿwa* (mission) of the Almohad dynasty, which supplanted the Almoravids in 1147.

The Abbasid imprint on Islamic society was so strong that no one could conceive of continuity in the world without an Abbasid caliph. The aforementioned Ibn al-Tiqtaqa described how even after Baghdad had fallen there was great reluctance even amongst the non-Muslim

---

[21] Ibn Wasil, *Mufarrij*, 3:180–182.

[22] Doris Behrens-Abouseif, "The Citadel of Cairo: Stage for Mamluk Ceremonial," *Annales Islamologiques* 24 (1988), 30; Stephen Humphreys, *Islamic History: A Framework for Inquiry* (Princeton, 1991), 44; Marina Rustow, *The Lost Archive: Traces of a Caliphate in a Cairo Synagogue* (Princeton, 2020), 11–14. See al-Qalqashandi, *Subh al-Aʿsha*, ed. Nabil Khalid al-Khatib (Beirut, 2012), 5:453.

Mongols to do away with the position of caliph. "[The Abbasids] had in the hearts of their people," according to the author, "a position not approached by that of any other in the world. So much so that, when the Sultan Hulaku conquered Baghdad and wanted to kill the Caliph, Abu Ahmad Abdallah al-Mustaʿsim, they told him that, if the Caliph were killed, the order of the world would be deranged, the sun veiled, the rain and crops withheld."[23] Ibn al-Tiqtaqa was looking back on the Abbasid past in a "mirror for princes" style, but according to one historian was also reflecting, as St. Augustine did in 410 CE, after the fall of the Rome to Goths, on the meaning of the fall of the capital of an empire in the divine plan of history.[24]

After the fall of Baghdad and the move of a shadow Abbasid caliphate to Cairo, starting with the reign of the Mamluk sultan Baybars, many political leaders, including the Mamluks, looked to the caliph as a source of legitimacy. But there were increasing experiments to discover a new legitimacy by applying the tasks that had made the Abbasid family central in the Islamic world. The Mamluks therefore became pioneers in the development of a strong interest in protecting and refurbishing the holy cities of Mecca and Medina, and protecting the pilgrimage caravans to Mecca. The Mamluk sultans emphasized their religious functions as "custodians of the two sanctuaries" (*khadim al-haramayn*), which ironically was from ancient times the honorific purportedly given by the Prophet to his uncle, al-Abbas – the task of providing water for the pilgrims and guarding the keys of the Kaʿba. The Ottomans would later inherit these tasks when they took over the Mamluk domains. Patronage of the *ʿulama* and construction of madrasas would also thrive under the Mamluks as religiously honorific tasks, but there was never really a substitute for the actual presence of the caliphs in Baghdad. Only there could one discover the historical continuity of the caliphate, and only there could the memory of caliphs such as al-Mansur, al-Rashid, and al-Maʾmun be truly evoked.

In looking back on Abbasid history one finds a range of lasting influences and contributions of the Abbasids. The rise of the dynasty stimulated theories on government and law, encouraged a more expansive role for the Hashimite family with its Alid and Abbasid wings, and

---

[23] Ibn al-Tiqtaqa, *al-Fakhri*, 141, trans. Whitting, 135.

[24] James Kritzeck, "Ibn al-Tiqtaqa and the Fall of Baghdad," in *The World of Islam: Studies in Honor of Philip Hitti*, ed. James Kritzeck and R. Bayly Winder (Princeton, 1959), 184.

in time fostered a balanced interaction between Sunni and Shiʿi currents in spite of occasional discord. Caliphs such as al-Nasir and al-Mustansir managed this interaction more successfully than many later rulers in the region. In their administrations the Abbasids encouraged an atmosphere of openness to other religions, and employed individuals of diverse faiths – most prominently, a significant cluster of Christians who over the years served as ministers and court officials. With their capital standing at the crossroads of cultures, the Abbasids became the shepherds of international commerce, ethnic mixing, and cosmopolitanism. The caliphs themselves reflected this diversity, some with mothers who were Greek (al-Wathiq, al-Muʿtamid, al-Muqtadi, and al-Radi), Turkish (al-Muktafi, al-Nasir, and al-Zahir), Armenian (al-Qaʾim, al-Mustanjid, al-Mustadiʾ), and Abyssinian (al-Muqtafi and al-Mustaʿsim).

There is perhaps one other important imprint that the Abbasids left in regional terms, and that is in their forging of the idea of Iraq as a unique entity, thereby shaping the foundations of the modern nation-state of Iraq. In recent years some publications that are apologetics for Western colonialism and the US invasion of Iraq in 2003 which fragmented the country have been misleading in denying any sense of cohesion for the land between the Tigris and Euphrates, or even that it should be called Iraq – preferring Mesopotamia instead. The Greek term "Mesopotamia" was the name that the Romans once gave to their easternmost province, and it was picked up in the modern period by British colonial officials – and in a restricted sense. Ancient geographers actually defined the label broadly – with Strabo defining it as all the land between the Tigris and Euphrates, while Herodotus viewed Mesopotamia as stretching from the Taurus to the Persian Gulf.[25] Classical Arab geographers, such as al-Muqaddasi and Ibn Hawqal, recognized the region of Mesopotamia as "Iraq," and, while this label could ebb and flow in territorial definition the way Misr (Egypt) did, in both cases rivers defined the core of these regions.[26] Abbasid methods of provincial administration reinforced this sometimes, such as when the term "al-Iraq" was inscribed on a gold dinar for the year 199/814

---

[25] Hamish Cameron, *Making Mesopotamia: Geography and Empire in a Romano-Iranian Borderland* (Leiden, 2019), 7–12.

[26] Abu'l-Fida, *Taqwim al-Buldan*, ed. M. Reinaud (Paris, 1840), 291. The thirteenth-century al-Qazwini even stretched the term Iraq to include Mosul: *Athar al-Bilad wa Akhbar al-ʿIbad* (Beirut, n.d.), 419.

(see coin illustrations), and medieval chroniclers enhanced the label further when they spoke of "the people of Iraq" (*ahl al-ʿIraq*). The foundation of Baghdad as a new capital and the inevitable immediate trade connections this city encouraged with towns such as Basra and Mosul created an economic zone of revenue generation for what would become the home province of the early Abbasid caliphs.

Caliphs in distress tried on more than one occasion to relocate to Mosul. Al-Muʿtadid seems to have spent more time there than he did in Baghdad, and in later centuries Mosul with its provincial dynasties helped strengthen the hand of later Abbasid caliphs when they sought to revive their authority – as happened when Nur al-Din Zangi sided with the caliph al-Muqtafi against the Seljuks. With the largest tax revenue of the Abbasid state coming from the Tigris–Euphrates region, Iraq was the home province of the dynasty. And even when the authority of the caliphs declined politically under Buyid and Seljuk rule, by their trenchant presence in Baghdad for five centuries the Abbasids kept the particularity of the Iraq province going. The importance of this Abbasid heritage to the identity of the region, along with the interconnectedness of its cities, were no doubt self-evident factors to British colonial officials, such as Gertrude Bell and Sir Percy Cox, when they set out after World War I to shape the boundaries of the modern nation-state of Iraq, and placed a Hashimite monarch on the country's throne in 1921.[27] Bell, in particular, described things in almost messianic terms, when she said of Faisal's installation as king on 23 August 1921: "It has been 700 years since an Arab king walked among his Mesopotamian subjects."[28]

The Sources for Writing Abbasid History

Given the range of influences of the Abbasid caliphate on the medieval and modern periods, it is surprising how little work has been done to survey Abbasid history from beginning to end. In contrast, one can

---

[27] Michael Seymour, *Babylon: Legend, History and the Ancient City* (London, 2013), 235. As Gertrude Bell explained to the British ambassador in France in 1921 regarding the interdependency of Iraqi cities, "If Mosul goes, Baghdad goes": Liora Lukitz, *A Quest in the Middle East: Gertrude Bell and the Making of Modern Iraq* (London, 2006), 160; and on Mosul, 192–195, 217.

[28] Lisa Cooper, *In Search of Kings and Conquerors: Gertrude Bell and the Archaeology of the Middle East* (London, 2017), 232.

find more readily available surveys of political history for provincial dynasties, such as the Buyids, Ghaznavids, Seljuks, and even the Saffarids and the Aghlabids. For the Abbasids, however, the picture remains scattered, and needs to be compiled from a variety of specialized studies and primary sources in order to fill the gaps for the later, under-studied phases (tenth to thirteenth centuries) and sketch a general history of the dynasty. Although in the late nineteenth and early twentieth centuries significant attention was paid to early Abbasid history and archaeology, the pendulum swung the other way after World War II, with a new emphasis on the provinces of the caliphate and the provincial dynasties. This shift maintained the neglect of the later Abbasid centuries, and added to it a sidelining of the topic of the caliphate in general.

This lopsided situation began to change in the 1980s with new contributions on the early Abbasids by M. A. Shaban, J. Lassner, and E. Daniel (and P. Crone and G. Hawting on the Umayyads). The writings of Hugh Kennedy on both the Umayyads and the Abbasids helped energize a renewed look at the history of the caliphate, and brought this topic back to the academic center stage and the general reader at the same time. His surveys of the Abbasids included the detailed *The Prophet and the Age of the Caliphates* and, more recently, *When Baghdad Ruled the Muslim World* (also published under the title *The Court of the Caliphs*), which he labeled as "lighthearted"; but in both cases he tended to stop with the Buyid entry into Baghdad, and his work still awaited further analytic development and enhancement by information from other primary sources. We may also need to bear in mind that throughout the hiatus in Western studies on the caliphate, there was a steady stream of publications on the Abbasids in Arabic by Iraqi scholars. The list of those includes such names as Abd al-Aziz al-Duri, Saleh Ahmad al-Ali, Farouk Umar, Mustafa Jawad, Nasir al-Naqshbandi, Yusuf Ghunayma, Isa Salman, Gurgis Awwad, and Naji Ma'ruf, whose work can be found in journals such as *Sumer*, *al-Maskukat*, and *al-Majma' al-'Ilmi al-'Iraqi*, in addition to monographs by some of them.

The state of evidence for Abbasid history has also provided a challenge for the historian. In material terms, we find, for example, that there is an ample resource of Abbasid coins in museum collections around the world, but these have never been systematically analyzed, and there is as yet no full catalog of Abbasid coinage similar to the one we have for the Umayyads.[29] Abbasid archaeology, however, unlike numismatics, has left few traces. In spite of the detailed picture given by the eleventh-century Khatib al-Baghdadi of the Round City of al-Mansur, once located on Baghdad's west side, we lack any remnants of his Golden Gate Palace with its iconic green dome. From a topographic point view, certain shrines, such as the Mosque of Abu Hanifa and the tomb of Ma'ruf al-Karkhi (along with the Kazimayn Mosque), can help in locating respectively the Rusafa of al-Mahdi on the east side and the Round City on the west side, since each of these was adjacent to these religious structures. Some compensation for those studying the profile of the Abbasid court and the urban rhythm of the Abbasid town can be sought with the varied state of ruins at Samarra, Raqqa, and Ukhaydir.

Art historians and archaeologists, such as K. A. C. Creswell, Ernst Herzfeld, and Gertrude Bell, pioneered the surveying and excavation of Abbasid monuments at Samarra in the period just before World War I, and more recently important studies on archaeology have appeared by Alastair Northedge (on Samarra), Michael Meinecke (on Raqqa), and more generally by Marcus Milwright and Alan Walmsley, but all these remain small in proportion to the historical presence of the Abbasids. The main Abbasid city on the east side succumbed to the destruction wrought by the Mongols in two waves (Hulegu's in 1258 and Tamerlane's in 1393 and 1400). Today, a few exceptions can evoke the medieval atmosphere: a bridge over the Harba river, attributed to al-Mustansir, is the only known all-brick bridge in Iraq; the Mustansiriyya madrasa dating to 1234 (even if heavily restored); and a wrongly attributed "Abbasid palace" (al-Qasr al-Abbasi), which is more likely a madrasa. The Khaffafin Mosque, once constructed by Zumurrud Khatun, al-Mustadi''s wife, and the Qumriyya Mosque, begun by al-Nasir and completed by al-Mustansir, were both rebuilt in later centuries. A market building called Khan Mirjan, dating to the Jalayrids in 1359, possibly resembles Abbasid structures that were built in the twelfth and thirteenth centuries to a much closer extent than the restored structures.

In order to write Abbasid history we are left with a limited set of primary written sources for each phase of the caliphate's existence, and

---

[29] Michel G. Klat, *Catalogue of the Post-Reform Dirhams: The Umayyad Dynasty* (London, 2002).

it may be worth providing an overview of these. For the early period and the high caliphate during the eighth and ninth centuries the historian has recourse to the most famous of the Arabic chronicles, *Tarikh al-Rusul wa'l-Muluk* (*The History of the Prophets and Kings*) by Muhammad b. Jarir al-Tabari (d. 310/923). This chronicle, which stops in 302/914, can be cross-examined with information provided by the *Tarikh* (*History*) of Ya'qubi (d. 284/897), which stops in 259/872, the accounts of Baladhuri (d. 279/892) in his *Ansab al-Ashraf* and *Futuh al-Buldan*, and the factual compendia book on Islamic heritage, *al-Ma'arif*, by Ibn Qutayba (d. 276/889). And to these one can add some other general histories, such as *al-Akhbar al-Tiwal* by al-Dinawari (d. 282/895) and *Muruj al-Dhahab* of al-Mas'udi (d. 345/956). All these primary sources usually also double as the key sources for writing the histories of the earlier Rashidun and Umayyad caliphates, but they differ regarding the Abbasids in that their authors were either contemporary with events they describe or closer in chronological distance to past events, and this has lent these authors a façade of reliability when it comes to reporting on the Abbasid period.

A useful bridge can then be found in a cluster of geographical treatises that span the tenth century, the most famous of which are undoubtedly Ibn Khurdadhbih's *al-Masalik wa'l-Mamalik* (*The Book of Routes and Realms*), al-Muqaddasi's *Ahsan al-Taqasim fi Ma'rifat al-Aqalim* (*The Best Divisions for the Knowledge of the Regions*), and Ibn Hawqal's *Surat al-Ard* (*A View of the World*). These books provide information on regional economic resources, landmarks, a combination of history and legend surrounding locales, and the tenth-century take on ethnography. The heyday of the administrative class of the court during this same period also makes available some manuals of administration, such as *Kitab al-Kharaj wa Sina'at al-Kitaba* (*The Book of Revenues and the Craft of Writing*) by Qudama b. Ja'far (d. 337/948), *al-Wuzara' wa'l-Kuttab* (*The Book of the Ministers and Scribes*) by al-Jahshiyari (d. 331/942), and *al-Wuzara'* (*The Ministers*) and *Rusum Dar al-Khilafa* (*The Rules and Regulations of the Abbasid Court*) by Hilal al-Sabi' (d. 448/1056). A widely cited work, *Kitab al-Awraq*, by al-Suli (d. 335/946), the renowned chess master and courtier, focuses heavily on poetry and the gossipy side of the Abbasid court, but gives the view of someone associated with the ruling dynasty. Although the work of the humanists and the litterateurs can be dated in origin largely with the work of al-Jahiz (d. 255/869), it is really in the tenth century that a new wave of moralizing and entertaining literature takes off, with writers such as al-Tanukhi (d. 384/994), Abu'l-Faraj al-Isfahani (d. 356/967), al-Tha'alibi (d. 429/1038), or the twelfth-century heritage compendium *al-Tadhkira al-Hamduniyya* by Ibn Hamdun. Historical writing was influenced by the new overt approach to draw lessons from history in the *Tajarib al-Umam* (*The Experiences of Nations*) by Miskawayh (d. 421/1030), whose goal was instructing rulers on wiser political control than the enlightenment of the average citizen. At the western extremity of the Islamic world, in al-Andalus, a new phenomenon developed in the tenth century with the growing interest in all that was happening in the central Islamic lands, and particularly in Iraq. *Al-'Iqd al-Farid* (*The Unique Necklace*) by Ibn Abd Rabbih (d. 328/940) in many ways provides a succinct anthology of what was required in a high-culture education alongside religious knowledge. Ibn Abd Rabbih reconciles elements from the literary writings of al-Jahiz and Ibn Qutayba, and one cannot but note the paradox of a writer working under Umayyad patronage – and in the year they declared themselves caliphs (929) – and yet expending great effort in preserving Abbasid heritage.

The literature of the *'ulama* flourished during the eleventh and twelfth centuries, a period that is usually described as a "Sunni revival" accompanying the emergence of the madrasa. The hallmark of this literature is the biographical dictionary (*tabaqat*) of scholars based in one town or another. The fourteen-volume *Tarikh Baghdad* by Khatib al-Baghdadi (d. 463/1071) gives the illusion of great promise for all manner of detail on the political and social history of the Abbasid metropolis. In reality, this is a biographical dictionary, mainly of religious scholars but also, albeit briefly, of key figures who lived in Baghdad, or were connected with the Abbasid dynasty in some way, up until the time of the author. Ibn al-Dubaythi (d. 637/1239) produced a sequel (*Dhayl Tarikh Baghdad*) with a similar approach later on, and later there was another, by Ibn al-Najjar (d. 643/1245). Khatib's *Tarikh* is heavily infused with hadiths of dubious authenticity, information about the teachers and students of scholars, and much lore about these scholars. His work sets the benchmark for the resource needed to study a field, which the longtime Harvard Islamicist Roy Mottahedeh has called "ulamalogy." The book invited copycats in towns around the Islamic world, with similar biographical dictionaries for Isfahan, Qazwin, Nishapur, and Samarqand, and with the most voluminous being produced in Syria for towns such as Aleppo, by Ibn al-Adim (d. 660/1262), and the record set for Damascus by Ibn Asakir (d. 571/1175), with his *Tarikh Madinat Dimashq* reaching up to seventy volumes in the modern published version.

Writing Abbasid history for the period from the eleventh to the early thirteenth centuries benefits from *al-Muntazam* by Ibn al-Jawzi (d. 597/1202). His seventeen-volume work combines the biographical dictionary format with the annalistic one, listing important events, but is too focused on Baghdad, and stops at 574/1178. Historians would have been at a great disadvantage were it not for *al-Kamil fi'l-Tarikh* of Ibn al-Athir (d. 630/1233), who lived through the turbulent period of the Crusades, the early Mongol invasions, and great powers such those of the Khwarazm shahs in Transoxiana and the Ayyubids in Egypt. Based in Mosul, and writing under the patronage of its wily Atabeg prince, Badr al-Din Luʾluʾ, Ibn al-Athir tried to maintain neutrality toward the main dynasties of the period, and he reflects an environment of high culture different from that of Baghdad. Although he drew mainly on Tabari's accounts for the earlier Abbasid period, he streamlined those, and often included valuable information on contemporary events in the Mediterranean world and Central Asia. The main value of his work is for the period after where Tabari's stops, and the way he avoided privileging accounts that Miskawayh, for example, would have deployed as exempla in an earlier period. Through his attempt to remove the hagiography and exempla, and by trying to pay attention to different regions of the Islamic world, Ibn al-Athir paved the way for history as an independent and academic discipline.

The Ghaznavid and Seljuk periods, while covered by Ibn al-Athir, benefit from other less ambitious works, such as *Zayn al-Akhbar* by Gardizi (fifth/eleventh century), *Tarikh al-Dawla Saljuqiyya* by al-Husayni (d. after 622/1225), and *Rahat al-Sudur wa Ayat al-Surur* by al-Rawandi (d. 601/1204). Less is known about these authors than Ibn al-Athir, but they all seem to have had access to courtly circles and privileged information, and sometimes themselves received the patronage of princes. The maverick scholar al-Biruni was clearly not the only one who wrote under direct patronage from dynasts such as the Ghaznavids. Although focused on the Seljuks, the Persian historians provide valuable information sometimes not found in the Arabic sources, such as al-Rawandi's mention of an attempt by the Abbasid caliph al-Muqtafi to have the Seljuk sultan Masʿud kidnapped when he arrived for prayers on a religious holiday – an attempt that didn't materialize because the sultan failed to show up that day. Additional details on the political and military calculations of the princes in western Iran ('Iraq al-'Ajam) are also provided by al-Rawandi but not Ibn al-Jawzi or Ibn al-Athir.

While Ibn al-Athir's chronicle stops in 628/1231, other works help continue the chronology at a distance from Iraq. In India, there is the *Tabaqat-i Nasiri* written in Delhi around 658/1260 by Juzjani, and although the work centers more on the careers of the sultans of Delhi, such as Iltutmish, it contains important references to the Abbasids. The true sequels to Ibn al-Athir can be found in the subsequent period in Syria and Egypt under Ayyubid and Mamluk patronage. Writers such as Abu Shama (d. 665/1266) and Ibn Wasil (d. 697/1297) provide important elisions of information for the thirteenth century and the twilight period of the Abbasid caliphate. The trend toward the voluminous oeuvre then builds up all the way till the fifteenth century in a wave that forms the true emblems of Mamluk universal histories, such as those by Ibn Kathir (d. 774/1373), al-Dhahabi (d. 748/1348), Ibn al-Furat (d. 807/1405), al-Maqrizi (d. 845/1441), Ibn Taghribirdi (d. 874/1470), and Ibn Iyas (d. 930/1530). Along with these, two encyclopedic works that contain much history ought to be mentioned: *Nihayat al-Arib fi Funun al-Adab* by al-Nuwayri (d. 733/1333) and *Masalik al-Absar fi al-Mamalik wa'l-Amsar* by Ibn Fadl Allah al-Umari (d. 745/1345).

Sibt ibn al-Jawzi (d. 654/1257), grandson of the more famous Ibn al-Jawzi of al-Nasir's reign, also produced a work of history and biography known as *Mir'at al-Zaman fi Tarikh al-A'yan* (*A Mirror in Time for the History of Notables*), which has only recently been published in its entirety, and with a sequel by a native of Ba'albek, Qutb al-Din al-Yunini (d. 726/1326), together reaching up to twenty-two volumes. Sibt's education and writing reflects a hybridity between the last days of Baghdad's intellectual grandeur and that of the increasingly more central role for the religious experience of Damascus, where he eventually settled. His contribution reflects the 'ulama worldview of the intellectual elite, and what they considered necessary knowledge about the past. This type of composition was to have a long run, virtually up until the modern period, and was updated and organized around a century rather than a town, as had been the case with Khatib al-Baghdadi and Ibn Asakir. A historian of the Abbasids can find new information in even a seventeenth-century source, such as *Shadharat al-Dhahab fi Akhbar man Dhahab* by Ibn al-ʿImad al-Hanbali (d. 1089/1678).

Abbasid Baghdad in its last decades lacks an easily usable history that can be identified as local. Ibn al-Saʿi (d. 674/1274), who was the first librarian of al-Mustansiriyya madrasa, wrote a multi-volume historical work that has been lost. A book entitled *al-Hawadith al-Jamiʿa*, once attributed to Ibn al-Fuwati (d. 723/1323) but now acknowledged to be anonymous, dates to the late thirteenth century. It provides valuable information on the reigns of al-Mustansir and al-Mustaʿsim, but one can easily notice in its historiography, as well as in much Arabic historical writing of the conquered east, the shadow of Ilkhanid pressure, which stifled the more vivacious spirit that characterized earlier writers on the Abbasids. Arabic poetry, the multi-layered anecdote, and digressions on characters on the margins of society, which reached a peak in the tenth century, all disappeared in the humorless world of the Ilkhanids. Concise dynastic histories, arranged by the reigns of caliphs, by authors such as al-Irbili (d. 717/1317) and Ibn al-Kazaruni (d. 697/1297), round out the survey of the Abbasid caliphate up until al-Mustaʿsim, but these remain mainly cursory and centered on the key political figures of each reign. And another work from the same period, *al-Manaqib al-Abbasiyya waʾl-Mafakhir al-Mustansiriyya*, remains in manuscript.

This sketch of primary sources, often familiar in name to specialists but sometimes inhibiting full access due to their size, gives us a glance of the historical literature that must be mined for writing Abbasid history. The fragmented nature of the evidence ensures that further research can often turn up new facts or provide an opportunity for a fresh reading of historical accounts previously thought to be fully understood. In surveying the Abbasid world, one needs to keep track of developments in three spheres that interacted over the course of a five-century period: the caliphate as a political institution that defined legitimacy and was open to a range of social perceptions and imagination; the Abbasid empire, which fostered networking across frontiers and encouraged cohesiveness and mobility in the region of the Middle East and North Africa; and, finally, the Abbasid capital, Baghdad, which was an urban magnet and a crucible of ideas.

The history of the Abbasid caliphate was not an isolated unit within the spectrum of medieval Islamic history but, as this survey shows, one that was deeply integrated into the social and religious patterns that shaped other Islamic dynasties over a long period. And, in spite of efforts to understand the contexts of change, the question will always remain whether Islam as a religious system shaped the history of the Abbasids or whether it was shaped by their unfolding political history. The dynamic interaction of the caliphs with various Islamic trends shows the transformation of both over the course of history. The Abbasid capital Baghdad, like other medieval Islamic cities such as Bukhara, Cairo, and Cordoba, mirrors the favorable side of the modern world: an open society where freedom of markets, ideas, and multiculturalism played out, and the record of their histories shows how these factors stimulated energetic waves in the areas of learning, commerce, crafts, and the arts. But Abbasid history also shows, no less than today, the havoc caused by nature and nations in factors such as climate change and invasions. While their history provides a model of how Islamic civilization fused ancient legacies with contemporary cultures, it also provides a cautionary tale of how the momentum of progress is always a perilous one in the face of a political challenge.

2 | From Revolution to Foundations (750–775)

The Roots of Umayyad–Hashimite Rivalry

In the early summer of 129/747 a group of dissidents boldly gathered in a village just outside the town of Marw in northeastern Iran to declare a rebellion against the Umayyad caliph in distant Damascus. They were sympathizers of the family of the Prophet, the Hashimites, whom they considered more worthy of the office of caliphate. Some in the crowd favored an Imam descended from the Prophet's cousin Ali, others from Muhammad's uncle, al-Abbas, but all in this "Hashimiyya" movement were agreed that religious criteria would eventually find *al-rida min al-Muhammad* (the one satisfactory or agreed upon from the family of Muhammad). And the Qur'an verse they chose to inscribe on their first coinage reflected this ambiguity, stating: "No reward do I ask for this except for affinity to those near of kin,"[1] taken here to mean the kin of the Prophet.

That night they welcomed in their midst a recently arrived visitor from Jordan, a charismatic emissary of Persian origin named Abu Muslim al-Khurasani, who carried dispatches from the guide of the movement, Ibrahim b. Muhammad b. Ali b. Abdallah b. al-Abbas (known as Ibrahim al-Imam), and brought two black banners bearing symbolism: one was named "the clouds" and the other "the shadows," and these were unfurled among the assembled crowd, who were all clad in black. The millennial message to the anxious crowd was clear: just as the clouds cover the earth, the Abbasid movement would one day rule the wide lands; and just as the shadows always exist, an Abbasid Imam would always lead it. This was a turning point in what was known as the *da'wa* or "call" that would culminate with the establishment of the *dawla*, or final state.

[1] Qur'an 42:22.

28

Ever since the turn in the Islamic hijri calendar to the year 100/718 in the brief reign of the caliph Umar b. Abd al-Aziz there had been a surge in chiliastic visions in Islamic society, and an expectation of a messianic figure or "Mahdi," who would bring about renewal and usher in a utopian age of justice and righteous rule. Riding this wave of millennialism, the Hashimite movement heightened expectations by taking the *da'wa* to the frontier region of Khurasan, far from the Arabian heartlands, thereby creating a sense of *hijra* (migration) that emulated the Prophet's *hijra* from Mecca to Medina in 622, which started the Islamic calendar and laid the foundation of the first Islamic state. Just as the Ansar ("helpers") of Medina aided Muhammad in defying the ruling clans of Mecca, Iranians in Khurasan were now viewed as the new helpers of the Hashimite kinsmen of Muhammad, who would help them regain political leadership, long lapsed outside the Prophet's family after the end of the caliphate of Ali in 40/661.

This was not the first time the ruling Umayyad dynasty had faced a challenge from the Hashimite family, but it was the first time it had come from the Abbasid branch, which they had previously viewed as politically the quietest or even friendly, whose core members lived in a mansion in Humayma in Jordan, among the more luxurious palatial countryside villas of the Umayyads.[2] This was a region of leisurely retreat for Arab aristocrats, who savored its intermediate position between urban and desert environments, and its mix of Arabic and Hellenistic Roman cultures. It was not a place for brewing rebellion, and the famed castles and mansions at Mshatta, Khirbat al-Mafjar, and Qusayr Amra, whose ruins still stand today and are familiar to tourists and archaeologists, were once iconic for the lifestyle of indulgence that surrounded the rule of some Umayyad caliphs.[3] In what was helpful timing for the Abbasids, these various courts were badly shaken, and some destroyed, by an earthquake that took place in 747 – an event that probably appeared as a sign of divine retribution to the opposition. Umayyad surveillance had long been vigilant against dissidence, but

---

[2] The Humayma site, located some 175 miles south of Amman, was excavated and analyzed in the 1990s; the findings are in a report by Rebecca Foote and J. P. Oleson, "Humeima Excavation Project, 1995–96," *Fondation Max van Berchem Bulletin* 10 (1996); and more generally Alan Walmsley, *Early Islamic Syria: an Archaeological Assessment* (London, 2007).

[3] K. A. C. Creswell, *A Short Account of Early Muslim Architecture* (London, 1968), 93–96, 157.

tended to center its efforts on the activities of the Alid branch of the Hashimite family, which had mounted challenges to the Umayyads in the town of Kufa and southern Iraq from the outset of their rule in 40/ 661. Kufa was the base of the fourth caliph, Ali, during a short reign dogged by constant contention with Mu'awiya, the governor of Syria and eventually the founder of the Umayyad dynasty, who was based in Damascus. It was also nearby to Kufa, at Karbala, that Ali's son al-Husayn had died in battle while struggling to fend off a large Umayyad force in 61/680 – an event that galvanized the Shi'a (lit. "partisans") of Ali and started the ideology of martyrdom in the decades prior to the revolution. The search for atonement for having let Husayn down haunted the Alid partisans as they searched for a charismatic leader from the Hashimite family who would avenge his memory.[4]

In spite of dissidence, the Umayyad state kept growing through conquests, which by the early eighth century had grown with exceptional speed to reach as far as North Africa and Spain in the west, and the borders of China and India in the east – the largest empire the world had yet seen. The perennial question of who should have succeeded the Prophet in leadership – the caliphate – was never resolved and gave rise to varied opposition movements, such as the rising of al-Husayn, and movements of political assertiveness by al-Mukhtar, the Kharijites, and Abdallah b. al-Zubayr. A turning point for the opposition came in 125/ 743 when a descendant of al-Husayn, Yahya b. Zayd, took the action to the eastern frontier province of Khurasan and declared a rebellion in Juzjan, after an unsuccessful rising by his father, Zayd b. Ali b. al-Husayn, in Kufa in 122/740. Yahya was an inexperienced young rebel, and his political efforts were no match for the titanic power of Umayyad governors who had just defeated the Khan of the Turgesh Turks, across the northeastern frontier in Transoxiana. However, he was instrumental in expanding the geography of Shi'i activism to the east, and in successfully sowing a seed of Hashimite sympathy. The tragedy of the rebel's capture and death by crucifixion awakened the province of Khurasan, and made many in the region disillusioned with Umayyad rule. In Khurasan that year, it was said, no son was born without being named Yahya or Zayd.[5] This perhaps included Yahya

---

[4] G. R. Hawting, *The First Dynasty of Islam: The Umayyad Caliphate, AD 661–750* (Carbondale, IL, 1986), 49–53.

[5] Elton L. Daniel, *The Political and Social History of Khurasan under Abbasid Rule, 747–820* (Minneapolis and Chicago, 1979), 39.

b. Khalid al-Barmaki, the future patriarch of the renowned family of ministers to the Abbasids. And it was probably after the rising of Yahya b. Zayd that the Abbasids became vocal in the Hashimiyya movement.

In the early years of Umayyad rule the opposition had mainly centered on Ali and his descendants, who were viewed as closest to the Prophet Muhammad, since they were descended through Muhammad's daughter Fatima, and as religiously special, endowed with gnostic knowledge that was handed down confidentially from the Prophet to Ali, and in succession to later Imams. In the period immediately after the Prophet, known to historians as the reign of the Rashidun caliphs or "the rightly guided caliphs" (Abu Bakr, Umar b. al-Khattab, Uthman, and Ali) in 632–661, the Abbasid family did not seem much interested in politics. Al-Abbas, the Prophet's uncle, mainly held the honorific task of being the custodian of the Well of Zamzam and providing water to pilgrims who came to Mecca. He was respected as an elder of the Hashimite family, but he made no claim for political leadership. This changed with his son, Abdallah (d. 68/687), who sided with Ali during the civil war, first against Aisha and later against Mu'awiya. After Ali was assassinated Abdallah seems to have given up on politics, and devoted himself to the study of the Qur'an and the sayings of the Prophet.

There is a hazy quality about Ibn Abbas, whom the medieval sources depict at times as an inspired sage and at others as a teacher of hadiths and literary heritage. Although his political views are unknown, he seems to have started to distance himself from Ali when the latter's efforts at state building began to falter. Throughout those years he continued to reside in Mecca, but probably made trips to Syria, and he maintained friendly relations with Mu'awiya. Ibn Abbas lived through two dramatic Hashimite rebellions after Mu'awiya's death; the first was al-Husayn's at Karbala in 61/680; the second, in 64/684, also in Iraq, was led by a zealous figure, al-Mukhtar b. Ubayd al-Thaqafi, on behalf of Muhammad b. al-Hanafiyya, a son of Ali but from a wife other than Fatima. Ibn Abbas remained neutral toward these events, but reportedly encouraged his son, Ali b. Abdallah, to migrate with the Abbasid family from the Hijaz to the area of Syria under Umayyad rule.

With Ali b. Abdallah settled in Humayma, the activities of the Abbasid family seem to have undergone a quiet change, perhaps under the influence of Shi'i ideas. Although Abdallah b. Abbas occupied a central place in later Sunni memory as a reference point for Qur'an commentary and transmitting hadiths of the Prophet, neither of his two successors, Ali

b. Abdallah (d. 118/737) and his son Muhammad b. Ali (d. 125/743), showed any continuity of interest in Ibn Abbas's scholarly activities, which were continued by other scholars from Medina, such as 'Urwa b. al-Zubayr and Sa'id b. al-Musayyib. The new Abbasid patriarchs seem to have enjoyed some kind of honorable rank at the Umayyad court, perhaps engaged in trade, as the archaeology of Humayma indicates, and aspired to style themselves in religious terms as Imam figures of sorts.

While the Umayyad caliph Abd al-Malik was battling the tenacious rebellion of Abdallah and Mus'ab b. al-Zubayr in the Hijaz and Iraq, the Abbasid patriarch, Ali b. Abdallah, carried on friendly relations with the Umayyads, getting the privilege on one occasion of being invited to sit next to Abd al-Malik.[6] There is no evidence that the Abbasids were politically active during the reign of Abd al-Malik, and in fact the entire Hashimite and Alid cause was dormant in that period, with the torch of opposition shifting to the Kharijites and Abdallah b. al-Zubayr. Abd al-Malik was probably even instrumental in giving the "Abbasid-friendly" birth name al-Abbas b. al-Walid b. Abd al-Malik to one of his grandchildren, who later was the famous builder of the Anjar fortress and leader of many military incursions against the Byzantines in Asia Minor. In contrast, the name Ali was never given to a member of the Umayyad family.

With the reigns of Abd al-Malik's successors – al-Walid, Sulayman, and Hisham – the Alid cause was rekindled, and the Abbasid attitude seems to have undergone a change, with clearer political aspirations, by the time of Muhammad b. Ali b. Abdallah b. al-Abbas. The Abbasids were at that period still part of a wider cluster of potential challengers to the caliphate, but some sources claim that they (specifically the aforementioned Muhammad b. Ali) acquired the title to the Imamate through official transfer from the Alid Abu Hashim (d. 98/716), offspring of Muhammad b. al-Hanafiyya.[7] As Hashimite members of the Prophet's family, the Abbasids had the potential to organize their own

---

[6] *Akhbar al-Dawla al-'Abbasiyya*, ed. Abd al-Aziz al-Duri et al. (Beirut, 1971), 154; Ibn al-Athir, *al-Kamil*, 5:198.

[7] al-Ya'qubi, *Tarikh* (Beirut, 1970), 2:297; al-Tabari, *Tarikh al-Rusul wa'l-Muluk*, ed. M. J. de Goeje (Leiden, 1879–1901), III, 24–25; *Akhbar al-Dawla*, 179, 186. For a discussion of this source, see Elton Daniel, "The Anonymous History of the Abbasid Family and Its Place in Islamic Historiography," *IJMES* 14 (1982).

underground opposition, but they seem to have devised some arguments, such as the "Abu Hashim transfer," as one way to appease unconvinced Alids, or at least to create divisions among the latter.

The Abbasids also probably followed a strategy of gaining political legitimacy through affinity with the ruling family, for example when Muhammad b. Ali wedded Rayta bint Ubaydallah, the widow of Abdallah b. Abd al-Malik b. Marwan. This marriage was controversial enough for Muhammad b. Ali to need to obtain permission directly from the Umayyad caliph Umar b. Abd al-Aziz, who was known to have parted ways with the Marwanid children on various matters of policy and opinion. The new tie to Rayta was symbolically important because it seemed to invest the Abbasids with the same tribal power structure that had helped the Umayyads, and as such allowed the offspring of the union, Abu'l-Abbas al-Saffah, to claim priority as the first of the Abbasid caliphs to rule, in spite of his youth relative to his brothers, after the death of Ibrahim al-Imam. Propaganda favorable to the Abbasid dynasty later depicted the rise of al-Saffah (called Ibn al-Harithiyya, in reference to Rayta's Harithi family roots) in hagiographic terms, as someone born in the auspicious year 100 AH, whose accession was foretold by soothsayers, and as someone saved from Umayyad surveillance and persecution in terms that mildly echo the way the newborn Moses was saved from Pharaoh, or Jesus from Herod.[8]

The Revolution

The headlines of Umayyad imperialism were abundant throughout the reigns of the Marwanid children, and especially in the reign of Hisham b. Abd al-Malik (r. 724–743), but underneath, the ruling family was finding it harder to maintain a grip on power.[9] Continued expansion was becoming less popular, tribal tensions were surfacing on all fronts, and pious voices were starting to repudiate the indulgent lifestyle of certain Umayyads, which contributed to discord within the ruling

---

[8]   Tabari, *Tarikh*, III, 24–26; Baladhuri, *Ansab al-Ashraf*, vol. 3: *al-Abbas Abd al-Muttalib wa waladuhu*, ed. Abd al-Aziz al-Duri (Wiesbaden, 1978), 82; *Akhbar al-Dawla*, 201, 234, 401. According to some, Rayta was Abd al-Malik's widow: al-Mas'udi, *Muruj al-Dhahab*, ed. Charles Pellat (Beirut, 1965–1970), 4:94.

[9]   Khalid Yahya Blankinship, *The End of the Jihad State: The Reign of Hisham b. Abd al-Malik and the Collapse of the Umayyads* (Albany, 1994).

family itself and the eventual assassination of one of its caliphs, al-Walid II (r. 743–744). In this climate, the Hashimite cause grew alongside the pious opposition and found a potential for followers especially among non-Arabs, in Iraq and the east. Persia had a long history of toleration for persecuted religions, such as Judaism (banished from Jerusalem after Heraclius' victory over the Sasanids in 628), and Nestorian Christianity (condemned at the Council of Ephesus in 431), both of whose followers fled the oppression of the Byzantine empire by migrating to Mesopotamia. But Sasanid Persia also tolerated the propensity for new religious ideas that included elements of syncretism and renewal, most prominently evident in the movements of Buddhism, Manicheism, and Mazdakism, even if toleration could turn to hostility with the change of rulers.[10] The political and the religious could quickly combine in this central region, which was a place of intersecting ideas coming from Central Asia, India, and the Fertile Crescent. Islamic ideas about the Mahdi easily fit in this mosaic world, and a renewing figure – an Imam – took on for a diverse public meanings that ranged widely, from a legitimate political figure, who would bring about upright government, to a new prophetic figure, who might change the laws of the faith, and become the next in the line of the prophets from Adam to Muhammad.

The Abbasids observed the repeated but failed efforts by the Alids to gain the caliphate, and learned from their mistakes. They avoided using Iraq as a base for rebellion, and waited for an opportune moment to strike at the Umayyads. The social base of their appeal was increasingly the non-Arab converts to Islam (*mawali*, lit. "clients," mainly referring to Persians), who were starting to feel Umayyad inequity for taxing them as if they were still non-Muslims. The Hashimite cause therefore became a magnet for an egalitarian tendency of sorts, which even included elements of a class struggle within Iranian society itself between peasants and small-time merchants on the one hand, and the old landed Persian aristocracy (*dihqans*) on the other. But above all, the angst remained centered on the historical tragedy of the Hashimite family, which resonated with religious passion and desire for a grand moment of political redemption that would right the injustices previously inflicted on the family of Ali, and bring about the utopian reign of a religiously credible figure (a Mahdi) at the same time. For a while

[10] Touraj Daryaee, *Sasanian Persia* (London, 2009), 72–75.

members of the Abbasid family, including the future second caliph al-Mansur, had joined other movements, such as the revolt, between 127/744 and 129/747, led by Abdallah b. Muʿawiya b. Abdallah b. Jaʿfar b. Abi Talib, a member of a third branch of the Hashimite family, along with the Alids and Abbasids. He had based his movement in Isfahan, but as the rebellion crumbled under Umayyad battering and internal discord, the Abbasids began to organize something political of their own.

From their base in Humayma, the Abbasid leaders, first Muhammad b. Ali, then his son, Ibrahim b. Muhammad, connected with key agents in Kufa, such as Bukayr b. Mahan, whom they dispatched to Khurasan in the guise of merchants to start a call on behalf of the Abbasid family. These agents were entrusted with raising funds for the cause and recruiting new followers, and remaining within the broad parameters of the Hashimiyya movement. In 127/744 a delegation of these followers, Qahtaba b. Shabib and Sulayman b. Kathir, came on pilgrimage to Mecca, where they met the new leader of the family, Ibrahim al-Imam. There must have been sufficient evidence of potential political support, for the Imam sent back with them his Persian freedman, Abu Muslim, to try and branch out in helping to recruit more non-Arab followers. The network of the Hashimite conspiracy now spanned cities as varied as Mecca, Kufa, Marw, and Humayma.[11]

The story of the Abbasid revolution and the cause of the Hashimite Imams is deeply entwined with the role that Khurasan played as the territorial base of the opposition movement. In later periods, starting with the ninth century, Khurasan would come to represent the home of many hadith scholars whose names reflect attribution to its cities, such

---

[11] The background of the Abbasid revolution has taken up much interest among historians, producing a spectrum of opinions. Some have argued that those who organized it were mainly the Arab settlers in Khurasan: Faruq Omar, *The Abbasid Caliphate, 132/750–170/786* (Baghdad, 1969), M. A. Shaban, *The Abbasid Revolution* (Cambridge, 1970); Moshe Sharon, *Black Banners from the East* (Jerusalem, 1983). Others view it as a revolt of disaffected *mawali*: Julius Wellhausen, *The Arab Kingdom and Its Fall*, trans. M. G. Weir (Calcutta, 1927). Some lean more toward a greater role for the Iranian rebels: Daniel, *Political and Social History*; Saleh Said Agha, *The Revolution Which Toppled the Umayyads* (Leiden, 2003). H. A. R. Gibb's view that the revolution resulted from the combined efforts of "the Arab colonists and Islamized Persian aristocracy of Khurasan" remains the most convincing: "An Interpretation of Islamic History," in *Studies on the Civilization of Islam*, ed. Stanford Shaw and William Polk (Princeton, 1962), 10.

as Bukhari, Tirmidhi, Nasa'i, and Bayhaqi, and others without such an indication in their names, such as Muslim b. al-Hajjaj from Nishapur, and Ahmad b. Hanbal from Marw. And Tabari, the compiler of a famous world history that starts with Creation and ends in the early tenth century, would highlight this influential role for the east in the disproportionate attention he gave to coverage of Khurasan in telling the story of the caliphate. There is much idealization therefore in the way Khurasan was portrayed in this early phase as a land of puritanical belief and unyielding loyalty, chosen almost by providence to bring salvation and closure to the tribulations of early Islamic history. This message is best illustrated in a statement that Ibrahim al-Imam made as he sought to encourage his operatives, who were entrusted to make the revolutionary summons to the people of Khurasan:

> But look to the people of Khurasan! There, the numbers are great, perseverance is clear, and the hearts free of hatred. These people are not split up into sects nor divided into creeds; they are the most obedient to God, and the ones with the finest morality among His subjects. They know not the vile and are a shield against the Turks ... I am indeed optimistic about the people of al-Mashriq (the East), of the place of the rising of the lamp of the world, the light of mankind.[12]

Khurasan was portrayed as everything that Iraq – that old land of Babylon, enticing for material greed and alluring with temptation – was not. Never a place for devoted followers, and only good at treachery, the new cities of Kufa and Basra in southern Iraq became implicitly in Tabari's scheme of Islamic history the political equivalents of the Bible's Sodom and Gomorrah. But mythology aside, Khurasan was a land of great potential for harnessing political support. A number of factors contributed to making this province strategic. Since the Sasanid period, Khurasan had kept a measure of autonomy and distance from the Sasanid capital Ctesiphon, and retained its own provincial nobility, which was never entirely subdued. When the Arab conquerors first arrived in Khurasan, they struck roots in this region through tribal settlements, which they did not emulate in other Iranian provinces. Based mainly in Marw, the Arab armies had contingents in important cities, such as Balkh, Tirmidh, Abiward, and beyond the Oxus river in Ferghana and Shash (Tashkent). Geographically, Khurasan opened up

<hr>

[12] Muqaddasi, *Ahsan al-Taqasim*, 293–294, trans. Collins, 240–241 (with modification); also *Akhbar al-Dawla*, 205–208.

to the more ethnically and religiously diverse lands of Transoxiana (Soghdiana) – what the Arabs called "the land behind the river" (or *ma wara' al-nahr*), where autonomous Persian elites, Soghdians, and Turks had defied Sasanid power even before Islam. And just to the southeast of the river the province of Tukharistan (Bactria) with its major city of Balkh provided another frontier direction that led to northern India. The Oxus provided a symbolic boundary between the Iranian world and that of Turkic Central Asia, the Iran and Turan of Firdawsi's epic of ancient Persian kings, the *Shahnameh*. There were, however, various cultural mixes and diverse communities in this frontier area, sheltered by valleys and mountain ranges that allowed the emergence and continuity of statelets, which Frye has compared to the mosaic pattern of the ancient Greek city-states.[13]

Ambitious local leaders straddling the frontier could draw on Arab tribal support or look across the Oxus for help from neighboring foreign princes and outside empires. Social groups held in caste-based bondage to local princes found in Islam's egalitarian spirit an appealing reason for conversion.[14] A revolt starting in Khurasan had the danger not only of gathering a provincial army but embroiling a wider set of foreign powers, as happened when the regions of Ferghana and Shash went to war in 749, with one seeking help from China and the other from Islamic Khurasan. The military lesson of this was so strongly felt by veteran Umayyad generals that one of them, Mujashshir b. Muzahim al-Sulami, famously advised an incoming governor when he was on his way out, in 113/731: "Whoever holds command of Khurasan should never cross the Oxus River with a force of less than fifty thousand troops."[15] Getting involved in that frontier region was a military nightmare long before the British and Russians fought out the Great Game in Afghanistan in the nineteenth century in the recesses of the Khaybar Pass, and suffered staggering military setbacks. Few had successfully established a cohesive hold on power in this region, as did the gifted Umayyad commander Qutayba b. Muslim, uniting the Qays and Yaman tribes, Arab and Persian troops before the region unraveled after his death in 96/715. With his alliances amongst local elites and daring military expansions, Qutayba was, as H. A. R. Gibb has noted,

---

[13] Richard Frye and Aydin Sayili, "The Turks in the Middle East before the Seljuks," *JAOS* 63 (1953), 201.
[14] E. Esin, "Tarkhan Nizak or Tarkhan Tirek?" *JAOS* 97 (1977), 328.
[15] Tabari, *Tarikh*, II, 1532.

"instrumental in giving the first impulse to the recovery of a national sentiment amongst the Persians of Khurasan,"[16] and this was about to play out again under a different leadership during the Abbasid revolution, with energy directed against the Umayyads in Damascus.

When the Abbasid political call arrived in the east, Khurasan was simmering with various tensions: tribal tensions between Qays and Yaman; Arab vs. non-Arab; and provincial interests against the Umayyad center in Damascus. The last Umayyad governor, Nasr b. Sayyar, did his best to patch things when in 128/745 he put down a rebellion near Marw by al-Harith b. Surayj, a pious rebel and veteran of the conquests. But Nasr was unable to control the movement of another challenger, Juday' al-Kirmani, who was jockeying to become governor of the province, and whose defeat prompted his son to join the Hashimiyya movement. Nasr could see the gathering storm, and in vain wrote to his superiors in Iraq and Syria warning of the dangers of this powder keg in his frontier region; but the caliph, Marwan b. Muhammad, was too busy confronting challenges to his rule within the Umayyad family to address the problem. One letter of distress by the governor finished with poetic words, hoping that this would spur quicker action:

> I see the coal's red glow beneath the embers,
>   And 'tis about to blaze!
> The rubbing of two sticks enkindles fire,
>   And out of words come frays,
>   "Oh! Is Umayya's House awake or sleeping?"
>   I cry in sore amaze[17]

The caliph was unmoved. A stubborn military figure, Marwan had previously been a successful field commander who helped the Umayyad caliph Hisham roll back Khazar incursions in the Caucasus, and raided as far once as the Khazar capital Itil on the Volga river in 120/738. After these campaigns his experience was mainly as governor of Armenia and Azerbayjan, which had neither the Arab tribal settlements nor the religious sympathies of Khurasan, and so he underestimated the problems in the east. It took him some time to realize that what was emerging in Khurasan was not merely a squabble within the tribal ranks of the army,

---

[16] H. A. R. Gibb, *The Arab Conquests in Central Asia* (London, 1923), 30.
[17] Tabari, *Tarikh*, II, 1973; trans. R. A. Nicholson as *A Literary History of the Arabs* (London, 1966), 251.

but a systematic *da'wa* whose roots stretched all the way back to a shadowy Imam figure who was ensconced in Damascus's Jordanian backyard. Once he finally caught word of the seditious plots of the Abbasids, Marwan had Ibrahim arrested and brought to Harran, where the Imam was probably killed in an act of Umayyad vengeance.

The revolutionaries – or Khurasaniyya, as the military wing were known – were livid at this provocation, but they kept their nerve and maintained their unity under the general slogan of seeking to install as caliph someone who was "truly worthy" or "agreed on" (*al-rida*) from "the family of the Prophet" without specifying who, and from which branch of the family, Abbasid or Alid.[18] After several military clashes with the revolutionaries, the last Umayyad governor of Khurasan, Nasr, fled Marw for Nishapur, and then to Rayy, where he died in 131/749 before trying to make another stand. Abu Muslim's troops led by the rising figures, Qahtaba and his son, Hasan, together with Khazim b. Khuzayma, crossed the Iranian plateau in a rapid march aimed at capturing the key town of Kufa before the Alids could use it to further their leadership ambitions. Settling the potential conflict with the Alids seemed more pressing than dealing with the last Umayyad caliph, and the Abbasids rushed to promote their candidate as Imam and general leader of the revolution. Abu'l-Abbas, the twenty-three-year-old younger brother of Ibrahim al-Imam, was brought out to the public at the main mosque in Kufa. Inarticulate and overwhelmed by the rapid pace of events, he must have stuttered, and just let his uncle, Dawud b. Ali, give the official announcement of Abbasid rule. The latter gave words that summarized years of aspiration, saying: "Now authority has finally been put in order. Now the sun has again risen from the East ... and now the legitimate rights have returned to where they should belong."[19] He continued:

Praise be to God ... who has brought to us our inheritance from Muhammad our Prophet ... now are the dark nights of this world put to flight, its covering lifted, now light breaks in the earth and the heavens, and the sun rises from the springs of the day while the moon ascends from its appointed place. He

---

[18] P. Crone, "On the Meaning of the Abbasid Call to al-Rida," in *The Islamic World from Classical to Modern Times: Essays in Honor of Bernard Lewis*, ed. C. E. Bosworth et al. (Princeton, 1989), 98–99.

[19] Baladhuri, *Ansab al-Ashraf*, 140.

who is the expert in wielding the bow and arrow takes it up, and the arrow returns to him who shot it ... By God, we did not rebel seeking this authority to grow rich in silver and in gold; nor to dig a canal or build a castle. What made us rebel was the shame of their taking away our rights; our anger for our cousins ...

Men of Kufa, surely we continued to be wronged and bereft of our rights, until God ordained for us our shi'a, the people of Khurasan, and by them revived our rights ... He has made manifest among you a Caliph of the clan of Hashim, brightening thereby your faces and making you to prevail over the army of Syria, and transferring the sovereignty and glory of Islam to you. He has [now] graced you with an imam whose gift is equity, and granted him good government ... [and] know that authority is with us, and shall not depart from us until we surrender it to Jesus the son of Mary.[20]

With southern Iraq now under its control, the Abbasid family turned its attention to a final confrontation with Marwan b. Muhammad. Abdallah b. Ali, another uncle of Ibrahim al-Imam, led an army of disaffected Arab tribesmen and a force of the Khurasaniyya in a decisive battle at the river Zab, south of Mosul. This region, known as al-Jazira – in Arabic literally "the island" because it lay between the Tigris and the Euphrates, although it was recognized as stretching deep into Asia Minor – could tilt to Syria or Iraq, but Abbasid ingenuity brought it to their side. Through promises of forthcoming reconciliation, various tribal supporters of Marwan deserted to the Abbasid side, and he fled after a sour battle, on 11 Jumada II 132/24 January 750, taking with him the insignia of the caliphate – the staff, the ring, and the mantle of the Prophet (the *burda*) – across Syria until he reached Egypt. A military detachment, led by Salih b. Ali, pursued Marwan all the way to Egypt, where it caught up with him, some six months after the battle of Zab, at a village named Busir, south of Fustat. There the last of the Umayyads held his ground and put up a fight, sword in hand, against unequal odds until he was killed. The insignia of the caliphal authority was finally taken and passed on to the new rulers.

In the months after the Abbasid victory near Mosul, the black banners swept into Syria as they stamped out vestiges of the old regime, and pursued members of the Umayyad family. Although stories have

---

[20] Tabari, *Tarikh*, III, 31–33; trans. John Alden Williams in *al-Tabari: The Early 'Abbasi Empire*, 2 vols. (Cambridge, 1989), 1:154–157.

been exaggerated, the Abbasids mostly singled out descendants of the last ruling Umayyad caliph in this purge, as well as members of the family of Hisham b. Abd al-Malik. The Abbasid fear of an Umayyad comeback was not without justification. In the seventh century the Islamic community had seen the territory ruled by Abd al-Malik b. Marwan dwindle to a narrow sliver in Syria, when he struggled against the Mecca-based "rebel" Abdallah b. al-Zubayr, who controlled Arabia, Iraq, and Khurasan; and yet, almost by a miracle, Abd al-Malik, the second founder of the Umayyad dynasty, had made a comeback. In various provinces, therefore, the sudden Abbasid success could have been viewed as temporary effervescence in another phase of an Arab tribal juggling for power that had been going on since the civil war within the Umayyad house started in 744. The name of Hisham b. Abd al-Malik still cast a long shadow as the last true Umayyad king, and anyone directly related to him could gather supporters. The famous story of Abd al-Rahman b. Muʿawiya b. Hisham, who eluded the Abbasids in Syria, who were hot on his trail, and escaped across North Africa, arriving amidst his Berber maternal relations in modern-day Morocco, and then organized a force that invaded Spain and set up an independent Umayyad principality by 756, was not just a phenomenal achievement, but one that could be repeated elsewhere. Al-Mansur could only be impressed by Abd al-Rahman, referring to him once as "the Falcon" for his daring flight to the west.[21]

In contrast with Abd al-Rahman's dramatic escape, the caliphate of the first Abbasid, Abu'l-Abbas al-Saffah, was still something of an anticlimax. Fourteen years younger than his brother Abu Jaʿfar, and much younger still than his powerful uncles, the first Abbasid caliph was less in control of matters than it may seem at first. In fact, unlike caliphs from al-Mansur onwards, each of whom assumed a regnal title, Abu'l-Abbas did not have one, and was, according to the medieval writers, such as Tabari, Jahshiyari, and Yaʿqubi, simply known by his *kunya*, Abu'l-Abbas. It was only in the later medieval sources that writers filled in the blank by giving Abu'l-Abbas the sobriquet al-Saffah ("the blood shedder"), which was originally associated with his uncle Abdallah b. Ali, for his purge of Umayyad princes.[22] Be that

---

[21] The story of Abd al-Rahman is told in Ibn al-Athir, *al-Kamil*, 5:493–496.
[22] Bernard Lewis, "Regnal Titles of the first Abbasid Caliphs," in *Dr. Zakir Husain Presentation Volume* (New Delhi, 1968), 15.

as it may, the title stuck, and Abu'l-Abbas came to rule in the shadow of powerful figures around him, the future al-Mansur, Abdallah b. Ali, and Abu Muslim.

The third in this triumvirate, Abu Muslim, was probably the most powerful, given his revolutionary background and access to military resources in Khurasan, and he was not keen on having a strong caliph. The Hashimite *da'wa* had long given great latitude to Abu Muslim in political and military affairs to the extent that no one could envisage a role for the Abbasid Imams (Alid or Abbasid) after gaining the caliphal title beyond that of being a holy man who would be a symbolic leader after the years of military dictatorship of Marwan b. Muhammad.[23] Abu Muslim had dominated all key decisions up until then, including eliminating the chief Alid propagandist in Kufa, Abu Salama, and refusing to pardon the last Umayyad governor in Wasit, Yazid b. Umar b. Hubayra. In his home province of Khurasan, Abu Muslim called all the shots, even waging a small war in 751 to test the waters in Central Asia, first through Turkic and Soghdian proxies and then by sending an army under Ziyad b. Salih to back the region of Shash (Tashkent) against Ferghana, the latter being a client protectorate of China. These events culminated with the famous battle of Talas (modern Taraz on the border of Kazakhstan and Kyrgyzstan), generally remembered in popular legend as the occasion on which Muslims for the first time learned the secret of paper making from Chinese prisoners of war. The battle, however, was historically more critical in stopping the advance of Chinese influence in the Transoxiana: were it not for Talas, Tehran and much of the Iranian world could well be speaking Chinese today.

Abu Muslim's pushback of China may have also created a snowball effect as a Turko-Soghdian commander in the Chinese army, An Lushan, started an eight-year rebellion in 755 that nearly brought down the Tang dynasty (618–907), and emboldened Tibet to wage war against China for over half a century.[24] An Lushan, like many

---

[23] Elton Daniel, "The Islamic East," in *The New Cambridge History of Islam*, vol. 1: *The Formation of the Islamic World, Sixth to Eleventh Centuries*, ed. Chase Robinson (Cambridge, 2010), 471–472.

[24] Barry Cunliffe, *By Steppe, Desert, and Ocean: The Birth of Eurasia* (Oxford, 2015), 349, 352–353, 379. Maurice Lombard, *The Golden Age of Islam*, trans. Joan Spencer (New York, 1975; repr. Princeton, 2004), 43; Christopher Beckwith, *Empires of the Silk Road* (Princeton, 2009), 146. Beckwith argues that the rebellion of An Lushan reads like a "mirror image" of Abu Muslim's and that the Soghdian warrior-merchants in the Chinese and

Soghdians, was probably a Manichean, a religion with a universalist message that competed with Islam for control of eighth-century Central Asia. To what extent Abu Muslim held an affinity to Manicheism is not clear – especially since at least another key advisor of al-Mansur, Ibn al-Muqaffaʿ, had a root in this religion before his conversion – but Abu Muslim undoubtedly contributed to the shaping of a syncretistic religious moment on the Khurasani frontier in the 750s. In contrast to the Umayyad period, when Khurasani discord tended to be tribally based, Khurasan would reverberate with a variety of syncretistic Iranian revolts in the decades following the revolution. From a purely political viewpoint anchored in the years immediately following the revolution of 750, however, it is sobering to think that Abu Muslim had a hand in regime change of two vast empires, and it is understandable to see the first Abbasid caliph anxious about how to restrain the revolutionary commander even if Abu'l-Abbas realized that this task might best be left to his more assertive brother and nominated successor, Abu Jaʿfar al-Mansur.[25]

Consolidation with al-Mansur

From the Abbasid perspective in Iraq, the significance of the various actions of Abu Muslim was the disproportionate role he had played as kingmaker and shaper of policies in the transition from Umayyad to Abbasid rule. The Abbasid state in the reign of al-Saffah stood at a crossroads. It had owed a great debt to the forces of Khurasan, which were led by Abu Muslim, but as Abu Jaʿfar understood best, it could not have established its rule in Iraq and Syria without the help of Arab tribal forces, not just of the Yaman who supported the *da ʿwa* but also of the Qays who had generally supported the last Umayyads but also harbored doubts, and could be swayed under the right circumstances. The new caliph also faced other challenges: from within the Abbasid family, his uncle Abdallah b. Ali viewed his military victory

Arab empires probably knew each other and kept in touch via shared interests in the Silk Road trade system.

[25] Al-Mansur's later purge of Abu Muslim also paved the way for Abbasid affinity with a beleaguered Chinese emperor. A tenth-century Chinese history of the Tang dynasty states that in 756 the Abbasid caliph sent an embassy to China, and that the emperor "Tai-tsung (r. 762–779) retook with the help of [the caliph's army] both capitals [of China] (i.e. Luo-Yang and Ch'angan)": Robert Hoyland, *Seeing Islam as Others Saw it* (Princeton, 1997), 253.

over the Umayyads as entitlement for him to lead the new state; and from without, there was the longstanding Alid claim to the caliphate. After the short reign of al-Saffah, al-Mansur acceded to power, in June 754, and found that he had to deal with all these problems, but tried to tackle them one at a time.

Abd al-Malik reportedly once said, "Two lions can never share leadership in a forest," and this maxim became clear as soon as al-Mansur assumed power. The immediate threat that Abdallah b. Ali posed with his claim to the caliphate, having inherited Marwan b. Muhammad's Arab tribal army in northern Syria, was quickly viewed as a threat to both the new caliph and Abu Muslim, and it did not take much convincing to have Abu Muslim move against him. While the latter raised a large army in Iraq and moved northwest, Abdallah b. Ali was moving around northern Syria in the areas of Harran and Nisibin, unsure where the confrontation would happen. In a battle fought in the northern Euphrates region in Jumada II 136/ November 754, Abdallah b. Ali found his forces no match for the Khurasaniyya. It did not help that a comet made a prolonged appearance, stretching from east to west, according to a Syrian chronicle, like a "javelin of fire," over the camp of Abdallah b. Ali, leading to the demoralization of his troops.[26] Defeated in battle, Abdallah fled towards Basra, where he sought safe haven with his brother, Sulayman b. Ali, the governor of the city, and sought his mediation for a pardon from the caliph. Sulayman was respected as a patriarch of the Abbasid family, and his descendants would retain some distinction in later centuries, particularly through the line of his daughter, Zaynab, known as the Zaynabis in the twelfth century. Al-Mansur could not turn down this request, but it clearly irked him enough to remove Sulayman from the governorship the following year.

The real force to be reckoned with, however, al-Mansur realized, was Abu Muslim himself. The power base he had established for himself in Khurasan was quite significant, and he had taken on the role of kingmaker by removing the Alid claim to power during the revolution and placing the Abbasids on the throne in Kufa, but there was no guarantee his loyalty would continue. The problem was magnified in light of a divergence between him and the new caliph on how

---

[26] *Theophilus of Edessa's Chronicle*, ed. and trans. Robert Hoyland (Liverpool, 2011), 296.

to reconstitute the caliphate. Abu Muslim favored a "Khurasan only" policy, which privileged the military elements of his home province exclusively, while al-Mansur's objective was more prudent in trying to reconcile Persian and Arab tribal support, even to the point of reconciling with the Qays tribes that had supported the last Umayyad ruler. To this end, al-Mansur showed great conciliation toward various commanders of the armies that had fought on the Umayyad side, issuing pardons, and even assigning them governorships and commands.[27]

Indirectly, al-Mansur's policy vision rose above the former Qays and Yaman tribal dispute and any Arab–Persian divide. To accomplish this, he had to contain the fledgling charisma of Abu Muslim. After defeating Abdallah b. Ali, Abu Muslim had departed for the east, fuming at the fact that al-Mansur had prevented him from punishing the followers of his defeated uncle. If Abu Muslim reached Khurasan, al-Mansur feared, the situation could lead to secession, and so he sent after him a high-level delegation led by the caliph's nephew and eloquent heir apparent, Isa b. Musa. Although Abu Muslim had reached Rayy, some 600 miles away from Iraq, for some reason he was duped. Using the ruse of a friendly invitation to court, Isa b. Musa had Abu Muslim turn all the way back to Iraq, ostensibly so that the caliph could sort out any lingering misunderstandings. Al-Mansur never really thought his policies were subject to misunderstanding, and as soon as the Iranian leader arrived with just a small retinue, he had him upbraided in a kind of mock trial and then promptly executed. Abu Muslim's downfall in the summer of 755 came only a few months after the defeat of Abdallah b. Ali, which reflects the caliph's determination to finish off his opponents as early as possible. He had taken a gamble on the continued loyalty of the Khurasaniyya after removing Abu Muslim, but he was sending an ideological as well as a military message. The Abbasid caliph was the true master of the scene, as Imam and ruler, and the road was being paved for governing in a more centralized way.

The new image of the emerging Abbasid caliphate was that of a *dawla*, a term that means a nation-state in modern Arabic but in this early medieval period meant a lot more. *Dawla* signified not just a change in polity but a broader sense of "dramatically changed times," capping "a

---

[27] Amikam Elad, "Aspects of the Transition from the Umayyad to the Abbasid Caliphate," *Jerusalem Studies in Arabic and Islam* 19 (1995).

historical process that had come full circle."[28] The Abbasids were not
simply the more successful victors of a key battle in 750, but the true
successors to the Prophet whose image resonated with messianic charisma. Their rule was about to establish a unique continuity with several
aspects of political heritage: linkage with previous Near Eastern and
Persian monarchies; succession to the Prophet Muhammad; and even
a linkage with biblical figures – the early patriarchs, Abraham and his
immediate descendants, as well as the Israelite kings, David and Solomon.
Every Abbasid caliph from Mansur forward adopted a title that conveyed
a divinely guided quality – al-Mansur (the Victorious), al-Mahdi (the
Guided), al-Hadi (the Guide), al-Rashid (the Wise), al-Amin (the
Trustful), and al-Ma'mun (the Well-Entrusted). And it was only later –
from al-Mu'tasim's reign onward – that Abbasid titles were crafted in
a constructed phrase: al-Mu'tasim bi'llah (the one seeking refuge with
God), al-Mutawakkil 'ala-allah (He who puts his trust in God), and al-
Mu'tadid bi'llah (He who seeks strength from God), and al-Mustadi'
(the seeker of illumination from God).

In the new picture of Abbasid government, members of the Abbasid
family played a prominent role as governors of the richest provinces of
the Fertile Crescent region and Egypt. Various uncles of al-Mansur
were appointed to core power centers, including: Sulayman b. Ali
(Basra), Isma'il b. Ali (Mosul), Salih b. Ali (Syria), and Dawud b. Ali
(the Hijaz). The caliph soon also turned to the Khurasaniyya to staff
official administrative and military posts.[29] However, unlike the
Umayyads, who sometimes allowed a governor, such as al-Hajjaj
b. Yusuf, to govern Iraq for twenty years (694–714), Abbasid governors had much shorter terms – frequently not more than one year. The
Khurasaniyya were not entirely native Iranians, but descendants of
Arab families who had long settled in Khurasan, mixed with the local
population, and opposed the Umayyads on regional and ideological
grounds. They were increasingly referred to as the Abna' – an abbrevi-
ation of the phrase *abna' al-da'wa* or *abna' al-dawla* ("sons of the
Abbasid revolutionary call" or "sons of the new state"), which classed

---

[28]   Jacob Lassner, "The 'Abbasid *Dawla*: An Essay on the Concept of Revolution in
       Early Islam," in *Tradition and Innovation in Late Antiquity*, ed. F. M. Clover
       and R. S. Humphreys (Madison, WI, 1989).
[29]   Hugh Kennedy, *The Early Abbasid Caliphate: A Political History* (London,
       1981), 52–53, 59–68, 78–82; Jacob Lassner, *The Shaping of Abbasid Rule*
       (Princeton, 1980), 129–136.

them in metaphoric terms as nobility, and anticipated the honoring at court of their descendants. This was a novel way for a ruler to invent group solidarity based on a historical achievement and a sense of religious mission, and was very different from the Umayyad tribal system, which was diminished by Qays and Yaman divisions.

Key leaders of the *da'wa* (*nuqaba'*), who had formed the nucleus of the revolution, were rewarded with senior military posts. They had the unique ability to draw on support not only from their hometown settlements in Khurasan but their ancestral homes of tribal origin as well, whether in Arabia, Syria, or Iraq. Among these were Khazim b. Khuzayma al-Tamimi, Malik b. al-Haytham al-Khuza'i, Mu'adh b. Muslim al-Dhuhli, Uthman b. Nahik al-'Akki, al-Musayyab b. Zuhayr al-Dabbi, and various members of the family of Qahtaba b. Shabib al-Ta'i'. Some of these leaders, such as Hasan b. Qahtaba (d. 181/797), lived long enough to serve al-Mansur's successor, al-Mahdi, and could even be found at al-Rashid's court afterward, which lent stability to the system over the long term. On various occasions we see the second caliph later in his reign turn to members of this inner circle when he faced a challenge, and they proved invariably loyal and successful in accomplishing their missions, none trying to secede in a province or decline a post.[30]

But al-Mansur was equally interested in balancing the Khurasaniyya with the Arab military aristocracy, whose tribal leaders were descendants of illustrious governors or commanders from Umayyad times. This included figures such as Salm b. Qutayba b. Muslim al-Bahili and Muhammad b. Khalid b. Abdallah al-Qasri; and this policy continued up until Harun al-Rashid's time with other figures, such as Yazid b. Hatim b. al-Muhallab b. Abi Sufra and his brother Rawh, and Rafi' b. al-Layth b. Nasr b. Sayyar. Barring the odd exception, as with Rafi' b. al-Layth's agitation in Khurasan toward the end of al-Rashid's reign, these military cadres generally showed themselves steadfast in loyalty. Rawh al-Muhallabi epitomized the career expected of an intrepid Abbasid official, as he served a record five caliphs. He fought against the last Umayyad governor at Wasit in Iraq, became al-Mansur's chamberlain in Baghdad, led a campaign against the Byzantines, was assigned as governor to Tabaristan, then transferred

---

[30] Patricia Crone, *Slaves on Horses: The Evolution of the Islamic Polity* (Cambridge, 1986), 173–196.

to govern Sind, brought back to Basra, and finally sent as governor to
North Africa to hold the hardest of assignments, which required bringing the unruly military of Qayrawan under control.

Coming from the powerful Azd tribe of Oman, and with the fame of
his ancestor, al-Muhallab, who had once served the Umayyads as commander, Rawh may have had opportunities to dissent, but he preferred
to stay the course with the Abbasids. Others with lesser-known ancestors
in their backgrounds but proven tribal clout were also included in the
Abbasid system, such as Ishaq b. Muslim al-ʿUqayli and his brother
Bakkar, who were important leaders among the Qays tribes in the
Jazira region of northern Syria and Iraq; and Maʿn b. Zaiʾda al-
Shaybani and his cousin, Mazyad b. Zaiʾda.[31] Gradually an unstated
equilibrium emerged in al-Mansur's system of government among different elements, and it is all the more remarkable that he was able to
engineer all this without having an official post for a vizir or minister.

While al-Mansur did not show any bias in terms of favoring one
military group over another, his search for a new capital showed a turn
to the east, away from the old base of the Umayyads in Syria. It was not
clear early in his reign where in Iraq he was going to settle, but it was
obvious that he wanted to have his capital somewhere there. Iraq had
been a part of the Persian empire since before the advent of Islam, and
was the site of various ancient Near Eastern monarchies, such as those
of the Assyrians and the Babylonians, whose palatial ruins across the
landscape in the time of al-Mansur would have been in much better
shape than when they were rediscovered in the modern period, and
these structures may have provided another source of inspiration for
Abbasid imperial pretensions. As late as the time of al-Buhturi (d. 261/
897), the ruins and walls of Sasanian Ctesiphon still boasted images of
Khusraw's battles at Antioch preserved in full color, and al-Buhturi
refers to this in his description of Persian troops, who appear dressed in
green and yellow garments.[32]

Iraq was the province that the Sasanids, and later Arab geographers,
referred to as *dil-Iranshahr* (the heart of the land of Iran), and represented the richest agricultural land of the former Persian empire,

---

[31] I. Bligh Abramski, "Umayyad Elements in the Abbasid Regime," 133/750–322/
932," *Der Islam* 65 (1988).

[32] The poem is translated in Samer Ali's *Arabic Literary Salons in the Later Middle
Ages: Poetry, Public Performance, and the Presentation of the Past* (Notre
Dame, IN, 2010), 158–159.

endowed with irrigation by the key rivers, the Tigris and Euphrates. The Parthians had founded Ctesiphon near the Tigris in central Mesopotamia as their winter capital, retaining Ecbatana (Hamadan) in the Zagros as their summer capital. The fortunes of these capitals were tied together in political and cultural ways such that Iraq spoke the official language, Pahlavi (Middle Persian), even though Aramaic was spoken more widely among the populace. The Abbasids wanted to build on this political tradition by governing directly from this strategically important region, which benefited from the desert protecting Iraq's southwestern flank, as the Zagros mountain range provided a protective barrier in the east. Al-Mansur experimented with a new site named Hashimiyya in southern Iraq, probably the former fortress of Ibn Hubayra near Kufa, as a temporary capital, and even minted coins bearing this town's name. His continuing search for a capital reflected the fact that he wanted something central and with urban prospects, unlike the first Islamic cities, Kufa and Basra, which were founded on the edge of the Arabian desert and reflected a nomadic mindset of proximity and longing for the hinterland.

Before finalizing a decision on where to build his new capital, however, al-Mansur took the more crucial step of designating a successor. Naming a successor was a crucial test for the loyalty of the troops, and a necessary ideological statement. In a bold move – not least because there a successor had already been named by al-Saffah, in the person of Isa b. Musa, the caliph's nephew – al-Mansur designated his young son, Muhammad, as second successor (eventually convincing Isa in 147/764 to accept becoming second after Muhammad) and gave him the title al-Mahdi ("the divinely guided one"), in a gesture that was meant to close the door on future messianic expectations amongst both the Alids and the Iranians. When the caliph next appointed al-Mahdi as governor of Khurasan in 141/758, he was further emphasizing that his message was mainly directed to Khurasan to abide by its loyalty to his branch in the Abbasid house as both spiritual and political leaders. The fifteen-year old al-Mahdi settled in the town of Rayy, which was renamed al-Muhammadiyya in his honor, and it was here that his son Harun al-Rashid would be born in 151/768, and be nursed by Iranian women from Rayy, which added to the symbolic bond between Iran and the caliphate.

There was foresight in al-Mansur's move to have al-Mahdi stationed in the east (where he remained till 768) because Khurasan had started showing signs of nationalist exuberance for a Persian leader after Abu Muslim's downfall. Agitation began with a certain Sunbadh, originally from Nishapur, who rebelled in 138/755 and preached that Abu Muslim had not died but had gone into occultation, and would one day come back with Islamic and Mazdean messiahs – the Mahdi and Mazdak. This rebellion, along with others (that of Ishaq the Turk ca. 140/758 in Juzjan; Ustadhsis in 147–151/765–768 in Herat, Badhghis, and Sistan; and al-Muqanna, ca. 160/776–163/779, in Marw al-Rudh, Balkh, and Bukhara), are usually referred to collectively as the Abu Muslimiyya rebellions.[33] They manifested various motives, including Persian national feeling, elements of class struggle between peasants and land-lords, and religious syncretism that blended features of Zoroastrianism and Islam. Some viewed Abu Muslim as a revolutionary Persian king, while others harbored what is known as a "Khurramiyya" heresy that suspended the Islamic sharia and the rituals of praying and fasting, denied the existence of heaven and hell, and taught the doctrine of transmigration of souls and the anticipation of a Persian messianic figure.

It remains difficult to know exactly what these movements stood for because most of the information about them comes to us from their enemies, and particularly the eleventh-century minister to the Seljuk sultanate and author of the famous mirror for princes, *Siyasatnameh*, Nizam al-Mulk. The label *zandaqa* (heresy) would become an all-purpose stigma leveled against any movement harboring some or all elements of these doctrines. The Abbasids had once benefited during their underground phase of the *da'wa* from some Buddhist and Manichean ideas about renewal movements, divine election, gnostic knowledge, and a cyclical view of history; but, once established in power, they increasingly distanced themselves from these views. The presence of the heir apparent, Muhammad al-Mahdi, in proximity to Khurasan and his mixing with Iranian society and culture fostered renewed support among the Iranian elite for the Abbasid dynasty, and must have defused the polarization for the time being.[34] Within his Arab circle of support, al-Mansur also used the opportunity to

---

[33] Robert Canfield, "Theological 'Extremism' and Social Movements in Turko-Persia," in *Turko-Persia in Historical Perspective*, ed. Robert Canfield (Cambridge, 1991), 132–160.

[34] Jere Bacharach, "*Laqab* for a Future Caliph: The Case of the Abbasid al-Mahdi," *JAOS* 113 (1993).

appear as a strict defender of Islam against heresy, which added another layer to the caliph's legitimacy as a champion of establishing orthodoxy.

The Alid Revolt of al-Nafs al-Zakiyya

While al-Mansur was preoccupied with the east, and the military unrest in North Africa, a more potent challenge to his rule came from the Hijaz. There an Alid rebel, who was descended from Ali through the line of al-Hasan, raised the banner of a claim for the caliphate in the town of Medina. Muhammad b. Abdallah b. al-Hasan b. al-Hasan b. Ali b. Abi Talib, who would be known as al-Nafs al-Zakiyya ("the Pure Soul"), received support from as far away as Basra, where his brother, Ibrahim, led another rising against the caliph.[35] Some twelve years after the revolution, this leader now disclosed that the Abbasids had effectively hijacked the caliphate from the Alids. In the perilous underground years preceding the revolution, it was now said, al-Mansur had once given the *bay'a* (oath of allegiance), along with other Hashimite elders, at a gathering near Mecca, to a still-young Alid star, Muhammad b. Abdallah (al-Nafs al-Zakiyya), in the event that the revolution was ever destined to succeed. And it was only as a result of later Abbasid domination, and betrayal of the early promises, the Alid now affirmed, that al-Mansur had assumed power. The sobriquet given to the rebel, Muhammad al-Nafs al-Zakiyya (the Pure Soul), evoked the high messianic regard and expectation that people in the Hijaz had for his person, and their view of his special place in history. Various signs were additionally read as portents for his predestined divine election, such as the similarity of his name to the that of the Prophet (Muhammad b. Abdallah); the fact that he was born in the year 100/718 after the *hijra*, a centennial moment with millennial overtones; and the alleged similarity of his physical features to those of the Prophet.

Even more unusual about this revolt is that it received the backing of seemingly bookish and proto-Sunni scholars, such as the hadith scholar Malik b. Anas in Medina, and the jurist Abu Hanifa in Iraq. These two figures, who would later be looked on as founders and pillars in the shaping of Islamic law, did not participate militarily, but apparently

---

[35] Kennedy, *The Early Abbasid Caliphate*, 67–70.

argued the invalidity of former pledges of allegiance to al-Mansur, since these were viewed as having been given under duress. Although in future centuries religious scholars of Sunni Islam would become politically quietist, and rally to the side of the Abbasid state against the Alids, the situation in the 760s was still in flux. It speaks to the pious utopianism of the Alid rebel that he decided to declare his rebellion from the strategically humble base of Medina, purely out of his belief that the city of the Prophet would give him the security necessary for success. Since the Hijaz depended for its grain supply on the regions of Egypt and the Fertile Crescent, however, it was only a matter of time before al-Mansur weakened this revolt with an embargo that he placed on food supplies to the Medina. The military resources of Arabia were no match for those of Khurasan, and whatever discord existed between branches of the Abbasid family over the projected succession to al-Mansur now dissipated as the family closed ranks to defend its hold on power against the Alids.[36]

We get a sense of the competing claims within Islam over the caliphate from the letters that were exchanged between the caliph al-Mansur and the Alid rebel before they went to war. These letters not only outline the political perspectives of each side during the conflict but also enshrine indirectly the seeds of what would turn into areas of sectarian difference between Sunnis and Shi'is more broadly later on. It is therefore useful to quote the exchange at some length.

In an initial letter the Alid laid out the Shi'i argument for his political legitimacy, namely direct descent from the Prophet through his daughter, Fatima, stating:

Surely the rights are ours, and you have only laid claim to this command, and made rebellion for it by means of our Shi'a (Arabic: faction), obtaining what was meant to grace us. For my forefather was the legatee (*wasi*) and was the Imam, and how could you inherit his dominion when his descendants were still living? Moreover, you knew that no one has ever sought this rule who had the like of our genealogy and honor ... Our progenitors include a prophet, Muhammad; the first of the pious forefathers in Islam, Ali; the noblest of all wives, the pure Khadija first to follow the Prophet in prayer; the best of all daughters, Fatima the chief of women among the people of paradise. Among those born in Islam, they include al-Hasan and al-Husayn, the two chiefs of the

---

[36] For details on this revolt, see A. Elad, *The Rebellion of Muhammad al-Nafs al-Zakiyya in 145/762: Talibis and Early Abbasis in Conflict* (Leiden, 2016).

youth of paradise ... I am most central of the Banu Hashim in genealogy and purest of them in paternity, unmingled with non-Arabs and uncompromised by slave women concubines ... I am nearer to the caliphate than you and more fulfilling of the compact.

The Abbasids, always insecure about their more distant kinship tie to the Prophet through his uncle al-Abbas, and aware of their delayed joining of the opposition against the Umayyads, found it necessary to spin a convoluted argument, but the caliph still responded energetically, giving a different perspective. He stated:

Your words have reached me, and I have read your letter. Now if your pride glories in the kinship of women, in order to delude thereby the uncouth and the rabble, still God does not make women the equal of paternal uncles and forefathers nor like the paternal relatives and male kindred, for God has made the paternal uncle like a father, and in His Book gives the mother a lower place.

Now God sent Muhammad, on whom be peace, when he had four paternal uncles, and God sent down these words: "Warn your clan, your nearest kin," and he did warn them and summon. Two of them accepted, and one was my ancestor [al-Abbas]. Two of them refused, and one was your ancestor [Abu Talib]. Hence God cut their nearness to the Prophet (when they did not enter Islam), and set nothing at all between them and him, whether obligation or inheritance [for a non-Muslim uncle cannot inherit from a Muslim].

You have asserted that you are the most central of the Banu Hashim in genealogy and purest of them as to father and mother, unmingled with non-Arab blood and uncompromised by slave-woman concubines ... you have transgressed your limit, and boasted yourself above one who was your better in person and paternity, first and last: Ibrahim the son of the Messenger of God [whose mother Mariya was a Coptic slave-girl] and over the begetter of that son! What were the best of the descendants of your ancestor in particular except sons of concubines?

As to your saying that you are sons of the Messenger of God, on whom be blessings and peace, God the Exalted says in His Book: "Muhammad is not the father of any of your men." Rather, you are the sons of his daughter, who was a very near relative but took no inheritance, and did not inherit any government, nor was leadership in prayer permitted to her, so how can you inherit [this] through her?

As for what you have boasted about concerning Ali and his precedence over others, when the Messenger of God, on whom be blessing and peace, lay near death, he ordered another man (i.e. the first caliph, Abu Bakr) to lead the prayers. After that the people accepted one man after another as Caliph and did not take Ali … Then there was his son, al-Hasan b. Ali, and he sold the Caliphate to Mu'awiya for rags and silver and went to the Hijaz, while his Shi'a submitted to Mu'awiya's rule. Thus he gave the government to one who was not its owner and took money from one who was not its trustee. That was not lawfully his to do, but if anything of the Caliphate was yours, then you have all sold it and received its price.

After that the Banu Umayya killed you and drove you from the lands so that Yahya b. Zayd was killed in Khurasan … At last we rebelled against them and sought retaliation for you. We took revenge for your blood and caused you to inherit their lands and their homes. We exalted your ancestor and held that he possessed great merits, and you have taken that as an argument against us.

You know well that our clan's post of honor in the pre-Islamic period was giving water to those on the Great Pilgrimage and custody of the Well of Zamzam, and this passed to al-Abbas from among all his brothers. Your ancestor disputed this with us, and Umar pronounced in our favor against him, so that we kept his post in both the Jahiliyya and in Islam. Moreover, famine struck the people of Medina, and Umar did not entreat his Lord on their behalf or seek his favor save by agency of my ancestor (al-Abbas).

How can you boast yourself above us when we fed you in the time of unbelief, and ransomed you from captivity, and garnered more of the nobility of our ancestors, and inherited as you did not from the Seal of the Prophets, and sought retaliation for you and obtained what you were too weak for, and you could not take revenge for yourselves? So peace be upon you, and the mercy of God.[37]

Both letters make it clear that debating politics over the caliphate between the Abbasids and the Alids was tantamount to debating two different readings of the events of the first century of Islam. The arguments also digress to adduce additional support from the still coalescing sharia rules to their side. A key point of difference in this latter area is that whereas in Shi'i Islam, Fatima (and women more generally) can fully inherit the estate of a deceased father when they have no male siblings, in Sunni Islam the law has the daughter share this inheritance with other distant kinsmen, such as uncles. Until today this point of divergence in the application of Islamic laws of inheritance is very emblematic of the split between Sunnis and Shi'is, but few realize that it rests on a political question in origin – whether Fatima could inherit the Prophet's political leadership.[38] Although Sunnis would not agree

[37] Tabari, *Tarikh*, trans. Williams, 1:99–103.
[38] Tayeb El-Hibri, *Parable and Politics in Early Islamic History: The Rashidun Caliphs* (New York, 2010), 60–61.

with all the points made by al-Mansur, the claim that Fatima could not exclusively inherit from the Prophet would have universal Sunni juristic support, or else the door was opened for Shi'i arguments on the Imamate. These letters represent opposing views that would have circulated on both sides of the Sunni–Shi'i divide for generations, with varying degrees of argument and provocation. But they continued to resonate with an ancient root of division between the two camps in historical and legalistic terms.

In the end, and despite all the reasoning that went into each side's argument, the matter was decided on the battlefield, where the Alid opponent fought to the death. Al-Mansur was caught off guard by the revolt with barely a few thousand troops with him, since the bulk of his troops had been dispatched to the east, North Africa, and the Byzantine front to reestablish control there. But, as always, al-Mansur was politically a man with nine lives, as he now appealed to Abbasid unity by entrusting to his nephew, Isa b. Musa, the task of leading the Abbasid campaign to the Hijaz. The dire experience of this revolt brought to the second caliph the lesson that he should never be too thin on Abbasid troops on his homefront. And he also came out with the added lesson that religious authority, such as that which Malik and Abu Hanifa projected, needed to be controlled, or at least coordinated with the interests of the state. Both al-Mansur and his successors would experiment with different ways to control scholars of Islamic law, and would continue to guard against Alid challenges. The suppression of the Alid revolt brought al-Mansur closer to a complete hold on power, but medieval chroniclers could not but emphasize that it was he who thus first caused the split to grow between the Alid and Abbasid branches in the Hashimite family.[39]

The Foundation of Baghdad

The real beginning of Abbasid rule can be dated to the year 145/762, when al-Mansur defeated the Alid challenger and consolidated control over his Arab and Persian constituencies. It was also in this year that the caliph finally decided on a location for his new Abbasid capital, with the foundation of Baghdad. The new capital was chosen in central Mesopotamia at a point where the Tigris and Euphrates rivers came

---

[39] al-Suyuti, *Tarikh al-Khulafa'* (Beirut, 1994), 326.

closest, and some 15 miles north of the old Sasanid capital, Ctesiphon. Although medieval accounts say the caliph sent out scouts to test various locations for a capital in Iraq, it is likely that his final decision on a location so close to Ctesiphon had already been shaped by the Persian elite around him, and especially Khalid b. Barmak, whose family played an influential role in the administration of the caliphate later on.[40]

Medieval sources show the caliph deeply involved in the detailed planning of the city. Three different astrologers, a Zoroastrian with the auspicious name Nawbakht ("New Luck") (d. 160/776–777), Mashallah (d. 200/815), a Jew from Basra, and Ibrahim b. Habib al-Fazari (d. 161/777), a Muslim – and famous as the first maker of an Arabic astrolabe on the Greek model and as translator of the *Siddhantas* (*al-Sind-hind*) Indian treatise on astronomy – all pored over astronomical calculations to find an auspicious date for beginning the construction of the city, and they agreed on choosing 2 August 762. On that day, these star-gazers concurred, Jupiter would be in Sagittarius and in the ascendant, and that the city's horoscope promised long life for the dynasty, grandeur, and the added "special quality" that no caliph would ever die in it.[41] This later led some chroniclers to try and prove the "theory" by pointing to how various caliphs happened to be outside the city when they died.[42]

The area of Baghdad was located in a plain of agricultural settlements, with a scattering of Christian monasteries. An older town named Baghdad, which meant "Given by God" or "the Gift of God," is mentioned in records of the early Assyrian monarch Tiglath-Pileser I (r. 1115–1077 BCE), when his son conquered this town, though it was never of any great importance.[43] The new Abbasid city, however, was now intended to be the successor to former capitals of ancient Near Eastern empires, including the Akkad of Sargon, Babylon of Nebuchadnezzar, and Sasanid Ctesiphon. In fact, in the early twentieth century bricks bearing the mark of Nebuchadnezzar were often found built into the quay by the river, clearly reused by al-Mansur in building

---

[40] C. Wendell, "Baghdad: *Imago Mundi* and Other Foundation-Lore," *IJMES* 2 (1971), 123.

[41] Wendell, "*Imago Mundi*," 122.

[42] al-Tha'alibi, *The Book of Curious and Entertaining Information, The Lata'if al-Ma'arif of al-Tha'alibi*, trans. C. E. Bosworth (Edinburgh, 1968), 125–126.

[43] Richard Coke, *Baghdad: The City of Peace* (London, 1935 [1927]), 22.

the city.[44] The new Abbasid city was officially named Madinat al-Salam, with clear chiliastic overtones evoking the finality of the Abbasids' Islamic statehood and its anticipation of paradise. This was the name that later appeared in all official references to the city, ranging from inscriptions on coinage (*sikka*) to writings on textiles (*tiraz*) that were woven in the royal factory; but the name Baghdad stuck in popular usage.

The original plan of the capital was the Round City of al-Mansur, which had at its center the caliph's Palace of the Golden Gate and his mosque. The caliph's palace was topped by a fabled green dome, which in the culture of the time was viewed as a celestial image, and a metaphor on the caliph's "closeness to the powers of heaven."[45] A statue of a mounted horseman carrying a spear atop the dome provided an additional talisman of the caliph's power against the enemies of the state. The overall effect revived the Roman and Sasanid pretensions of a universal monarch, and formed a key factor in the pious religious opposition that faced al-Mansur in the early part of his reign. Beyond the esplanade around the palace but within the circular walls of the city were located the various departments of government and the barracks of the caliph's officials. The circular plan of the city, according to the eleventh-century al-Khatib al-Baghdadi, "has advantages over a square city, in that if the monarch were to be in the center [of a square] some segments would be closer to him than others, while, regardless of divisions, the sections of a round city are equidistant to him when he is in the center."[46]

Modern scholars, however, have read more intellectual and cultural reasons into the round design. There is evidence for idealization in a round city plan that comes from previous Persian heritage, such as Parthian Darabjird and Hatra, and Sasanid Firuzabad – all with an inner circular enclosure and four equidistant gates, as in Baghdad – and an apparent fusion of Zoroastrian, Buddhist, and Indian ideals, presenting the city as a model of a cosmic plan.[47] A keen modern observer of the Round City has argued that Baghdad was "nothing less than an Islamic *mandala* worked out on the huge scale of urban

[44] Coke, *Baghdad*, 22.   [45] Wendell, "*Imago Mundi*," 119.
[46] Khatib al-Baghdadi, *Tarikh Baghdad*, 1:73; Lassner, *The Topography of Baghdad*, 162, 232 n.6.
[47] Wendell, "*Imago Mundi*," 104; John Hoag, *Islamic Architecture* (New York, 1975), 23.

architecture."[48] With al-Mansur's renaissance spirit and avid interest in pre-Islamic cultures ranging from Persia and India to ancient Greece and China, there is much reason to find foreign influence in his thinking, and how he chose to build his fortress city, and to articulate his divine right to rule. To these influences, al-Mansur also added biblical infusions, with his attempt to connect Abbasid rule with the biblical David and Solomon when he ordered that five antique iron gates – reportedly once constructed for Solomon's Jerusalem by wizardly creatures – be brought to Baghdad. He had these placed on the four gates of the Round City, and the fifth placed at the entryway to the caliph's palace, the Golden Gate. The implications of all this were unmistakable: the Abbasids were now official heirs to both prophetic and monarchical authority in a capital that they named Madinat al-Salam ("the City of Peace"), which evoked its biblical ancestor, Jerusalem, another former "city of peace."

Today we can only imagine what the Round City of al-Mansur looked like from the textual descriptions, since it has been obliterated over time. Located on the western bank of the Tigris, it is likely to have stood just south of the famous Shi'i mosque and shrine of al-Kazimayn. The Round City's western Basra Gate was said to lead directly to the shrine of the mystic Ma'ruf al-Karkhi, which remains an important landmark in the city today.[49] We may gain a more physical sense of the city if we consider the only remaining Abbasid structure from that period, Ukhaydir. This palace mansion, which is located some 120 miles south of Baghdad and was built around 771, gives clues on building methods and the rise of the Abbasid courtly space in the mid-eighth century. With an orientalist sense of discovery, the World War I-era archaeologist Gertrude Bell described Ukhaydir as "enchanting," and a palace of "solitary magnificence,"[50] while K. A. C. Creswell more soberly pointed out the novel features in its architecture, including the first shift from the Umayyad round arch to the Abbasid pointed arch, its intersecting vaults unknown in Sasanian architecture, and defensive elements (machicolation) that would not enter European castle architecture until the fourteenth century.[51] Ukhaydir was a castle home

---

[48] Wendell, "*Imago Mundi*," 122.
[49] Guy Le Strange, *Baghdad during the Abbasid Caliphate* (London, 1900), 351–356.
[50] Gertrude Bell, *Palace and Mosque at Ukhaidir* (Oxford, 1914), xii.
[51] Creswell, *Early Muslim Architecture*, 192–193.

(with dimensions of 111 x 82 m), which is set within a fortress (175 x 169 m). It boasted walls 2.5 meters thick and 20 meters high, with rounded towers that are 5 meters in diameter. The original Round City of Baghdad would easily have included features of similar architectural design.[52] And al-Mansur was proud to disclose to a confidant that, in case of a siege, he even had access to an underground tunnel for escape that reached up to 2 farsakhs (6 miles) outside the city.[53]

Symbolism aside, however, Baghdad was also a strategic economic choice for a capital. The city lay in the midst of the richest agricultural region in the Middle East, opened up new possibilities for the use of water transport through the Tigris and Euphrates, and developed a propensity for international trade. The historian and geographer Ya'qubi gives the iconic image of Baghdad from a vantage point a century later, after it became fully developed:

> I begin with Iraq only because it is the center of this world, the navel of the earth, and I mention Baghdad first because it is the greatest city, which has no peer in extent, size, prosperity, abundance of water, or health of climate, and because it is inhabited by all kinds of people ... On its flanks flow two great rivers, the Tigris and the Euphrates, and thus goods and foodstuffs, come to it by land and by water with the greatest ease ... Goods are brought from India, Sind, China, Tibet, the lands of the Turks, the Daylam, the Khazars, the Ethiopians, and others to such an extent that the products of the countries are more plentiful in Baghdad than in the countries from which they come.[54]

These were the advantages for trade looking to the Gulf waterway, but one could add that, looking north, the adjoining Euphrates river provided an added advantage, since this river at the great bend in its course east of Aleppo is no more than 125 miles away from the closest point to the Mediterranean coast near Antioch. Although trade goods from the north did not have the prestige of those coming from the east, this network of

---

[52] The traces of a kindred palace to Ukhaydir and Mshatta can also be found in Constantinople (on the Asian side of the city), where the emperor Theophilus (r. 829–843) built a palace in imitation of al-Ma'mun's palace at Rusafa: Alessandra Ricci, "The Road from Baghdad to Byzantium and the Case of the Bryas Palace in Istanbul," in *Byzantium in the Ninth Century: Dead or Alive?* ed. Leslie Brubaker (Ashgate, 1995); Hussein Keshani, "The Abbasid Palace of Theophilus: Byzantine Taste for the Arts of Islam," *al-Masaq* 16 (2004).

[53] Khatib al-Baghdadi, *Tarikh Baghdad*, 1:77.

[54] al-Ya'qubi, *Kitab al-Buldan*, ed. M. J. de Goeje (Leiden, 1892), 233–242; trans. Bernard Lewis in *Islam: From the Prophet Muhammad to the Capture of Constantinople*, 2 vols., vol. 2: *Religion and Society* (Oxford, 1987), 69–71.

transport on waterways in close proximity to each other played a vital role in facilitating military and administrative communication.

Baghdad served as the political base of the Abbasid empire, but it was also strategically suited to facilitate the drive for intercultural contact epitomized in the Qur'anic verse: "O mankind, We have created you male and female, and made you into nations and tribes, so you may know (explore) one another."[55] If Damascus once epitomized a city on the periphery of both the Arabian desert and the Mediterranean world, Baghdad was unabashedly central for all cultures – in the words of a recent author, "the axis on which the world turned," while Iraq was "a vortex that pulls inward and fuses what lies around it."[56] In an effort to expand the settlement quickly in the city, al-Mansur built another palace in 773 that he named al-Khuld (eternity), outside the Round City by the riverside, opposite a monastery; and around this palace flourished the market area of al-Karkh; and he built the Rusafa Palace, across the Tigris river, which he reserved for his designated successor, al-Mahdi. The Rusafa district later included a cemetery of the Abbasid caliphs from the late ninth century onwards as well as the tomb of Abu Hanifa, which became an important shrine. From al-Rusafa, settlement expanded east to the Shammasiyya, a predominantly Christian area located on a picturesque summit where in 829 al-Ma'mun established an observatory for astronomical study.[57] And to the south of the Shammasiyya later grew the Mukharrim quarter, south of which the Dar al-Khilafa (caliphal palace) was established in the tenth century. Three pontoon bridges were also constructed to connect the two banks of the river; one of them was reserved for use by women.[58]

With its various nodal points of courtly and commercial activity, the new capital rapidly developed a unique urban life sustained by merchants and a new breed of consumers increasingly demanding commodities of luxury and the unusual. Within the span of half a century this mecca of commerce became an arbiter of style to other cities and populations, giving rise to a new Arabic verb, *tabaghdada* (to act like a Baghdadi), which connoted someone projecting urban sophistication – the equivalent of modern pretensions in cities such as Paris and

[55] Qur'an 13:49.
[56] Garth Fowden, *Empire to Commonwealth: Consequences of Monotheism in Late Antiquity* (Princeton, 1993) 161, 17–18.
[57] Ibn al-Qifti, *Ikhbar al-Ulama' bi-Akhbar al-Hukama'* (Beirut, n.d.), 234–235.
[58] Khatib al-Baghdadi, *Tarikh Baghdad*, 1:116.

New York. Future visitors to the city would compare it to a garden of paradise, and figures as widely different as the jurist al-Shafiʿi (d. 204/ 820) and the secular belles letterist al-Sahib b. ʿAbbad (d. 385/995) are quoted praising it as an ideal setting for learning. Much as in a modern airline travel poster, Shafiʿi's name was enlisted to say that going to Baghdad is not arduous travel but feels like going to a second home, while al-Sahib b. ʿAbbad states that Baghdad among the nations is like a teacher among students (more proverb-like in Arabic: *Baghdad fi'l-bilad ka'l-ustadh fi'l-ʿibad*).[59]

The city quickly also became a magnet for different religious communities and their leaderships, as the Nestorian Catholicos, Timothy (d. 823), moved his base from nearby Ctesiphon to Baghdad, and the Babylonian Jewish academies of Sura (near Hilla) and Pumbedita (at Anbar) soon relocated to Baghdad from southern Iraq. The tenth-century al-Shabushti described at length the monasteries that dotted the region near Baghdad and gave favorable descriptions of the orchards, gardens, and vineyards that usually surrounded monasteries, describing how these locales served as parks for the enjoyment of visitors of different faiths, and had taverns that entertained others seeking quality wine or romantic escapades.[60] Such a cooperative atmosphere among adherents of different faiths, often associated later with the environment of medieval Islamic Spain, was equally robust in this early period in Iraq as well. Unlike the secluded and ghettoized environment experienced by the Jewish minority in medieval European towns, the Christian and Jewish quarters in this new Islamic city were located in a central area of Baghdad, near the area of Karkh and the Round City, and were directly integrated in the city's commercial and financial life. The Abbasids conferred special favor on Nestorian Christianity such that many ministers in the ninth and tenth centuries and the majority of physicians to the elite belonged to this sect, while the influence of Judaism's Talmudic academies in Iraq on the shaping of Islamic law probably spanned the entire first century of Abbasid rule.[61]

---

[59] Yaqut, *Muʿjam al-Buldan* (Beirut, 2015), 3:461, 463; Michael Cooperson, "Baghdad in Rhetoric and Narrative," *Muqarnas*, ed. Gülru Necipoğlu, 13 (1996).

[60] Hilary Kilpatrick, "Monasteries through Muslim Eyes: The *Diyarat* Books," in *Christians at the Heart of Islamic Rule: Church Life and Scholarship in Abbasid Iraq*, ed. David Thomas (Leiden, 2003), 22–23.

[61] In highlighting the atmosphere of assimilation, al-Jahiz adds that many prominent Christians were able to avoid paying the *jizya* (poll-tax), generally

In a telling sign of this ongoing intercultural awareness, Tabari, who did not even mention in his chronicle the battle of Poitiers in 732 – an event that occurred too far west for his interests – records that in a rare confluence in the year 244/858 several major holidays of Islam, Judaism, and Christianity (the Adha festival, Passover, and Palm Sunday) happened to coincide on the same day. It was not just a report on calendars, but was no doubt a reference to a moment that added festiveness to the social climate in Baghdad.

Early Abbasid Statecraft

Al-Mansur's string of successes against his various challengers can make his achievements seem mainly in the area of military domination, when in fact his reign marks a formative moment in the shaping of the Abbasid state and its guiding principles.[62] He was greatly helped in achieving this task by an emerging cadre of court secretaries, known as the *kuttab*, of whom the most prominent examples were Khalid b. Barmak and Abdallah b. al-Muqaffa'. A Manichean for much of his life before his conversion to Islam, Ibn al-Muqaffa' (d. 139/757) was an avid reader of Persian and Indian political and philosophical learning, but also a student of Abd al-Hamid al-Katib, a chancery official who pioneered the adaptation of Arabic rhetorical techniques for the purpose of administrative and diplomatic writing in the late Umayyad period.[63] Ibn al-Muqaffa''s name is today mostly familiar from his entertaining book of fables, *Kalila wa Dimna*, which tells parables on morality and advice applicable in the human realm through dialogs and interactions of animals. Contrary to modern uses of *Kalila wa Dimna* as a children's book, Ibn al-Muqaffa', who rendered it into Arabic from Persian and more ancient Indian texts, such as the *Panchatantra*, had intended his book less for entertainment than for the serious task of delivering political messages, albeit in the indirect way of stories.

Less well known but even more important from Ibn al-Muqaffa''s pen was his *Risala fi'l-Sahaba*, in which he advises the caliph on how to

mandatory on all non-Muslims: al-Jahiz, *Rasa'il a-Jahiz*, ed. Abd al-Salam Muhammad Harun (Beirut, 1991), 2:316–317.

[62] Lassner, *The Shaping of Abbasid Rule*.

[63] J. D. Latham, "Ibn al-Muqaffa' and Early Abbasid Prose," in *The Cambridge History of Arabic Literature*, vol. 2: *Abbasid Belles Lettres*, ed. J. Ashtiany, et al. (Cambridge, 1990).

choose his staff, and organize his government and military. He advises the caliph to select for his entourage as devoted companions (*sahaba*) only those who have proven loyalty and special qualities such as intelligence, courage, or notable status, thereby starting the Abbasid phase of reliance on key Persian ministers, such as the Barmakids.[64] He then focuses on the Khurasaniyya troops, whom he praises as the most loyal praetorians of the state because their service was based on a religious bond (*da 'wa*) to the dynasty, but recommends additional steps to ensure their continued trust, such as payment of their salaries on time, guarding the value of their money against inflation, instructing them in the basics of the faith, and above all discouraging troops from engaging in financial matters and trade.

In Ibn al-Muqaffa''s writings we find glimmers of the famous Persian flowchart of Sasanid political wisdom, stretching back in attribution to Khusraw I Anushirwan (r. 531–579), and sketched out in this rough sequence: the monarchy depends on the army, the army on money, money comes from the land-tax, the land-tax comes from agriculture. Agriculture depends on justice, justice on the integrity of officials, and integrity and reliability on the constant watchfulness of the king.[65] This circle of duty or rights for the ruler and his subjects (*ra 'iyya*) was considered in medieval times the equivalent of the modern notion of a nation-state's constitution, and it was viewed as universal political wisdom. A modern observer of political theories has also argued that Ibn al-Muqaffa''s discussion of "imperial companions" "lies within the boundaries of the canon set in Hellenistic thought for the Royal *philos* or 'friend'," such as represented in Alexander's reliance on a similar circle of "royal companions," and in Aristotle's treatment of *philia* "as the paradigmatic form of political relations."[66]

The burden of government was an immense responsibility according to Ibn al-Muqaffa', and he compared the wielder of military power to someone riding a lion down the street. People may be afraid of him, but he is undoubtedly the most terrified of all. It is a sobering image for all time on the relation between civil and military spheres of authority, which could only be maintained with a guiding idea of loyalty to rulers or principles. At the same time that he emphasizes the importance of

---

[64] Ann Lambton, *State and Government in Medieval Islam* (Oxford, 1981), 52.

[65] Peter Brown, *The World of Late Antiquity* (London, 1971), 166.

[66] Patricia Springborg, *Western Republicanism and the Oriental Prince* (Austin, 1992), 266–267.

proper dealing with the military, Ibn al-Muqaffaʿ dwells heavily on the role of religion in governing the state. Although Islam is almost never directly referenced in his writings, he considered religion an important foundation for the state. Sasanid political philosophy had long held from its first purported mirror for princes, *ʿAhd Ardashir*, that kingship and religion were twins, with religion being broadly defined as a moral philosophy and what moderns would characterize as the rule of law. And building on this idea while also noting the discrepancies of Islamic legal practices in the provinces, and with various emerging scholars on legal thinking, such as with Malik b. Anas (in Hijaz) and Abu Hanifa (in Iraq), Ibn al-Muqaffaʿ advised the caliph on the need to promulgate a uniform religious legal code for the empire.

In this early period the Abbasids did not promote a single system of religious law throughout the empire, but they were active in trying to shape the writing of religious culture. This they did with their patronage of writers who worked on writing a formal master narrative of Islamic history, and more specifically the biography (*Sira*) of the Prophet Muhammad. And since the *Sira* was viewed as the culmination of monotheistic history, it meant that the project involved the writing of a story as if in a revised form of a biblical narrative, yet this time from Creation to the Abbasid revolution. The Qurʾan has little to say on the details of stories of the ancient prophets, but the ancestor of the Abbasid house, Abdallah b. Abbas, had since the seventh century been active by way of Quraʾnic exegesis in developing a genre of Arabic/Islamic commentary (*qisas*) that filled in the gaps in detail surrounding various Qurʾanic verses. This process of narration was continued by students of Ibn Abbas, and culminated in the early Abbasid period when the caliph al-Mansur entrusted Ibn Ishaq (d. 150/768) with the task of writing down the *Sira* (ostensibly for the instruction of al-Mansur's young successor, al-Mahdi). Ibn Ishaq was probably already active in the late Umayyad period, but the process of final redaction of all historical accounts (including the *Sira*), which he did under Abbasid rule, must have been the most critical phase in the shaping of Islamic textuality and culture.

Such stories accomplished an important task in providing a more cleansed version of biblical tales that served the Islamic idealization of the ancient past; but in the process they made the key contribution of giving a highly flattering portrayal of the ancestors of the Abbasid house – al-Abbas and his son, Abdallah b. Abbas. These ancestors became the "antediluvian" equivalents of the patriarchs of the Old Testament whose progeny would mysteriously work their way to the top of Islamic salvation history. Al-Abbas, for example, was portrayed as the chief protector and spokesman of Muhammad when the latter first met the Medinese supporters who invited him, in 622, to make the *hijra* from Mecca to Medina, and start building the first Islamic state in their city. And Abdallah b. Abbas was given the blessing of the Prophet as an "Imam–sage" figure who held the keys of deep knowledge to the meaning of the Qur'an, and was in possession of general expertise in all matters of the faith. Ibn Abbas would go on to become the first example of a compiler of hadith,[67] while lore connected to his name was associated with a flexible attitude to Islamic law through the use of *rukhas* (sing. *rukhsa*, "dispensations") that relaxed strict rules.[68]

Ibn Ishaq's work was later continued by al-Waqidi, who extended the stories further in his *Maghazi*, which he wrote during al-Rashid's reign, and continued the pattern of depicting al-Abbas and Abdallah b. Abbas as the wisest of their society after the Prophet and hence as deserving of leadership (unlike the imprudent Alids). Such building of narratives with religious and moral implications helped create a climate of Islamic culture centered on the privilege of the Abbasid family in history, but in the end stories were just stories and subject to interpretation. They were not the Ten Commandments or the Code of Hammurabi, which forcefully defined law or showed legal authority under the control of the state.

If there was a time to press ahead with a centralizing religious program, it was in al-Mansur's reign. As new situations developed in Islamic society in the complex urban and multicultural environment of the Middle East, there was a need for a coherent system of legal answers. Instead, two key trends started emerging to answer such questions in the eighth century: the Hanafi school, which emphasized rational analysis of situations based on reasoned opinions (*ra'y*); and the Maliki school, which followed the letter of established customs and traditions (*sunna*) to reach a solution. The former was based in Iraq, and as such was colored by the highly developed intellectual and analytic methods of Mesopotamia, while the latter was based on the more rudimentary Arabian environment of the Hijaz, and eventually

---

[67] Tayeb El-Hibri, "Umar b. al-Khattab and the Abbasids," *JAOS* 136 (2016).
[68] Ibn Habib, *Kitab al-Tarikh*, ed. Jorge Aguade (Madrid, 1991), 160.

defined *sunna* as the normative practices of key Companions of the Prophet and the early society of Medina in general (*'amal ahl al-Madina*), and therefore not just the Prophet's own *sunna*.[69] Al-Mansur tried to draw close to both Abu Hanifa and Malik, to co-opt their clout, and tried to have them serve as officials in the apparatus of the state, but was unsuccessful, and just let the juristic situation grow without official supervision.[70]

The Abbasids may have had reason to avoid direct control over the sharia because they had confidence in their political power and preferred to keep the definition of caliphal authority open between the different perceptions of the Arab and Persian constituencies. The Qur'anic verse that reads "David, behold, We have appointed thee a viceroy (*khalifa*) in the earth; therefore judge between men justly, and follow not caprice, lest it leads thee astray from the way of God"[71] was probably assumed by the Abbasids sufficient to project caliphal authority in all spheres. The caliph here was defined as "God's Caliph," having wide latitude to judge his subjects, and this was probably viewed as sufficient to define caliphal authority over jurists.[72] Resistance from jurists, such as Abu Hanifa and Malik b. Anas, who may have grumbled about the pretensions of Abbasid political authority, may have been stinging but did not seem important when Abbasid military power was felt across the lands in full force. And even if religious scholars sought to limit a caliph's authority, they did not know how to do it in this early Abbasid period given the scattered picture of Islamic legal practice in various locales, and the as yet non-canonical situation of what passed for *sunna* and hadith. It later took a charm offensive from Harun al-Rashid toward Malik, al-Shafi'i, and other important jurists of the time to make it respectable for Abu Hanifa's students, such as Abu Yusuf and Ibn Abi Layla, to join in Abbasid state service as judges and advisors. This development helped project harmony between the two branches of religious power, and deferred any confrontation between the state and the circle of pious scholars. The meaning of terms such as "Imam" and "caliph" remained

---

[69] Noel Coulson, *A History of Islamic Law* (Edinburgh, 1964), 47–52.
[70] Muhammad Qasim Zaman, *Religion and Politics under the Early Abbasids* (Leiden, 1997), 147–166.
[71] Qur'an 38:26; A. J. Arberry, *The Koran Interpreted* (London, 1955), 2:160.
[72] P. Crone and M. Hinds, *God's Caliph: Religious Authority in the First Centuries of Islam* (Cambridge, 1986).

ambiguous, and it would take until well after the Mihna of al-Ma'mun to demote the Abbasid office of political leadership from any claims on divinely sanctioned authority.[73]

There were other religious gestures that al-Mansur began developing to strengthen his legitimacy in a public way, and this included leading the pilgrimage to Mecca, and investing in the construction and upkeep of mosques. Since the dynasty's ancestor, al-Abbas, was said to have once held, before and after the emergence of Islam, the religiously honorific task of providing water to pilgrims in Mecca, al-Mansur tried to show the revival of this privilege with the attention he gave to improving the pilgrimage sanctuary, and preparing the pilgrimage caravan from Iraq to Mecca. The continued attention he gave to the pilgrimage sites would culminate in the late medieval period with the Mamluk invention of the title Khadim al-Haramayn ("custodian of the two holy cities [Mecca and Medina]"), which the Ottomans picked up after they conquered the Hijaz,[74] and continues into the modern period as the title of the king of Saudi Arabia. But in origin, such great emphasis on the upkeep of Mecca was rooted in this early Abbasid period, and their dynastic search for functions that could help their political legitimacy. Al-Mansur's clear intent to make Mecca the cornerstone of Abbasid legitimacy was reflected in his move in 137/ 755 to renovate the Ka'ba mosque, which had not undergone any renovation since the reign of al-Walid b. Abd al-Malik (r. 705–715). An inscription from 140/758 attested to the completion of the phase of work in al-Mansur's reign with a decorative mosaic inscribed in black on a gold background that named al-Mansur, and included the Qur'anic verse "Muhammad is the Messenger of God, he was sent with guidance and the religion of truth, that He may uplift it above every religion, though the unbelievers be averse."[75] This statement was famously continued by the Abbasids on Islamic coinage when they first took power, and later also appeared on their banners.[76]

---

[73] John P. Turner, *Inquisition in Early Islam: The Competition for Political and Religious Authority in the Abbasid Empire* (London, 2013), 7–8, 20–21, 27–28. A revival in Abbasid religious authority, however, restarted later, in the reign of al-Qadir.

[74] Arnold, *The Caliphate*, 141.

[75] Qur'an 9:33; al-Azraqi, *Akhbar Makka*, ed. F. Wustenfeld (Leipzig, 1858), 311–312.

[76] al-Sabi', *Rusum Dar al-Khilafa*, ed. Mikhail Awwad (Baghdad, 1964), 95.

Al-Mansur greatly helped establish the foundations of the Abbasid state almost by the sheer force of his personality. Shrewdly authoritarian but never arbitrary, he vetted all information about his officials. An idealizing portrait in Tabari's chronicle states that postmasters in all outlying districts used to write him every day on the prices of staple commodities (wheat and corn and other foods), on decisions issued by the judges in their regions, about what the governor had done, and what wealth had been returned to the treasury.[77] This statement was probably meant to hark back to older Sasanid ideals of the need for attentiveness by rulers, and may have been meant to show the importance of keeping a rapid postal network across the empire. In his final testament to his son, al-Mahdi, he admitted his rough path to power and harsh policies, but flattered himself on keeping a treasury so rich that even if tax revenues were to cease for a decade, the new ruler could still pay his troops and run the state.

His style of micromanagement remained till the end of his reign; we read that on his last pilgrimage trip he chanced upon some unflattering poetic graffiti, targeting him, scribbled on a wall. He wasted no time in summoning his officials and upbraiding them for letting public order decline to the point that someone would be bold enough to write such nonsense. Since no one else could see the ominous lines, this story, which Tabari's chronicle gives, was therefore clearly meant allusively to evoke "the Writing on the Wall" parable – as in the case of Belshazzar of Babylon in 539 BCE (Daniel 5:5–6). The caliph then resigned himself to the inevitable. He died on his way back from pilgrimage, surrounded by all his high officials who were still in awe of his domination. And, to ensure his continued "Genghis Khan-like" aura of mystery, they had him buried secretly and dug an additional one hundred graves in order to mislead any enemies who sought to desecrate his grave, as had been done to some Umayyad caliphs. Yet it is interesting that, for all of al-Mansur's autocratic style, it is said that once, when he went to propose marriage to a Yemenite tribeswoman, Arwa bint Mansur al-Himyari, she made a condition that he would not take another wife or consort besides her, or do so without her permission.[78] With a lack of records for consorts for his reign, he may well have kept this promise for the woman who became the mother of his successor, al-Mahdi.

---

[77] Tabari, *Tarikh*, III, 435.   [78] Ibn Abd Rabbih, *al-'Iqd al-Farid*, 5:114.

3 | *The Golden Age of the Abbasid Caliphate (775–833)*

al-Mahdi and al-Hadi

The insignia of caliphal power – the staff, the ring, and the mantle of the Prophet – was sent to the new caliph, the thirty-two-year old al-Mahdi, who was in Baghdad. The two decades of al-Mansur's reign had given al-Mahdi an opportunity to develop in personality and build up some experience. He had known the Abbasid homestead at Humayma as a child, and this gave him an important root in the Abbasid foundational years and the revolution. He benefited from having leading commanders of the Khurasaniyya around him when he was still an adolescent as he marched to the east in 141/759 to direct the campaign that put down a rebellion by the governor Abd al-Jabbar al-Azdi, and he actively pacified the east after the Abu Muslimiyya revolts. When he came back to Baghdad in 151/769 with his newly born son, Harun, his father settled him in Baghdad on the east bank of the Tigris in a newly constructed palace area of al-Rusafa, where he based his military supporters, including the emerging Barmakid family.

With barely a respite, he was assigned in 155/771 to Raqqa in northern Syria, where he was put in charge of building the city of Rafiqa (lit. "Companion City," i.e. to Raqqa). This city, hastily built from mud brick, became part of a larger Raqqa–Rafiqa urban complex that was intended to provide an alternative to Damascus for stationing loyal Abbasid troops. The city lay just north of the ancient Silk Road that in the third century had connected Palmyra, Dura Europos, and Hatra through trade, but it was more strategically located on the upstream part of the Euphrates with easy reach down to Baghdad, and within close proximity to Asia Minor to provide an advance point for launching campaigns against the Byzantines. Medieval Arab geographers considered Raqqa part of a cluster of towns (including Harran, Diyarbakir, Amid, Mayyafariqin, and Mosul) that made up the province of Jazira (lit. "the island," i.e. between the Tigris and Euphrates). This province, today spanning the northern parts of Syria and Iraq as well as much of southern and central Turkey, in antiquity straddled the borderlands between the Roman and Persian empires and was bordered geographically in the north by Armenia. Jazira harbored a diversity of Arab tribal federations that could sway power when empires went to war, and which required constant maintenance in terms of honor and economic advantage. The early Abbasid caliphs understood more than any modern political analyst the risks and strategic value of this region as the glue between the eastern and western provinces of the empire, and in later years Raqqa would become the preferred base and capital of Harun al-Rashid, who resided there from 180/796 till the end of his reign.[1]

Al-Mahdi continued the attention his father gave to religious activities, and in some ways did so with greater vigor. He is mentioned by Tabari as having built several mosques in Basra and elsewhere, but little evidence of these remains today except for one in the city of ʿAsqalan (Ascalon), where epigraphy on a panel, probably dating to when al-Mahdi was still a nominated successor and active in building al-Rafiqa, reads: "Al-Mahdi, [son of] the Commander of the Faithful, has ordered the building of this minaret and this mosque, at the hands of al-Mufaddal b. Sallam, and Jahwar b. Hisham, in the month of Muharram, in the year 155 [771]."[2] When he visited Jerusalem in 163/780 he ordered the rebuilding of the Aqsa Mosque, turning the prayer space into twice the size that it is today,[3] and in a pious gesture ordered the inclusion on his coinage of the famous Islamic honorific formula usually mentioned by pious Muslims after the Prophet's name ("Salutations and blessing be upon him"); this inscription on coinage continued until 184/800, in al-Rashid's reign.[4]

But by far his most sustained attention was paid to Mecca, where he used his pilgrimage trips to improve and expand the structure of the Kaʿba Mosque. On his 160/777 pilgrimage he ordered the removal of the many veils that had piled up on the Kaʿba, had the structure washed

[1] Michael Meinecke, "Rakka," *EI*[2].
[2] Guy Le Strange, *Palestine under the Moslems: A Description of Syria and the Holy Land from AD 650 to 1500* (London, 1890), 401.
[3] Miriam Rosen-Ayalon, *Islamic Art and Archaeology in Palestine* (Walnut Creek, CA, 2006), 36.
[4] Stanley Lane Poole, *Catalogue of the Collection of Arabic Coins Preserved in the Khedivial Library in Cairo* (Oxford, 1897), 42–46, 56–58.

and enhanced with various kinds of aromatics added to its stones, and ordered the expansion of the prayer space. Having noticed that the Ka'ba was unevenly positioned in the courtyard of the mosque, al-Mahdi in 164/781 ordered the acquisition of properties adjoining the mosque in order to expand the space for prayer and have the Ka'ba better centered for circumambulation.[5] Many of the marble pillars used in these expansions were brought by sea from Syria and Egypt through Jidda, and some pillars with commemorative inscriptions in Kufic script bearing his name as the caliph who ordered the renovations stand in the mosque to this day. In Medina he probably found the Umayyad mosaics in the Prophet's mosque still in good condition, but he made sure to remove the name of al-Walid b. Abd al-Malik from an inscription, and placed his name there instead.

With governing stints in Iran and Syria, and journeys on pilgrimage to the Hijaz, al-Mahdi was amongst the early Abbasids to do the "Grand Tour" of the empire (others included al-Mansur, al-Hadi, al-Rashid, al-Ma'mun, and al-Mu'tasim). This experience gave him exposure to regions and cultures outside Baghdad, which would increasingly become a scarce opportunity for future heirs apparent, such as al-Amin. These journeys made the successor a familiar figure to different regional and social groups, and rallied the support of the military to him as a credible leadership figure. In Iraq, al-Mahdi's rule seemed secure, and he devoted more time to transforming the Abbasid state in the direction of professional government departments. The court became more of a formal institution run by a chief minister, and a new class of government secretaries (*kuttab*) started emerging.[6] Within this picture also, the service of the Barmakid family of viziers starts to stand out for their role in shaping policies of centralization, better tax collection, and the planning of military campaigns. The Barmakids were originally from Balkh ("Baktra" in the pre-Islamic period, from which the "Bactrian" region), where they had served as Buddhist priests of its temple (*nawbahar*) before their conversion to Islam in the Umayyad period. The medieval geographer Ibn al-Faqih compares their pre-Islamic social status to that of the Quraysh, the tribe of the Prophet Muhammad, and states that Balkh was viewed as

[5] Azraqi, *Akhbar Makka*, 317; Oleg Grabar, "Upon Reading al-Azraqi," *Muqarnas* 3 (1982).

[6] Richard A. Kimber, "The Early Abbasid Vizierate," *Journal of Semitic Studies* 37 (1992).

pilgrimage center for visitors from as far away as Central Asia and China.[7] The city was once the religious capital of the Kushan empire, and was said in legend to be the original home of the Persian prophet Zoroaster.[8] Today Balkh has been eclipsed by the nearby town of Mazar-i Sharif, which is said to include the shrine of the Prophet's cousin, Ali,[9] but in the early Islamic period Balkh was considered by geographers the "mother of cities" in the Iranian world. In political terms, Balkh rose to importance in 118/737 when the Umayyad governor of Khurasan, Asad b. Abdallah al-Qasri, briefly shifted the province's capital from Marw to Balkh during the war with the Turkic empire in Central Asia.[10] This interlude was probably crucial in raising a coterie of Persian elite, such as the Barmakids and the Samanids, to newfound prominence.

Khalid b. Barmak probably joined the Abbasid underground earlier than Abu Muslim, and he was Ibrahim al-Imam's representative in Jurjan. Al-Mansur later assigned him for seven years as governor in the east, where he was based in Tabaristan, while his son Yahya was his deputy in Rayy, and he helped al-Mahdi settle into the task of governing there. Al-Mansur, however, kept Khalid at arm's length, as he did with all his senior military leaders. In the reign of al-Mahdi, however, Khalid came into the spotlight in Baghdad for his skill in creating a better bookkeeping system for state revenues. Yahya b. Khalid became also increasingly associated with the future successor, Harun al-Rashid. In an unusual development, the Abbasid and Barmakid families established a special bond when Harun was born. Yahya's wife, Zubayda bint Munir, was said to have nursed al-Rashid, while al-Khayzuran, al-Rashid's mother, nursed al-Fadl b. Yahya.[11] The milk brotherhood between Harun and al-Fadl projected an image of partnership between the caliphs and their Persian ministers in a world still healing after the revolutionary years. The political use of kin ties were already strong within the Abbasid house, since al-Mahdi was married to the daughter of al-Saffah, and al-Mahdi's daughter 'Ulayya would

[7] Ibn al-Faqih al-Hamadani, *Mukhtasar Kitab al-Buldan*, ed. M. J. de Goeje (Leiden, 1885), 323.
[8] Gibb, *The Arab Conquests in Central Asia*, 10.
[9] The more generally recognized location of Ali's tomb is at al-Najaf, located a few miles west of Kufa.
[10] Hugh Kennedy, *The Great Arab Conquests* (New York, 2007), 289.
[11] al-Jahshiyari, *Kitab al-Wuzara' wa'l-Kuttab*, ed. Mustafa al-Saqqa et al. (Cairo, 1938), 136.

be married to the son of Isa b. Musa, the divested successor to the throne, but since marriage between an Iranian and a Hashimite princess was not allowed, al-Mahdi devised this step of artificial kinship between the Abbasids and the Barmakids to strengthen their ties. Khayzuran, the mother of al-Hadi and al-Rashid, increasingly started to play a significant role in court politics.

In the area of caliphal succession, al-Mahdi followed al-Mansur in making an early arrangement, naming his son Musa al-Hadi as first successor, to be followed by Harun. It was the latter, however, who attracted the support of the court, the *kuttab*, and the Abna'. In 163/780 and 165/782 he was assigned to lead military campaigns against the Byzantines, where he was accompanied by Khalid b. Barmak and his son, Yahya. Although the expedition forayed deep in Asia Minor, it probably was not intended to make great territorial gains, but to reestablish deterrence and a stable border region. A Byzantine incursion against the town of Edessa had invited a reprisal, which saw Harun reach as far as the Bosporus, and exact a heavy tribute from the Byzantines. It was in the light of Harun's clever maneuvering on this campaign that he was now given the title al-Rashid ("the wise").

Al-Mahdi's decade-long reign is described without much political drama in the medieval chronicles, but with the occasional anecdote involving poetry or interactions with commoners. He was given a favorable image in general for his generous giving and for issuing amnesties to political prisoners, and he tends to come across as a cultured figure imbued with curiosity and a desire for leisurely discovery. One anecdote describes him running an experiment to test which kind of fur endured rain and snow best to remain dry and warm,[12] while another shows him straying from his hunting party one day, and finding hospitality in a Bedouin tent, sharing a drink and a jocular conversation.[13] The caliph was said to be passionate about the hunt, and patronized the writing of a book on falconry.[14] Stories about al-Mahdi show him a less dour figure than his father, and in real life this lighter side must have influenced those around him: his daughter, 'Ulayya, became an accomplished poet, and one of his sons,

[12] al-Mas'udi, *Kitab al-Tanbih wa'l-Ishraf*, ed. M. J. de Goeje (Leiden, 1894), 63.
[13] al-Mas'udi, *Muruj al-Dhahab*, trans. Paul Lunde and Caroline Stone in *Meadows of Gold: The Abbasids* (London, 1989), 37.
[14] Dimitri Gutas, *Greek Thought, Arabic Culture: The Graeco-Arabic Translation Movement in Baghdad and Early Abbasid Society* (New York, 1998), 74.

Ibrahim, a famous musician. There is a leisurely and anecdotal character to al-Mahdi's biography, even till its end, with one account stating that his death was an accident while he was out hunting and chasing a gazelle in thickly wooded area, while another version claims he died from eating a poisoned pear. Apparently, in the latter account, a disgruntled concubine hoping to eliminate a rival for the affections of the caliph placed the pear as bait for the other woman, but al-Mahdi took the fruit by mistake.

Little is known about al-Mahdi's first successor, al-Hadi, who ruled for barely a year. He seems to have been a tempestuous personality who did not get along with senior officials, particularly the *kuttab* at the palace. He had acquired some experience as heir apparent when his father sent him to Jurjan in 167/784 to negotiate with Wandad Hurmuzd, a chieftain of the Qarinid family in the highlands of Tabaristan province adjacent to the Caspian Sea, who had started a rebellion. Al-Hadi was accompanied on this mission by commanders from the Abna', including Ali b. Isa b. Mahan, a future controversial governor of Khurasan. That the Iranian Barmakids were not involved in this mission of mediation and leading the Abbasid military force shows a possible tension between the elites of Khurasan and Tabaristan. Al-Mahdi had taken direct charge of this situation by sending his successor al-Hadi, and it was resolved in a way that protected Qarinid pride. Although al-Hadi's success in gaining the submission of the province in 169/786 was impressive, the episode may have driven a wedge between the Barmakid courtly circle of the court secretaries (the *kuttab*) and the army commanders (the *quwwad*). Barmakid suspicions that al-Hadi's new ties with the Qarinids could endanger their privileges caused them to increasingly promote al-Hadi's brother, Harun, for the succession. It did not help al-Hadi that his mother, Khayzuran, who was deeply political, sided with the Barmakids, and that al-Hadi showed an autocratic tendency, such as when he quickly reacted to events by trying to change the course of succession in favor of his son, Ja'far. The chroniclers provide little substance when covering al-Hadi's short reign, except for describing an Alid rebellion that took place in Mecca by a Hasanid descendant of Ali, named al-Husayn b. Ali. Although this uprising was easily defeated, it resulted in the escape of two of the rebel's supporters, siblings of the former al-Nafs al-Zakiyya: Yahya b. Abdallah, who escaped to

Daylam, and the more successful Idris b. Abdallah, who escaped to North Africa where, like the Umayyad Abd al-Rahman before him, he was able to rally Berber support to his cause and eventually founded the Idrisid dynasty in the Maghreb with its new capital at Fez.

Harun al-Rashid and the Caliphate in Its "Golden Prime"

The Caliphate in Myth: Islamic and Orientalist

The rapid transition from al-Mahdi to al-Rashid after the short one-year reign of al-Hadi shows almost sure signs of a stealthy assassination, usually attributed to a conspiracy by the Barmakids and al-Khayzuran, who feared the many changes he was implementing. It would also be sacrilege if the most storied of the Abbasid caliphs, Harun al-Rashid, who presided over the dynasty's golden age, were to accede to the throne merely in the course of normal succession, and the chroniclers have him enter the political stage in circumstances that almost ended his reign from the start. Al-Hadi's increasing pressure to place his son, Ja'far, as heir apparent evidently presented a problem for the caliphate's dynastic system. According to long-honored customs on the rules of succession that dated to Umayyad times, it was frowned on for a leader to change a line of succession, especially when a succession arrangement had already been secured through binding oaths from court officials and commanders. And since Harun refused to relinquish his rights, the situation deteriorated, as al-Hadi turned to pressure, and ordered that his brother be imprisoned until the matter could be decided. It was shortly afterwards that al-Hadi's reign abruptly came to an end.

To those with a religious take on events, Harun's situation was reminiscent of that of the biblical Joseph, who underwent a transformation of fortunes from imprisonment to a sudden assumption of a place of power at Pharaoh's court. And since medieval chroniclers took a long view of historical change, the cycle of predestination was probably read to include the future reign of al-Rashid's son, al-Ma'mun, who also rose to power amid contention with his brother and on the basis of renewed Khurasani support. The auspicious turn of fortune on that fateful night came to be referred to as the "Night of the Three Caliphs" – when al-Hadi died, al-Rashid acceded to the throne, and the new caliph received news that he had a newly born son, whom he named Abdallah (the future al-Ma'mun).

The tripartite scheme in al-Rashid's succession resonated with the story of the famous Sasanid shah Khusraw Anushirwan, and provides a window for the literary critic. The rich tapestries of medieval chronicle accounts used kernels of fact around which they spun moralizing messages and lengthy narratives stretching in an intertextual way across reigns and dynasties.[15]

The reign of Harun al-Rashid has long captured the imagination of later generations as the high point of the Islamic caliphate. The hyperbole about his reign can be found from the late medieval period, where one chronicler compares its days to wedding festivities,[16] and another gives more elaboration:

The reign of al-Rashid was one of the best of reigns, most replete of them in dignity, splendor and charity, and the one which most increased the extent of the realm. Al-Rashid received taxes from the greater part of the world, and ... there never collected at [a] Caliph's doors so many scholars, poets, canon lawyers, Qur'an readers, judges, clerks, boon companions and bards as collected at the door of al-Rashid; each one of them used to meet with the most generous treatment, and he raised him to the highest rank. [The caliph] was outstanding, a poet, an authority on history, [lore] and poems, of nice taste and discrimination, respected by both (his) intimates and the common folk.[17]

The fifteenth-century al-Qalqashandi leans more toward myth making when he describes the caliph's reach over tax revenues covering almost the entire known world. When a drought once struck Iraq, and the people of Baghdad became desperate for rain and prayed for rain on seeing clouds reaching over their city, al-Rashid, the writer claims, addressed the cloud from his palace balcony with famous words: "Travel where you shall over the lands, your revenues (i.e. from the agricultural harvest brought forth from this rain) will surely come back to my treasury!"[18]

In Western cultures, the image of the caliph from *The Thousand and One Nights* has also added to the romance with its portrayal of

---

[15] For a survey of the various modalities of this exercise of literary crafting of history, and examining backprojections in the sources on al-Rashid's reign, see Tayeb El-Hibri, *Reinterpreting Islamic Historiography: Harun al-Rashid and the Narrative of the Abbasid Caliphate* (Cambridge, 1999).

[16] Suyuti, *Tarikh al-Khulafa'*, 344.

[17] Ibn al-Tiqtaqa, *al-Fakhri*, 195–196, trans. Whitting, 192.

[18] al-Qalqashandi, *Ma'athir al-Inafa fi Ma'alim al-Khilafa*, ed. Abd al-Sattar Farraj (Beirut, 2006), 95.

medieval Baghdad as a city of boundless power, affluence, and magic. These fantasy stories often portrayed Harun al-Rashid and his minister, Ja'far, like medieval *flâneurs*, journeying the city in disguise, interacting with different social classes and seeking adventure. The *Nights* have left a lasting impression on Western imagination of the "Orient" ever since they were translated into French and English in the early eighteenth century. They inspired Tennyson's famous refrain on the "golden prime" of Harun al-Rashid in the poem "Recollections of the Arabian Nights" (1830) and Thomas Dibdin's opera *Il Bondocani* (1812), and these were followed by poets such as Henry Wadsworth Longfellow and W. B. Yeats, who also composed verses inspired by the Abbasid caliph.[19] Prose saw the caliph in the guise of a character in a novel – and a spy novel, no less. His ability to assume different identities, keep secrets, elude enemies, and turn the tables on his opponents suddenly made his name a metaphor for movement between two worlds and achieving the impossible. Rudyard Kipling's *Kim*, the story of a British agent engaged in rivalry against Russia for control of Afghanistan in the nineteenth century, described its main character as someone who "was hand in glove with men who had led lives stranger than anything Haroun al-Rashid dreamed of."[20]

As they undertook missions to help establish British political influence in the Middle East in the late nineteenth and early twentieth centuries, various orientalists who did double duty as enablers of empire and amateur scholars came back to England to write biographies of Harun al-Rashid. Edward Palmer, Harry St. John Philby (father of the more famous double agent Kim Philby), and John Bagot Glubb served in different locations (Sinai, Arabia, and Jordan), but all shared a sense of political awe and wonder in the face of Harun's dominance. Mark Sykes (of Sykes–Picot fame) described the caliph as "a capable warrior, a wise administrator," someone endowed "with a perception far in advance of his years," and "a worthy pinnacle of the structure of a mighty state."[21]

A British spirit struggling for control in Afghanistan, Egypt, Iraq, the Hijaz, and Gallipoli was no doubt fascinated by how the caliph moved

[19] Byron Porter Smith, *Islam in English Literature* (London, 1967), 208; Sari Nasir, *The Arabs and the English* (London, 1976), 56.
[20] Priya Satia, *Spies in Arabia: The Great War and the Cultural Foundations of Britain's Covert Empire in the Middle East* (Oxford, 2008), 357.
[21] Mark Sykes, *The Caliphs' Last Heritage* (London, 1915), 222, 227.

freely to, and controlled, all these flashpoints, which later gave Britain enormous hardship. The colonial biographers of Harun al-Rashid were curious to know the secret of his success to help them better manage their interactions with Arab and Muslim societies.[22] To all these writers, the reign of al-Rashid became a reified symbol of a distant Orient, in which Abbasid, Mamluk, and Ottoman elements blended to shape a Western imaginary of effective authoritarian power, which was still thought by romantics to have the potential to turn the tables on Western ascendancy.[23]

The American inheritance of this orientalist legacy took a more glossy turn, as the cliché images of the *Arabian Nights* was converted into film and took deeper root. This trend reached a peak in the 1950s when America kept up friendly relations with Iraq's Hashimite monarchy and maintained an interest in oil exploration there, which indirectly helped encourage a wave of films centered around Baghdad and the *Arabian Nights* setting, featuring stars such as Maureen O'Hara and Paulette Goddard. A more sober thinker on the Abbasid heritage in this time was perhaps the American architect Frank Lloyd Wright, who in 1957 produced a myriad of drawings in what is known as his "Plan for Greater Baghdad project." This included designs for a cultural center, a university, an opera house, and even a statue of Harun al-Rashid on top of a spiraling tower, located on an island – which he named "the island of Edena" – in a "Statue of Liberty" style, but with an outstretched sword.[24] His vision of the central space of the Baghdad university campus was of a circular form reminiscent of the Round City of al-Mansur, free of vehicular traffic and with university faculties and departments providing a substitute for the caliph's former placement of government offices around the central palace. And the vision of the "Round City" was blended further with modernity by including tall television antennas, a fact especially important because Iraq was the first Middle Eastern country to have television.[25] Writing to the Iraqi Development Board, Wright explained that his plan "would make of

---

[22] El-Hibri, *Reinterpreting Islamic Historiography*, 19–21.

[23] For a direct attempt to compare the British and Arab empires and their reasons for decline, see John Bagot Glubb, *The Course of Empire* (London, 1965), 397–408.

[24] Mina Marefat, "Wright's Baghdad: Ziggurats and Green Visions," *DC Papers* (Barcelona, 2008), 145–155. Wright's fascination with the *Arabian Nights* from childhood is also widely referenced.

[25] Neil Levine, *The Urbanism of Frank Lloyd Wright* (Princeton, 2016), 374.

Baghdad a modern mecca for travelers and a place in which to find the strength and beauty of ancient-culture – alive today."[26] And of his design of the proposed cultural center he added that his project "was intended to glorify the great circular city of Harun al-Rashid [*sic*], the romance of the Thousand and One Nights – [and] the story of Adam and Eve in the Garden of Eden."[27]

The legendary literature on Harun al-Rashid will always continue to inspire fictional writing, but there is also a historical Harun who was a real political figure, who charted policies, led military campaigns, and interacted with scholars and scientists of his time, and probably did preside over a moment that was in some ways the zenith of the caliphate. Al-Rashid entered his reign as a hesitant prince, and in the shadow of his mother, al-Khayzuran, and the Barmakid ministers who paved his way to power. He felt indebted to them and inexperienced, and therefore delegated great powers to Yahya the Barmakid, whom he viewed as mentor and second father figure, stating as he entrusted him with the royal seal: "I have invested you with the management of my subjects' affairs, removing the burden from my shoulders to yours. Govern them as you think right; appoint to office whom you will, and remove whom you will. Conduct all affairs as you see fit."[28] The hesitations of al-Mansur and al-Mahdi about appointing a minister with such vast powers were now removed as the Barmakid family, Yahya and his two sons, al-Fadl and Ja'far, became like mayors of the palace, running the empire as if it was their own.

The caliph benefited politically from a wide range of support, and especially on the Khurasan side. The Khurasani wing of the army was now in its second generation of lieutenants, known as al-Abna', but it maintained the same bonds of loyalty to the caliph it had once provided to the Abbasid revolution and al-Mansur. Some veteran commanders of al-Mansur, such as al-Hasan b. Qahtaba, could still be found active in the military during al-Rashid's reign. And above all, the Abbasid family itself continued to show a strong sense of solidarity as a ruling house. In fact, despite his youth, al-Rashid – a mere twenty-one-year-old when he acceded to power – astonished medieval observers for receiving the homage not only of princely members of his generation

---

[26] Levine, *The Urbanism of Frank Lloyd Wright*, 363.
[27] Levine, *The Urbanism of Frank Lloyd Wright*, 374.
[28] Tabari, *Tarikh*, III, 603–604, trans. Williams, 2:185.

but of senior members of the Abbasid family as well: his uncle, Sulayman b. al-Mahdi; his father's (al-Mahdi's) uncle, al-Abbas b. Muhammad; and his grandfather's (Abu Ja'far's) uncle, Abd al-Samad b. Ali b. Abdallah b. al-Abbas (d. 185/801). The latter figure in particular would have garnered great prestige for the caliph, since he gave an almost direct link to the times of the Prophet, as his grandfather was none other than the direct cousin and Companion of the Prophet Muhammad and famous authority on hadith, Abdallah b. al-Abbas. Such loyalty from older generations of the Abbasid family built up a reverence in the public for the Abbasid caliphs as if they had ruled for a very long time – indeed, as if they had just succeeded the Prophet.

The proclamation declaring the accession of the new caliph gave great promise of lenient times ahead. When the courtier Yusuf b. al-Qasim read it out to the assembled audience at Harun's investiture, its message underscored a policy of pardons and bounty to the elite and subjects:

God, He is exalted and magnified, has taken to Himself His Caliph, Musa al-Hadi the Imam, and has drawn him to Himself. He has appointed as Musa's successor a rightly guided, well-pleasing one (*rashidan mardiyyan*) as Commander of the Faithful for you, one who is compassionate and merciful towards you, one who will receive cordially those of you who act righteously and who will show himself tender-hearted by pardoning those of you who act evilly. The Caliph ... promises for you, from his heart, compassion and mercy towards you and the sharing out among you of your stipends when you justly deserve them. He will bestow on you presents from what God has bestowed on His Caliphs, stored up in the state treasury, which will be of such magnitude that you will not require your regular pay allotments for so-and-so number of months ... So give praise to God and renew your thanks, and this will inevitably bring you an increase in His beneficence towards you ... Make petition to God for the Caliph's long life and for yourselves, that through him you may enjoy long-lasting favor ... Give (the Caliph) your right hands in the clasp of homage and adhere to your professions of allegiance – may God protect you and defend you, bring about righteousness through and at your hands, and take you as His helpers just as He takes His righteous devotees![29]

The friendly tone of this speech shows continuity with al-Mahdi's lenient policy, and a departure from the heavy-handed tone of al-Mansur's days.

---

[29] Tabari, *Tarikh*, III, 600–601; trans. C. E. Bosworth in *History of al-Tabari*, vol. 30: *The Abbasid Caliphate in Equilibrium* (Albany, 1989), 93–94.

The various power groups around the caliph were being assured of equal acceptance, implicitly including those who had preferred or backed al-Hadi. The Barmakids stood as the architects of this new policy, and they dominated all others around them, including the caliph. The Barmakids are recognized in the medieval sources as efficient administrators who collected a higher share of tax revenue from the Iranian provinces and mediated the allegiance of its various leaders. Al-Fadl is represented as a man of sound policies and actions and Ja'far as possessing social flair and savvy discourse,[30] while Yahya towers above both as the wise counselor who blends time-honored sound principles of government with moralizing imperatives. The chronicles portray him mediating pardons on behalf of persecuted Umayyads and Alids, and cautioning against decisions that could endanger the Abbasid state, such as a proposal floated at court to dig a canal linking the Red Sea and the Mediterranean. Yahya warned that such a canal could make the coasts of Arabia and the cities of Mecca and Medina vulnerable to Byzantine naval incursions, and thereafter the idea was discarded. Above all, the Barmakids share praise for being generous givers, and for attracting scholars and men of talent to the court, such as their promotion of the careers of litterateurs such as al-Waqidi and al-Asma'i, whom they introduced to the caliph. Islamic coinage, which normally excluded all names except for the inscription of the profession of faith, included the name of Ja'far for a solid decade (176–186/792–802) until his name was replaced by the word "caliph" in 188/804.[31]

The first decade of al-Rashid's reign, when the Barmakids were in power, saw the caliph's pursuit of an energetic religious policy that had its roots in the reigns of al-Mansur and al-Mahdi. The caliph undertook a pilgrimage to Mecca from his first year in power, and seven additional trips over the course of his reign, becoming the most frequent pilgrim caliph among the Abbasids as well as the last caliph to set out on a trip to Mecca. In an age of premodern travel, these treks through the desert were arduous undertakings, but, together with the caliph's various other journeys, later on, to Syria, the east, and the Byzantine front, they show a very energetic personality at work. The pilgrimage climate of his reign probably encouraged greater study of Arabian ethnography, such as with the compilations of al-Asma'i (d. 216/831) of Arabian folklore and poetry, and the attempts of court linguists, such

[30] Jahshiyari, *Kitab al-Wuzara'*, 198.   [31] Lane Poole, *Catalogue*, 49–51.

as Sibawayh (d. 183/799) and al-Kisa'i (d. 189/805), to discover the pure, archaic roots of Arabic speech among various tribes, and to set about establishing the rules of Arabic grammar, syntax, and most authentic styles of expression. The work of Sibawayh and al-Kisa'i built on the previous foundations established by al-Khalil b. Ahmad al-Farahidi (d. 175/791), and no doubt helped in deciding the vowels and method of reading the Qur'anic text by expert reciters, such as Hafs (d. 189/805) and Warsh (d. 197/812), which are still famous today.

If al-Mansur had laid the foundations of the writing down of Islamic texts, such as with his patronage of Ibn Ishaq's *Sira*, al-Rashid moved more toward patronage of the systematization of details of Islamic culture, in doctrine, law, and the correct recitation of the Qur'an. And just as al-Mansur was contemporary with jurists who became founders of Islamic legal schools, such as Abu Hanifa (d. 148/767) and Malik b. Anas (d. 179/795), al-Rashid continued the interaction with Malik b. Anas, as well as al-Shafi'i (d. 204/820), a newly rising figure in Islamic law. The latter would become famous for laying the ground rules of Islamic jurisprudence in his famous epistle, the *Risala*, which was the first legal work to produce a comprehensive system of law based upon the four sources: the Qur'an, the *sunna* (custom), *qiyas* (analogy), and *ijma'* (consensus).[32] While the founding figures of Islamic law did not form close ties to the Abbasid court, the caliph was able to cultivate stronger ties with their students, such as Abu Yusuf (d. 182/798), in Baghdad, who was eventually appointed chief judge of the caliphate, and Muhammad b. al-Hasan al-Shaybani (d. 189/805), who served as judge in Raqqa – both having been students of Abu Hanifa. The caliph was also successful in associating with other religious scholars of varying profiles: jurists, such as al-Layth b. Sa'd and Abu Ishaq al-Fazari; and ascetics with a more independent mindset, such as Abdallah b. al-Mubarak and al-Fudayl b. 'Iyad.

From different angles, al-Rashid's circle of scholars were laying the foundations of what became traditional beliefs about Islamic heritage: the Qur'anic text as well as its exegetical frame, and the narrative of early Islamic history. The task of establishing Abbasid political legitimacy expanded during Harun al-Rashid's reign to include a particular

---

[32] P. W. Baker and I. D. Edge, "Islamic Legal Literature," in *Religion, Learning, and Science in the Abbasid Period*, ed. M. J. L. Young et al. (Cambridge, 1990), 144.

way of narrating the past. Religious tasks and rituals added to this program. Al-Rashid's pilgrimage journeys, while addressing a religious function, also served as a political tool for the state. They provided occasions for the caliph to connect with the public, and to cultivate loyalty to the caliphate. They would have been highly anticipated public events as Harun made his way through various regions from Baghdad or Raqqa to the Hijaz. At Mecca and Medina the caliph often took time out after performing the pilgrimage to visit the landmarks associated with political and military events recounted in the *Sira* of the Prophet, and to meet with local religious scholars, such as Malik b. Anas, to whom he brought his young children and future successors, al-Amin and al-Ma'mun, for sessions of hadith study.

Al-Rashid's wife, Zubayda (d. 216/831), also provided support for these trips with her famous construction of the pilgrimage road known as Darb Zubayda, from Kufa to Mecca, at great financial cost to herself. Modern archaeology has discovered a trail of fifty-four watering stations on this 875-mile highway, spaced at 15-mile intervals – the distance a person normally traveled per day.[33] This kind of visible role for an Abbasid princess in a state project was unknown in previous Islamic history, and demonstrated an element of openness and forward thinking in a culture otherwise known for the seclusion of women. In fact, Zubayda's acts of patronage would range more widely, as she has been credited with ordering the initial construction of the towns of Tabriz and Kashan.[34] Zubayda's groundbreaking role in charities, however, was not sufficient to give her a lasting role in political leadership. The memory of the Prophet's widow, Aisha, and her famous conflict with the fourth caliph, Ali, would linger on as a dangerous example, in the imagination of the pious, of how female intervention in politics could bring about division in the community and civil war.[35]

The Barmakids loomed large in the internal government of the empire for almost sixteen years after al-Rashid's accession to the caliphate. Their main policy objective increasingly became better

---

[33] Marcus Milwright, *An Introduction to Islamic Archaeology* (Edinburgh, 2010) 163.

[34] W. Bartold, *An Historical Geography of Iran*, ed. C. E. Bosworth, trans. Svat Soucek (Princeton, 1984), 178, 217.

[35] For a discussion of later medieval perceptions of Muslim women's involvement in politics, see Denise Spellberg, *Politics, Gender, and the Islamic Past: The Legacy of 'Aisha bint Abi Bakr* (New York, 1994), 140–149.

state centralization rather than territorial expansion, and they showed particular attention to the welfare of the Iranian regions as the anchor of the Islamic state. The high point of this can be noted in 178/794 when al-Fadl was sent as governor to Khurasan where he, according to the chronicler Tabari, "governed fairly, built mosques and fortresses, and invaded the land beyond the river." He also recruited a military force, which he called al-Abbasiyya, and sent some of its troops to Baghdad. When he returned to Baghdad, the caliph, along with various state officials (listed as *quwwad*, *kuttab*, and *ashraf*) reportedly met him on the outskirts of the city, and the event was capped with an appearance by poets, such as Marwan b. Abi Hafsa, who recited verses in praise of al-Fadl while he doled out purses of dinars to his well wishers.[36]

That the caliph would start turning against the Barmakid family after this successful tenure in the vizierate has therefore surprised historians, who have sought an explanation or reason. The famous episode of the sacking of the Barmakids in 187/803, which resulted in the imprisonment of Yahya and al-Fadl, and the execution of Ja'far al-Barmaki, has captured the imagination of writers since medieval times for its suddenness, and has fueled speculation on its motives. Pride of place, if not credibility, among these reasons has always been given to a purported sexual liaison between Ja'far and the caliph's sister Abbasa. It is said that the caliph was fond of having both of these cultured individuals in his company, but to evade the strictures of Islamic law against the familiar mixing of men and women in such occasions as the caliph's assemblies, a nominal marriage contract between Ja'far and Abbasa was contrived to allow interaction. However, at some point the two decided to take their intimacy further, leading to a tryst, a pregnancy, a period in hiding for Abbasa, and an offspring whisked off to Mecca; and, eventually, a shocked reaction from al-Rashid.[37] The whole story seems a bit of a stretch for critical historians, especially since interaction between men and women at the caliph's literary assemblies, and in royal courts in general, may not have been as rigidly restricted as may be imagined from a strict reading of the sharia. Chronology also runs against the purported legend, since Abbasa, who was a busy landowner of vast estates, and twice married to Abbasid princes, is said to have died in

---

[36] Tabari, *Tarikh*, III, 635.   [37] Ibn al-Tiqtaqa, *al-Fakhri*, 209.

182/798, much earlier than the fall of the Barmakids.[38] But factors of logic and historical context did not hinder the efforts of storytellers to shape a story of wine, song, and literary musing, and so the Ja'far–Abbasa episode should be allowed to stand on its own as a lingering canard. Storytellers spun yarns of melodrama about the Barmakid tragedy, and added much embellishment to the tragedy, highlighting universal themes on the transience of power, the fickleness of rulers, and the cycles of unpredictable fate.

Still, why Ja'far was the only member of the Barmakid family killed in the purge remains unclear. The story of Abbasa and Ja'far is unlikely to be true, but it would seem that al-Rashid did have a more personal grudge against Ja'far than against the other Barmakids. Whether it was a moment of overfamiliarity or indulgence on the part of Ja'far cannot be known, but some spark brought down the entire edifice of Barmakid power. There is likely to have been more than one reason for the fall of the Barmakids. The success of their policies undoubtedly stirred a measure of jealousy at court from their rivals, such as al-Fadl b. al-Rabi', the son of another family of chamberlains that had been active at the Abbasid court since the reign of al-Mansur. But it is also important to stress that the Barmakids were no angels. Khalid b. Barmak had once been instrumental in bringing false witnesses who testified that the caliph al-Mansur's nephew, Isa b. Musa, had abjured his rights to caliphal succession, and Yahya b. Khalid was complicit in al-Hadi's assassination. Although members of the Abbasid family were also behind both of these events, al-Rashid no doubt suspected that if the Barmakids could commit such treacherous acts once, they could do so again.

In addition, looking at the wider picture of Abbasid government, there may have been other, more policy-centered reasons for the sacking of the Barmakids than those provided by romantic anecdotes. The Barmakid rivalry with the majority of the Abna' commanders, for example, was something that dated back to al-Hadi's reign, and continued to fester in a way that caused tension in the Abbasid military. On the tribal front, the Barmakids showed very little understanding or patience in managing the egos of the Qaysi Arab tribal elite in northern

---

[38] Muhammad b. Habib al-Baghdadi, *Kitab al-Muhabbar*, ed. Ilse Lichtenstadter (Hyderabad, 1942), 61; al-Qadi al-Rashid b. al-Zubayr, *Kitab al-Dhakha'ir wa'l-Tuhaf*, ed. Muhammad Hamidullah (Kuwait, 1959), 235.

Syria and Iraq, which al-Mansur tried so hard to reincorporate into his support base after the revolution. From the Barmakid perspective, various officials and governing chiefs were equal subordinates to the state, and were expected to meet certain targets for tax revenue in Baghdad. The high frequency of governor turnover in various provinces, with many serving not more than one or two years, was intended to prevent them establishing any local roots. But what worked in the east could not work in the western provinces.

The year 179/795 brought a number of reactions to central rule. A revolt by the tribal chief al-Walid b. Tarif, in the region of Mosul, took on a Kharijite flavor, though with less ideological meaning than in Kharijite agitations dating back to the Umayyad period. The same year another rebel, al-Haysam b. Abd al-Majid al-Hamdani, started an uprising in Yemen, while Egypt continued to reel from a revolt that had started the previous year, over matters of excessive taxation. To deal with these challenges, al-Rashid called on outsiders to the Barmakid system to help: the Arab tribal chief Yazid b. Mazyad al-Shaybani, who reasserted control over Mosul; his overbearing Berber freedman Hammad, who was sent as governor to Yemen; and an older but tenacious commander of the Abna', Harthama b. A'yan, retook control of Egypt. Matters were patched, up but such flare-ups would not have happened if the Barmakids had attended to all the provinces equally.

Farther west, al-Rashid could only watch as the Umayyads in al-Andalus settled into greater political comfort. The once fugitive Umayyad prince Abd al-Rahman b. Mu'awiya b. Hisham set about solidifying control in Spain and began building the Great Mosque of Cordoba at the start of al-Rashid's reign in 786, as if in defiance; and the Hashimite Idris b. Abdallah, who survived the Alid rebellion in Medina in al-Hadi's reign – and was himself brother of the earlier rebel Muhammad al-Nafs al-Zakiyya – found his way to North Africa and with Berber tribal help started the Idrisid dynasty in 789, which became the first Alid (though not the first Shi'i) state in history. In Qayrawan (in modern-day Tunisia) disgruntlement also grew among the restive Abbasid troops in 179/795, and this was only stemmed in 184/800 when al-Rashid agreed to grant the province as a hereditary governorship to Ibrahim b. al-Aghlab in exchange for a fixed amount of tax revenues to be delivered to Baghdad. With such disappointing outcomes, lands west of the Nile might as well have been the other anonymous "lands beyond the river" (*ma wara al-nahr*), for the Barmakids, judging from their neglect of affairs there.

The Barmakids would have been blamed for these failures, and the situation may have been compounded by a growing suspicion that they were switching their political loyalty from the Abbasids to the Alids. When al-Fadl b. Yahya was entrusted in 176/792 with putting down an Alid rebellion in the Daylam province in the southwestern part of the Caspian sea, the caliph sounded skeptical when the Alid leader, Yahya b. Abdallah (brother of the Idrisid rebel), was given a promise of safety when he surrendered. It gave rise to rumors that the Barmakids were secretly sympathetic to the Alid cause, and rekindled fears of the independent-minded ways of Abu Muslim. Various elements were stacking up to make the caliph – who was with age increasingly becoming a micromanager – ready to turn on the Barmakids like a thunderbolt.

The change in al-Rashid's attitude can be gradually discerned in the sources. As early as 179/795 al-Fadl was removed from the governorship of Khurasan, while Ja'far was asked to give the seal of government to his father in 180/796. Yahya seems to have become aware of the estrangement, and asked the caliph for permission to let him travel and do a devotional trip (*'umra*) to Mecca in 185/801. Perhaps another sign of change can be found in the caliph's decision to start spending more time in Raqqa, which became his preferred capital from 180/796 till the end of his reign. Today Raqqa's dusty and arid environment may not seem the verdant ground a caliph would choose for a palatial capital, but back then it was different. The Islamic art historian Creswell argues that the course of the Euphrates has moved away from Raqqa by as much as a kilometer over time, while the geographer al-Muqaddasi describes some 360 springs that used to gush water to the city.[39] The entire area enjoyed agriculture and roads shaded by palm trees, while modern archaeology has uncovered evidence that shows how the city flourished, with palaces, markets, artisan workshops, and race-tracks.[40]

---

[39] Creswell, *Early Muslim Architecture*, 183; Muqaddasi, *Ahsan al-Taqasim*, 140; and on the shift in river course, see Keith Challis et al., "Corona Remotely-Sensed Imagery in Dryland Archaeology: The Islamic City of al-Raqqa, Syria," *Journal of Field Archaeology* 29 (2002–2004), where the authors also observe that the area formerly occupied by Abbasid palaces "is more extensive than hitherto believed" (148).

[40] A. Asa Eger, *The Islamic–Byzantine Frontier* (London, 2015), 156.

There was a statement of imperial assertion and autonomous will in al-Rashid's decision to move to Raqqa, emulating the example of the greatest of the Umayyad caliphs, Hisham b. Abd al-Malik, whose capital, Rusafa, was some 30 miles southwest of Raqqa, and included Hisham's tomb. But there were also important strategic policy considerations; one was foreign-policy related, given the geographic proximity of the town to the military flashpoints on the Byzantine frontier; and another domestic, in the way Raqqa lay at the heart of the tribal region of the Jazira. Based there, the caliph could keep closer control over the loyalty of tribal federations in the area, while Raqqa afforded him easy river transport for trade and resources down the Euphrates to Baghdad. These rising practical considerations were far more important than any sentimental notions the Barmakids had of being located close to the Arch of Khusraw at Ctesiphon. From 180/796 till the end of his reign, Raqqa became al-Rashid's favorite place of residence, even though Baghdad remained the capital.[41]

With the overthrow of the Barmakids, the caliph could count on projecting a more direct and authoritarian image when it came to charting policy. Whether al-Rashid was trying to imitate the example of al-Mansur in shaking off the hegemony of Abu Muslim is never explicitly stated in the sources, but the outcome had a similar effect, concentrating all power with the caliph. Looking across to the Byzantine empire, al-Rashid would have noticed how Irene, who had been empress in Constantinople since his adolescent days in 780, when he led expeditions against her armies, was suddenly overthrown by an army coup in 802. He was clearly aiming to avoid a similar fate by preempting the Barmakids with a purge in 803. During the last decade of his reign, al-Rashid took a variety of steps to reinforce his authority in the provinces. These usually included administrative reorganization, the building of walls of a town, or undertaking a public project. Towns that had been neglected, such as Isfahan, Qazwin, and Qumm, were upgraded administratively to become regional centers, which usually meant the setting up of a military base for Abbasid troops, increased spending on the town, and the establishment of stronger bonds with the capital. At Qazwin and Maragheh, for example, al-Rashid initiated the construction of fortification walls, while at Qumm he ordered the

[41] Meinecke, "Rakka."

construction of a new mosque in 806–807 "to symbolize the reality of caliphal authority."[42]

The Abbasids and Foreign Policy

The caliphate did not turn against the Iranian provinces of the empire after the overthrow of the Barmakids, but underwent a new articulation of sovereignty that perhaps drastically reduced the power of the vizirs. Although the caliph's new governor of Khurasan, Ali b. Isa b. Mahan, was unsuited for the task, and it took al-Rashid some time to understand this, the appointment reflected an attempt by the caliph to seek new governors with Iranian backgrounds other than the Barmakids, who had long dominated relations with Khurasan. When he made his first journey to Rayy in 189/805 to investigate the accusations against Ali b. Isa, the caliph used the fact that he had been born in Rayy to great advantage, as commemorated in poetry from the time. He then welcomed the two leaders who were representatives of the Iranian princely families of Tabaristan, Sharwin and Wandad Hurmuzd (the latter was the grandfather of Mazyar, who converted in the reign of al-Ma'mun), and gave them what is referred to as a promise of safety, but was more likely a treaty of friendship and alliance. He also welcomed a leader named Marzuban b. Justan, of the Daylam region.[43] These political ties were established through direct dealings with the caliph, without the mediation of the Barmakids.

To complement the affirmation of his authority in this new phase of his reign, the caliph began to resume the traditional warrior image of his office by turning his attention to the Byzantine frontier. Although al-Rashid gets a lot of attention among his medieval biographers for being a frequent leader of military expeditions against the Byzantines, this in fact is an exaggeration. This reputation stems partly from expeditions that he led in 163/780 and 165/782, during al-Mahdi's reign, when he built a fortress named Haruniyya (modern Haruniye) on the Byzantine frontier, while he was still a prince, and with a different title, al-Mardi, before he

---

[42] Paul Wheatley, *Places Where Men Pray Together: Cities in the Islamic Lands, Seventh to Tenth Centuries* (Chicago, 2000), 140, 162. Al-Rashid's name was inscribed on the town's wall: Abd al-Karim b. Muhammad al-Qazwini, *al-Tadwin fi Akhbar Qazwin*, ed. A. al-'Attaridi (Beirut, 1987), 4:187.

[43] Tabari, *Tarikh*, III, 705.

became al-Rashid.[44] During his reign, however, the caliph led military campaigns across the Byzantine frontier only twice. The main thrust of his policy in Asia Minor was to strengthen Abbasid control of the border region, and toward this effort he undertook the renovation of various towns, and encouraged Arab and Islamic migration and settlement all across towns in the region.[45] He also charted an administrative reorganization in the frontier of Asia Minor, separating the fortresses in northern Syria from those in northern Iraq, and creating in the process two zones in the frontier region – one named al-Awasim (the strongholds) and another, more easterly region, al-Thughur (the frontiers).[46] The general Abbasid line of defense ran through the towns of Tarsus, Adana, Mar'ash, Hadath, Malatya, Samosata, and Qaliqala (Erzurum) – an area covering roughly the entire eastern part of modern Turkey, which medieval chroniclers broadly called "al-Thughur al-Shamiyya" (northern Syria) and "al-Thughur al-Jazriyya" (northern Iraq). This entire region was heavily defended with Islamic fortresses that dotted the plains.[47]

Further north the caliph used Armenia and Azerbayjan as buffer zones against possible threats from the Khazar kingdom, which had a longstanding friendship with the Byzantines, and could boast one Byzantine emperor who was half Khazar, Leo IV (r. 775–780) – grandson of Leo III (r. 717–741), who famously foiled the great Umayyad siege of Constantinople in 717. In Armenia he maintained strong ties with the indigenous political elite, the leading aristocratic families known as the *naxarar*s, whose main branches, the Bagratunis (Bagratids) and Artsrunis, often sought foreign intervention as they competed for power. Armenia's geographical vulnerability to threats from the steppes north of the Caucasus had long made it turn to central powers, such as Sasanid Persia, and later the Abbasids, for protection. Al-Mansur strengthened the Abbasid hold on the province with higher taxation, and throughout the eighth century and up until the mid-ninth

[44] Michael Bonner, "al-Khalifa al-Mardi: The Accession of Harun al-Rashid," *JAOS* 108 (1988).
[45] Eger, *The Islamic–Byzantine Frontier*, 99, 156, 236; Mark Whittow, *The Making of Byzantium* (Berkeley, 1996), 212–213.
[46] Michael Bonner, "The Naming of the Frontier: 'Awasim, Thughur, and the Arab Geographers," *BSOAS* 57 (1994).
[47] Kennedy, *The Great Arab Conquests*, 365.

century Armenia remained uninterested in Byzantine political overtures. Al-Rashid accommodated the loyalty of the notables of
Armenia in the same way that he did in Tabaristan, but probably
with added ceremonial gestures of giving honorific titles to the
Armenian ruler, such as the granting of a crown and the title of king,
which is recorded for a Bagratid prince as late as al-Muʿtamid's reign in
884. With these trappings of privilege, Armenia remained aligned with
the Abbasids, but it also became sufficiently politically confident to
seek better terms from the Byzantines in the future, as the Abbasids
weakened and military power shifted in the mid-tenth century.[48]

In Azerbayjan, the character of al-Rashid's policy involved more
direct rule through a mix of Abnaʾ and Qaysi commanders. Figures
such as Yazid b. Mazyad al-Shaybani, Khuzayma b. Khazim, Yusuf
b. Rashid al-Sulami, and Saʿid b. Salm b. Qutayba came successively to
the province as governors, and brought with them their wider tribal
kinsmen (Nizar, Rabiʿa, and Yaman) for settlement. This was not new,
since the trend had begun in al-Mansur's reign when commanders
started streaming in as settlers.[49] With layer after layer of new arrivals,
the picture in Azerbayjan resembled somewhat the process of Arab
settlement in Khurasan in Umayyad times, but now reflected
a centralizing policy from Baghdad. Some of these settlers assimilated
strongly into Iranian culture, and in the case of the Mazyad family they
put down such deep roots in part of the region as the shahs of Shirwan
that they stayed on for centuries until the invasions of Tamerlane in the
fourteenth century.[50]

In general, Harun's policy in this northern region was largely an
extension of policies from al-Mansur's time. Instead of siding with one
Arab tribal affiliation at the expense of another, the Qays or the

[48] A. A. Vasiliev, *A History of the Byzantine Empire* (Madison, 1952), 1:314;
Whittow, *The Making of Byzantium*, 202–203, 212–217; S. Peter Cowe,
"Patterns of Armeno-Muslim Interchange on the Armenian Plateau in the
Interstice between Byzantine and Ottoman Hegemony," in *Islam and
Christianity in Medieval Anatolia*, ed. A. C. S. Peacock et al. (Farnham, 2015),
78–79. Cowe notes that the situation of a Bagratid king under Abbasid
suzerainty paralleled that of the Armenian Arsacids previously under the Roman
and Persian empires (63–428 CE).

[49] Yaʿqubi, *Tarikh*, 2:426.

[50] C. E. Bosworth, "The Persistent Older Heritage in the Medieval Iranian Lands,"
in *The Rise of Islam*, ed. Vesta Sarkhosh Curtis and Sarah Stewart (London,
2009), 39.

Yaman, the Abbasids included both, and the system of authority rested on bonds of loyalty to the family of the Abbasid caliphs, rewards of land grants in the province, and a continuity of mutual obligation. With steady stability in the Abbasid house, the system cohered, but if there was discord at the top, as happened with the succession crisis after al-Rashid, the province could turn into a "second Khurasan" mirroring Umayyad times, with military leaders taking sides or encouraging rebellion, as happened with Hatim b. Harthama, whose spark of agitation on al-Ma'mun's accession culminated in the Mazdakite rebellion of Babak al-Khurrami between 819 and 838.

As for the actual raids against the Byzantines in the first half of al-Rashid's reign, these were usually conducted by Abd al-Malik b. Salih b. Ali, the governor of Syria, and Abd al-Malik's son, Abd al-Rahman, in 175/791, 181/797, and 182/798. Abd al-Malik b. Salih had built up Arab tribal support in Syria to such an extent that he practically ran a mini-state within the Abbasid state. His raids in Asia Minor were successfully launched from Syria, and on one occasion, in 182/798, reached Ephesus on the Aegean. Reports of such success, and by a hero of Arab tribal groupings in Syria and Jazira, made him another potential danger to al-Rashid, like the Barmakids. In fact, Abd al-Malik's situation was more dangerous because he was a member of the Abbasid family, and possibly related to the Umayyads as well. There were persistent rumors that when the last Umayyad caliph, Marwan b. Muhammad, was killed in Egypt, one of his concubines was pregnant, and that Salih b. Ali, an uncle of al-Mansur, in a storyline that smacks of a novel, married her in a final gesture of Abbasid conquest of the Umayyads. Whether he found out later or already knew that she was pregnant but deliberately hid the information and married her to save her from the purges of his brother, Abdallah b. Ali, is not clear, but the fact he named his wife's newborn, Abd al-Malik, after Abd al-Malik b. Marwan, the famous father of the key Umayyad caliphs (al-Walid, Sulayman, and Hisham), shows a contrarian attitude that would normally have been unwise, at a time when the black banners were still roaming the Fertile Crescent region in victory after the revolution.

It is said that Harun al-Rashid knew this virtually open secret about Abd al-Malik's genealogical roots, and that he used to taunt the man about it on occasion, but that he also stated he could not harm Ibn Salih because of a long-recognized custom within the Abbasid house of not harming members of the ruling family. Whatever the reasons for the estrangement toward Abd al-Malik, the latter seems to have been just pushed aside as the caliph sought to assume more direct command of warfare in the Byzantine frontier region. The opportunity for Harun to assert a stronger presence arrived in 187/803 when the news came of a Byzantine incursion while the caliph was on an Iranian journey. The new Byzantine emperor, Nicephorus, had quite reasonably estimated that the caliph was preoccupied with affairs far away from Asia Minor, and decided to breach the line recognized as the boundary, and seize the city of Tarsus.

Tarsus and Malatya were cities that had been solidly under caliphal control since the daring Umayyad siege of Constantinople in 715–717, but Nicephorus, having just overthrown the Byzantine empress Irene, sought to make a show of his military strength to his people, and reportedly wrote a letter to the caliph borrowing a simile from the game of chess:

The queen who was my predecessor put you in the rook's square, and herself in the square of the pawn, and sent you such wealth as truly should have been sent by someone like you to someone such as she, but that was by the weakness of women and their foolishness. When you have read my letter, return the money which she has sent to you.[51]

Harun, who was probably an avid chess player, took this challenge to heart and hurried back from the east in winter weather to reassert control over the Byzantine border region and restore the lost territory.

But now that he had been provoked into military action, al-Rashid felt he needed to do more. In the following year he reportedly initiated a mobilization estimated at 135,000 and in 190/805 set out on an offensive that struck inside the province of Cappadocia, which was the home region of Nicephorus. Different wings of the Abbasid army fanned across the frontier area, and a naval expedition was simultaneously sent to capture what remained of Cyprus under Byzantine control, and made a raid on Crete as well. The naval squadron played a key role in deflecting Byzantine attempts to land troops in the bay of Antalya and attack the Abbasid army from the rear.[52] But beyond strengthening the frontier area, the campaign had achieved only the modest conquest of the town

---

[51] Tabari, *Tarikh*, III, 695, trans. Williams, 2:260–261.
[52] Christophe Picard, *The Sea of the Caliphs: The Mediterranean in the Medieval Islamic World*, trans. Nicholas Elliott (Cambridge, MA, 2018), 221.

of Heraclea (modern Eregli), which was commemorated in poetry and with a victory monument in Raqqa. It was all "vintage Harun" in the way he used a campaign seemingly for strategic reasons but with a limited goal, and leveraged it for wider political and religious propaganda. Just as he had the jurists on his side in Baghdad, he now attracted a cadre of ascetic warriors, such as Ibrahim b. Adham and Abdallah b. al-Mubarak, who were galvanized by these skirmishes and preached the duty of jihad on the Byzantine frontier against a historical enemy. Harun built a victory monument in Raqqa to commemorate the Heraclea expedition, and the campaign ended "Saladin-style" with the emperor seeking a favor from the caliph, and the latter agreeing to it chivalrously. Apparently a bride promised to Nicephorus's son was still among the population of the conquered Heraclea, and the emperor asked if the caliph would allow her to depart, and used the occasion to request a certain perfume and a tent. The Byzantine maiden was sought out, according to Tabari, and al-Rashid ordered that she be decked out and seated on a throne in a tent with precious furnishings, and sent her to Constantinople with the tent and trousseau, along with the perfume, some dates, figs, and healing drugs, in a great show of chivalry.[53] Abbasid–Byzantine relations remained quiet for over two decades after this expedition, and Nicephorus probably only appreciated dealing with a foe like Harun when he finally met his death in battle against the ferocious Bulgars in 811.

At the same time that the caliph was paying attention to the Byzantine frontier, he also showed an interest in other foreign powers, and an awareness of the Abbasid state's international context. Just as the caliphate showed vigilance against the Byzantines, there was anxiety in Baghdad about the rising threat of powers in Central Asia. Chinese sources on the Tang dynasty (618–907), which mention embassies dating as far back as the Umayyads in 716, also mention several embassies by the "Arabs with black robes," including one from Harun al-Rashid's envoys to the Chinese court at Chang'an, called by the Arabs "Khumdan," in 798.[54] Chang'an is today known as Xi'an,

[53] Tabari, *Tarikh*, III, 710.
[54] D. M. Dunlop, "Arab Relations with Tibet in the 8th and 9th centuries AD," *Islam Tetkikleri Institusu Dergisi* 5 (1973). A Chinese source on the Tang dynasty states that in the reign of Chen-yuan (r. 785–805), "the black-coated Arabs (i.e. the Abbasids) began a war with Tibet, and the Tibetans were obliged every year to send an army against the Arabs. On this account the Chinese

the famous city with the archaeological find of terracotta soldiers, and still home to 50,000 Muslims of Arab, Persian, and Soghdian descent.[55] Al-Rashid's embassy seems to have taken place at a time when Abbasid military readiness in Transoxiana was increasing, where the great walls of Samarqand were rebuilt, and a new fortress was built in Badakhshan and named after the caliph's wife, "the fortress of Sitt Zubayda." The purpose of these ties with China would have been to establish a political alliance against the rising power of Tibet, but would have also centered on discussing closer trade ties, particularly regarding high-value luxury goods, such as silken textiles, aromatics, and ceramics. Unlike the people of ancient Greece, Rome, or medieval Europe, who had no direct contact with China, Arab merchants famously established trading communities, mostly in the coastal town of Guangzhou/Canton (known to the Arabs as Khanfu).

It took five months to reach this city by ship, sailing from Basra through the Persian Gulf, but the distance was no barrier to the growth of a community of Muslim, Christian, Jewish, and Zoroastrian traders in Khanfu who did business even with the heavy rate of 30 percent that China exacted on all goods being exchanged at that port. Stories of this prosperous trade have been preserved in the account of "Sulayman the Merchant," who described the people, customs, and commodities of China.[56] By the late ninth century Khanfu had become home to an estimated 120,000 foreign merchants, who received an official proclamation of imperial protection in 829. But the social and economic disparities created by this commerce provoked a rebellion led by Huang Chao in 264/878, targeting all foreign merchants there as well as the emperor's capital, Chang'an. After this setback, Arab traders stopped coming directly to Guangzhou, and went back to trading goods at

frontier enjoyed more peace": Hoyland, *Seeing Islam as Others Saw it*, 253. These events provide a crucial window on the background of the revolt of Rafiʿ b. al-Layth and al-Maʾmun's political movement in Khurasan later on.

[55] Gary Nabhan, *Cumin, Camels, and Caravans: A Spice Odyssey* (Berkeley, 2014), 149.

[56] William Bernstein, *A Splendid Exchange: How Trade Shaped the World* (New York, 2008), 117–118. This treatise, along with the later and more firmly attributed travel account of Abu Zayd al-Sirafi, has recently been translated to English in *Two Arabic Travel Books: Accounts of China and India (Abu Zayd al-Sirafi)*, ed. and trans. Tim Mackintosh-Smith (New York, 2014). Mackintosh-Smith considers the "Sulayman" treatise largely a compilation attributed to a merchant by that name, but nevertheless views it as "one of the richest in all the literature of travel and geography" (p. 10).

intermediate points, such as the island of Sri Lanka and the Malay Peninsula, as was customary in previous centuries.[57]

In the west, al-Rashid also seemed mindful of building relations with the rising kingdom of the Carolingians. The story of the embassies between Harun al-Rashid and Charlemagne is famous in the western sources, but these embassies are not mentioned in the medieval Arabic sources (as is also the case with those to China). Being cozy with an infidel leader – particularly for a "ghazi-caliph" – may not have been the best press for al-Rashid at that time in Islamic culture, but there is no reason to dismiss the historical authenticity of these missions. There was, in fact, an earlier exchange of embassies between Charlemagne's father, Pepin the Short (r. 751–768), and the caliph al-Mansur.[58] The most famous of the Harun–Charlemagne embassies occurred in 797, when envoys of Charlemagne arrived in Baghdad, and a return embassy from the caliph arrived in 801, landing at Pisa, which included an envoy from Baghdad, and another from the caliph's governor in North Africa, Ibrahim b. al-Aghlab. This mission was followed by another embassy from Baghdad in 807, bearing precious textiles, a tent, and curtains for a canopy of different colors (described by the *Annales regni Francorum* as one "of unbelievable size and beauty"), silken robes, perfumes, and a brass water clock with twelve horsemen who stepped out of twelve windows on the hour as chimes sounded.[59] There is also mention among

---

[57] Regina Krahl, et al., eds., *Shipwrecked: Tang Treasures and Monsoon Winds* (Washington, DC, 2010), 12, 49; D. M. Dunlop, *Arab Civilization to 1500 AD* (London, 1971), 158. News of this rebellion is also recorded by Ibn al-Athir, who refers to the rebel as a "Khariji" (Arabic for "outlaw," but also used in Islamic history to refer to the sect of the Kharijites): Ibn al-Athir, *al-Kamil*, 7:319. On the restrictions on foreign merchants in China in general during this period, see Edward Schafer, *The Golden Peaches of Samarkand* (Berkeley, 1963), 22–25.

[58] Jeff Sypeck, *Becoming Charlemagne: Europe, Baghdad, and the Empires of AD 800* (New York, 2006), 80.

[59] *Carolingian Chronicles: Royal Frankish Annals and Nithard's Histories*, trans. Bernhard Walter Scholz (Ann Arbor, 1970), 87. In total, there were two missions from Charlemagne to Baghdad (in 797 and 802), and two Abbasid embassies (in 801 and 807). These exchanges were different from the four missions sent by the patriarch of Jerusalem to Charlemagne – in 799, 800, 803, and 807 – conveying gifts of relics, and receiving in return great financial support: Steven Runciman, "Charlemagne and Palestine," *English Historical Review* 50 (1935).

the gifts of a goblet called "the cup of Khusraw," which was said to have once been a cup of King Solomon.[60]

It was the embassy of 801, however, that captured the attention of contemporary observers the most, since it included an exotic animal not seen in Europe since Roman times: a white elephant, nicknamed Abul Abaz (from the Arabic Abu'l-Abbas). The conveyor of this elephant was a returning emissary of Charlemagne, known only as "Isaac the Jew," the sole survivor of the original three-man mission to Baghdad (the others, Lantfrid and Sigimund, having died during the journey). Isaac may have hailed from the famous Jewish trading community along the Rhone river, famous for its involvement in long-distance trade and well known to the Latin West as Rhodanici ("the people of the Rhone") and to the Arabs as al-Radhaniyya.[61] In spite of the romantic tale that the elephant came from Baghdad, however, it is more likely that it came from Africa, and was dispatched with the Abbasid and Aghlabid emissaries from Qayrawan (in modern Tunisia). Seeking the shortest possible route, the latter had the cumbersome cargo dropped off at Genoa, and then the arduous elephant journey commenced across the Alps.[62] It would take from autumn till spring – traveling at elephant speed – before the ambassadors finally appeared at Aachen with the animal, which astonished Western viewers and captivated the memory of later historians.[63] Einhard wove an exuberant story of the diplomatic mission that flattered Charlemagne, making it seem as if the caliph sought nothing but to

[60] Andreas Fischer, "Introduction," in *Western Perspectives on the Mediterranean: Cultural Transfer in Late Antiquity and the Early Middle Ages, 400–800 AD*, ed. Andreas Fischer and Ian Wood (London, 2014), ix–xxiv.

[61] Sypeck, *Becoming Charlemagne*, 85–89; M. Gil, "The Radhanite Merchants and the Land of Radhan," *JESHO* 17 (1974).

[62] Gaston Wiet, *Baghdad: Metropolis of the Abbasid Caliphate*, trans. Seymour Feiler (Norman, OK, 1971), 33.

[63] According to Runciman, "[The elephant] had a considerable influence on Carolingian art before he succumbed to the rigours of the North" ("Charlemagne and Palestine," 608). These "rigours" included the fact that the elephant was last reported present at Charlemagne's campaign against the Saxons in Denmark, after which it died at Lippeham in Westphalia in 810 (*Carolingian Chronicles*, 92). It has been hypothesized that an elephant etched in the stone porch of Basel Cathedral begun by Haito (d. 836), a bishop-cum-ambassador in Charlemagne's reign, may be a depiction of the Abbasid elephant: Julian Huxley, *From an Antique Land* (London, 1954), 188.

appease the emperor – even if the reality was more likely the other way around.[64] Einhard writes regarding Charlemagne:

> His relations with Harun, King of the Persians, who ruled over almost the whole of the East, India excepted, were so friendly that this prince preferred his favor to that of all the kings and potentates of the earth and considered that to him alone marks of honor and munificence were due. Accordingly, when the ambassadors sent by Charles to visit the most holy sepulchre and place of resurrection of our Lord and Savior presented themselves before him with gifts, and made known their master's wishes, he not only granted what was asked, but gave possession of that holy and blessed spot. When they returned, he dispatched his ambassadors with them, and sent magnificent gifts, besides stuffs, perfumes, and other rich products of the Eastern lands. A few years before this, Charles had asked him for an elephant, and he sent the only one that he had.[65]

There is no reason to accept the magnified image given by Einhard of Charlemagne's importance amongst leaders as true, but it is reasonable to assume that politically the Abbasids and the Carolingians would have found common ground to interact based on their mutual hostility to the Umayyad principality in Spain, and, more importantly, to the Byzantines.[66] Charlemagne's rivalry with the Byzantines in Constantinople was especially important, since they objected to his assumption of the title of emperor, considering themselves the only true Roman emperors. The Byzantines had long refused to recognize his annexation of coastal territories in eastern Italy, which they considered officially theirs since better times some two or three centuries earlier. But with the warming of relations between two of their main enemies, there was nothing that the Byzantines could do except compromise. In his study of Charlemagne's ties to Baghdad, F. W. Buckler has argued that at a critical moment in 803 when Nicephorus was pressured by campaigns from the Abbasids in Asia Minor, the Byzantine emperor found himself agreeing to the Carolingian land grab around the Venetian coast and grudgingly recognizing Charlemagne's new title of emperor – though admittedly

---

[64] Michael McCormick, *Charlemagne's Survey of the Holy Land* (Washington, DC, 2011), 80, 166.

[65] Einhard, *The Life of Charlemagne by Einhard* with a foreword by Sidney Painter (Ann Arbor, 1960), 42–43.

[66] The shared enmity to the Byzantines probably motivated the last Abbasid embassy sent by al-Ma'mun to the Carolingian Louis the Pious in 831.

only as "emperor of the Franks," since the Byzantine maintained his rank as "emperor of the Romans."[67]

The political purpose of Charlemagne from these embassies, however, and the courtesies extended by the caliph to the emperor, whether in terms of permission of access to Church of the Holy Sepulchre or the purported sending of the keys of Jerusalem to him, has been distorted by later historical memory and Western competition with Islam.[68] In the later medieval period, and amidst the rise of the Crusades, Charlemagne's image became reimagined as an exemplar of crusading against Islam, and a leader aspiring to be a pilgrim.[69] The modern period, with its zealous national claims on territory and reshaped narratives of the past, further contributed to the distortion of these Abbasid–Carolingian embassies, which were infused with added layers of meaning. Around the time of World War I these ninth-century ties jostled tensely with the memory of the Crusades in the psyche of European diplomats who drew the maps and the spheres of interest in the European mandate in the Middle East. In the tussle of political negotiations and treaties, colonial France, for example, would read Harun al-Rashid's act of sending gifts, including keys of the Church of the Holy Sepulchre, to Charlemagne as an official surrender by a medieval caliph of Islam's sovereignty over Jerusalem, and this purported event would be invoked by some French officials in diplomatic conferences in 1919.[70]

al-Rashid's Succession Plans

Harun al-Rashid's attentiveness to foreign-policy issues generally stands in stark contrast to his greatest blunder: handling the internal issue of succession to the throne. The first step he undertook in this

---

[67] F. W. Buckler, *Harunu'l-Rashid and Charles the Great* (Cambridge, MA, 1931), 27.

[68] Runciman states that Charlemagne was probably granted facilities for pilgrims from the West coming to Jerusalem, and the privilege of including Latin priests in the service of the Church of the Holy Sepulchre, but that Harun's concessions were in no way political ("Charlemagne and Palestine," 610–612).

[69] William R. Cook and Ronald B. Harzman, *The Medieval Worldview* (Oxford, 1983), 192–193; Nicholas L. Paul, *To Follow in Their Footsteps: The Crusades and Family Memory in the High Middle Ages* (Ithaca, 2012), 174, 224–226.

[70] André Clot, *Harun al-Rashid and the World of the Thousand and One Nights*, trans. John Howe (London, 1989), 251.

direction came in 175/791, when the caliph appointed as heir apparent his five-year-old son al-Amin, born to Zubayda, illustrious daughter of Jaʿfar, the son of al-Mansur. In 182/798 al-Maʾmun, who was only six months older than al-Amin, but born to a Persian concubine said to be from the region of Badhghis (near Herat), was designated as second in line for the succession. Till this point the succession arrangement seemed normal, but in 186/802 the caliph went overboard in trying to draft a more detailed succession document known as the "covenant of Mecca." In addition to confirming the first and second nominations for succession, the new plan designated al-Maʾmun as viceroy during al-Amin's reign over an extended eastern province whose boundaries ranged from Hamadan and the Zagros mountains to the extremity of Transoxiana, and stipulated that al-Maʾmun would eventually rule as caliph after al-Amin, and over a unified realm.

This was the famous plan for which al-Rashid would be remembered – trying to "divide" the empire between his children. And in order to ensure public obedience to the plan as well as the faithfulness of the successors, al-Rashid took his sons on pilgrimage to Mecca in 802, and there had them swear an oath of allegiance to this covenant document, and that they would honor the succession agreement. Al-Amin was not to attempt to remove al-Maʾmun from the succession, nor could he interfere in his region of Khurasan and the east, while al-Maʾmun must honor al-Amin and abide by his directions. All the leading officials of the state, including the Barmakids, were present on that occasion, and when the ceremony was over, the documents were reportedly placed in precious casings inside the Kaʿba.

The historian today can be skeptical of all the details of privilege laid out in the document in favor of al-Maʾmun, since the latter, after al-Rashid's death, would enter into a conflict over jurisdiction and independence with al-Amin, which turned into a succession crisis and civil war. In trying to justify al-Maʾmun's later political challenge to al-Amin, his supporters may well have exaggerated the autonomy assigned to him by al-Rashid in the succession covenant. A more modest reading of the covenant of Mecca may find simpler reasons from the plan, namely confirming the first and second succession. This had become necessary, since previous Abbasid experience had shown that newly acceding caliphs often tried to alter the line of succession from their brothers to their own children. While al-Rashid may have further positioned al-Maʾmun as governor of Khurasan, and envisaged an important symbolic role for him in the east given his partly Iranian background, it is difficult to accept the full details on al-Ma'mun's autonomy provided in the extant version of the succession covenant of 802 as entirely authentic. The violent overthrow of al-Amin by al-Ma'mun required an apologetic that took the form of a detailed rewriting of the succession covenant to show al-Amin's breaches of the document. Whatever the full truth, there is no doubt that the succession plan became the spark for conflict, as the brothers became magnets of national tensions and political ambitions in the eastern and western parts of the Islamic world.

The fall of the Barmakids happened a year after the succession covenants took place in Mecca. Whether the events were linked is unclear. It is possible that the caliph viewed such domineering ministers as standing in the way of the proper implementation of the covenants. Al-Rashid, who had previously relied on the Barmakids to mediate control, especially in the east, envisaged a new method of governance through the Abbasid princes. The appearance of Ja'far's name on coins minted in Baghdad between the years 176/792 and 187/803, accompanying the name of al-Amin as successor, and al-Fadl's in the east accompanying al-Ma'mun's between 183/799 and 187/803, shows the hegemony of the ministers right up to the drafting of the covenants and soon after.

In the years that followed the downfall of the Barmakids, the caliph returned to relying more on the Abna' commanders to run the government. In the key province of Khurasan, however, his choice for governor proved particularly bad when he sent Ali b. Isa b. Mahan to take charge of this complex region. Unlike most of the Abna', who led austere lives (including one Abdallah b. Malik, who undertook a pilgrimage to Mecca on foot to atone for once having backed al-Hadi for the succession), Ali b. Isa, whose name indicates Persian ancestry, which the caliph viewed as useful for governing in the east, was immersed in commerce and luxurious living, and had no greater interest than the extraction of revenues. It did not take long before his inept policies produced a reaction in Sijistan (Sistan) in the uprising of the Kharijite Hamza b. Abdallah in 182/798,[71] while in Khurasan a more dangerous movement rallied around the ambitious governor

---

[71] In contrast with Tabari's minimal mention of Hamza's revolt, a full description is included in the *Tarikh-e Sistan*, trans. Milton Gold (Rome, 1976), 123–127.

of Samarqand, Rafi' b. al-Layth, grandson of the last Umayyad governor of Khurasan, Nasr b. Sayyar. Rafi' was able to forge an alliance with neighboring foreign leaders, who bordered Transoxiana, causing great alarm in Baghdad. Al-Rashid's standard options of using the Barmakids and the Abna' to stabilize the east had now been exhausted, and he decided to set out on a campaign to the east to deal with these challenges in person.

This was the first time that a caliph ever undertook a journey that far inside Khurasan, and as such it was meant to deliver important political and psychological messages. The caliph was accompanied on this journey by al-Ma'mun, who brought along al-Fadl b. Sahl, a rising advisor from the former circle of the Barmakids. As they journeyed east with the Abbasid troops on the Khurasan Road that stretched from the Zagros mountain to the Iranian plateau, both al-Rashid and al-Ma'mun would have found time to stop near Hamadan, and see the Achaemenid rock reliefs at Bisitun, which depicted Darius I (r. 522–486 BCE) greeting the Zoroastrian god Ahuramazda and triumphantly receiving the homage of nine rebel-king prisoners from Mesopotamia and Iran who were being led before him. A trilingual inscription (in Old Persian, Elamite, and Babylonian [an Akkadian dialect]) accompanied the monument at Bisitun, and although in Harun's time no one understood these languages, the visual message of imperial conquest and restoration was clear. What meanings such images would have conveyed to the caliph, his son, and al-Fadl b. Sahl will never be known, but the historical site surely inspired the imagination of the Abbasid caliph now in a similar situation of trying to subdue a rebel, and may have evoked in his prospective successor, al-Ma'mun, a national sensibility regarding the heritage of Persian monarchical rulership and the notion of divine right to rule.

When the expedition reached Khurasan, the caliph ordered a halt at Tus; he sent al-Ma'mun to Marw, where he set up a command base, and sent the main army under the leadership of Harthama b. A'yan to take control of distant Samarqand. Already ailing before leaving Baghdad, al-Rashid's health became worse when he settled in Tus, and soon after he died, opening the way for rivalry over the succession between his sons, al-Amin in Baghdad, and al-Ma'mun in Marw. The relatively stable reign of al-Rashid would come to represent a reference point of nostalgia for medieval chroniclers writing after the civil war between the brothers. For religious writers his reign symbolized a time of harmony before the onset of *fitna* (conflict), while for literary writers it represented a story of a prosperous time. Sunni writers saw in him a loyal champion of hadith, unlike the philosophically innovative al-Ma'mun, while literary writers depicted his court as the purveyor of massive wealth and patronage for scholars and all those with talent.

In spite of elements of extra myth, however, the reign of al-Rashid does appear to have been a time of prosperous economic activity, with international networks of overland and sea trade in which Baghdad stood as the most important metropolis. The archaeological finds of Abbasid coins in areas as varied as South Asia, the Baltic Sea, and the East African coast of Zanzibar show a Baghdad-based global network of trade.[72] The sudden appearance of Abbasid coins in Russia and northern Europe, starting in the 780s, clearly reflects the apparent subsiding of hostilities between the Abbasids and the Khazar kingdom north of the Caucasus, and the opening up of a new market for commerce.[73] The commodities exchanged for Abbasid silver in those years ranged widely: Ceramics and silk textiles from China, musk from Central Asia, spices from South Asia, teak wood from India, gemstones from the island of Sarandip (Sri Lanka), ivory from Africa, and furs, wax, and honey from Russia and Scandinavia are just a few from a long list of items. The discovery of the Belitung shipwreck near the isthmus between the islands of Java and Sumatra in 1998 tells the story of one ship trying to make its five-month, monsoon-propelled journey from China to Iraq, probably sometime between April and September – the window of return voyages – in the first half of the ninth century while laden with a massive cargo of pottery.[74]

The caliphate in the early Abbasid period, to a greater extent than in the Umayyad period, showed the dynamic role Islam could play not just in shaping a state but also an economy. Trade was glamorized in the Islamic belief system as the most noble profession, with the Prophet

---

[72] Richard Hodges and David Whitehouse, *Mohammed, Charlemagne, and the Origins of Europe: Archaeology and the Pirenne Thesis* (Ithaca, 1983), 156–157.

[73] T. S. Noonan, "Why Dirhams First Reached Russia: The Role of Arab–Khazar Relations in the Development of the Earliest Islamic Trade with Eastern Europe," *Archivum Eurasiae Medii Aevi* 4 (1984).

[74] The discovery motivated an exhibition and catalog on this find: Krahl et al., eds., *Shipwrecked*, and a later study by Alain George, "Direct Sea Trade between Early Islamic Iraq and Tang China: From the Exchange of Goods to the Transmission of Ideas," *JRAS*, series 3, 25 (2015).

Muhammad representing the first merchant, and his example would be followed even by religious scholars, the *'ulama*, whose names are often followed by a reference to their trade profession – often dealing with textiles.[75] And to address fears regarding the dangers associated with long-distance journeys of commerce, apocryphal traditions were invented to strengthen a merchant's resolve. The second caliph, Umar, is said to have commented: "I prefer dying on my camel's saddle while travelling on business, to being killed in the Holy War; has not God himself mentioned those that travel on business before those that fight 'on the Path of God'" (a reference to Qur'an 73:20)?[76]

The activity of long-distance trade with unknown parts of the world also stimulated the rise of legends, which were sometimes intended by merchants not only to enhance the price of their commodities but also to deter any would-be competitors. This was especially prevalent in the case of aromatics, such as musk and camphor, and merchants tried to conceal their real place of origin in China, the Gobi, and Taklimakan desert,[77] just as they kept the Chinese in the dark about where ivory and incense (commodities from Africa and Arabia, respectively) came from,[78] going as far as to tell avid devotees of cotton apparel in China that cotton could only be obtained by shearing an animal unique to the West (i.e. in the Islamic world).[79] A legend animated by commerce, therefore, combined with lore about distant foreign cultures, and mythic tales of supernatural forces encountered on frightful journeys, to add new layers of fiction to literature such as the *Arabian Nights*.[80]

The War of Succession between al-Amin and al-Ma'mun

With everyone rushing to make a dinar, we may well wonder whether al-Mansur would have approved of the obsessively market-oriented world of his grandson's reign. And yet it was precisely at this hour of

[75] "If there was a trade in Paradise," the Prophet reportedly once said, "I would become a cloth merchant there": S. D. Goitein, "The Rise of the Near Eastern Bourgeoisie," *Journal of World History* 3 (1956–1957), 588.

[76] Goitein, "Near Eastern Bourgeoisie," 587–588.

[77] Nabhan, *Cumin, Camels, and Caravans*, 147–148.

[78] Bernstein, *A Splendid Exchange*, 116.

[79] Nabhan, *Cumin, Camels, and Caravans*, 155.

[80] Nabhan, *Cumin, Camels, and Caravans*, 137, 146–147, 155; Anya H. King, *Scent from the Garden of Paradise: Musk and the Medieval Islamic World* (Leiden, 2017).

greatest promise for stability in the Abbasid state and society that conflict blew up between the two successors of al-Rashid. The safety provided by the geographic distance between the new caliph, al-Amin, based in Baghdad, and al-Ma'mun, based in Marw, on the eve of al-Rashid's death, was an invitation for trouble. As al-Ma'mun easily brought the revolt of Rafi' under control, and the Abna' army of al-Rashid clamored to head back to Baghdad, disputes started to emerge between the brothers. The traditional outline of the discord between the two usually assigns its beginning to al-Amin, who began to assert a centralizing policy, demanding revenues from certain towns in the east, trying to appoint and send officials to the region, and eventually asking al-Ma'mun to return to Baghdad for consultation. These initial requests from al-Amin were viewed as an intrusion by al-Ma'mun who refused to cooperate, and styled himself with a politically provocative title, Imam al-Huda ("guide to righteousness"). When al-Ma'mun gradually increased his refusal of al-Amin's commands, including the latter's attempt to designate his infant son as successor to al-Ma'mun, the polarization grew, and when al-Amin dropped al-Ma'mun from the succession to the caliphate in favor of his own son, the road was paved for open conflict.

Al-Amin and al-Ma'mun are each portrayed as acting, in the early period of the conflict, in the shadow of a capable minister, al-Fadl b. Rabi' in Baghdad, and al-Fadl b. Sahl in Marw, each of whom was trying to protect a privilege or political party, whether the Abna' in Baghdad, or a rising coalition of Persian support in the east. Al-Fadl b. Sahl, who belonged to the Barmakid world of ministers and the scribal class (the *kuttab*), came from aristocratic roots in Khurasan and was well connected with frontier princes in the east as well as with the Iranian class of landed notables. Using his connections, he set about organizing a movement that championed al-Ma'mun as caliph, and he put the newly formed Khurasani army under the leadership of Tahir b. al-Husayn, whose family had once contributed to the Abbasid rise to power during the revolution, but had long been of purely local import-ance in the area of Herat. Badhghis, the province adjacent to Herat and home of al-Ma'mun's maternal roots, twice registered on the caliph-ate's radar screen as a place of trouble: once when it sheltered Tarkhan Nizak, who tried to challenge the Umayyad conqueror, Qutayba, in 91/709; and another when it was used as a base by the schismatic Ustadsis against the Abbasids in 147/765. Al-Ma'mun's cause quickly attracted allies across Khurasan and Transoxiana, reached inside Central Asia, and cohered into an opposition movement based in Marw and ranged against the incumbent caliph in Baghdad.

It is difficult to find entirely neutral accounts of the civil war between al-Amin and al-Ma'mun because these were shaped after the war ended in a way favorable to al-Ma'mun. The latter is portrayed from the beginning as innocently unsuspecting of plots from Baghdad, and simply abiding by al-Rashid's Meccan covenants of 802 that lent Khurasan autonomy, while al-Amin is presented as greedy, treacherous, and acting in breach of the covenants. The difference between the brothers is also shown reflected in terms of probity and lifestyle, and the chronicler Tabari describes the contrast on the same page, almost in a split-screen depiction. When confronted by the polarizing conflict, al-Ma'mun is said to have gathered religious scholars around him, and to have become introspective, and more active in implementing justice and redressing grievances – even holding court while sitting on felt mats. At this same time, al-Amin is said to have turned to hedonism and drinking, and from his first day in power turned the space in the Round City around al-Mansur's palace – once forbidden to any horse traffic – into a polo maydan for sport.[81] This picture of a sober and pious al-Ma'mun contrasts starkly with that of the scheming and indulgent al-Amin.

The factual record of Islamic history during this phase is deeply marred by problems of representation, and the road to understanding this complexity may be more a question for the literary critic than the historian. The Islamic world chronicles of the ninth century, such as Tabari's *Ta'rikh al-Rusul wa'l-Muluk* (*The History of Prophets and Kings*), dwell heavily on the affairs of Khurasan, from the Umayyad to the Abbasid periods, narrating rebellions of idealism, heresy, and heroism, culminating with the rise of al-Ma'mun. Sifting the wheat from the chaff is still an ongoing task for readers of these chronicles. The reality of al-Ma'mun's sudden rise is that it represented a provincial movement cloaked in religious garb and a pretense of political legitimacy. What perhaps helped al-Ma'mun the most was his dual identity as a Hashimite and an Iranian. This made him a symbolically important figure in two aspects – in religious terms as an Imam, and in national political terms as an Iranian leader. Al-Fadl b. Sahl is even described in

---

[81] Tabari, *Tarikh*, III, 742–747.

his strategy of propaganda as portraying al-Ma'mun's movement as a "second *da'wa*," as a form of revival of the Abbasid revolution from half a century earlier.

As the succession conflict escalated during the years 194–198/810–813, it also translated into a myriad of regional conflicts across the Islamic empire as various local leaders vied for power while pretending to champion the cause of one Abbasid leader against the other. The key battle between al-Amin's army, which was led by Ali b. Isa b. Mahan, and al-Ma'mun's troops, who were led by Tahir b. al-Husayn, took place at the town of Rayy, where al-Ma'mun's army swiftly defeated the Abna' and then advanced on to Baghdad in 198/813. After a siege that lasted over a year, al-Ma'mun's forces finally broke through into the city, and in the chaos that followed al-Amin was captured and quickly put to death on the orders of Tahir b. al-Husayn. The execution of the caliph must have gone against the strategy of al-Fadl b. Sahl, who then feared a backlash against al-Ma'mun and sought to mitigate the damage by transferring Tahir from the military leadership to a relatively inferior governorship in the Jazira province soon afterwards. The regicide of al-Amin was the first time that an Abbasid caliph had been violently overthrown, and this was something that no doubt shook the credibility of the Abbasid monarchical institution, altering how it was perceived by an Islamic, Arab, and Persian public.

Medieval chroniclers expended great literary effort trying to wrestle with the crisis of political legitimacy that beset the caliphate with this violent transition in power. The story of al-Amin, long accepted by historians as fact with all its chronicle details, has only recently undergone scrutiny as largely a literary construction surrounding a basic historical event. Arabic historical writing, best represented in the chronicle of Tabari, provides in the case of al-Amin the Near Eastern medieval equivalent to a Shakespearean tragedy, such as that centered on the downfall of the fourteenth-century English monarch Richard II – a parable of a legitimate monarch who made errors in judgment based on the bad advice of those around him, and in the end came to realize the lessons of politics and life, but too late.[82] Tabari's famous chronicle ranges widely in evocation when narrating the story of al-Amin, providing intertextual ties to the story of the downfall of third caliph, Uthman (r. 644–656), who also resisted abdication and was blamed

---

[82] El-Hibri, *Reinterpreting Islamic Historiography*, 72–75, 83, 167.

for surrounding himself with a circle of unscrupulous advisors; and Tabari creates literary bridges with the regicide of the Sasanid monarch Khusraw Parviz, who was overthrown (in 628) after his famous meteoric string of victories over the Byzantines in Syria, Egypt, and Asia Minor at the time that Islam was emerging in Arabia. All these evocations in the chronicles underscore the difficult task for the modern historian to unravel the mythic story from the history.

Had al-Ma'mun returned to Baghdad after the city was conquered, he may well have contained the fallout from the conquest. Instead, he decided to remain in Khurasan and became more reclusive, as the empire was now run from Marw. The pressure of local notables was probably strong, especially al-Fadl who adopted the title Dhu'l-Riyasatayn ("the one who holds the two powers"; i.e. over administration and warfare). But this openly pro-Khurasan government ignited renewed turmoil in the Iraq region and the central lands. In a gesture of religious propaganda, the new caliph's coinage now started including a Qur'an verse that evoked a message of divine support, stating: "God's is the command before and after; and on that day the believers shall rejoice in the help of God;"[83] and this inscription was included on Abbasid coinage in later centuries. And in another bid for favorable publicity, officials described the fairness of al-Ma'mun's government, and how this even attracted foreign rulers to embrace Islam. This includes for the year 199/814 a reference to "a king of Kabul" (Kabul shah), Qandahar, and Bamiyan (most likely a Hindu),[84] who sent his throne and crown to al-Ma'mun as a sign of his submission; and another reference to a king of Tibet (Khaqan al-Tubbat), who surrendered to the caliph a golden statue (probably of Buddhist origin) as a token of his conversion to Islam. All these objects were then sent to Mecca to be exhibited as trophies of the caliph's successful Islamic policy in the east. And in the cases of both these frontier monarchs, there are references to al-Fadl b. Sahl as the one who implemented these conquests, and seems to have exercised the vigorous diplomacy needed to bring Transoxanian and Central Asian leaders to heel.[85]

[83] Qur'an 30:3–4.
[84] Richard Frye, *The Golden Age of Persia: The Arabs in the East* (London, 1975), 45.
[85] Azraqi, *Akhbar Makka*, 157–159, 318–319; Christopher Beckwith, *The Tibetan Empire in Central Asia* (Princeton, 1987), 158–162. According to the tenth-century geographical treatise *Hudud al-'Alam*, Kabul housed temples that

These steps, however, did little to diminish the chaos in the heartland of the caliphate, as rebellions of different stripes continued. Al-Ma'mun, seemingly out of touch with the reality of events, indulged in innovative experiments to take advantage of the public anxieties about the turn of the second century in the Islamic hijri calendar. Such junctures are usually associated in Islamic religious culture with millenarian expectations of a religious revival under the leadership of a "mahdi," and so al-Ma'mun found it useful to proclaim himself on coinage as "God's Caliph." And to strengthen his pretensions further, he tried to reach out to the Shi'a, who valued the leadership of the Alid Imams, and invited Ali b. Musa al-Rida, grandson of Ja'far al-Sadiq, to come from the Hijaz, where he was living, to Khurasan, and had him proclaimed as heir apparent to the caliphate. This attempt at fraternity between the Abbasid and Alid branches of the Hashimite family was cemented through the betrothal of al-Ma'mun's daughter, Umm al-Fadl, to Ali al-Rida's son, Abu Ja'far Muhammad.[86] At the same time, the official color of the Abbasid state was switched from black to green.

Whether the caliph aimed to strengthen his ideological appeal in Khurasan and Central Asia by cultivating a more pronounced divine right of rulership through his new title is not clear, but these dramatic developments, especially the nomination of an Alid in place of an Abbasid, along with the caliph's continued use of Marw as his capital, provoked an uproar in Baghdad among the Abbasid family as well as the mercantile elite of the city, and they all joined in an opposition that put forward a counter-caliph in the person of Ibrahim b. al-Mahdi. As the situation continued to deteriorate in Iraq in light of the inability of the governor, al-Hasan b. Sahl, to control matters, the caliph finally realized that he needed to return to Baghdad. His journey, which took a year to complete, was marked with stops along the way, such as in the town of Tus, where Ali b. Musa al-Rida died in mysterious circumstances, probably poisoned. And in a calculated move, al-Ma'mun had him buried next to the tomb of the caliph al-Rashid. Both tombs today are in the famous shrine city of Mashhad, where the Shi'i devout come

attracted pilgrims from India. "The royal power of the *raja* of Qinnauj," according to *Hudud*'s anonymous author, "is not complete until he has made a pilgrimage to [Kabul's] idol-temples, and here too his royal standard is fastened": Scott Levi and Ron Sela, eds., *Islamic Central Asia: An Anthology of Historical Sources* (Bloomington, 2010), 33.

[86] Ya'qubi, *Tarikh*, 2:455; al-Qadi al-Rashid, *al-Dhakha'ir*, 101.

in pilgrimage to pay homage to Ali al-Rida. But whether the Shiʿa today direct their veneration to al-Rashid's tomb by mistake cannot be known, since al-Maʾmun reportedly effaced both tombs for a while to blur the distinctions and to confuse Shiʿi pilgrims as to the actual place of al-Rida's tomb.[87] Next on al-Maʾmun's return journey came the turn of al-Fadl b. Sahl, who was killed by assassins as the caliph reached the town of Sarakhs. Al-Fadl had been the architect of al-Maʾmun's bid for power from the beginning, but had also come to be viewed as a political liability with his early encouragement of conflict with Baghdad. With these two figures, who had alienated the Abbasid family and the Abnaʾ, out of the way, al-Maʾmun could expect a better reception in Iraq. He arrived in Baghdad in 204/819, and all disturbances in the city subsided as the populace looked forward to a restoration of Harun's legacy and a time of renewed peace.

The Age of Reunification and Transition

The political picture of the Abbasid empire on al-Maʾmun's arrival in Baghdad is largely one of disarray. Various provinces had lapsed into varying degrees of autonomy from Abbasid rule. In Egypt two governors were competing for power; Syria had come under the control of a Qaysi tribal strongman, and northern Iraq under that of another; and Yemen had undergone two Alid rebellions. But perhaps most dangerous of all was the situation in Azerbayjan and Armenia, where Hatim b. Harthama had started a rebellion in 201/816, in vengeance for his father. Harthama was Harun's longtime trusted commander, who had accompanied him on his journey to Khurasan, but later got entangled in the machinations of al-Fadl b. Sahl and Tahir b. al-Husayn during the civil war. His attempts to warn al-Maʾmun in Marw about the conspiracies around him had led to his murder by al-Fadl b. Sahl's men. In retaliation, Hatim b. Harthama started an uprising in Azerbayjan, which attracted members of the Khurramiyya sect, and when he died the movement was entirely taken over by Babak al-Khurrami, who established his base in the mountainous region south of the Araxes river and began building ties with the Byzantines. The Khurramiyya was a neo-Mazdakite messianic movement that challenged both Islam and Zoroastrianism, and was vaguely related to the stream of

---

[87] Thaʿalibi, *Lataʾif*, 133.

rebellions that sprang up in Khurasan after Abu Muslim's death. It espoused radical change, such as an end to hierarchical society, advocated the holding of all property in common, rejected the basics of Islamic rituals and laws, and put forward belief in Babak as a reincarnated messianic figure. The Khurramiyya rebellion continued throughout al-Ma'mun's reign, and was only finally suppressed in 223/838.

Reunifying the diverse provinces of the caliphate in the years after the civil war demanded the kind of military force that was not available to al-Ma'mun at that time, and he found himself over the course of the next decade using a mixture of diplomacy and incremental conquest to restore his control over the empire. The cornerstone of al-Ma'mun's new government was a continued reliance on the Tahirid family that had brought him to power. The task of achieving the first steps in the process of provincial recentralization was delegated to Abdallah b. Tahir, who commanded a new and more Iranian nucleus of the Abbasid army. After achieving reconciliation with the Abbasid family, and granting amnesty to his former opponents in Baghdad, al-Ma'mun dispatched Abdallah b. Tahir on the mission of reunification. This began in 209/824 with a move against the Qaysi Nasr b. Shabath al-Uqayli, a tribal rebel in northern Iraq, who was brought to submission after much negotiation, and the same Abbasid army then moved south, took control of Syria, and entered Egypt. Through military maneuvering and perhaps a negotiation of some privileges for the local governors, Ibn Tahir brought Egypt under Abbasid control in 212/827. When he finally returned to Baghdad, Ibn Tahir was received with a parade and a hero's welcome from the caliph, and was soon afterwards designated the new governor of Khurasan, thus beginning the most prosperous phase of Tahirid rule in the east (213–230/828–845).

The caliph's success in the west was not matched, however, in the north, where a series of armies that were sent out against the Khurramiyya in Azerbaijan met with complete defeat. The situation was largely the result of the disbanding of the Abna' armies during the chaotic years of the civil war. The empire's newly felt shortage of military resources finally reached a crisis point after the defeat of Muhammad b. Humayd by the Khurramiyya in 214/829. It is therefore not a coincidence that the first significant appearance of Turkish slave/ghulam military units – when Abu Ishaq (al-Mu'tasim) is reported to have commanded an army of 4,000 Turkish troops – happened around this time. This military development signaled a new strategy by al-Ma'mun for dealing with a crisis in Azerbayjan that threatened to bring down the entire Abbasid frontier in Asia Minor. The Tahirid governors of Khurasan, while aware of the military demands of the caliphate and its vulnerability, were reluctant to help out in the intractable war in Azerbayjan. The Khurramiyya rebellion cost the caliphate tremendous treasure and troops, and would only be effectively dealt with in al-Muta'sim's reign, when he mobilized his newly formed Turkic army into steady campaigns on that front.

During this period of recentralization the caliph set about taking additional steps in Baghdad that reasserted his newly established sovereignty, including a coinage reform that affected both the fineness and the style of dirhams and dinars. Whereas under earlier Abbasid caliphs such coins had included the names of caliphs, successors, and officials, and during the civil war coinage inscriptions had provided a playground for the names of ambitious governors, the newly reformed coins removed all names, including that of the caliph, leaving only Islamic religious statements. This perhaps simplified the test of political control in the provinces, and the continuity of the minting process. A remarkable artistic feature in the new coinage was a marked refinement in the style of the Arabic Kufic script.[88] These reforms happened at a time when the caliph was undertaking some reorganization of the tax assessments in Iraq, and making changes to the systems of measuring agricultural harvests as well.[89]

By 215/830 al-Ma'mun had regained control over most of the empire, and turned over a new leaf in Abbasid government, moving away from the traditional system of al-Mansur and al-Rashid. Provinces were now organized into larger administrative units, with towns such as Kufa and Basra merged under the Iraq province, and Khurasan expanded in scope. The principle of hereditary and autonomous governorship, once applied by al-Rashid to Qayrawan with his appointment of the Aghlabids, became more common in provincial administration. The Tahirids were the first and most prominent example of this in the east. Tahir b. al-Husayn was appointed governor of Khurasan in 205/820, and his family continued as governors there until 259/873, and they were also given charge of providing military

---

[88] Tayeb El-Hibri, "Coinage Reform under the Abbasid Caliph al-Ma'mun," *JESHO* 36 (1993).
[89] Tabari, *Tarikh*, III, 1039.

security in Baghdad, a task that became more important when the capital shifted to Samarra.

The Samanids were another Persian family that had helped al-Ma᾽mun in the early years of the succession crisis, and he rewarded them with governorships in Transoxiana. The children of Asad b. Saman were appointed in 204/819 to various towns: Nuh (Samarqand), Yahya (Shash), Ahmad (Ferghana), and Ilyas (Herat). Although in al-Ma᾽mun's reign the Samanids were subordinate to the Tahirid governor of Khurasan, few probably realized how rapidly this dynasty would take advantage of the trade opportunities that the geography of the province afforded, whether in terms of overland routes east to Central Asia or west to the Volga river region. Both the Tahirids, based in their capital, Nishapur, and the Samanids, based in Bukhara, remained deferential to caliphal suzerainty, and at least in the beginning maintained a steady contribution of tax revenues to Baghdad. To strengthen their legitimacy, both dynasties were staunch adherents of Sunni Islam and made efforts to attract religious scholars to their courts.

The political energy and regional interests that made Khurasan and Transoxiana bring the Abbasids to the caliphate in 750, and al-Ma᾽mun to power during the civil war in 813, encouraged the rise of a new Iranian elite that had old roots in local leadership. The Samanids, for example, came from a priestly and aristocratic background in Bukhara in the days before they converted to Islam in the late Umayyad period (with Asad b. Saman being named after Asad b. Abdallah al-Qasri as governor of Khurasan). The situation was similar with the princely Qarinid family in Tabaristan whose representative, Mazyar, converted to Islam under al-Ma᾽mun, and with al-Afshin, whose family had long defied control by the caliphate in the remote and isolated region of Ushrusuna, and became loyal to the Abbasids in al-Ma᾽mun's reign. With the new climate of Iranian cultural affinity and political opportunity created by al-Ma᾽mun's rise to power, various leaders were able to reshape their elite status and extend their regional influence within the garb of loyalty to Islam and the caliphate.

The picture of Abbasid–Iranian affinity in al-Ma᾽mun's reign would become complete with the caliph's betrothal to Buran, daughter of his one-time governor of Iraq, al-Hasan b. Sahl. Although in later times Abbasid matrimonials with members of the Buyid and Seljuk dynasties would become a frequent tool of political alliance, the Ma᾽mun–Buran event was the first Arab to Persian (and later Turkic) reachout. After the

Arab-centered century of the Umayyads, when ruler marriages were contracted only with Arab women, al-Ma'mun's tying the knot with a foreigner signaled a new official statement on multiculturalism. The wedding, which took place in 207/822 at Fam al-Silh, a small country town on a river channel turned into a palatial mansion north of Wasit, no doubt became the festive party of the century, with its extravagant atmosphere meant to inspire confidence in the dawn of a new age and partnership between Baghdad and Khurasan.[90] The tenth-century Tha'alibi says: "The dazzling splendor attained in this feast reached such a peak that [al-Hasan b. Sahl] entertained al-Ma'mun and all his military commanders and courtiers for forty days, and he (i.e. Hasan) provided a spectacle of unusualness and lavishness never before seen."[91] The Iranian host reportedly spent 4 million dinars on this celebration, and to signal the return of prosperous times, the festivities were concluded with a shower of gifts for the important guests. Attendants scattered among them tickets, each with the name of an estate written on it, and al-Hasan transferred ownership of the estate to whoever got hold of it. Measures of dirhams, dinars, musk, and ambergris would have been the standard gifts to those not lucky enough to get a title to land.

The result of al-Ma'mun's new policy of turning to Iranian allies for administrative support was the marginalization of the two groups that had once served as governors, the Abbasid family and the Abna'. The power of the Abna' was deliberately reduced in response to their previous support for al-Amin, but their political influence may have already been on the decline for some time with their increasing turn to commerce and attachment to their landed estates in Iraq. Still, despite the loyalty of the eastern potentates to al-Ma'mun, he gradually became wary of Baghdad's singular dependence on the Iranian element, and to counterbalance this he presided over the organization of two other wings in the military. The first of these was the newly created Turkish military slave corps, which was put under the direction of the future al-Mu'tasim,[92] who became the caliph's viceroy in the western provinces of Syria and Egypt and a likely candidate for succession. The second was the grouping of an Arab tribal army under the direction

[90] Ahmad b. Abi Tahir Tayfur, *Kitab Baghdad* (Cairo, 1949), 113–115.
[91] Tha'alibi, *Lata'if*, 99–100.
[92] Ibn Qutayba, *Kitab al-Ma'arif*, ed. Tharwat 'Ukasha (Cairo, 1969), 391; al-Maqdisi, *Bad' wa'l-Tarikh*, ed. Clement Huart (Paris, 1899–1919), 6:112.

of the caliph's son, al-Abbas, who became the governor of al-Jazira in northern Iraq and Syria and was put in charge of organizing campaigns against the Byzantines. This new tripartite structure of the Abbasid army allowed the caliph to balance his diverse troops (Arab, Iranian, and Turkish) and preserve the autonomy of caliphal decisions.

In the latter part of his reign al-Maʾmun increasingly took more personal charge of handling political and military questions, journeying to Egypt in 217/832 to examine the situation closely after his com-mander, al-Afshin, put down a revolt there. On the Byzantine front, the caliph started showing an interest in taking a more aggressive mili-tary posture from 215/830. After the two-decade lull in direct Arab–Byzantine confrontations since the last incursion by Harun al-Rashid in 190/806, this may well seem sudden. But during this period the Abbasids and Byzantines were evidently waging an indirect war through proxies, which was even more dangerous for the fate of the two powers than anything that happened just outside Tarsus or Malatya.

As the disarray grew in the Abbasid empire during the Amin–Maʾmun civil war, the Byzantines became enthusiastic supporters of the revolt of Babak al-Khurrami in Azerbayjan. The caliph meanwhile, having just wrapped up the discord and returned to Baghdad in 204/819, decided on a return gesture by supporting the rebellion of Thomas the Slav, a former officer in the Byzantine army and one-time colleague of the reigning emperor, Michael II (r. 820–829). This rebel, who had been in Syria between 803 and 813, represented both a social and religious challenge to the Byzantine empire, since his supporters included many who chal-lenged the power of the landowners, and he himself was an adherent of image-worship (an iconophile), against the iconoclastic Amorian emperor. Thomas received wide support across Asia Minor, was crowned emperor by the Patriarch of Antioch (with tacit support from the caliph), and went on to lay siege to Constantinople on land and by sea for fifteen months, starting in 821. It was only due to a Bulgar intervention on the side of Constantinople that the Byzantines were saved from this debacle, after which the rebel was captured and executed.[93] All this unsavory background in Abbasid–Byzantine rela-tions no doubt added a new desire to settle scores more directly as soon as one side felt ready. And ready al-Maʾmun certainly was, judging from the "all-star" commissariat he brought along, including the recently

[93] Vasiliev, *A History of the Byzantine Empire*, 1:274–276.

recruited Afshin of Ushrusuna and Mazyar of Tabaristan, who got to see a new landscape on the Mediterranean for the first time, and came face to face with a Greek-speaking society.

A successful cross-border raid by the emperor Theophilus in 831 revived the bellicose spirit, and despite profuse apologies from the emperor to Baghdad regarding what happened, the situation quickly deteriorated. Unlike previous caliphs, whose conflicts with the Byzantines tended to stabilize after a sharp confrontation, such as al-Rashid's conquest of Heraclea in 190/806, al-Ma'mun showed a surprising determination to escalate things, to the extent of an apparent ambition to subdue the entire empire. This can partly be gauged from the impossible conditions he put on Theophilus in 218/830 – that all his subjects either convert to Islam or all, including the emperor, pay the poll-tax – and from the extra military recruitments that the caliph called up from the regions of Syria, Jordan, Palestine, al-Jazira, Baghdad, and Egypt. The conquest of Constantinople had always been beyond the reach of Islamic power, but if it were to happen, such an event would be considered a sure sign of divine favor for an Islamic ruler, and almost a sign of the end of times.

For al-Ma'mun, this rivalry included additional layers in light of his interest in the classical heritage of the ancient Greeks, which he systematically tried to acquire, have translated into Arabic, and turn into the new patrimony of Islamic civilization. The Byzantines' neglect of the great works of science and philosophy dating to Alexander's time made them doubly guilty in al-Ma'mun's eyes – not just of being of the wrong faith, but of being willing to discard the knowledge accumulated by Hellenistic culture.[94] The conflict between al-Ma'mun and the Byzantines in 833 therefore took on a character beyond jihad to become a clash over reestablishing a synthesis between Hellenism and Islamic civilization in a way reminiscent of Alexander's dream of synthesizing the achievements of East and West under one imperial rule. Whatever the caliph's exact motives were, however, the military campaign ended with his sudden death after his armies had assembled in Tarsus. He was accompanied by his brother, Abu Ishaq (al-Mu'tasim) and his son al-Abbas, and there are conflicting reports about whether the caliph had intended to transfer the succession to the throne from al-Abbas to al-Mu'tasim, who in fact assumed the caliphal title soon after.

---

[94] Lyons, *The House of Wisdom*, 76–77.

The Philosopher Caliph

The last years of al-Ma'mun's reign are generally famous for being the time when he vividly displayed a strong inclination toward intellectual and philosophical matters, and began promoting the rationalizing theology of the Mu'tazila sect. To place this trend in context, it is probably useful to examine broader features of the intellectual side of the caliph. Almost by popular agreement, modern scholars have come to look on al-Ma'mun as the foremost patron of enlightenment, learning, and science in the Abbasid period. This reputation has largely been connected with his reported founding of Bayt al-Hikma (House of Wisdom), a library or study center, inspired perhaps by the ancient Library of Alexandria, where scholars skilled in Greek, Syriac, and other languages translated the great works of antiquity, such as Aristotle's *Metaphysics* and *Poetics* (but not the *Politics*), Euclid's *Elements*, Ptolemy's *Almagest*, and various medical works by Hippocrates and Galen.[95] Ironically, Mesopotamia was famous from ancient times for similar bibliophile efforts, such as with the Assyrian king Ashurbanipal (r. 668–627 BCE), whose library at Nineveh, discovered in the twentieth century, contained clay tablets of the Sumerian and Akkadian past, all stamped with the colophon "To Save for Days to Come."

As if through serendipity, the Abbasids were now repeating the same experiment of gathering scholarly works, but with the additional steps of translation into Arabic, and applying analysis to them. This famous "translation movement" has captured the attention of modern observers for being a state-sponsored project that covered a wide range of topics, involved a diverse group of participants, and lasted throughout the ninth and early tenth centuries. The possibility that scholars of various ethnic backgrounds, different religious affiliations, and multilingual skills could join together in a purely academic enterprise, and to study not the Islamic heritage of their patron Abbasid state but the intellectual output of foreign cultures, has struck observers as something very modern in outlook and conceptual intent.[96]

---

[95] On Islamic libraries, see Pinto, "The Libraries of the Arabs," 210–228.

[96] One writer has opined that a translation movement on this scale and importance did not happen again until the one patronized by Egypt's Muhammad Ali and his nineteenth-century successors, and energetically supervised by Rifa'a al-Tahtawi (d. 1873): Christopher de Bellaigue, *The Islamic Enlightenment: The Struggle between Faith and Reason, 1798 to Modern Times* (New York, 2017), 43.

It is probably useful when examining the translation movement to temper the usual overemphasis on al-Ma'mun as a pioneer in this endeavor by pointing out that the project of patronizing the translation of great works began in the founding days of Baghdad. From the reign of the caliph al-Mansur, and through the reigns of his successors, al-Mahdi, al-Hadi, and al-Rashid, the atmosphere of openness to outside knowledge continued, as scholars sought out all manner of intellectual heritage that filtered over the centuries through Persia, India, Central Asia, Alexandria, and Athens. Rather than emphasizing al-Ma'mun, it is probably more useful to recognize the general openness of all the early Abbasid caliphs to this research effort. Throughout those times we never encounter a clash between caliph and scientists, philosophy and piety; and much less a backlash against those active in translating texts, or an attempt to exclude certain scientists or scholars of translation based on their religious affiliation or specialization. The diversity of these specialists included the Jewish John bar Masarjawayh, presiding over the medical school in Baghdad;[97] the Nestorian Jurjis b. Bakhtishu', who served as court physician to al-Mansur, and Bakhtishu' b. Jurjis, who was physician to caliphs from Harun al-Rashid to al-Mutawakkil;[98] the Nestorian Theophilus of Edessa (d. 789), who served as astrologer and military advisor for the caliph al-Mahdi; the Zoroastrian Abu Sahl al-Fadl b. Nawbakht (d. 809), who was the keeper of Harun al-Rashid's library and translated works from Persian into Arabic;[99] and Muhammad b. Ibrahim al-Fazari (d. 191/806), who advanced the study of astronomy and astrology.[100]

There is no equivalent in this early Abbasid period to the Byzantine emperor Justinian closing down, in 529, the Academy of Athens, which taught the philosophy of Plato and Aristotle; to an earlier emperor, Zeno, who closed down the Nestorian school at Edessa in 489, leading to the relocation of this school to the Persian town of Nisibis; or to the Christian mob in Alexandria, incited by its bishop, Cyril, who hacked the philosopher and mathematician Hypatia to death in 415.[101] In

---

[97] De Lacy O'Leary, *Arabic Thought and Its Place in History* (New York, 1939), 110.

[98] L. E. Goodman, "The Translation of Greek Materials into Arabic," in Young et al., eds., *Religion, Learning, and Science in the Abbasid Period*, 480.

[99] Gutas, *Greek Thought, Arabic Culture*, 55.

[100] Freely, *Light from the East*, 36–37.

[101] Freely, *Light from the East*, 22, 24–25.

contrast to these instances fueled by religious intolerance, caliphs and/
or jurists sometimes invented ways to accommodate groups thought by
the Qurʾan to be beyond the pale, such as Thabit b. Qurra's community
of star worshipers of Harran, in northern Mesopotamia, who were
adapted to the *al-sabiʾa* group, mentioned in the Qurʾan, in reference to
rebels against ancient religions, who were combined with the "People
of the Book."[102] The inclusive spirit of the age is probably best summarized by the philosopher al-Kindi's famous observation in the introduction to his work *On First Philosophy*: "It should be no shame for us
to honor truth and make it our own, no matter whence it may come,
even though from far distant races and peoples who differ from us."[103]

The military campaigns of al-Rashid to Ankara and al-Muʿtasim to
Amorion, far from creating an iron curtain between cultures, often
resulted in the capture of Greek manuscripts from libraries as booty
that provided specialists, such as Hunayn b. Ishaq, with a treasure trove
to work with.[104] Both caliphs and scholars utilized the academic
opportunity afforded by the translation movement for different purposes, and both groups benefited from the still open atmosphere of
Islamic culture to outside ideas. L. E. Goodman has pointed to the
pragmatic spirit that characterized this age and underlay much of the
Abbasid policy in propelling this translation movement:

The cosmopolitan character of the movements that fostered knowledge of
Greek sciences is pronounced under the early Abbasids, who regarded the
achievement of a certain form of cultural integration under their Islamic
banner as a central mission of the dynasty. The increasingly systematic
sponsorship of translation from the Greek during these reigns, reflects the
policy of their monarchs and their viziers to adapt what they saw as the most
useful elements of the pre-Muslim substrate cultures as a matter of expedi-
ency or even urgency.[105]

This perspective finds confirmation in a ninth-century text, al-
Khwarazmi's treatise on Algebra, *The Book of Restoring and
Balancing*, where the author underscores the pragmatic use of his
findings:

---

[102] Freely, *Light from the East*, 43; Kevin van Bladel, *The Arabic Hermes: From
Pagan Sage to Prophet of Science* (Oxford, 2009), 65–67, 190–193.
[103] H. A. R. Gibb, *Arabic Literature* (Oxford, 1963), 65; Freely, *Light from the
East*, 49.
[104] Goodman, "The Translation of Greek Materials into Arabic," 487.
[105] Goodman, "The Translation of Greek Materials into Arabic," 478.

Fondness for science, by which God had distinguished Imam al-Ma'mun . . . has encouraged me to compose a short work . . . confining it to what is easiest and most useful in arithmetic, such as men constantly require in cases of inheritance, legacies, partition, law-suits, and trade, and in their dealings with one another, or where the measuring of lands, the digging of canals, geometrical computation, and other objects of various sorts and kinds are concerned.

Among the other uses of his text was probably the calculation of state taxes, including the obligatory annual *zakat* charity in Islam.[106] Skills in such computations were added by Ibn Qutayba (d. 276/889), a professional observer of the bureaucracy and the author of *Adab al-Katib*, to his overview of the requirements necessary in the training of state officials, alongside "knowledge of irrigation systems, surveying, architecture, instrument making, accounting, geometry, and astronomy."[107]

Where al-Ma'mun's reign differs from those of the earlier Abbasid caliphs is in the sharp turn patronage took, from interest in Indian science in the reign of al-Mansur, such as with this caliph's emphasis on the *Siddhanta* (*al-Sind-hind*) astronomical treatise, to interest in the Hellenistic works of ancient Greece in al-Ma'mun's reign. The jewel in the crown in this journey of translation was the *Almagest* of Ptolemy (second century CE), which was a study of the motion of the key planets, and yielded the coordinates that formed the basis for the making of the astrolabe, which facilitated the study of astronomy and astrology. The reign of al-Ma'mun witnessed the first formal setting up of an astronomical observatory, which was located in Baghdad. Al-Khwarazmi also pioneered the beginning of geographical study, with his book *Surat al-Ard* (*A View of the World*), which was based on the now lost *Geography* of Ptolemy. Al-Khwarazmi's work also yielded a pictorial depiction of the world named after al-Ma'mun (*al-sura al-ma'muniyya*), which in turn motivated later geographers, such as Istakhri, Balkhi, and Idrisi, to depict the earth with greater accuracy. These strides in geographical study were no doubt inseparable from al-Ma'mun's commissioning of the Banu Musa b. Shakir to measure the circumference of the earth with greater accuracy than had been done by Ptolemy. This they did through more than one measurement of the length of a terrestrial degree (mostly famous for the experiment done in

---

[106] Lyons, *The House of Wisdom*, 74.   [107] Freely, *Light from the East*, 33.

the plain of Sinjar near Mosul), and then extrapolating from these figures. The Arab scientists arrived at the measurement of 8,000 far-sakhs or 24,000 miles (closer to the modern calculation of 24,092 than was recognized in pre-Islamic times).[108]

In various fields, we find in al-Ma'mun's reign a new cadre of scholars solidly engaged with studying the Hellenistic legacy: Abu Yusuf Ya'qub b. Ishaq al-Kindi (d. 252/866), an analyst but not trans-lator, who became the first Arab to try and harmonize philosophy and religion, and built up a library – al-Kindiyya – that was the envy of other scholars; the aforementioned al-Khwarazmi (d. 236/850), pion-eer in algebra and from whose name the word algorithm derives, who simplified arithmetic by introducing the usage of arabic numerals from India and introduced the decimal system; Ahmad b. Muhammad al-Farghani (known in Europe as Alfrangus) in astronomy; Yuhanna b. Masawayh (d. 243/857) in medicine, who headed the Bayt al-Hikma center, and three brothers, the Banu Musa b. Shakir, who were famous for their engineering skills in designing irrigation canals, and for their astronomical observations which allowed the measuring of solar year with great accuracy. The Banu Musa also became famous for translating works from Greek and Pahlavi into Arabic in the area of mechanics, and, along with Hunayn b. Ishaq (d. 260/877), and al-Kindi, they formed a key trio supervising al-Ma'mun's scientific mis-sion and scouting talents for scholars who could join the translation movement.

al-Ma'mun, the Mu'tazila, and the Mihna

The question of why al-Ma'mun's name has been more closely associ-ated with the translation movement than those of other caliphs has to do with his greater interest in trying to bring religious belief in line with the methods of rational inquiry. An apocryphal story about al-Ma'mun's moment of intellectual awakening provides a tableau of the caliph as a Renaissance man. According to the famous account reported by Ibn al-Nadim, al-Ma'mun once had a vision of Aristotle in a dream, and a short but decisive conversation ensued between the awe-inspiring older philosopher and the caliph, as the latter began by asking, "What is good?" Aristotle replied, "What is good according

---

[108] Freely, *Light from the East*, 40.

to reason." Al-Ma'mun again asked, "Then what?" and the answer came, "Whatever is good according to religious law." When the caliph asked a third time, "Then what?" the philosopher said, "Whatever is good according to the majority." When the pesky caliph persisted in asking, "Then what?" the answer came: "There is no more! [but] whoever advises you about gold, let him be to you like gold, and stick to monotheism." Ibn al-Nadim then caps this by saying, "And this dream was one of the key reasons why al-Ma'mun sought out the ancient texts (i.e. for translation)."[109]

Without putting much credence in the historicity of the story, it seems fair, however, to argue that al-Ma'mun himself was a more innovative and complex personality than his predecessor caliphs. He was conscious of belonging to two different heritages, the Arab and Persian, personally delved into philosophical debates rather than just observed and listened to opinions, and was not inclined to compromise. He undoubtedly took the translation movement to greater heights, but his subjects raised objections when he tried to translate the intellectual conclusions of his age into a political ideology that he sought to impose on the religious scholars and society at large.

It is therefore crucial whenever surveying al-Ma'mun's interests in science and philosophy to consider his other famous policy of lending patronage to the religious stream known as the Mu'tazila. The ideas of this sect, which was marked by a rationalizing tendency, grew in the ninth century among scholars, who addressed questions of speculative theology (*kalam*), such as: what is meant by the divine word? how does the concept of divine justice square with the ideas of free will and predestination? and how can one understand the qualities of God without the risk of anthropomorphism? But the main confrontation between the caliph and the *'ulama* took place over a different question, which centered on the Mu'tazili idea of the "createdness" of the Qur'an. Al-Ma'mun's first clear patronage of the Mu'tazila came in 212/827, when he proclaimed the createdness creed as official state doctrine. The Mu'tazili line of reasoning behind this creed considered that mere assertions about the Qur'an as "the speech of God" risked making the word of God something that existed outside the frame of time and therefore co-eternal with the Creator. Philosophical belief in

---

[109]   Ibn al-Nadim, *al-Fihrist*, trans. Bayard Dodge as *The Fihrist of al-Nadim: a Tenth-Century Survey of Muslim Culture* (New York, 1970), 1:243.

a Prime Mover demanded that all contingent events be viewed as created in time (*muhdath*). Hadith scholars, however, who were dubious regarding any discussion of revelation and prophecy in relation to philosophy and linguistic detail, rejected this interpretation and abided by the letter of the text without attempts at redefinition. The Qur'an, to the traditionalists, was simply the "Word" of God, which cannot be characterized further. And so the battle lines were drawn between the state and the informal grouping of pious scholars.

When al-Ma'mun first declared the official adoption of the createdness creed in 212/827, he remained tolerant of other Sunni opinions on this issue for about six years. It was clear that his previous experiment in assuming the title God's Caliph for a brief period in 201–203/817–819, and claiming religious authority, had not gone away; and with religious judges, such as Yahya b. Aktham and Ahmad b. Abi Du'ad, appointed, in succession, as chief vizirs in these later years, the caliph was trying to bring religious law under state control. Then in 218/833 all hell broke loose against the traditionalist *'ulama*, who kept resisting as the caliph tried to impose the Mu'tazili createdness view on all hadith scholars in a program known as the Mihna (lit. "ordeal" or "inquisition"). In a missive sent to Baghdad just when he was preparing to start his invasion against the Byzantines from Tarsus in 218/833, al-Ma'mun ordered his Tahirid chief of police there to summon the hadith scholars and question them as to whether they accepted the new doctrine. Those who accepted it were released, and those who rejected it were to be imprisoned until they recanted.[110] In the end, all scholars submitted grudgingly, except for two, who became instant heroes of the traditionalist crowd: Muhammad b. Nuh and Ahmad b. Hanbal. The caliph ordered both of them to be brought to Tarsus in chains. Ibn Nuh died on the way, while Ibn Hanbal's journey continued until news came that al-Ma'mun had died.

Why the createdness creed interested al-Ma'mun to the point of making it official doctrine, and why the hadith scholars stood so solidly against it, is still not clear to modern scholars. Although it may seem that, by contextualizing the Qur'an as "created" in time, al-Ma'mun was trying to subordinate the sacred text's authority, there is no evidence that he was trying to override the authority of the Qur'an as

---

[110] Turner, *Inquisition in Early Islam*.

a source of religious law.[111] Rather, the confrontation with the 'ulama probably related indirectly, but more importantly, to the authority of hadith. Hadith had long been the primary field of specialty among traditionalists, who professed knowledge not only about the authority of hadith content but also about those who narrated it (i.e. those listed in its *isnad* [chain of transmission]). This exclusive exercise, which had grown to govern a variety of topics, including interpreting the law, Qur'anic exegesis, and narrating an authoritative version of early Islamic history (the *Sira* and biographies of the Companions of the Prophet), gave the 'ulama a religious authority that surpassed that of the caliph.

The Mihna sought to change this by applying scrutiny to the content of selected examples of religious commentary: the createdness creed; the controversy over the attributes of God (the issue of *tashbih* [anthropomorphism]); the beatific vision; and stories about Final Judgment. The ensuing debates quickly showed that these issues needed hadith to be interpreted in the way the 'ulama desired, and it was in this sphere that al-Ma'mun probably perceived the conflict to be truly happening.[112] By forcing the 'ulama to abide by a new official policy, the caliph was making state approval (together with the system of logic employed by the Mu'tazila) – and not the books of hadith – the source of final authority. Had he succeeded in enforcing the createdness creed, al-Ma'mun would have been on his way to creating a formal religious hierarchy tied to the court that would have been instrumental in centralizing the process of legal and theological interpretation in the empire.[113]

The crisis surrounding the createdness creed took place around the same time that the Byzantine empire was enduring the imposition of iconoclasm (815–843) by the Byzantine emperor Theophilus, though to what extent caliph and emperor were motivated by similar

---

[111] M. Hinds, "Mihna," *EI²*.

[112] Since the full "five principles" of Mu'tazili thought crystallized over a two-century period, culminating with the writings of al-Qadi Abd al-Jabbar (d. 415/ 1025), it remains difficult to know fully the position of the Mu'tazila in this early period beyond the two main questions of the Mihna, much less the full nature of al-Ma'mun's religious views. See Wilferd Madelung, "The Origins of the Controversy Concerning the Creation of the Koran," repr. in *Religious Schools and Sects in Medieval Islam* (London, 1985).

[113] John Nawas, "A Reexamination of Three Current Explanations for al-Ma'mun's Introduction of the Mihna," *IJMES* 26 (1994).

philosophical questions remains unclear. For about eight years, various kinds of pressure were applied by al-Maʾmun and his successors, al-Muʿtasim and al-Wathiq, particularly in the western provinces of Iraq, Syria, and Egypt, to make the *ʿulama* abide by the createdness creed. Scholars who refused to follow the official doctrine were forbidden to serve in an official capacity as judges, prayer leaders, or teachers; nor was their word in court testimony considered bona fide. In Egypt there are stories about some scholars being prevented from praying in the main mosque because they were in the opposition group.[114] The creed of the "created Qurʾan" was given great publicity when al-Maʾmun commanded that it be included in inscriptions at the entrances of some mosques.

In the end, however, the campaign not only failed but had a negative effect on the image of the caliphate as a source of religious authority, and increased the popularity of hadith scholars. The eastern provinces of Khurasan and Transoxiana, under Tahirid and Samanid rule, did not seem enthusiastic about enforcing the Mihna, and as a result became in effect safe havens for hadith scholars, as well as, jointly, a bedrock of future developments in Sunni learning. It was not the arguments of the *ʿulama* that won them support as much as their principled stance against political authority and their seeming devotion to simple belief.[115] Ahmad b. Hanbal (d. 241/855), who was originally from Marw, and whose name later became a lightning-rod for trad-itionalist Islamic movements, became famous primarily as one of the few scholars who held out against the Mihna till the very end. Like the preacher Abdallah b. al-Mubarak, another Marw native who emerged in al-Rashid's reign, Ibn Hanbal viewed the Abbasid court and the "academic" style of its Hanafi officials with suspicion. Although he was neither a jurist nor a skilled rhetorician, his Mihna trial captivated the public's attention, and reports about it quickly became embellished with heavy shades of hagiography and miracle.

When the caliph al-Mutawakkil finally decided to lift the Mihna in 233/848, the hadith group emerged stronger and a more cohesive network that commanded not just scholastic allegiance across the provinces but the loyalty of the Baghdad commune as well. The

[114] al-Kindi, *Kitab al-Wulat waʾl-Qudat*, ed. R. Guest (Leiden, 1912), 446.
[115] Michael Cooperson, *Classical Arabic Biography: The Heirs of the Prophet in the Age of al-Maʾmun* (Cambridge, 2000), 40.

Hanbalis (named after Ibn Hanbal) became the spearhead of Sunni Islam, resistant to mixing philosophy with religion, wary of the esoteric path of Sufism, and hostile to Shi'i Islam and to People of the Book. With few ways left for al-Mutawakkil to shore up his image as an adherent of a traditionalist reading of Islam, he proclaimed stricter boundaries on the dealings of Muslims with Christians and Jews. The official stipulations in the document known as the Pact of Umar were once thought to date to the reign of the second caliph of the Rashidun, Umar b. al-Khattab, or to the Umayyad Umar b. Abd al-Aziz, but are now recognized as more likely a product of al-Mutawakkil's reign, projected back to the time of the caliph Umar.[116] Many of the stipulations, such as the ban on the employment of Christians in the state, and on the building of new churches, for example, were not usually enforced, as evidenced by the continued presence of Christian ministers in the Abbasid court, and continued church development. Al-Mutawakkil's "Pact" was mainly intended to exaggerate the separation of believers and "unbelievers" for the purpose of political propaganda.

By the third quarter of the ninth century, hadith had become more rigid than it had ever been, codified in canonical texts, and its authority was matched only in importance by the reputations of its narrators. To traditional scholars of later times, and as in the case of many orthodoxies shaped in reaction in the histories of other religions, the name of al-Ma'mun became synonymous with something bordering on heresy, and he could easily find company in ancient Egypt with the heretic Pharaoh Akhenaten and in the Roman period with the emperor Julian, dubbed "the Apostate" by later Christian historians. In reaction to the Mihna, religious scholars even began to rehabilitate the image of the former enemies of the Abbasids, the Umayyads, as the first patrons of hadith study and thereby pioneers of a traditional approach to faith.

Al-Ma'mun's ambition to assert his new power using religious tools can also be gauged from other evidence toward the end of his reign. We find some of this inside the Dome of the Rock, where a famous inscription records the structure's foundation date. There the name of its

[116] Philip Wood, "Christians in the Middle East, 600–1000: Conquest, Competition and Conversion," in *Islam and Christianity in Medieval Anatolia*, ed. A. C. S. Peacock et al. (Farnham, 2015), 23–50; and for problems in dating the text of the Pact, see Mark Cohen, "What Was the Pact of 'Umar? A Literary-Historical Study," *Jerusalem Studies in Arabic and Islam* 23 (1999).

original builder, the Umayyad caliph Abd al-Malik, is clearly scratched out and replaced with the name "al-Imam al-Ma'mun," even though the date of the original construction was kept, 72/691–692.[117] Since another longer inscription at the north gate of the same structure mentions al-Ma'mun's name along with his brother Abu Ishaq (the future al-Mu'tasim),[118] and gives the year 216/831, it is almost certain that both inscriptions were made around the same time. Al-Ma'mun is very likely to have been in Jerusalem when the modification of the inscriptions occurred because after spending some time in Damascus, where he stopped after a Byzantine campaign, he headed to Egypt to deal with a revolt, arriving there at the very beginning of 217/832.[119] Those years were eventful for al-Ma'mun in different ways: campaigning against the Byzantines, increasing the tempo of his religious innovations, and traveling frequently between 215/830 and 218/833 across the Syrian region. It was also while he was in Syria that he sent out a missive to Baghdad ordering the governor to add the *takbir* (the invocation *allahu akbar*) after the prayer in the two key mosques of the city. His intention in taking this step is still not known, but it is probably linked to his continuing perception of himself as "God's Caliph" and his attempt to give a stronger religious resonance to his military campaigns. Seeing the Great Mosque of Damascus and the Dome of the Rock no doubt invited al-Ma'mun to compare himself with the Umayyads in terms of mosque building and war against the Byzantines, and he sought to assert his religious zeal in a competitive way. He had done some of that at the outset of his reign when in 199/814 he sent conquest trophies and a victory proclamation from Khurasan to be placed inside the Ka'ba in Mecca, and he was repeating the same experiment in 216/831 by affirming his ideological control over the Dome of the Rock as well.

Over the course of a two-decade reign, al-Ma'mun left more influences on Islamic society than several other Islamic monarchs combined, and his achievements are varied in the areas of politics, the military, religion, and culture. His tilt toward his Iranian identity brought about a decisive shift in the caliphate's power base toward Khurasan and Transoxiana. This encouraged the rise of a new class of political elite

---

[117] Oleg Grabar, *The Shape of the Holy: Early Islamic Jerusalem* (Princeton, 1996), 59–60.
[118] Grabar, *The Shape of the Holy*, 61.
[119] Tabari, *Tarikh*, III, 1105, Ya'qubi, *Tarikh*, 2:465.

around him (and his successor, al-Mu'tasim), and perhaps strengthened the pace of conversion to Islam in these regions. In the long term, his experiment of rule from Marw showed a firm commitment of Islamic interest in Turkic Central Asia, and his subjugation of Kabul opened the most direct road for later expansion into India in the eleventh and twelfth centuries. Later generations were divided, however, on how to judge this caliph's legacy. His forceful takeover of the caliphate by means of civil war was widely viewed as something that caused divisions in a hitherto more stable society.[120] Historians can even view it as the real end of the "Arab kingdom," or of the long Umayyad century. His zealous support of the Mu'tazila and the Mihna program also stands out as an experiment that led to divisions among religious opinions and created a polarized atmosphere that contributed to the hardline reactions of traditional Islam in later times.

In spite of this controversial legacy, al-Ma'mun also attracted a wave of admirers, and his image would enjoy a revival in the tenth century. While religious scholars stuck to a representation specific to the issues of the Mihna, a whole new stream of litterateurs and humanist writers refurbished al-Ma'mun's image as a paragon of eloquence, wisdom, skeptical thinking, and even freedom of speech. More anecdotes and stories were crafted and attributed to al-Ma'mun's reign than to that of any other caliph, with the possible exception of Harun al-Rashid – but with a clear subtext of rivalry between the two, since al-Rashid's anecdotes are less aphoristic than al-Ma'mun's. The litterateurs (*udaba*) of the late ninth and early tenth centuries forged a worldview entirely different from that of religious scholars, overlapping frequently with the writings and views of the professional bureaucrats (the *kuttab*). Those partaking in philosophy, mysticism, Mu'tazili thought, and new leanings in Shi'ism in the tenth century found in al-Ma'mun a point of common ground for expressing some of their views in popular and elite terms. Were a reader to collect the sayings and moralizing situations of al-Ma'mun, these would certainly form a volume larger than the *Meditations* of Marcus Aurelius.

Al-Ma'mun was frequently depicted presiding "Plato-style" over an assembly – or *majlis* – of scholars engaged in a session of dialog in an atmosphere where all sorts of opinions were exchanged. Topics ranged

[120] On the polarized views in the sources, with and against al-Ma'mun, see El-Hibri, *Reinterpreting Islamic Historiography*, 96–126.

widely to include such matters as the ideals of rhetoric and logic, and the definitions of science and love. And al-Ma'mun was always portrayed defending the reasoned approach, and seeking out the most sensible *ra'y* (opinion). The sayings and aphorisms attributed to him stand out as if they were time-honored wisdom from Greek and Sasanid antiquity. There was also a clear attempt by the humanists to put these sayings of al-Ma'mun on some footing of rivalry with the sayings of the Prophet (hadiths), with al-Ma'mun representing a philosopher king and an Imam to the non-conformists. Ibn Qutayba attributed speeches to al-Ma'mun imbued with the rhetorical approaches of Ali, while Abu'l-Faraj al-Isfahani, Ibn Abi Tahir Tayfur, al-Jahiz, and Ibn Abd al-Rabbih credited him with numerous anecdotes involving debate and general opinion. There is a brooding sense of ethical reflection in the language of al-Ma'mun that sometimes reflects a disillusionment with politics, such as when he tells his courtly circle that "the best life is that of an average man who does not know us and we don't know him,"[121] and answers a political critic by saying he would gladly give up the caliphate to someone if the Islamic community would agree on such a person.[122] All this, however, stands in stark contrast to the image of Harun al-Rashid, who, in spite of bearing the title al-Rashid (the wise), is rarely associated with wisdom statements, but rather appears as a monarch with unbridled power. The reality of al-Ma'mun's actual thinking and intentions will always remain a mystery, hidden behind the welter of literary stories and complex events spanning the many transitions of his reign.

In a sense, this ambiguity surrounding al-Ma'mun's intentions remains till the end of his reign; we are unable to tell whom he firmly intended to choose as his successor –his son, al-Abbas, or his brother, al-Mu'tasim. At an earlier point in his reign al-Ma'mun is said to have been eager to make Abu Ahmad b. al-Rashid his successor, but the latter died in 209/824.[123] Much had happened since then, with the rise of factions around al-Mu'tasim and al-Abbas, which would have made

---

[121] Gustave von Grunebaum, *Islam: Essays in the Nature and Growth of a Cultural Tradition* (Chicago, 1955), 26; S. D. Goitein, "Attitudes towards Government in Islam and Judaism," repr. in *Studies in Islamic History and Institutions* (Leiden, 1966), 206.

[122] Suyuti, *Tarikh al-Khulafa'*, 386.

[123] Sibt Ibn al-Jawzi, *Mir'at al-Zaman fi Tarikh al-A'yan*, ed. Kamil Salman Juburi (Beirut, 2013), 9:119.

the caliph hesitant to rush in making a choice. But considering the rising specter of increased military confrontation with the Byzantines, the chroniclers depict al-Ma'mun siding more with al-Mu'tasim, and suggest that the caliph sought to choose him as successor toward the end. The caliph may have also been eager to make sure his successor continued his support of the Mu'tazila, but without indicating how that would help the state in the long term. Whatever al-Ma'mun's actual intentions, the caliphate was quickly taken over by al-Mu'tasim, the most obvious strongman at the caliph's side, and the one most likely to recreate a bridge with the times of Harun al-Rashid.

4 | *From Triumph to Tribulation (833–990)*

The Caliphate at Samarra: Palace and Barracks

Soon after al-Maʾmun's death at the town of Podandus near Tarsus, al-Muʿtasim acceded to power, called off the invasion of Asia Minor, and returned to Baghdad. With the accession of al-Muʿtasim there began a clear and decisive shift in the political and military foundations of the empire toward a new regime that was militaristic and centered on the Turkic military corps. Whereas al-Maʾmun had created a coalition of Arab, Iranian, and Turkic troops that balanced one another, al-Muʿtasim relied exclusively on the newly recruited Turkic troops. The nature of his military power is still difficult to know precisely, and the terms "slave" and "Turk" used to describe his recruits have been the subject of considerable debate. Some of the new commanders who became his chief lieutenants were probably of aristocratic Transoxanian or Central Asian background, such as Afshin, prince of Ushrusuna, Khaqan ʿUrtuj, and al-Abbas b. Bukhara Khuda, who brought with them their personal military retinues (*chakar*s). In these situations, the loyalty of these troops to the caliph was mediated through a princely figure for some time before it became direct to the caliph.[1] The majority of the rank and file of the new army, however, was made up of slave troops who were dispatched from beyond the Oxus river by al-Muʿtasim's Samanid governor.[2] Little is known about these latter recruits, who are collectively labeled "Turks," a term that

---

[1] Beckwith, The Tibetan Empire in Central Asia, 39; and more recently Étienne de la Vaissière, *Samarcande et Samarra. Élites d'Asie centrale dans l'Empire abbaside* (Paris, 2007), 237, who speaks of the Soghdo-Turkic nobility.

[2] Gordon, *The Breaking of a Thousand Swords*, 8. The research of de la Vaissière (*Samarcande et Samarra*) rejects the view of "slave troops" for al-Muʿtasim's reign, and dates this phenomenon later to al-Muwaffaq's second phase of military reorganization in the 870s.

131

referred to diverse people in a region stretching from the Khazar domain in the Caucasus to the Central Asian steppes. Be that as it may, al-Muʿtasim's Samarran troops were both ethnically and linguistically – and probably for some time religiously – different from the mainstream of the Perso-Arab society of the empire, which created the first paradigm of a political rift between a ruling elite and Islamic society.

From al-Muʿtasim to al-Mutawakkil: The New Grandeur

Ninth-century writers such as al-Jahiz were intrigued by the arrival of the Turks, and tried to place them within a wider perspective on nations. Al-Jahiz considered that each nation had a special aptitude at something in which it became preeminent. The Chinese were viewed as skilled in craftsmanship, the Greeks in philosophy, the Sasanids in administration, and the Arabs in poetry, oratory, genealogy, and divination. But to al-Jahiz, it was the Turks – "the Bedouins of the non-Arabs" – who were most skilled in the realm of warfare, hunting, and horsemanship. The Turk is praised by al-Jahiz for his stamina on long journeys, formidable skills at archery, and ability to resort to various ruses in battle tactics. The Turk "spends more time in the saddle," according to al-Jahiz, "than on the ground," "can aim his arrows as accurately behind him as he does in front of him," has an ability for long night rides "covering twenty miles for other rider's ten," and, the Baghdad essayist affirms, the Turk has focused all his efforts on the activities of "raiding, hunting, and skirmishing."[3] The public admired the new troops for their discipline, as they probably represented the first standing army of the caliphate. But the infusion of such a vast army in a city of merchants soon created tensions between the civilian population and the professional military. The solution al-Muʿtasim devised for this was to create a new city that would become the new capital of the caliphate as well as the home of the Turkic troops. This was Samarra, which was built further upstream, some 60 miles north of Baghdad, in a lightly settled area on the eastern bank of the Tigris.

---

[3] Charles Pellat, *The Life and Works of Jahiz: Translation of Selected Texts*, trans. D. M. Hawke (London, 1969), 93–97; William H. McNeil, et al., eds., *The Islamic World* (Chicago, 1983), 119.

The remaining archaeological outlines of the city today show traces of a gigantic area of settlement covering some 14,000 acres along a 30-mile stretch of the east bank of the Tigris. For about half a century between 221/836 and 279/892 this was a hub of military power and the center of the empire; a city of palaces and private mansions that sprawled in a mix of power and luxury to the extent that it was dubbed *surra man ra'a* ("he who sees it is delighted"). Samarra served not only the practical purpose of providing a base of settlement for al-Mu'tasim's army, but, just as importantly, it formed a new courtly setting that enhanced the prestige of the Abbasid dynasty. The ruling authority was now set at a distance from the populace of Baghdad and protected by a new guard of foreign troops, and amid a new royal culture revolving around sprawling palatial grounds, public spectacle, and a seemingly ceaseless quest for leisurely indulgence. The relationship between Samarra and the metropolis of Baghdad, as Oleg Grabar has noted, became like that between Versailles and Paris during the seventeenth and eighteenth centuries.[4] Different caliphs competed in building their own palaces in the new capital, and sometimes a caliph would build palaces for each of his successors to the throne. The largest of these structures was al-Jawsaq al-Khaqani, built by al-Mu'tasim, and al-Ja'fari, built by his son and later successor, al-Mutawakkil. Al-Wathiq, al-Mu'tasim's immediate successor, built his own, al-Haruni; al-Mu'tamid built al-Ma'shuq; and the most sizable built for an heir apparent was Balkuwara, for al-Mu'tazz, al-Mutawakkil's son. Eventually, al-Mutawakkil, still not satisfied, went on to build his own city, al-Ja'fariyya, also known as Madinat al-Mutawakiliyya, to the north of Samarra.

The most remarkable feature of the Samarra palaces was their staggering size. The dimensions of al-Jawsaq's complex of palaces covered an area of 432 acres, of which 172 were gardens, while Balkuwara covered 89 acres, and both had stately entrances on the Tigris.[5] These were not the square-shaped, "70-meter-a-side" desert mansions of the Umayyads. The "trend to gigantism" that began with the Mshatta palace, located south of Amman, reached its culmination in Samarra.[6] The vast space of the Samarra palaces allowed for a range of state functions, but also for leisure and an opportunity for display. The reception area of the

[4] Oleg Grabar, *The Formation of Islamic Art* (New Haven, 1973), 166.
[5] To put these figures in perspective, a soccer field, roughly 1 hectare, is 2.6 acres or 10,000 square meters; Windsor Castle is 10 hectares or 26 acres.
[6] Walmsley, *Early Islamic Syria*, 103.

imposing arch at Bab al-'Amma showcased the grandeur of the ruler, and betrays influences from the famous Arch of Khusraw at Ctesiphon. A visitor would have approached this entrance from the Tigris, ascending an impressively broad stairway – the largest conceived in Islamic architecture before the eighteenth century[7] – and then approached the palace at the gateway known as Bab al-'Amma, where the caliph sat in judgment of public petitions on Mondays and Thursdays and received foreign visitors. State and military officials would have lined up on this reception stairway according to a complex system of military rank and palace function. Palaces at Samarra were often built at an elevation to allow for commanding views of the Tigris and the outdoor gardens, but also to provide for review stands and platforms which probably overlooked ceremonial parades and military processions. The ruler and his family had access to other outdoor leisure space that included sporting grounds consisting of racecourses and polo fields, parks with exotic animals (ostriches, deer, gazelle, and hare), and gardens interspersed with canals and fountains. The innovative elements in the Abbasid use of cascading landscape and architectural viewpoints have been shown to have directly influenced designs in later medieval Islamic courts, such as the palatial Madinat al-Zahra, just outside the Umayyad capital, Cordoba, in Islamic Spain, which became the equivalent pleasure city of the Umayyad princes who declared themselves caliphs in 316/929, and the military–palace complex of Lashkari Bazar, the Ghaznavid winter capital located on the Helmand river, near Bust, in southern Afghanistan.[8]

When Samarra was first excavated just before World War I by the German archaeologist Ernst Herzfeld, it yielded a treasure trove of information on its architectural design and artwork. Whereas Islamic art in the Umayyad period continued the Greco-Roman and Byzantine drive for accurate representation of nature, Samarra took an innovative turn toward abstraction in a decorative form known as the "bevelled" style, which gave an impression rather than being an accurate depiction of naturalistic scenes, and this style was popular enough that it can be found chiseled in the stucco walls of the city's various structures, in

---

[7] Jonathan Bloom and Sheila Blair, *Islamic Art* (London, 1997), 52.
[8] D. Fairchild Ruggles, "The Mirador in Abbasid and Hispano-Umayyad Garden Typology," *Muqarnas* 7 (1990); Markus Hattstein, *Islam: Art and Architecture* (Potsdam, 2015), 334–335.

wooden panels of various doors, and even on glass vessels. But the bevelled style still shared space with the more realistic side of human representation, which can be found in murals on the interior of palace walls, where images with clearly Central Asian and Far Eastern ethnic features started to enter the vocabulary of Islamic art for the first time.[9]

The Persian and Central Asian influences on Samarra were also reflected in the social and ceremonial organization of the courts, which witnessed an increase in the seclusion of the ruler and the formality of the monarchical institution. The royal order was now governed by a highly elaborate protocol of interaction with the sovereign. The ninth-century *Kitab al-Taj* (*The Book of the Crown*) provides a glimpse of how courtiers and visitors were to conduct themselves: who can sit where at an assembly, how to address the ruler, how to behave at banquets, and what to avoid saying or doing. The book also describes how rulers were expected to keep up certain time-honored rules and practices, such as directly addressing grievances and keeping tabs on what their officials were doing. The key model for these policies was Ardashir, the founder of the Sasanid dynasty in the early third century; and the second caliph, Umar, from the early Islamic period. There is also recognition of al-Mansur and al-Rashid as exemplars of discipline from the Abbasid period. And in a possible glimmer of democracy, the author of *al-Taj* also suggests that rulers should designate as successor to the throne one of their children who is popular with the public. *Kitab al-Taj* also describes the need for the sovereign to celebrate certain festivals with public receptions, such as the Mihrajan and the Nawruz – the latter marking not only the famous Persian New Year in the spring, but also the official calendar date for tax collection on agricultural lands, which made it an occasion of both political and cultural importance.

In addition to being a courtly and military city, Samarra was also a center of religious culture. After al-Mutawakkil abandoned the doctrines of the Muʿtazila and the Mihna program, and in an attempt to project the newly adopted traditionalist religious policy of the caliphate, he ordered the construction in 233/848 of the grand mosque of Samarra, which was completed in 237/852. The mosque of Samarra was a triumph of size and ornament. With bastioned walls and massive dimensions of

[9] G. Fehervari, "Art and Architecture," in *The Cambridge History of Islam*, vol. 2B: *Islamic Society and Civilization*, ed. P. M. Holt et al. (Cambridge, 1970), 710. P. M. Costa, "Early Islamic Painting: From Samarra to Northern Sicily," *New Arabian Studies* 3 (1993), 14–32.

240 x 156 meters (reaching to 444 x 376 meters if the open courtyard was included), it covered an area of 38,000 square meters (for comparison, the area of the Great Mosque of Cordoba is 22,000 square meters and Hagia Sophia is 7,000 square meters). With a fountain at its center, it evoked an indoor image of serene nature, and included expensive ornamentation in teakwood panels, stained glass, mosaics, and marble to such high standards that it was meant to outshine the fame of the Great Mosque of the Umayyads in Damascus.[10] The mosque's famous spiral minaret (the malwiya) rising to 55 meters – about the height of the leaning tower of Pisa and reminiscent of the ancient ziggurats at Babylon – has been the most iconic image of Samarra. It has thus far defied explanations of function, but it has over the centuries provided an inspiration that has influenced other structures with a spiral tower, such as the Mosque of Ibn Tulun in Cairo (completed in 265/879), and has left an equally lasting influence on modern architectural esthetics ranging from the spiraling building of the Guggenheim Museum in New York to the Burj Khalifa skyscraper in Dubai.

The mosque and the caliph's palace became extremities of interaction on occasions of political and religious publicity, such as when the caliph or heir apparent made the journey from the palace to the mosque for Friday prayer or religious festivals. Chroniclers such as Tabari described the pomp and ceremony that surrounded the caliph's procession. Turkish troops dressed in their newly designed uniforms and with horsemen in full armor lined the way through which the caliph's procession made its way. The court poet, al-Buhturi (d. 260/897), describes in a vivid poem al-Mutawakkil wearing the insignia of power, which included the ring, the staff, and the mantle of the Prophet (*burda*), and crowds of spectators cheering with religious invocations, and eagerly trying to point out where the caliph and members of his family were in the moving procession.[11]

It was a carefully staged spectacle by the Abbasid court on the day of the Fitr festival after the end of Ramadan, for example, which blended glamor and piety in an attempt to rally public support for the caliph. With its long and broad avenues – sometimes reaching as wide as 60 meters – Samarra was to be the place for various imperial celebrations, whether bringing home a vanquished enemy leader, honoring the

---

[10] Muqaddasi, *Ahsan al-Taqasim*, 22.
[11] Tayeb El-Hibri, "The Abbasids and the Relics of the Prophet," *Journal of Abbasid Studies* 4 (2017).

nomination of new successors to the throne, or witnessing the journey of the caliph to the Friday prayers. The capture of a rebel leader in Abyssinia, dubbed "Ali Baba," an almost certainly fictional name meant to bemuse the public, was commemorated, in 241/855, with a medal depicting on the obverse the bust of the caliph al-Mutawakkil in formal Persian garb, and on the reverse a man riding a camel being led by a rider, representing the rebel leader being taken in a procession through the streets of Samarra. Al-Mutawakkil's reign coincided with the centenary of the rise of the Abbasid dynasty, and such an occasion found its match with a caliph who was bent on outdoing himself in staging grand spectacles and celebrations.

The prosperity of Samarra and the high expenditures that the caliphs put into building palaces reflected the revived ability of the state to collect taxes from Iraq and the provinces. The courtly setting demanded new varieties of commodities from outside the empire, which in turn stimulated greater long-distance trade with Central Asia, South Asia, Africa, and Russia. Samarra stimulated the growth of creative crafts, and the city itself became an exporter of ceramics with the pioneering application of colorful designs on opaque white glaze imported from China, thereby setting in motion the famous "blue on white" esthetic that redefined the patterns of Chinese porcelain and flourished in Asia and Europe up until the period of the Renaissance. Samarran craftsmen also experimented with the introduction of poly-chrome luster-painted vessels and tiles, which involved the addition of metallic solutions (alkaline, tin, and quartz) that gave glazed ceramic a gem-like radiance. These visual and technological advances catered to the demands for decorative variety by the rich and powerful at Samarra, and examples of such Iraqi tiles with naturalistic and geometric vocabulary can be found until today in places as far away as Tunisia in the prayer niche of the ninth-century mosque of Qayrawan.[12]

The gardens and parks of Samarra's palaces would have also benefited from the phenomenon described as an "agricultural revolution" for this time period, as a myriad of newly imported exotic plants and ornamental flowers would have filled the carefully watered landscapes of these palaces by the Tigris.[13] The caliph al-Mutawakkil was particularly obsessed with

---

[12] Oya Pancaroğlu, *Perpetual Glory: Medieval Islamic Ceramics from the Harvey B. Plotnick Collection* (Chicago and New Haven, 2007), 17–19.

[13] Andrew Watson, *Agricultural Innovation in the Early Islamic World* (Cambridge, 1983).

roses, which he made a monopoly of the court for a while, and he dubbed the rose the "king of flowers," comparing its central place among flowers to his position as the "sovereign over rulers."[14] After hearing of the alluring aroma of aloeswood in India, he sent his courtier Ibn Hamdun on an expensive mission to Lahore to befriend its king, and try to acquire this scent. After a long but successful journey, Ibn Hamdun returned with only a small amount (half a ratl/pound) of this fabled item.[15]

The new courtly class that revolved around the Abbasid family at Samarra and managed the festive spectacles that caught the public's attention may have stimulated the rise of a new sensibility for refinement among the sober and the cosmopolitan. The flood of new luxuries, such as fabrics of different colors, furs, decorative wares, aromatics, and leather goods added new accents to pretensions of sophistication in the lifestyle of Abbasid society. And it may have added to the marketing frenzy that the caliphs, unlike their contemporary Tang Chinese and Byzantine emperors, did not place restrictions on their subjects' wearing of silk garments or of garments of a certain color, such as purple (restricted in Byzantine territory for the emperor's use only).[16] In this new environment of Abbasid society, a new Arabic term came to be coined in the ninth century for elite living, the art of social interaction, and creative speech: *zarafa* (being "interesting"). A treatise on this mode of life, *al-Zurf wa'l-Zarafa*, by al-Washsha' (d. 325/936), provides advice on how one should say the right words, read the oblique messages in people's behavior, dress smartly for different occasions and seasons, eat according to etiquette at receptions, and send the right gift and accompanying poetic verse. This culture of coded language and inferences became embedded in Islamic civilization, and grew to such an extent that an eighteenth-century observer of Ottoman society, Lady Mary Wortley Montagu, would remark on this communicative subtlety by saying: "There is no colour, no flower, no weed, no fruit, herb, pebble, or feather that has not a verse belonging to it."[17] Social entertaining in Abbasid Baghdad became a formal affair, and was no longer the casual "welcome-

---

[14] al-Tanukhi, *Kitab al-Faraj ba'd al-Shidda*, ed. A. al-Shalji (Beirut, 1978), 4:414.
[15] King, *Scent from the Garden of Paradise*, 64–65.
[16] Xinru Liu, *Silk and Religion: An Exploration of Material Life and the Thought of People, AD 600–1200* (Oxford, 1996), 140.
[17] Jason Goodwin, *Lords of the Horizons: A History of the Ottoman Empire* (London, 1998), 133.

anytime" of bedouin hospitality, which came to be frowned on by Khatib al-Baghdadi as déclassé or "party crashing," and he devoted a monograph to the topic.[18]

Literary activity in the Samarra period in the mid-ninth century reached a peak with the writings of talented figures such as al-Jahiz in prose and Abu Tammam, al-Buhturi, and Ali b. al-Jahm in poetry. These poets pioneered the development that came to be known as the "modernist" style of composing verse, avoiding older themes tied to the Arabian desert environment (as was common in Umayyad poetry), and drawing more on the new urban culture with its different cosmopolitan musings and evocations of psychological depth.[19] The court lavishly rewarded the panegyrics of these poets, whose function resembled that of the press today, publicizing the achievements of leaders and glorifying them to a curious public. The Abbasid court also showed a strong zeal for music and creative song. Leading courtesans, such as 'Arib and Shariya, who were famous for their melodious voices, performed at court-funded public spectacles as each built up her own fan base. The ninth century witnessed the rise in trends of competitive critiques touching on various fields, and music proved to be a major battleground for categorizing talent in an areas such as performance, voice, and technique. To keep the door open for emerging new singers, such as Farida, Qalam, and Mutayyam, one critic noted that he counted the songs of 'Arib that were truly original, and he could only find 100![20]

In spite of their focus on Samarra, the concerns of the first three caliphs who built the city were very different. The first of these, al-Mu'tasim, was a military personality who probably sought to emulate al-Mansur in reestablishing the foundations of the state. He is generally portrayed in the chronicles as an unusually energetic and athletic figure, whose physical strength is characterized in legendary terms: it is said that he could wipe out engraved inscriptions on coins by rubbing them with his thumb, and could string bows in freezing weather with his bare hands when none of his troops would dare expose their skin to the elements. He had little education, and as a child reportedly cheered when he heard that

---

[18] Khatib al-Baghdadi, *al-Tatfil* (Cairo, 1983), trans. Emily Selove as *Selections from the Art of Party-Crashing in Medieval Iraq* (Syracuse, 2012).

[19] Ali, *Arabic Literary Salons*; Beatrice Gruendler, "Modernity in the Ninth Century: The Controversy around Abu Tammam," *Studia Islamica* 112 (2017).

[20] Agnes Imhof, "Traditio vel Aemulatio? The Singing Contest of Samarra, Expression of a Medieval Culture of Competition," *Der Islam* 90 (2013), 7.

his tutor had died. Noting this, his father, al-Rashid, skipped over him in the plans for succession, assuming that he would get nowhere in life as a statesman, compared with al-Amin and al-Ma'mun. In an ironic twist of fate, however, he not only seized power, but, as it turned out, all future Abbasid caliphs came from his line of descent.

The most notable military achievements of his reign were the suppression of the movement of Babak al-Khurrami in Azerbayjan in 223/838, after a sustained strategy organized by his talented commander, al-Afshin, and the massive military campaign against the Byzantine town of Amorion ('Ammuriyya) in 223/838. This famous expedition, which the caliph led in person, came after the Byzantine emperor Theophilus had raided and sacked the town of Zipatra in Asia Minor in an attempt to test the defenses of the caliphate while al-Mu'tasim was distracted in suppressing the Khurramiyya revolt. Defying negative expectations, and going against the advice of his astrologers, al-Mu'tasim marched into central Asia Minor in freezing conditions and targeted Amorion, Theophilus' hometown, reducing it to ruins after a long siege that was later commemorated in a famous poem by Abu Tammam. The symbolic gestures made by the caliph included bringing back the two iron gates of Amorion, one of which he put at an entrance of his palace, while he sank the other in the Tigris.[21] The impact of the campaign was sufficiently strong on Constantinople that Theophilus wrote to other rulers, such as Louis the Pious, the Holy Roman Emperor, Venice, and even the Umayyads in Cordoba asking for military help.[22]

Al-Mu'tasim's successor, al-Wathiq, with his exclusive interest in literary topics and song, was very different from his father. We know little about the personality and the politics of al-Wathiq, dubbed "the little al-Ma'mun" by al-Ma'mun himself when a child, and he seems to have left much of the affairs of state to his chief judge, Ahmad b. Abi Du'ad, and his vizir Ibn al-Zayyat. Perhaps reflecting al-Ma'mun's tendency to curiosity – al-Ma'mun tried to excavate the Pyramids when he visited Egypt – al-Wathiq is said to have dispatched two missions of exploration. The first of these was sent to discover the existence of "Alexander's Wall," which is mentioned in the Qur'an as the final boundary between civilized society and that of Gog and Magog.

---

[21] Khatib al-Baghdadi, *Tarikh Baghdad*, 3:334; Sibt Ibn al-Jawzi, *Mir'at al-Zaman*, 9:265.
[22] Vasiliev, *A History of the Byzantine Empire*, 1:277.

This mission traveled east to Khurasan, where it received supplies from the Samanid governor before continuing further east to a point that may well have been the Great Wall of China. The second mission was sent to verify the existence of the Cave of the Seven Sleepers, a group of early Christians who were reportedly sheltered in Asia Minor from Roman persecution in a decades-long sleep. The Qurʾan briefly mentions this story, which is known in Christian lore as having happened in the reign of the Roman emperor Decius (r. 249–251), with the sleepers awakening in the reign of Theodosius II (r. 400–450).

These quests for archaeological and cultural discovery reflected the same spirit as that shown in al-Maʾmun's reign, which radiated with curiosity toward the world around the caliphate. These journeys of exploration proceeded from an atmosphere of political stability in the Abbasid capital and an attitude of confidence within Islamic civilization as scholars sought to catalog knowledge about other cultures and regions of the world in a "Napoleonic" style of superiority and pretension to objectivity. Scholars such as Yaʿqubi and Ibn Khurdadhbih positioned Baghdad in the ideal geographic zone among the seven climes of the world, and travel writers attributed to foreign leaders, such as the Chinese emperor, flattering references to the king of the Arabs as the most important among a group of five kings (followed in importance by the Chinese, Turkic, Indian, and Byzantine kings). While each of these was viewed as possessing a unique quality, the Chinese emperor describes the caliph as the one ruling over "the most magnificent of empires, with the most extensive lands for crops and grazing, the greatest wealth, the most intelligent men, and the furthest flung renown."[23]

After a short reign, al-Wathiq was followed by his brother, al-Mutawakkil, whose policy turned sharply away from those of his immediate predecessors. Al-Mutawakkil tried to consolidate power in the caliphal office, removing hegemonic figures, such as the commander Itakh and the vizir Ibn al-Zayyat. And in an attempt to bring the caliphate closer in line with popular opinion, the caliph ended the state-sponsored program of the Mihna and pro-Muʿtazila policies, and instead started backing the Hanbali and hadith scholars as propagators of orthodoxy. This was a crucial turning point in Islamic history, since it signaled the triumph of Sunni ideology, and the success of its hadith scholars in becoming the official spokesmen on matters relating to the

[23] *Two Arabic Travel Books (Abu Zayd al-Sirafi)*, 79–81.

interpretation of Islamic doctrine, thereby ending the caliph's ability to shape Islamic law and culture.

Al-Mutawakkil inherited a caliphate that had been greatly strengthened by the military triumphs of al-Muʿtasim. However, he began to discover, more than his predecessors had, the challenge of maintaining the loyalty of the military behemoth at Samarra that his father had created. The poet Ali b. al-Jahm once referred in a panegyric addressed to al-Muʿtasim to "the seventy thousand archers of the Imam (i.e. the caliph)" who stood at the ready to take on an enemy.[24] But in the absence of war, this idle military could only preoccupy itself with self-aggrandizement and turn on its Abbasid masters. Viewed by the Turks as a political lightweight and man of leisure, al-Mutawakkil did not command the loyalty that al-Muʿtasim once did, while the atmosphere of excessive palace construction and the wall-to-wall settings of poetic and musical preoccupation at court only made the caliph ever more distant from both his military and religious bases of support.

What finally tipped the caliphate of al-Mutawakkil into the abyss was the financial situation created by his extravagant lifestyle and steady demands for new palace construction. With the grand memory of al-Mansur, Harun al-Rashid, and al-Muʿtasim before him, al-Mutawakkil could only feel that he had fallen short when he compared his achievements with theirs, and this led him to go overboard in ostentation. By the end of his reign, he had given further expression to this insecurity when he demanded the construction of the new city of al-Jaʿfariyya (named after him), where he built his most magnificent palace yet – the Qasr al-Jaʿfari. Several sources give lengthy lists of the palaces al-Mutawakkil built, sometimes providing the cost of each in an effort to highlight the exorbitant expenditures of the caliph, and thereby signaling the reasons for the eventual decline of the Abbasid government in the mid-ninth century.

Samarra and Military Chaos

Less than a year after al-Mutawakkil moved into the new palace of al-Jaʿfari, and, during what seems to have been a masquerade party at court at which the caliph and his trusted courtier, the highly literate al-Fath b. Khaqan, drank themselves to a stupor, a group of Turkish

---

[24] Ali b. al-Jahm, *Diwan* (Beirut, 2010), 211.

officers brandishing swords broke into the party venue. Mistaken at first for latecomers who were adding more spice to the atmosphere of the charade with their hostile appearance, the attackers soon worked up their courage and assassinated both the caliph and al-Fath b. Khaqan. The conspiracy against the caliph took place with the prior knowledge of al-Mutawakkil's eldest son, al-Muntasir, who had grown fearful that his father was about to shift the succession to his other son, al-Mu'tazz. It was an abrupt and momentous event. Until then the idea of military intervention in politics had been successfully suppressed, with the downfall of various figures who had tried: al-Abbas b. al-Ma'mun, 'Ujayf, al-Afshin, and Itakh. With al-Muntasir the idea had finally succeeded, and it put in place a paradigm of palace coups for later Turkish commanders.

The situation was exacerbated when al-Muntasir immediately moved to depose his siblings, al-Mu'tazz and al-Mu'ayyad, from the line of succession, and sent an edict to this effect to various provinces. Aside from provoking their potential backers in Samarra, this move may have added to the disillusionment in the provinces regarding the perceived decline of Abbasid rule, and the need to search for local alternatives of government. This was the beginning of a renewed trend to decentralism in the caliphate, and in a few years it would send provinces gradually out of the control of Samarra and into different orbits: Transoxiana under the Samanids, Sijistan (Sistan) under the Saffarids, and Egypt under the Tulunids. The gulf between the state and the religious establishment after the experience of the Mihna had exacerbated the isolation of the caliphal institution, and the geographical distance of the Abbasid rulers in Samarra from Baghdad made it difficult for caliphs to scramble for public support when they needed to challenge the Turkic military.

Al-Muntasir died suddenly only six months after assuming power; he seems to have been the victim of his former military supporters who felt that he regretted his actions, and was about to turn on them. The decade after al-Mutawakkil saw the rapid rise and fall of several short-lived caliphs: al-Muntasir (r. 861–862), al-Musta'in (r. 862–866), al-Mu'tazz (r. 866–869), and al-Muhtadi (r. 869–870). Each of these rulers was installed and undone by one military faction or another, represented by a particular commander. The gallery of mischievous generals is a crowded one, and includes names such as Baghir, Bugha, Utamish, Wasif, Salih b. Wasif, Bayikbak, and Musa b. Bugha. There was no single reason for these agitations, nor any clear division between camps backing one caliph or another, although there probably was a general antipathy in the Abbasid house between the children of al-Mutawakkil and those of al-Wathiq, and among the military between the Turks on the one hand and other groups such as those from Ferghana (Faraghina), and the western regions (Maghariba) on the other. Accustomed to financial plenty in al-Mutawakkil's time, now diminished with his assassination, and with the decline in provincial revenue receipts, officers now jockeyed for governorships, land grants, and monetary resources. The harem may have also played a role in this drama, since the women linked to the Abbasid house hoarded great treasures, which they sometimes used to foment military intrigue.

After al-Muntasir the army officers tried to reach outside al-Mutawakkil's branch of the family for the succession, and agreed on al-Musta'in (r. 862–866), who seemed a docile figure. However, he immediately finished off Baghir, the ringleader of conspirators, who had struck al-Mutawakkil with the fatal blow, which made other officers anxious that they would soon follow. When the Turkish military decided to have al-Mu'tazz installed as counter-caliph, al-Musta'in fled to Baghdad, where he sought the protection of the Tahirid military governor of the city, Muhammad b. Abdallah b. Tahir, and built an extensive wall around the city on the east bank to block threats. For the next two years, war raged between a Samarra-backed candidate for the caliphate, al-Mu'tazz, and a Baghdad-backed one, al-Musta'in. The conflict ended in stalemate, and eventually an agreement by al-Musta'in to abdicate in exchange for a covenant of safety, which was given but later broken by a rising officer named Ahmad b. Tulun.

This civil war between al-Mu'tazz and al-Musta'in in 251–253/864–866 was even more damaging than that between al-Amin and al-Ma'mun, not only because it brought destruction to the old city of Baghdad on the western bank of the Tigris but also because it was fought across the agricultural lands stretching outside Baghdad. Both sides applied economic embargoes against each other, and the Turkic military resorted to a scorched-earth policy to force al-Musta'in out of Baghdad, destroying irrigation canals, dykes, and bridges that made al-Anbar a swamp region.[25] Such military damage in the Tigris–Euphrates region was especially detrimental given the economic

---

[25]   David Waines, "The Third Century Internal Crisis of the Abbasids," *JESHO* 20 (1977), 289–292.

dependence of Iraq on environmental and political stability. In order to succeed, the Mesopotamian region required a steady system of irrigation "technology" through a network of dykes, levees, reservoirs, and canals to make the flow of its rivers beneficial for agriculture. Unlike the Nile, which flooded gradually when its waters reached Egypt after a long journey, and at an opportune time in late summer before the sowing season, the Tigris and Euphrates often had a potentially destructive pattern of flooding, and at an early moment in the harvest season. The relatively short distance of these rivers from their original catchment sources (the Tigris from south of Lake Van, and the Euphrates from Mount Ararat) where melting snows quickly gushed forth meant that a stable government was necessary to maintain the security of the dykes and canals that could temper sudden river overflows.[26] The blistering summer heat in Mesopotamia posed the added challenge of sapping the agricultural soil, and resulting in great salination, which also required an organized and labor-intensive effort to remove the salt from the agricultural land.

The absence of a stable government that could maintain the irrigation networks and desalination efforts during the mid-ninth century made agriculture risky, and led many farmers to flee their lands, which created food shortages and an economic decline that continued for almost three decades.[27] The military chaos in Samarra, and the long-simmering resentment of the luxurious living of Baghdad residents, also stimulated a rebellion in southern Iraq, known as the Zanj revolt. This revolt by the African slaves who worked on clearing the salty marshes near the Persian Gulf region was led by an Arab and espoused the Shiʻi cause, but it had all the signs of a social uprising. The slogans included on the Zanj coinage included verses from the Qurʾan favored by previous Kharijite rebels, and the rebellion successfully attracted support for many years, taking up most of the attention of the Abbasids between 255/868 and 270/883. The rebellion disrupted commercial traffic coming through the Persian Gulf region, and forced traders who usually used the Tigris and Euphrates to find alternative routes to transport their goods. It was around this time that the southern coast of Fars started to grow at the expense of Basra as a dock and conveyer of commerce through an overland route that passed through the

---

[26] Hans Nissen and Peter Heine, *From Mesopotamia to Iraq* (Chicago, 2009), 2–3.
[27] Waines, "The Third Century Internal Crisis of the Abbasids," 299–300.

Persian Gulf. Before long, the geographer al-Muqaddasi would describe the port city of Siraf on the coast of Fars as "the point of access to China, after 'Uman," adding, about the rise in its prosperity, "I have not seen in the realm of Islam more remarkable buildings or more handsome ... built of teakwood and baked brick. They are towering houses, and one single house is bought for more than one thousand dirhams."[28]

Al-Mu'tazz tried to make progress in standing up to the army and removed two key leaders, Bugha al-Saghir and Wasif. But another, Salih b. Wasif, rallied troops around him and overthrew al-Mu'tazz. The new faction chose al-Muhtadi, who was a son of al-Wathiq, to succeed him, still sidelining the children of al-Mutawakkil. Al-Muhtadi (r. 869–870) is usually portrayed assuming a pious image, in an attempt to repeat the example of the short-reigned ascetic Umayyad caliph, Umar b. Abd al-Aziz. The new Abbasid caliph reportedly sat in judgment for people's petitions of grievance, removed all trappings of courtly ostentation, and even punished troops for drinking wine. This was a poor starting point for reforming the military, and he soon found himself at odds with them. When al-Muhtadi brought down a particularly big fish among the officers, Bayikbak, in the usual attempt to regain caliphal power, the troops rallied around Musa b. Bugha and surrounded the court. The caliph tried to rally the public behind him, but this was not forthcoming. Samarra, unlike the Baghdad of later times, did not have much of an activist public, and the caliph was left to deal with the military on his own; he followed his immediate predecessors as a victim of the Turks in 256/870, having ruled for a little over a year.

A glimmer of recovery finally came with the next caliph, al-Mu'tamid (r. 870–892), the son of al-Mutawakkil, who was greatly helped by his brother al-Muwaffaq, a sober figure with some military experience. How of all the Abbasid princes al-Muwaffaq came to be accepted by the military to lead the way out of the prevailing chaos toward a stable government remains a mystery. Al-Muwaffaq was reportedly in Mecca when he received the invitation from al-Mu'tamid, a year after his accession, to help him in the administration. Whether he had gone there on pilgrimage, trade, or simply to avoid the conflict surrounding al-Muhtadi is not clear. Prior to this he had been on the side of al-Mu'tazz, and he may have been instrumental in the

---

[28] Muqaddasi, *Ahsan al-Taqasim*, 426, trans. Collins, 378.

selection of al-Muʿtamid to the caliphate from behind the scenes. A lot remains unknown about al-Muwaffaq's original connections with the Turkic military, but it is evident that no sooner did he return from the Hijaz to the capital than he set out on military expeditions like an expert soldier. Success was partially brought about when he introduced an informal arrangement of separating the ceremonial authority of the caliph from the military one, which al-Muwaffaq held. While al-Muʿtamid's name therefore was invoked in the *khutba* of the Friday prayer and appeared on Abbasid coinage, and he kept the title of Commander of the Faithful, his brother ran the government, led the army, and appointed ministers and generals.[29] This new formula in Abbasid politics signaled the start of a dozen years of re-patching Abbasid authority in the provinces, and in Iraq especially. The chronicler Tabari describes at length a solid decade in which al-Muwaffaq, aided by his son, the future al-Muʿtadid, became deeply involved in the war against the Zanj revolt, and bore the scars of battle, which no doubt raised the credibility of the Abbasid leadership.

The First Provincial States: Tahirids, Samanids, Saffarids, and Tulunids

As the Abbasid caliphate struggled to regain control in Iraq, the trend toward autonomy strengthened in the provinces. Ever since the time of al-Maʾmun, who disbanded the Arab tribal armies and relied more on Persian troops, there had been a climate of political confidence in the east that encouraged some degree of autonomy. The Tahirid descendants of Tahir b. al-Husayn, who commanded al-Maʾmun's army during the war of succession against al-Amin, were the first in al-Maʾmun's reign to be recognized as viceroys to the caliph in the east and with their authority stretching over nearly the whole of the Iranian regions. Although officially they remained governors within the Abbasid frame, using the title *amir* rather than that of kingship (*malik* or sultan), the Tahirids set a model that others would try to emulate later, seeking more independence and grand titles in the future. Tahirid success in autonomy was based on their abiding by mainstream ideas, such as patronage of Sunni Islam, the expression of loyalty to the caliph, and avoidance of the Alid cause. Tahirid governors, especially during the successful tenure of

---

[29] Ibn al-Tiqtaqa, *al-Fakhri*, 247.

Abdallah b. Tahir, also projected themselves as patrons of religious scholars and of Arabic literary heritage. Figures such as the jurist Abu Ubayd b. Sallam (d. 224/839) and the prose writer Ibn Qutayba (d. 276/889) provided counterparts to those prominent a generation earlier in Baghdad, such as al-Waqidi and al-Jahiz, in al-Ma'mun's reign.[30] These symbolic cultural trends were accompanied by a new economic policy that sought to address the local needs of peasants and improve the conditions of agriculture. Abdallah b. Tahir is credited with building a better system of irrigation through the use of qanats (subterranean irrigation canals), regulating water rights, and alleviating tax burdens. A manual composed on these qanats during his governorship would remain an official guide until the Ghaznavid period.

Tahirid stability was greatly aided across the Oxus river by the Persian Samanid family in the cities of Bukhara and Samarqand, where they acted as sub-governors to the Tahirids. Transoxiana had long been viewed as an unstable frontier region, with its various Persian, Turkic, and Soghdian ethnicities, but it did not take long for the Samanids to turn it around into an economic powerhouse as they discovered a windfall of trade opportunities on their northern frontiers. Sitting on the area that contained the most important silver mines in the Middle East, the Samanids were in a position to engage in long-distance commerce with Central Asia and China in the east, and Russia, the Baltic region, and Eastern Europe in the west. The geographer al-Muqaddasi provides a list of such commodities that traded between Khwarazm and the Baltic and Volga regions, including "sables, miniver, ermines, and the steppe foxes, martens, foxes, beavers, spotted hares, and goats [i.e. goat hides]; also wax, arrows, birch bark, high fur caps, fish glue, fish teeth [most likely walrus tusks], castoreum, prepared horse hides, honey, hazelnuts, falcons, swords, armor, khalanj wood, Slavonic slaves, sheep and cattle."[31] And all this came just from the northern European sector of trade.

Commerce trends that began in the reign of Harun al-Rashid accelerated under the Samanids as they took over the driving seat of

---

[30] C. E. Bosworth, "The Tahirids and Arabic Culture," *Journal of Semitic Studies* 14 (1969).

[31] Muqaddasi, *Ahsan al-Taqasim*, 324–325; trans. in W. Bartold, *Turkestan Down to the Mongol Invasion* (London, 1928) 235; Florin Curta, "Markets in Tenth-Century al-Andalus and Volga Bulgharia: Contrasting Views of Trade in Muslim Europe," *al-Masaq* 25 (2013), 312.

international trade. As provincial rulers tried to copy the caliphs in lifestyle, and as a new, gentrified stratum in society tried to copy the princely manner in dress, cuisine, and leisure in Baghdad and other cities in Iran and the Mediterranean world, the opportunities for commerce seemed boundless. Trade transactions were no doubt rapid and involved large quantities. A view on this market-oriented world can best be captured in a statement recorded by the tenth-century traveler Ibn Fadlan as a prayer of a Rus that says: "I wish that you send me a merchant with many dinars and dirhams who will buy from me whatever I wish and will not dispute anything I say."[32]

Bukhara and Samarqand under Samanid rule became market hubs that also addressed the burgeoning military demand in Samarra and among various provincial dynasties for Turkic slave troops. Unlike the Tahirid state, which remained mostly feudal and agrarian, reflecting the traditional economy and rural lifestyle of pre-Islamic Iran,[33] the Samanid state used its strong Central Asian connections to reshape its ambitions. The Samanids went beyond the Tahirids in developing their power, drawing on the Abbasids in the way they organized their court, bureaucracy, and provincial administration.[34] They also developed their military along the lines of the ghulam/slave system of Samarra, and this included now an elaborate and gradual training program, which culminated after years of experience with assignments for recruits as commanders and governors of districts. Nizam al-Mulk, the eleventh-century Persian chief minister of the Seljuks, later looked back on the Samanids in his government treatise, *Siyasatnameh*, as a model for state organization, and considered the loyalty of elite ghulam troops as more durable than the filial loyalty of family members. Whereas children always look to succeed their father as monarch, he opined, the ghulams work only to strengthen his rule.[35]

The Samanids followed the Tahirids in maintaining nominal loyalty to the Abbasid caliphs, and in supporting the emerging orthodoxy of Sunni Islam. But to an even greater extent they became patrons of the

---

[32] Cunliffe, *By Steppe, Desert, and Ocean*, 406.
[33] On the rural culture of pre-Islamic Iran, see Goitein, "Near Eastern Bourgeoisie," 597; Jahshiyari, *Kitab al-Wuzara'*, 186.
[34] R. N. Frye, "The Samanids," in *The Cambridge History of Iran*, vol. 4: *From the Arab Invasion to the Saljuqs*, ed. R. N. Frye (Cambridge, 1975), 143–147.
[35] Nizam al-Mulk, *The Book of Government or Rules for Kings*, trans. Hubert Darke (New Haven, 1960), 120–121.

'ulama, and it was under their rule and in their regions that hadith scholarship prospered. The major compilers and redactors of the sayings of the Prophet, such as Bukhari (d. 256/870) and Muslim (d. 261/ 875), all came from towns in the Khurasan/Transoxiana regions under Tahirid and Samanid control, and the 'ulama were the only class of visitors to the Samanid court exempted from bowing to the ground when greeting the ruler. Libraries flourished under Samanid rule, the most famous being that of the *amir* Nuh b. Mansur (r. 976–997) at Bukhara, which Ibn Sina made much use of; and he even served for some time as its librarian.[36]

The court of the Samanids quickly surpassed that of the Tahirids as a magnet for scientists and scholars. The list of those whom the Samanids encouraged is a long one, and it includes pioneers in various fields: literary scholars such as al-Tha'alibi (d. 429/1038) and al-Hamadani; physicians such as Abu Bakr al-Razi (d. ca. 311/923) and Ibn Sina (Avicenna) (d. 428/1036); mathematicians such as Abu'l-Wafa al-Buzjani (d. 386/996); and geographers such as Abu Zayd al-Balkhi (d. 322/933) and al-Muqaddasi (d. 381/991). The geographers stand out in this period for pioneering what came to be known as the "Balkhi school of geography," which described towns, regions, and topography in almost pictorial terms, and was contrasted with the "Baghdad school." Whereas the Balkh school placed Mecca at the center of the world, the latter placed Baghdad at its center.

In terms of patronage, the Samanids were innovative in the way they encouraged cultural expression in Persian, such as in the poetic works of Rudaki and Daqiqi, who composed verse in New Persian, and of Bal'ami, who completed an abridged translation of Tabari's world chronicle into Persian. The Persian language began to revive in written form around this time, using the Arabic alphabet and borrowing Arabic poetic meters, and started to make inroads as a language of bureaucracy. But these were modest first steps in a world where Arabic still reigned supreme. The geographer al-Muqaddasi could not but notice that people in Khurasan spoke the purest Arabic that he encountered in all regions he traveled, east and west,[37] while al-Biruni (d. 440/1048) probably reflected the elite attachment to Arabic as a language of high culture when he famously remarked: "I would rather be abused in Arabic than

---

[36] Pinto, "The Libraries of the Arabs," 218.
[37] Victor Danner, "Arabic Literature in Iran," in *CHIran*, vol. 4, 581.

praised in Persian."[38] For those finding Arabic difficult, a hadith was attributed to a Companion of the Prophet that says: "if someone says a prayer in Persian or makes an error (i.e. in Arabic), an angel is entrusted to render it correctly [in Arabic] and lift it to on high."[39]

But if the Tahirids and the Samanids provided cordial forms of autonomy from the caliphate, a more rogue type of autonomy was presented by the Saffarids in the region of Sistan, south of Khurasan. The Saffarids were former soldiers in the Abbasid army stationed in Sistan and Kirman, who turned into local vigilantes. Their region, which was long neglected by the caliphate, had experienced social unrest in the reign of al-Rashid with a Kharijite rebellion that eased for a short while under the Tahirids. In 239/854 the situation boiled over again in military action when the Saffarid brothers, Ya'qub and Amr b. al-Layth al-Saffar, who had increasing aspirations for local leadership, drove out the Tahirid governor from the town of Bust, and gradually built up their challenge, rebelling not just against the Tahirids but also the Abbasids. With no claim to Iranian elite status or privilege, the Saffarids, unlike the Tahirids and the Samanids, were open about their commoner background (their title Saffar ["the coppersmith"] refers to their former craft), and they gave expression to Sistan's disgruntlement with Khurasan.

It seems that, although the Tahirids were uniformly praised in the sources for bringing prosperity to Khurasan, they did so at the expense of the welfare of other Iranian regions, which had to shoulder a heavier financial burden to keep Khurasan comfortable.[40] Various previous attempts to challenge the Tahirids, such as those of al-Afshin of Ushrusuna and Mazyar of Tabaristan, were in some sense political outbursts against the hegemony of the Tahirids, who successfully presented such rebels to the caliph as mere heretics.[41] The Saffarids finally

---

[38] G. von Grunebaum, *Classical Islam: A History, 600 AD–1258 AD* (New York, 1970), 129. C. E. Bosworth, "The Interaction of Arabic and Persian Literature and Culture in the 10th and Early 11th Centuries," *al-Abhath* 27 (1978–1979) (repr. in *Medieval Arabic Culture and Administration* [London, 1982], 71).

[39] Khatib al-Baghdadi, *Tarikh Baghdad*, 11:164; and a related hadith, Abu Nu'aym al-Isbahani, *Dhikr Akhbar Isbahan*, ed. Sven Dedering (Leiden, 1931–1934), 2:52.

[40] Daniel, *Political and Social History*, 198.

[41] John P. Turner, "al-Afshin: Heretic, Rebel or Rival," in *Abbasid Studies II: Occasional Papers of the School of Abbasid Studies, Leuven, 28 June–1 July 2004*, ed. John Nawas (Leuven, 2010).

burst the Tahirid bubble when they quickly marched on Nishapur in 259/873, ending Tahirid rule, and declared their intention to march on Baghdad as well. This was overdoing things a bit, since the Abbasids had no deep attachment to the Tahirids, and were even willing to consider Ya'qub for the governorship of Khurasan. The latter, however, elated by his regional success, refused any compromise. In Baghdad, al-Muwaffaq organized the defense, and, although he was a military man like Ya'qub, unlike him he took more cautious defensive strategies, often allowing his enemies to extend themselves too far so he could fight them on his own doorstep and exact better terms for negotiation once he had brought them down to size. With great exuberance, the Saffarids came out, in 262/876, with an invading army – and, to taunt the enemy further, brought along the last Tahirid governor of Nishapur, Muhammad b. Tahir, in chains – to within 50 miles east of Baghdad, at Dayr al-'Aqul, only to find there a well-assembled Abbasid army in high spirits with the caliph al-Mu'tamid and al-Muwaffaq at their lead. Still, it was a hard-fought battle in which the left wing of the Abbasid army, led by Musa b. Bugha, fell back under the initial assault, with many fallen Turkish commanders. The tide only turned to the Abbasid advantage, according to Ibn al-Athir, when al-Muwaffaq himself led the next offensive, and encouraged by this the Abbasid troops escalated their assault. After suffering defeat, the Saffarids backed off from Iraq, and retreated to Sistan. They still roamed freely in the Iranian regions, and the next caliph, al-Mu'tadid, sought to accommodate their presence by extending to them recognition as governors of Khurasan in 279/892.

Restless and eager to accomplish more, the next Saffarid leader, Amr b. al-Layth, now set his sights on dominating the region of Transoxiana, which led to his final undoing. The caliph knew the folly of such an ambition, but cynically gave the Saffarids the go-ahead, complete with an edict of appointment to the region, while retaining his agreement with the Samanids as the rightful governors of the region. A vanguard army sent out by the Saffarids against the Samanids was soundly defeated, but Amr b. al-Layth remained stubborn about pressing forward, and the ensuing confrontation between the two sides near the Oxus was as strange as the diplomatic intrigue surrounding Amr's appointment as governor. As the latter moved about the region with a small band of guards scouting dissent against the Samanids, the people of Balkh reportedly arrested him when he entered their town and handed him over to the Samanid leader, Ismaʿil b. Ahmad, who in turn sent him to Baghdad in 287/900, where he was executed. Al-Muʿtadid rewarded Ismaʿil by granting him title to the former Saffarid dominions, and sending him a crown and a sack of precious pearls.[42] The Saffarid–Samanid war illustrated the greater economic and military abilities of a power based in Transoxiana, but it also provided the first instance of a caliph using his diplomatic skill to entangle distant powers against each other – a trend that would be repeated between Baghdad and the Ghaznavids, Seljuks, Khwarazm shahs, and Ghurids in future centuries.

Just as the eastern parts of the Abbasid empire experienced the rise of the Samanids and the Saffarids, the western provinces, Egypt and Syria, witnessed a new experiment with the rise of the Tulunids. Ahmad b. Tulun was originally sent to Egypt in 254/868, while still a junior member of the Turkic military of Samarra, as a representative of Bayikbak, a more senior Turkic officer and his kinsman, who was appointed as governor to Egypt but chose to remain in Samarra. Soon after he arrived, Ibn Tulun undertook various steps that seemed to outline his desire for autonomy and promote his popularity. He encouraged agricultural development, collected taxes effectively, and raised his own army of slave troops, from Greek, Turkic, and Nubian backgrounds. He also emulated the Samarra model with his founding of a garrison city for his troops – al-Qataʾiʿ – where he copied Samarra down to its architectural forms, decorative and esthetic styles. The Mosque of Ibn Tulun, which still stands in Cairo today, includes a minor spiral design for its minaret that emulates to some extent the minaret of the Great Mosque of Samarra. With his leadership established in Egypt, it did not take long before Ibn Tulun started to withhold the majority of Egypt's tax revenues from Baghdad, and he extended his control over Syria while projecting himself as its zealous defender against the Byzantines.

Al-Muwaffaq realized the strong points of the Tulunid state, such as its geopolitical distance from Iraq, but also understood its vulnerability in the way that it lacked a genuine base of social support, which was unlike the Samanid state, which had a "nationalist" character. Recognizing this gap

---

[42] al-Azdi, *Tarikh al-Mawsil*, ed. Ahmad Mahmud (Beirut, 2006), 2:155; Ibn al-Athir, *al-Kamil*, 7:501–502; Ibn Taghribirdi, *al-Nujum al-Zahira fi Akhbar Misr waʾl-Qahira* (Cairo, 1963–1972), 3:911.

as well, and hoping to increase his political legitimacy, Ibn Tulun invited the Abbasid caliph, al-Muʿtamid, to escape the hegemony of his brother, al-Muwaffaq, and come to Egypt. In a moment of frustration, al-Muʿtamid gave this idea a try when he came to northern Syria, in 269/882, to meet the Tulunids; but he was intercepted on this journey by al-Muwaffaq's men and brought back to Baghdad. Although unsuccessful, the experiment showed the rise of Egypt as a regional power with a newfound ability to shape Middle East politics in a way that it had not done since the times of Cleopatra.[43] Ironically, Ibn Tulun's idea to host the caliph would succeed later under the Mamluks, when they hosted the Abbasid caliphate after the Mongol conquest of Baghdad in 1258.

Abbasid Revival with al-Muʿtadid and al-Muktafi

The opportunity for the Abbasids to reassert their influence over Egypt came slowly after Ahmad b. Tulun died in 270/884, and was succeeded by his son, Khumarawayh. Al-Muwaffaq's strategy of fighting near the Iraq home turf, previously applied against the Saffarids, was applied again to the Tulunids, when the latter's army ventured into Syria as far as Raqqa, found their supply lines overstretched, and needed to negotiate a retreat. In return, the Abbasids allowed the Tulunids to hold the governorship of Egypt on hereditary terms in 279/892 but with a promise of payment of taxes in arrears – 300,000 dinars for previous years, and similar amounts in a forward arrangement. This financial boost would have been timely for the newly revived Abbasid state, as the next caliph, al-Muʿtadid, used it to raise more troops, and reextend his military power.

Unlike his father, however, al-Muʿtadid had recourse to additional political tools in handling the Tulunids, and in 282/896 he went a step further by proposing to marry Qatr al-Nada (lit. "Dewdrop"), the daughter of Khumarawayh; the Tulunids greatly welcomed this prospect as a way to gain honor and link themselves with the Abbasid caliphal family. In reality, and with the Tulunids expected to pay for a betrothal fitting for a caliph, and have the bride conveyed with an appropriate trousseau and in high luxury to Baghdad, the whole idea turned out something of a financial trap. The famous Baghdad jewelry

---

[43] Bernard Lewis, "Egypt and Syria," in *The Cambridge History of Islam*, vol. 2B, 184.

merchant Ibn al-Jassas acted as the middleman who led Qatr al-Nada's convoy to Iraq in 282/895, and the new bride soon entered Arabic legend for having had the most expensive of weddings.[44] The entire process pushed the Tulunid treasury to near bankruptcy, and only a few months after the wedding Khumarawayh was assassinated.[45] The army of al-Muʿtadid's successor, al-Muktafi, then found reason to challenge the Tulunids in battle in Syria, and the Abbasids took back control of Egypt in 292/905. At a time of rising threats from the deserts of northern Arabia, when the Qaramita were raiding the towns of Syria and Iraq, the Abbasid state gained credibility as the only remaining power capable of providing a defense of Syria.

The reign of al-Muʿtadid was therefore a time of rolling back much of the rising trend toward autonomy in Egypt and Iran. It was remarkable that, after all the chaos Samarra had endured, the caliphate could still bounce back as the vigorous welder of a Near Eastern empire stretching from western Iran to Egypt. Al-Muʿtadid came to be compared by medieval observers to Harun al-Rashid for reviving the military fortunes of the state as he led armies in person on campaign against the Byzantines. An experienced soldier, al-Muʿtadid restored direct Abbasid control over al-Jibal in western Iran, and appointed his son and designated successor, al-Muktafi, as governor of this province, which comprised the cities of Rayy, Qumm, Qazwin, Zanjan, Hamadan, and Dinawar. Between 210/830 and 285/898 the region had been governed by the Dulafid Arab tribal family, descended from Abu'l-Qasim Isa b. Dulaf (d. ca. 225/840), a folk hero of chivalry in medieval Arabic literature. However, with the Dulafid attempts at autonomy, the power vacuum left by the Tahirids, and the attempts by the Saffarids to expand, the caliph moved to assert direct control over this province, which provided access to Iraq.

The highlands of western Iran (ancient Media) were always an area of strategic concern for governments in Baghdad. The Diyala river, which joined the Tigris as a tributary just south of Baghdad, originated from al-Jibal province, thereby highlighting a vital geographic link. Even more important were the overland links. Western Iran was separated from

---

[44] Ibn al-Athir, *al-Kamil*, 7:473; al-Dhahabi, *Duwal al-Islam*, ed. Hasan Marwa (Beirut, 1999), 1:252; Ibn Taghribirdi, *al-Nujum al-Zahira*, 3:61–63. Lunde and Stone, *Meadows of Gold*, 331.

[45] al-Tanukhi, *Nishwar al-Muhadara wa Akhbar al-Mudhakara*, ed. Abboud al-Shalji (Beirut, 1971), 1:262; Ibn Taghribirdi, *al-Nujum al-Zahira*, 3:53, 88.

Khurasan by the central desert, which gave al-Jibal more points of contact with Mesopotamia than with the east. The Great Khurasan Road helped facilitate this further. This road, which began at Baghdad then reached to the foothills of the Zagros mountains at Hulwan, continued on to Kirmanshah, Bisitun, Hamadan, and Saveh, and terminated at Rayy – the town that was the arrival and departure point of caravans to various destinations in Central Asia and north of the Caspian. Branch roads from the Khurasan Road connected to other important cities, with a road going south from Hamadan leading to Nihawand, Qashan, Qumm, and Isfahan, and roads leading north to Zanjan, Dinawar, Qazwin, Maragheh, and Azerbayjan. The Khurasan Road was traditionally the main route of invaders, including the army of the Abbasid revolution, and whoever controlled it could influence the politics of the Iranian plateau and harvest the economic advantages of dominating the commerce of Rayy.[46] As late as al-Mutawakkil's reign, al-Jibal was combined with Iraq as the appanage assigned to al-Muntasir, when the caliph sought to assign zones of honorary administration to his three nominated successors (al-Muntasir, al-Muʿtazz, and al-Muʾayyad), and it was against this background of administrative practice that al-Muʿtadid was trying to revive Abbasid control there. In subsequent centuries, and well into the reign of al-Nasir, the Abbasids would continue to try and extend their control over the Jibal region, after the collapse of the Seljuks there in 1194.

The success of al-Muʿtadid in reviving Abbasid political sovereignty was in part the result of his creation of a new army based on the ghulam system. Reaching back to al-Muwaffaq's desperate efforts to suppress the Zanj revolt, and benefiting from the opportunities of the slave trade offered by the Samanid state, the Abbasids revived the Samarra experiment to build up a ghulam army made up of Turkic and other ethnic groups. The medieval sources provide us with Arabic names of the new leading commanders of al-Muʿtadid's army – Badr, Muʾnis, Rashiq, Yumn, and Khafif – that sound less menacing than Bugha and Baghir of

---

[46] David Durand-Guédy, *Iranian Elites and Turkish Rulers: A History of Isfahan in the Saljuq Period* (London, 2010), 33. Durand-Guédy also notes how this affinity between Jibal and Mesopotamia was even reflected in language, with the continued dominance of Arabic in towns such as Isfahan, even with the advent of New Persian in Khurasan. See also David Durand-Guédy, "What Does the History of Isfahan Tell us about Iranian Society during the Seljuq Period?" in *The Age of the Seljuqs*, ed. Edmund Herzig and Sarah Stewart (London, 2015), 62.

the Samarra years but tell us little about their background (Turk, Slav, Greek, or African).[47] We are better informed, however, on the shaping of the new army into units known by names such as al-Hujariyya and al-Sajiyya. Alongside these were other units of Arab and Kurdish tribal forces.

To gain the sustained loyalty of troops, it was necessary for the Abbasid state to provide a system of rewards and honorifics that showed the caliph's attentiveness to military achievements. We gain glimpses of this merit-and-reward system with al-Mu'tasim, who decorated his commander Ashnas with a higher military rank in 225/840 and granted honors to al-Afshin after the latter's victory in the Azerbayjan campaign against Babak al-Khurrami. In the case of al-Afshin, Tabari's chronicle reports that the caliph placed a crown on al-Afshin's head, girded him with two sashes studded with jewels, and asked poets to recite panegyrics in the commander's honor.[48] With al-Mu'tadid, there is an even more elaborate description of such a ceremony of military decoration. The tenth-century al-Mas'udi describes one such event in 283/896:

Al-Mu'tadid returned to Baghdad. Pavilions were erected in the capital and the streets were hung with banners. The Caliph drew up his army in perfect battle array before the Shammasiya Gate and then crossed the town to the Hasani Palace. To honour Husayn ibn Hamdan, the Caliph gave him a splendid gala robe and clasped a gold chain about his neck. A number of knights of his entourage and important men of his family were also presented with robes of honour. As a reward for their courage and prowess, they rode in triumph before all the people and, on the orders of the Caliph, Harun al-Shari (the Kharijite rebel captured by Ibn Hamdan) was mounted on an elephant. He was dressed in a sleeved robe of silk brocade and on his head was a tall headdress of raw silk. His brother followed, mounted on a Bactrian camel. They came immediately after Husayn ibn Hamdan and his escort. Al-Mu'tadid followed them, wearing a black robe and a tall pointed headdress; he was riding an ash-grey horse. To his left was his brother Abdallah b. al-Muwaffaq and behind him his page Badr, his vizier Ubaydallah and the vizier's son, al-Qasim.[49]

Such public honoring of a military figure underscores the bond of mutual support between the caliph and his commanders. And it may explain

[47] Hugh Kennedy, *The Armies of the Caliphs* (London, 2001), 156.
[48] Tabari, *Tarikh*, III, 1233.
[49] Mas'udi, *Muruj al-Dhahab*, 5:157–158, trans. Lunde and Stone, 168–175.

why some military chiefs, such as the Hamdanids in this case, remained tenaciously loyal to helping al-Mu'tadid's successors reestablish their grip on power even when Abbasid power was later on the decline.

Stable military loyalty to the caliphate was undoubtedly a key asset for the caliph, but the reestablishment of Abbasid authority also reflected an increased trend toward the professionalization of government. Increasing attention was paid in the late ninth century to reexamining the administration of various provinces, and the fiscal system in general. In 282/895 al-Mu'tadid famously shifted from April to June the date of the Persian New Year (Nawruz), which marked the beginning of the fiscal year when taxes were collected; it came to be known as *nawruz al-khalifa* (the caliph's New Year).[50] The aim of this reform was to account for crops more accurately when they were completely ready for harvest, unlike under the early date of the previous system, which used to elicit much angst among farmers about premature assessments in April. The caliph's new reorganization seems also to have touched the leisure side of life with his introduction of a "weekend" for government employees, designating Friday, along with Tuesday, as weekly days of holiday.[51]

The staff of al-Mu'tadid's government were in general a class of professional bureaucrats, who carefully charted policy and had an accurate picture of the topography and resources of various provinces. The dawn of geographical science began around this period with a book by a highly placed postal agent of the court, Ibn Khurdadhbih (d. 272/885), who wrote a kind of "rough guide" on the provinces of the Islamic world. His *Book of Routes and Realms*, probably initially intended to familiarize military and civilian officials with the landscape under Abbasid control and beyond, included a survey of the distance between towns, an outline of the roads, and landmarks such as mountains and rivers; it covered, with evidently accurate references, as far away as the Korean Peninsula, and less clear references to the so-called Waqwaq Islands, variously placed by some at Japan, Sumatra, or Madagascar.[52] Another book by a highly placed official, Qudama b. Ja'far (d. 334/948), *The Book of Revenues and the Craft of*

[50]   al-Biruni, *Kitab al-Athar al-Baqiya 'an al-Qurun al-Khaliya*, ed. E. Sachau (Leipzig, 1923), 266; Ibn al-Athir, *al-Kamil*, 7:469.

[51]   Adam Mez, *The Renaissance of Islam*, trans. Salahuddin Khuda Bukhsh and D. S. Margoliouth (London, 1937), 88.

[52]   On this genre of books, see Zayde Antrim, *Routes and Realms: The Power of Place in the Early Islamic World* (Oxford, 2012), 102–107.

Writing, composed around 316/928, went further by sketching in encyclopedic terms the formal profile of various government departments (*diwan*s) and the norms that should guide the practices of administrators. Qudama's work went beyond the philosophic musings of Ibn al-Muqaffa' to describe the theory of professional governance, which later entered the Islamic juristic writings of scholars such as al-Mawardi.[53] Qudama concluded his work with a new item on the rights of the vizir at court, and how the sovereign ought to give him wide powers, grant him honors and promotions when necessary, and not listen to slander against him or confiscate his property.[54] These were undoubtedly heady days for a new class of government clerks and courtiers, who were about to find themselves invested with tremendous authority, and access to wealth.

Advancing in government service in Baghdad at the turn of the tenth century was no longer a matter of selection by chance, as had been the case was with Ibn al-Zayyat, former vizir to al-Mu'tasim and al-Wathiq, but a career path for which one trained in different skills. These included a knowledge of tax assessment, the layout of the empire's land and its agricultural potential, principles of the calendar, Islamic law, exempla from history, and how to speak and write eloquently. Acquisition of these skills marked the moment of genesis for the "Men of the Pen" class that would pervade various Islamic dynasties down the centuries, and would contrast with the military class, the "Men of the Sword." Ibn 'Abdus al-Jahshiyari (d. 331/942), former chamberlain of Ali b. Isa, minister to the caliph al-Muqtadir, penned a history on former Abbasid vizirs that contained lessons for those aspiring to serve at court, and dwelled extensively on the Barmakids in order to honor the historical achievement of his former role models. Ibn Qutayba (d. 276/889), a *diwan* official and famous essayist, often compared to al-Jahiz, went beyond the latter's discursive compositions to write a formal treatise, *Adab al-Katib* (*The Craft of the Bureaucrat*) on the theory of the appropriate style of writing at the chancery. This covered a range of topics, including: the use of introductory formulae in correspondence, applying the right titles for persons of rank, the use of

---

[53] Paul Heck, *The Construction of Knowledge in Islamic Civilization: Qudama b. Ja'far and his Kitab al-Kharaj wa Sina'at al-Kitaba* (Leiden, 2002), 16, 27, 219–221.

[54] Qudama b. Ja'far, *Kitab al-Kharaj wa Sina'at al-Kitaba*, ed. Muhammad al-Zabidi (Baghdad, 1981), 484–485.

certain scripts depending on the occasion, and even the proper choice of various sizes of paper. Ibn Qutayba also marks the first turn toward the encouragement of lengthy and ornate prose that became the hallmark of Arabic rhetorical style in later centuries, reversing the emphasis on brevity and efficiency in prose pioneered by Ibn al-Muqaffaʿ and long held as a scribal tradition in bureaucracy by the Barmakids.[55]

It would not be long before the craft of chancery would encourage refinement in Arabic calligraphy itself, and this too developed in the early part of the tenth century. Ibn Muqla (d. 328/940), a court official and later minister, is credited with beginning the move away from the cumbersome Kufic calligraphy of the previous century toward a more legible cursive style that undoubtedly facilitated the task of reading for the public in a way almost as central as a printing revolution. This method was refined even further at the end of the tenth century by Ibn al-Bawwab (d. 423/1022), when the Sunni revival was reformulating religious texts and reaching out for broader social support. Ibn Muqla's technical contribution also included the laying of foundations for various styles of Arabic calligraphy that he narrowed to six scripts: *naskh*, *muhaqqaq*, *rayhani*, *thuluth*, *riqʿa*, and *tawqiʿ*. He outlined a set of geometrical principles and regulations of proportion for these scripts. Soon, the first three types of script became popular for the writing of the Qurʾan, and the fourth for grand inscriptions. But Abbasid bureaucracy and courtly interests were to benefit the most from the last two, *riqʿa* and *tawqiʿ*. According to the art historian David Roxburgh, these two types of script, which became preferred in the Abbasid chancery, were characterized by a reduced emphasis on diacritics and vocalization (dots and short vowels), and by a flexible manner of linking letters together – not normally linked in other scripts – so as to make it (almost intentionally) harder to read by the uninitiated.[56] The refinement of Arabic script was therefore clearly following other developments during the late ninth/early tenth century that centered on strengthening the professional tasks associated with the court and the government.

In urban terms, this period was also pivotal because it was in the reign of al-Muʿtadid that the capital was moved back to Baghdad, but to a point downstream and on the east bank of the Tigris, at a location

---

[55]   C. E. Bosworth, "Administrative Literature," in *Religion, Learning and Science in the ʿAbbasid Period*, ed. M. J. L. Young, et al. (Cambridge, 1990), 161–162.

[56]   David Roxburgh, *Writing the Word of God: Calligraphy and the Qurʾan* (New Haven, 2007), 25–26.

that remains the nucleus of Baghdad today. Al-Muʿtadid built the new caliphal residence, Dar al-Khilafa, which remained the official palace of the Abbasids until 1258. The project was an ambitious one that continued under his successor al-Muktafi, who famously completed building its core unit, al-Taj Palace, for which he made extensive use of bricks and stones from the nearby Arch of Khusraw palace complex at Ctesiphon. This building revival at the Abbasid court also invited a renewed emphasis on court ceremonial around this time, as a new Arabic word, *rasm* (pl. *rusum*), "protocol," was coined to describe ceremonial and the proper procedure for advancing petitions and transactions at the caliph's court. The name recognition of the Abbasids grew once again on the international stage. In medieval Europe the caliph came to be viewed as the head of the leading empire within the Islamic world in terms not too different from the perception of the Holy Roman Emperor. Probably confirming this, an embassy reportedly arrived at the court of al-Muktafi in 293/906, sent by Bertha, who styled herself a Frankish queen of vast domains in northern Italy, and sent gifts and a proposal of marriage to the caliph.[57] That the Arabic sources document this diplomatic exchange, unlike the case of Charlemagne earlier, also shows the expansion of literary writing to cover more foreign regions than those of the Byzantines, Turks, and China.

Although only a decade long, al-Muʿtadid's reign also left a lasting cultural imprint, with his continued support of the translation movement and patronage for scholars. Ishaq b. Hunayn (d. 298/910) gained fame in this period for continuing the translation movement, while Thabit b. Qurra (d. 289/901) served as court astrologer in addition to his role in revising previous translations of Greek texts to a higher degree of accuracy.[58] The caliph himself was a learned person, said to be fluent in

---

[57] Bertha was daughter of Lothair II of Lorraine, while her son, Hugo, ruled as king of the Franks after her death in 925. She may well have sent this letter while her father still ruled as king, and their motives may have been connected to the rising pressure of the Arab colony in Fraxinetum, which they were trying to contain. On the gifts and the embassy, see al-Qadi al-Rashid, *al-Dhakhaʾir*, trans. Ghada al-Hijjawi al-Qaddumi as *Book of Gifts and Rarities* (Cambridge, MA, 1996), 93–96, 283; Daniel G. König, *Arabic-Islamic Views of the Latin West: Tracing the Emergence of Medieval Europe* (Oxford, 2015), 200–201; and, on various Bertha(s) around this time, Liudprand of Cremona, *The Embassy to Constantinople and Other Writings*, ed. John Julius Norwich (London, 1993).

[58] Goodman, "The Translation of Greek Materials in to Arabic," 486. In relation to astronomical study, Wiet has noted the existence in the Bibliothèque

Greek;[59] he had been tutored by the philosopher and physician al-Sarakhsi (d. 283/896), who was a student of al-Kindi, and kept the prolific religious scholar Ibn Abi'l-Dunya (d. 281/894) in his company as advisor and tutor to his son, al-Muktafi. Also associated with the Abbasid court at this time was the physician and philosopher Abu Bakr al-Razi (d. 313/925 or 320/932), known in the West as Rhazes, who was a maverick critic of religions, composed a compendium of all medical knowledge up to his time, and headed the newly founded hospital in Baghdad, named al-Muʿtadidi hospital after the caliph. In the area of astronomy, al-Muʿtadid's court extended support to the astronomer al-Battani (d. 317/929) (Latin, Albategnius), who became famous for reconciling Indian, Persian, and Greek astronomical tables, compiled new tables for calculating the orbits of the moon and certain planets, and would be credited centuries later by Copernicus in the sixteenth century as a source for his heliocentric theory of the solar system. In fact, the originality of one of al-Battani's observations would not be understood until the twentieth century: he referred to "a little cloud" always present in the constellation Andromeda, which was evidently the earliest observation of what are now recognized as galaxies, and specifically in this case the spiral galaxy M31.[60]

Alongside the academic leaps in scientific and philosophical thought, late ninth- and early tenth-century Baghdad witnessed a sprouting of curiosity on the margins of conventional fields. Literary figures, such as Ibn Durayd (d. 321/933), went beyond the culture of high expression to explore the etymology of curious and arcane words, making the profession of "literary critic" a fashionable trade, and a highly rewarded one at caliphal courts and the salons of the elite.[61] Some forms of poetry were increasingly turned into song, and although the melodious tunes of these have been lost – due to a lack of musical notation – their lyrics survive in compilations, such as Abu'l-Faraj al-Isfahani's famous *Kitab al-Aghani* (*The Book of Songs*).[62] Abbasid courtesans were highly famed if they

---

nationale in Paris of an astrolabe, dated to 905, with the name of one of al-Muktafi's sons on it (*Baghdad*, 67).

[59] Sabiʾ, *Rusum*, 89.

[60] Steven Weinberg, *To Explain the World: The Discovery of Modern Science* (New York, 2015), 108.

[61] Hugh Kennedy, *When Baghdad Ruled the Muslim World* (Cambridge, MA, 2005), 245–247.

[62] Kennedy, *When Baghdad*, 125, 248–249; George Sawa, *Music Performance Practice in the Early Abbasid Era, 132–320 AH/750–932 AD* (Toronto, 1989), 1–32.

sang or played a musical instrument, and even more if they were skilled at the game of chess. Abu Bakr al-Suli (d. 335/947), courtier extraordinaire for five caliphs, penned a treatise on the art of playing chess, *Kitab al-Shatranj*. Although the roots of this game date back to the reign of Harun al-Rashid, interest in chess reached a high point during the late eighth and early tenth centuries, when chess proliferated in wider social terms and a whole etiquette grew on how to behave when playing the game.[63] The modern study of chess pieces by art historians has shown the wide provenance of this game in the Islamic world, and has uncovered rock-crystal pieces artfully carved in Samarra's famed "bevelled style."[64] Creativity also flourished in the culinary arena, with the composition of Ibn al-Sayyar's *Kitab al-Tabikh* in the early tenth century,[65] capping a long tradition dating back to Ibrahim b. al-Mahdi (both a member of the dynasty and noted food critic), in which it was men who set the high standards of Abbasid cuisine. The layout of the Abbasid banquet centered not merely on game as the product of a grand hunt, as was customary in Western medieval cultures, but on a variety of dishes blending vegetable, herb, and spice in a fusion that reflected creativity and the refinement of living.

al-Muqtadir: The Caliphate of Squander

The efficient government established by al-Muʿtadid continued under the short reign of his son, al-Muktafi (r. 902–908), and the expansion of Abbasid influence continued. On land Abbasid authority was firmly extended to Syria and Egypt, and on the sea an Arab naval expedition that ventured from the Syrian coast joined up with a naval force from Crete in 904, and seized Thessalonica, the second city of the Byzantine empire, but did not try to hold it. Had al-Muʿtadid or al-Muktafi ruled for longer, the Abbasid state could have had the chance to stabilize, and control the regions between Egypt and western Iran, by far the richest of the former lands of the caliphate, in economic terms. But without the stabilizing factor of a long reign, their efforts were overtaken by the designs of ambitious ministers and military commanders who sought to

---

[63] Deborah Freeman Fahid, *Chess and Other Games: Pieces from Islamic Lands* (London, 2018), 14–15.

[64] Freeman Fahid, *Chess and Other Games*, 164–166.

[65] Lilia Zaouli, *Medieval Cuisine of the Islamic World*, trans. M. B. De Bevoise (Berkeley, 2007), 10.

assert themselves. When al-Muktafi, who had been ailing since the reign of al-Muʿtadid, died in 908, Abbasid politics took a sudden turn toward domination by court ministers, and there began a three-decade period of ministerial intrigue and rivalry between two families that dominated the office, the Banu al-Furat and the Banu al-Jarrah, who competed for influence over the state.

To avoid any resistance from an empowered Abbasid prince, the chief minister, al-Abbas b. al-Hasan al-Jarjaraʾi, working in league with Ali b. Muhammad b. al-Furat, chose a thirteen-year old son of al-Muʿtadid, and gave him the title al-Muqtadir. Contemporary writers, and especially observers of the ministry during this transition in power, dwell heavily on the morality lesson of letting ministers exploit a power vacuum. Al-Sabiʾ in his book on ministers, *al-Wuzara*ʾ, describes the devious advice Ibn al-Furat gave to al-Jarjaraʾi on the better prospects of manipulating a child caliph and exploiting governmental wealth,[66] rather than bringing in the experienced Abdallah b. al-Muʿtazz.[67] The coming discord is also given a predestined flavor when it is reported how al-Muqtadir's father, al-Muʿtadid, once foretold the doom of this child's reign. Al-Muʿtadid happened to be passing by outside the palace once when he saw Jaʿfar (al-Muqtadir) surrounded by a coterie of other children. Jaʿfar was eating from a bunch of grapes when he suddenly decided to hand the remaining grapes, so rare in that season, around among his friends, who finished them all. In the mentality of the time a royal sharing his own food with others was viewed as a bad omen, a sign that he would share power with others, and this made al-Muʿtadid recoil from Jaʿfar with restrained rage, divulging to his confidant that this was a sign of things to come.[68]

Other ministers briefly set up a counter-caliph, Ibn al-Muʿtazz, an erudite poet prince, who had been educated by literary scholars such as al-Mubarrad (d. 286/899) and Thaʿlab (d. 291/904), was himself the author of a treatise on rhetorical style, *Kitab al-Badiʿ*, left a collection of poems, and was equally attuned to matters of state. But his chances to rule were doomed when it quickly became apparent that he did not

---

[66]   al-Sabiʾ, *al-Wuzara*ʾ, ed. Hasan al-Zayn (Beirut, 1990), 70; briefer version in Ibn al-Athir, *al-Kamil*, 8:10; discussion in Letizia Osti, "Abbasid Intrigues: Competing for Influence at the Caliph's Court," *al-Masaq* 20 (2008), 8–9.
[67]   Sabiʾ, *al-Wuzara*ʾ, 70.
[68]   Harold Bowen, *The Life and Times of Ali b. Isa, the "Good Vizier"* (Cambridge, 1928), 99; Khatib al-Baghdadi, *Tarikh Baghdad*, 7:216–217.

have access to the treasury to pay the troops, and al-Muqtadir's party put up a quick show of military intimidation that seemed enough to dispel his momentum. Ibn al-Muʿtazz, the "one-day caliph," as he came to be known, was hunted down and killed together with his supporters in 296/908. Given the way both military and ministerial figures, such as Muʾnis and Ibn al-Furat – who in later years became bitter rivals – found agreement in backing al-Muqtadir at the outset of his reign, it seems that those who stood to benefit from the regency were many, and that they only subsequently fell out over how to draw personal advantages from the system. Soon, in 912, Byzantium would also witness the accession of a youth to the throne – the seven-year-old Constantine VII – accompanied by a succession of regents as well, and the courtly circles in Baghdad and Constantinople were undoubtedly aware of each other's experience.

Toward the beginning of al-Muqtadir's reign there was a measure of continued Abbasid success. The caliph's commander, Muʾnis, rebuffed several attempts by the newly emerging Fatimids in 301/913, 302/914, and 306/918 to invade Egypt from North Africa, and warded off Byzantine threats in Asia Minor and Qaramita incursions in southern Iraq. Abbasid authority still reached widely in the provinces in those early years of the tenth century, and a list of revenues drafted at the order of Ali b. Isa and dating to 305/917–918 showed provincial contributions of tax revenues still coming in from Egypt, Syria, Jazira, western Iran, Fars, and Ahwaz.[69] Attempts at provincial autonomy were rejected in the capital, such as that by the governor of Armenia and Azerbayjan, Yusuf b. Abi'l-Saj (d. 315/928), who offered an annual sum of 700,000 dinars to the central treasury in exchange for autonomy. In 307/919 a military expedition, led by Muʾnis, was sent out to Ardabil and, after a series of battles, captured Yusuf and brought him to Baghdad, where he was imprisoned for a while. On the Byzantine front, in 302/914 the minister Ali b. Isa sent out a military campaign that led to negotiations over a prisoner exchange in 305/917. It was on the heels of these activities that diplomatic relations led to the arrival in Baghdad, in 305/917, of a Byzantine embassy from Emperor Constantine VII, seeking closer cooperation.[70]

---

[69] Hugh Kennedy, *The Prophet and the Age of the Caliphates: The Islamic Near East from the Sixth to the Eleventh Century* (London, 2004), 196.

[70] Sabiʾ, *Rusum*, 11–14.

The power of the Abbasid state was put on full display on this occasion, and the ceremony receives a detailed description in the medieval chronicles. Al-Muqtadir and his ministers invested heavily in putting on a show of wealth and military strength. The Byzantine envoys were led through elaborate passages in the palace grounds flanked by hundreds of soldiers, and exotic animals, including a hundred lions, until they reached a garden where a tree with branches and leaves of silver and gold was displayed. Through mechanical devices the tree would sway as if through the effects of wind, while mechanical birds sang in its branches.[71] This was reportedly the object that impressed the envoys the most, and was later copied in the Byzantine court ceremonial.[72]

It was also around this time that more distant kingdoms corresponded with the caliphate, seeking to establish ties with Baghdad. An embassy was sent out from al-Muqtadir's court to the Bulgar ruler on the Volga river in answer to his request for more information on the Islamic faith and for help in building a fortress. This resulted in the famed journey of Ahmad b. Fadlan in 308/921, in which he encountered the Viking people who had come for trade in the Volga region, leading him to write a vivid travel narrative that provides one of the earliest accounts of the society and culture of the Vikings. Ibn Fadlan was not the first Muslim to travel on an official mission to the Norsemen; he was preceded in 230/845 by Yahya al-Ghazal, who was sent by the *amir* of Cordoba to Denmark to try and convince them stop raiding al-Andalus.[73] But Ibn Fadlan's writings have gained him Hollywood fame with their adaptation into a fictional production in the form of a cinematic film called *The 13th Warrior*. Ibn Fadlan's journey was nevertheless historically real, and he was probably successful in his mission, since the Volga Bulgars seem to have converted to Islam and the son of their king reportedly came to Baghdad on his way for pilgrimage a few years later.[74] In terms of tenth-century politics,

---

[71] Khatib al-Baghdadi, *Tarikh Baghdad*, 1:102–103; translation of the reception
     account in Grabar, *Formation of Islamic Art*, 168–171; Lassner, *The
     Topography of Baghdad*, 86–91.
[72] Steven Runciman, "Baghdad and Constantinople," *Sumer* 12 (1956);
     Gerard Brett, "The Automata in the Byzantine 'Throne of Solomon'," *Speculum*
     29 (1954).
[73] A. El-Hajji, "The Andalusian Diplomatic Relations with the Vikings during the
     Umayyad Period (AH 138–366/AD 755–976)," *Hesperis-Tamuda* 8 (1967).
[74] Richard Frye, *Ibn Fadlan's Journey to Russia: A Tenth-Century Traveler from
     Baghdad to the Volga River* (Princeton, 2005), 112.

these missions highlight an attempt by the caliphate to expand its image to the outside world as the symbol of religious authority, alongside its imperial pretensions. Baghdad and Constantinople were around this time entering a race to reach out to regions north of the Black Sea, trying to enlist support from the Bulgars and Rus on the Volga, with each power attempting to convert one of these groups to its religion. The Bulgars on the Volga greatly leveraged their position as intermediaries between Muslim and Scandinavian traders to become a "silver bridge" between powers, acquiring Islamic dirhams, issuing imitation dirhams, and using them to trade with the Baltic and east European region. Although it started out with almost nothing, the town of Bulgar on the Volga quickly surpassed Kiev in terms of urban growth in light of its economic connections with Baghdad and the Islamic world.[75]

The grandeur that al-Muqtadir's court projected to the outside world, however, was an illusion. Ministerial intrigue, harem luxury, and superficial leadership were rapidly taking the caliphate downhill.[76] Al-Muqtadir was easily swayed by rumor, and entered a cycle of reshuffling the office of chief minister, often between the Banu al-Jarrah and Banu al-Furat families, resulting in twelve ministers over the course of his reign, with some doing more than one stint in office. Both of these families were converts to Shi'i Islam from Nestorian Christianity,[77] and both were known as competent bookkeepers, but the Banu al-Furat stood out for their financial greed, intrigue with the harem, and the use of any opportunity to retaliate against staff from the rival camp of the Banu al-Jarrah. Tax-farming favors were issued from the Baghdad court to provincial officials in return for cooperation, and military officers were paid in land grants in place of money (*iqta'* or *daman*). This gradually shrank the tax-resource base of the caliphate

---

[75] Curta, "Markets in Tenth-Century al-Andalus and Volga Bulgharia," 312–314.

[76] Nadia El Cheikh, "The 'Court' of al-Muqtadir: Its Space and Its Occupants," in *'Abbasid Studies II, Occasional Papers of the School of Abbasid Studies, 28 June–1 July 2004*, ed. J. Nawas (Leuven, 2010); Nadia El Cheikh, "Caliphal Harems, Household Harems: Baghdad in the Fourth Century of the Islamic Era," in *Harem Histories: Envisioning Places and Living Spaces*, ed. Marilyn Booth (Durham, NC, 2010).

[77] This was also the case with their predecessors the Ibn Wahb family: Gutas, *Greek Thought, Arabic Culture*, 131–132; Maaike van Berkel, "The Bureaucracy," in *Crisis and Continuity at the Abbasid Court: Formal and Informal Politics in the Caliphate of al-Muqtadir (295–32/908–932)*, ed. Maaike van Berkel et al. (Leiden, 2013), 98; John Donohue, *The Buwayhid Dynasty in Iraq 334 H/945 to 403 H/1012* (Leiden, 2003), 183–186.

and the durability of a standing army, leading to an escalating two-decade problem of tax-farming, bribery, and increasing dependency on mercenary troops that chroniclers would look back on with regret in 334/946, the year the caliphate threw its doors open to the Buyids in desperation.

The court administration in al-Muqtadir's reign generally revolved around two figures: Ali b. Isa, of the Jarrahid family, who was known for his exacting bookkeeping and piety, and has been labeled "the good vizir"; and Abu'l-Hasan Ali b. Muhammad b. al-Furat, who is described as "the prince of darkness."[78] Little is known about the personal life and beliefs of Ali b. Isa, but it is telling that members of his family were briefly supporters of Ibn al-Mu'tazz's bid for the caliphate, and he barely managed to return to Abbasid service. Reviews of his handling of state matters are consistently favorable, and show him thrifty in spending, and trying to curtail favors from the court and the trend toward land grants.

In contrast, Ibn al-Furat is consistently portrayed as shady and trying to build up his power at the expense of state interests. He had been distanced from high office by al-Muktafi, but his vast knowledge of the provinces, what they could yield in revenue, and how to make it easier for governors to remit this revenue to the capital made him indispensable. He kept meticulous records, to the extent that whenever he was brought in as minister, it is said that the price of paper and candles went up due to his increased demand for these items. He was highly articulate, and his sophisticated manner won him the admiration of the caliph, but he was frequently also rumored to be playing a double game, and corresponding in secret with the Qaramita rebels or enticing governors, such as Yusuf b. Abi'l-Saj, to rebel. One example of his machinations can be seen on the occasion of the famous Byzantine embassy to Baghdad in 305/918. Instead of focusing attention on the caliph, he demanded that the Byzantine envoys meet with him first, and he put on a great show of opulence and luxury, showing off a gilded ceiling in the audience hall where he received them. The meaning of this was to imply that he was effectively in charge of the Abbasid state, and foreign leaders had to take his interests into account.

In a more domestic way, there is also ample evidence about the tools he used to build up a system of allies and cronies. He was famous for

---

[78] Kennedy, *The Armies of the Caliphs*, 159.

making his home a center of patronage and networking, and for frequently staging lavish banquets at which much business was conducted on the side. The kitchen of his household was always teeming with huge quantities of food being prepared, bakers who were active around the clock, and more working on pastries. The guests were usually the staff of various government departments, scribes, and secretaries, but also military personalities (officers in both the infantry and cavalry) and their auxiliaries. All of these would have especially enjoyed the "open bar" hall at his mansion, where smartly dressed waiters offered the guests chilled drinks of various sorts. And it was a trademark of Ibn al-Furat's hospitality to send his guests away with a candle – perhaps even a scented one – and, more importantly, ice, which was considered a high luxury item. Hilal al-Sabi' provides a description of a banquet that Ibn al-Furat once held for important state functionaries, and describes how new courses kept coming to the table for two hours, while Ibn al-Furat carried on amiable conversation with his guests. When the latter had finished dining, they moved to another assembly setting in the dining hall, where the real business of the evening began as Ibn al-Furat listened to the guests, and then met individually with some of them to hear their requests or whatever "secrets" certain people had brought him.[79] In light of this record of lavish entertaining, it is no wonder that some wrote panegyric poems about Ibn al-Furat. Ali b. Isa, in contrast, is never described as holding such banquets, and hardly receives poems of praise – in fact, there is one short poem of derision toward him.

While most observers of al-Muqtadir's reign tend to focus on the key figures of his government and their image in the medieval sources, it is often overlooked that significant trends of an economic nature started to unfold under his rule. In 308/920 inflation and grain shortages led to riots against the state until the court opened its own reserves of staple goods;[80] there was also an increasing decline in the fineness of the silver coinage, in varying degrees across regions, and a growing tampering with the formerly strict weight regulations.[81] It was not long after, in

---

[79] Sabi', *al-Wuzara'*, 116, 141–142.
[80] Hugh Kennedy, "The Reign of al-Muqtadir (295–320/908–932): A History," in van Berkel et al., eds., *Crisis and Continuity at the Abbasid Court*, 30.
[81] Stefan Heidemann, "Numismatics," in *The New Cambridge History of Islam*, vol. 1: *The Formation of the Islamic World, Sixth to Eleventh Centuries*, ed. Chase Robinson (Cambridge, 2010), 661.

the mid-tenth century, that the Fertile Crescent region famously began experiencing a shortage of silver coinage, and Baghdad would stop minting silver coins altogether in 1010 in favor of coinage of gold and base metals only;[82] silver coinage was only reminted in Baghdad in 1233. The causes and impacts of these monetary developments have yet to be fully explored, but they no doubt also coincide with the rising pull of the feudalistic economy that would be further encouraged under the Buyids, and the rise in new tribal powers that brought a pastoral lifestyle.

By the end of al-Muqtadir's reign, in 315/927, tax revenues from Egypt and Syria had ceased coming to Baghdad completely, and the arbitrary extortions being applied by ministers only grew worse. The age of the great Muslim financiers of Baghdad, such as Ibn al-Jassas, who could famously show off the finest jewelry to the court at a moment's notice, was about to enter its twilight when his wealth was confiscated in 302/914.[83] This growing environment of arbitrariness and insecurity in Baghdad propelled an exodus of other members of the mercantile class of Jews and Zoroastrians to Syria and Egypt.[84] The caliph al-Radi would later lament not having someone like Ibn al-Jassas around to bail out the state instead of letting it turn more to a system of feudal land grants (*iqtaʿ*).[85] The morality lesson of the long-term impact of damage done by al-Muqtadir's reign would be best expounded later in the century in the highly pragmatic historiography of Miskawayh (d. 421/1030), who in many ways foreshadowed the social and political analysis of Ibn Khaldun (d. 808/1406).

Ali b. Isa tried his best to address the problems of the Abbasid treasury through a fair and uniform assessment of taxes that encouraged farmers and clamped down on corruption and bribery among officials, but he faced a serious problem at the Abbasid court with al-Muqtadir's unrealistic financial expenses and the intrusions of the queen mother, Shaghab. During al-Muqtadir's reign the harem garnered increasing influence over state decisions, and this was mediated through Shaghab, who had little understanding of the changing times, but had a hegemony that could censor information or prevent it from

---

[82] Andrew M. Watson, "Back to Gold – and Silver," *Economic History Review* 20 (1967).

[83] al-Suli, *Kitab al-Awraq: Akhbar al-Radi*, ed. James Heyworth Dunne (Beirut, 1934–1936), 61, 71, 76, 83–84; Khatib al-Baghdadi, *Tarikh Baghdad*, 4:231.

[84] Micheau, "Baghdad in the Abbasid Era," 239.   [85] Suli, *al-Awraq*, 16.

reaching al-Muqtadir. A former concubine of Greek background (like Qabiha, mother of al-Mu'tazz, before her), and accustomed to clout from al-Mu'tadid's reign, Shaghab interfered in the appointment of officials and believed that the harem took priority over the court. Generally referred to as "al-Sayyida" (the Lady) in the chronicles, she controlled vast revenues from her landed estates, indulged herself in the luxuries of the harem, and spared no expense to keep up her lifestyle. Marie Antoinette famously played a village maiden frolicking with milking pails in the Versailles grounds. Shaghab did one better. After seeing Baghdad girls with muddied feet by the shore of the Tigris filling vessels with water and doing chores, Shaghab ordered her servants to fill up a space in her palace grounds with aromatic dark amber, in imitation of mud, and waded with her harem friends to have the same – albeit comfortable – 'Les Miserables' look as the girls she saw working by the river quay.[86] And in a moment of spending rage, Shaghab once had Ali b. Isa fired, during his second term as vizir, when his secretary refused to wake him up to approve expenditures for a shopping list brought by her harem servant.[87] Throughout those years al-Muqtadir showed no ability to curb the ambitions of those around him, made sudden shifts in favor that brought him new animosities, and kept up the party atmosphere at court with extravagance. A commemorative coin from his reign summarizes his own indulgent lifestyle, depicting him on the obverse seated and holding a wine cup in his hand, and on the reverse seated and playing the lute. In many ways, al-Muqtadir's reign planted lasting roots of disaffection with the idea of Abbasid central rule, and led to a continuous search in the provinces for alternative forms of political authority and an open climate for new religious and ideological experiment.

The Shi'i Challenge: The Zaydis, Qaramita, and the Fatimids

The intersection of problems around this time could not have been worse for the interests of the Abbasid state. Whereas in the ninth century the caliphate had faced provincial decentralization that could be remedied with diplomacy and military campaigns, in the tenth century – and on

---

[86] See editor's note to Tanukhi, *Nishwar al-Muhadara*, 1:292.

[87] Ibn al-Athir, *al-Kamil*, 8:98, and Maaike van Berkel, "The Young Caliph and His Wicked Advisors: Women and Power Politics under Caliph al-Muqtadir," *al-Masaq* 19 (2007), 9.

top of provincial trends for autonomy – a new type of ideological challenge surfaced with the emergence of Shi'i chiliastic movements. These did not simply demand local autonomy, but put forward a claim to universal leadership of the Islamic world, reviving the Alid challenge to the Abbasids for the office of the caliphate. It was as if the Abbasid *da'wa* was being re-created, but instead of coming from Khurasan, it came from the west and in the garb of an Isma'ili Shi'i movement. The tenth century would prove to be the heyday of Shi'i ideologies in various states (Zaydi, Twelver, and Isma'ili), so much so that historians would refer to this period as "the Shi'i century."

Perhaps the violent overthrow of al-Mutawakkil and the decade of military anarchy in Samarra in the mid-ninth century provided an early background that stimulated yearnings for an alternative government. To medieval society regicide often symbolized an overturning of the natural order, like an earthquake or a drought, and could turn the political disillusionment of many into a quest for new religious salvation. It is not a coincidence therefore that Twelver Shi'ism, also known as Imami Shi'ism, suddenly came up with the idea of the occultation of the Twelfth Imam in 260/873. The Twelfth Imam was a child when he reportedly disappeared in 873, at the height of the atmosphere of Abbasid political chaos, raising expectations among his followers that he would come back in time as the Mahdi, the messianic figure expected to bring final justice and righteous rule. It was not long after this that the Zanj revolt in Iraq and the Zaydi movement in Tabaristan in the late ninth century provided further links with the revival of the Shi'i political cause.

Tabaristan had successfully rebelled against the Tahirids in 250/864, and invited the Zaydi Imam, Hasan b. Zayd (d. 270/884), from Rayy to become the region's chief. This was the first major Alid rebellion since the early part of al-Ma'mun's reign, when a descendant of the Hasanid line, Muhammad b. Ibrahim (known as Ibn Tabataba), together with an Abbasid soldier of fortune named Abu'l-Saraya, raised a brief challenge in Kufa in 198/814. The Zaydi state in Tabaristan succeeded for a while, and ended in 287/900 when Hasan's brother, Muhammad, sought to invade Khurasan, which brought about the conquest of Tabaristan by the Samanids.[88] More critical perhaps was the fact that another Alid, closely related to Ibn Tabataba, named Yahya b. al-Husayn (*al-hadi li'l-haqq*) (d.

---

[88]   Wilferd Madelung, "The Minor Dynasties of Northern Iran," in *CHIran*, vol. 4, 206–207.

298/911), whose grandfather had tried unsuccessfully to make inroads in Tabaristan, migrated to Yemen, where he was made welcome and founded the town of Sa'da, some 150 miles north of San'a, in 284/ 897.[89] This would become the base of a new Zaydi Imamate, and would continue up until the modern period as a source of political influence, until overthrown by a republican coup in Yemen in 1962. Little did anyone realize back in Abbasid times what a lasting presence the Zaydis would have in Yemen, much less the repercussions of their role in shaping the politics of the Arabian Peninsula in the modern period.

Shi'i eclecticism in the tenth century found even more unusual expression in the Qaramita wave of bedouin raids, starting in 289/ 902. These raids on southern Iraq and Syria, which began soon after al-Mu'tadid's death, originated from the eastern coast of Arabia and added a new, ostensibly Isma'ili Shi'i voice to these movements. The emergence of the Qaramita less than a decade after the final defeat of the Alid Zanj revolt and in the same frontier environment of southern Iraq shows the unusual reformulation of an ideology, as the anti-Abbasid movement transformed from one framework to another: Kharijite to Alid, and finally to Isma'ilism. After the sacking of the minister Ibn al-Furat in 312/924, who was viewed as harboring an affinity to the Qaramita, the raids of the latter increased in severity and expanded in scope. Raids on Basra and Kufa almost threatened Baghdad itself in 315/927, and the Qaramita's brief takeover of Mecca in 317/930, when they seized the Black Stone and took it to Bahrain, tested the limits of Abbasid credibility and defensive capability. The Qaramita raided caravans across the Fertile Crescent and Hijaz regions, completely interrupting pilgrimage traffic from Iraq between 317/930 and 327/940.[90] The Abbasids tried at times to buy off the Qaramita with financial sums, and at others to entrust a hired commander with the task of fighting them, but neither solution was completely successful. And with the caliph unable to undertake the basic task of securing the safety of pilgrims going to Mecca, the image of the Abbasids eroded further, and motivated even the Sunni Umayyads in

[89] The Zaydi founder's full lineage is Yahya b. al-Husayn b. al-Qasim b. Ibrahim b. Isma'il b. Ibrahim b. al-Hasan b. al-Hasan b. Ali b. Abi Talib. For more, see Wilferd Madelung, "Zaydiyya," *EI²*. Yahya shares ancestry with al-Hasan b. Zayd b. Muhammad b. Isma'il at Isma'il b. Ibrahim.

[90] Donohue, *The Buwayhid Dynasty*, 259.

Spain to start claiming the title of caliph for themselves in 316/929, during the reign of Abd al-Rahman III.

In North Africa, another messianic threat emerged in the form of the Fatimid *da'wa* for a caliph/Imam from the Isma'ili branch of the Alid family. The roots of this movement probably began in the late ninth century in the Syrian town of Salamiyya, located between Homs and Hama, when a certain Ubaydallah al-Mahdi, claiming descent from Ali, sent out missionaries to Iraq, Iran, Arabia, and North Africa. Just as the Shi'i *da'wa* of the Qaramita connected with the social unrest of bedouins on the frontier, the Fatimid movement also found support with the Kutama Berber tribes in North Africa. The Aghlabid state at Qayrawan and the Rustamids in Tahert fell during the rise of this early Fatimid state organized by its regional propagandist, Abu Abdallah al-Shi'i. And with the arrival from Syria of its original Imam figure, Ubaydallah al-Mahdi, the movement was ready to expand toward Egypt and eventually try to dominate Syria, Iraq, and the rest of the Islamic world. The climax of Fatimid power would come later, in the reign of al-Mu'izz, who founded the city of Cairo in 358/969 and claimed on behalf of the Fatimids the title of caliph, of what was by then a third caliphate, alongside the Abbasids and the Umayyads.

Although the Fatimid Isma'ili threat grew later in the tenth century, al-Muqtadir laid the groundwork for Abbasid vulnerability. In 313/925 the Byzantines increased their incursions on the frontier, and in 315/927 Mu'nis had to rush from fending off a Byzantine attack on Samosata to cope with a Qaramita attack on Kufa, with each mission probably requiring a different method of warfare. The province of Jibal in western Persia was also threatened by a newly rising leadership from the Daylam region on the southern Caspian, and the Abbasids completely lost control there in 319/931. With blank checks always available for harem expenditures, salaries for the standing army always in arrears, and defeats on different fronts, it was only a matter of time before the troops and the public would agitate. Year after year during this period, Ibn al-Athir describes refugees coming from frontier towns in Asia Minor to Baghdad, seeking help against the Byzantines and finding little support. In 316/928 Ali b. Isa finally submitted his resignation from the ministry, ostensibly on grounds of old age, and the following year a brief attempt was made to dethrone al-Muqtadir in favor of al-Qahir. In the edict of deposition, Mu'nis explained the reasons for the mutiny to al-Muqtadir as follows:

The army is displeased with the wasteful allocations, by way of money and land grants, that are assigned to the harem and court staff, and it is despondent about the interference of the latter groups in shaping policies and in managing the kingdom. And the troops demand that all these [culprits] be expelled from the palace and that they return the funds they appropriated [to the treasury].[91]

The chasm between the caliph and Mu'nis now became open, and signaled the growing discord between the army and the court. But al-Muqtadir, still resilient, promised changes, and was brought back through lobbying two days later. As the caliph this time tried to assert his own influence more energetically, ministers successfully intrigued to drive a wedge between him and his commander, Mu'nis. The latter represented the troops who were dissatisfied with the lack of payment from the Abbasid court, and had tried in vain to curb mischievous ministers and the harem. The dysfunction of the Abbasid court in handling the grievances of the military and finding an effective chief minister, however, dragged on in al-Muqtadir's last years until Mu'nis finally withdrew north to Mosul in 320/932, and sided more clearly with the military opposition. With al-Muqtadir in no way capable of a fight but insisting on one, he ventured outside Baghdad to suppress the dissidents. In a chaotic battle that Mu'nis avoided joining, the caliph was killed, and change finally came, but almost too late, with much of the state in disarray. Ibn al-Athir places blame on both Mu'nis and al-Muqtadir, blaming the former for emboldening challenges to the office of caliph, and the latter for neglecting affairs of state, involving the harem in decisions, and dismissing competent ministers.[92]

In the next few years, a series of short-reigned caliphs followed: al-Qahir (r. 932–934), al-Radi (r. 934–940), and al-Muttaqi (r. 940–944), all of whose reigns coincided with the beginning of new religious tensions in Baghdad between the Hanbalis and the Shi'is, forcing the caliphs to choose sides and risk reactions. None of them was able to rally much military loyalty, and they all found few allies. Al-Radi, a son of al-Muqtadir who had been groomed for succession from his childhood, tried a new but drastic solution when he combined all military and political authority in a new post of Chief Prince (*amir al-umara'*), which he entrusted to the adventurer governor of Wasit, Muhammad b. Ra'iq, in 324/936. This step reduced the office of the caliph to a mainly

---

[91] Ibn al-Athir, *al-Kamil*, 8:200.   [92] Ibn al-Athir, *al-Kamil*, 8:243, 323.

religious symbol, and was a prelude of things to come under the Buyids and Seljuks. In order to strengthen his hold on power Ibn Ra'iq used the pretext of political reforms to disband the Abbasid army, which left the caliphate in search of some other military system that could provide security in the Baghdad region. For this, the Abbasid government turned to itinerant Turkish military figures, who typically led their own militias after being discharged from the services of neighboring dynasties in Iran. Such medieval parallels to the Renaissance era's *condottieri* brought ambitious commanders such as Bajkam (d. 329/941) and Tuzun (d. 334/945), who exacerbated the debacle of the caliphs by subjecting the court to intimidation and financial extortion, while providing little security in Baghdad itself. The Baghdad public was already inferring from this state of affairs that their city's fortunes had reached their nadir, and when, on a night of severe thunder and torrential rains in 329/941, the celebrated green dome of al-Mansur's Golden Gate Palace in the original Round City finally collapsed, it seemed clear that the fortune of the caliphs was on the retreat.

Al-Muttaqi tried to assert his authority by seeking alternative groups of supporters, including an attempt to revive Arab tribal support. For this, he turned to the rising family of the Hamdanids, former lieutenants in the Abbasid army, whose chief, Abu'l-Hayja Abdallah b. Hamdan, had Kurdish maternal kin ties and built a regional state based in Mosul with mild Shi'i leanings. Al-Muttaqi bestowed the new titles Nasir al-Dawla and Sayf al-Dawla on the Hamdanid children of Abu'l-Hayja, al-Hasan and Ali. Nasir al-Dawla briefly took over the task of Chief Prince, and helped eliminate Ibn Ra'iq, but the Hamdanid's priority was Mosul, and so al-Muttaqi had to come to him there when he faced pressure from a new Chief Prince, Tuzun. This was also the time when Mosul was making its first showing as a rising city that helped provide a springboard for many aspiring state builders. It was, according to al-Muqaddasi, a city with a potential for wealth, as the point of convergence for caravans coming from the north (Armenia, Azerbayjan, and Arran). In addition, the diversity of the city's ethnography (Arab, Kurd, and Assyrian), geographic distance from Baghdad, and its ability to fall back on a neighbor or hinterland (Syria, Iraq, Asia Minor, and Azerbayjan) for support proved useful to a cavalcade of local statelets from the Kharijites in early Abbasid times to the Hamdanids, and later the Zangids, in the time of the Crusades. The Hamdanid Nasir al-Dawla showed much chivalry in hosting the caliph, and the latter found additional support from the Ikhshidid governor of Egypt, Muhammad b. Tughj (d. 334/946), who invited the caliph to come to Syria or Egypt. Deeply pious but with little political acumen, al-Muttaqi thought the situation in Baghdad could be salvaged through negotiation with the Turkic Tuzun, and was misled into returning to Baghdad by promises of safety given by the latter, who assumed the sobriquet Abu'l-wafa' ("faithful to covenants"). On his return, the caliph was deposed, blinded, and another, al-Mustakfi, was put in his place.

The Buyids

All these scattered developments coincided in the 940s with the rise of a new family, the Buyids (Buwayhids), who came from the mountainous Daylam area in the southwest region of the Caspian, and, after previously serving a regional Iranian vigilante, Mardawij (d. 323/935), turned their attention to expanding their own authority over the areas of Rayy and Hamadan. The Buyid leader Ahmad b. Buya kept encroaching south until he controlled the region of southeastern Iraq (Khuzistan), Kirman, and the Fars province, and was in a position to play a role in seizing control over the fertile agricultural lands of the Sawad in southern Iraq. The opportunity finally came when a desperate al-Mustakfi called on him to step in as the latest Chief Prince to try and provide security in Baghdad and the Iraq region. The caliph bestowed honorific titles on each of the three Buyid brothers as they took control of different regions: Mu'izz al-Dawla (Ahmad) in Iraq, Rukn al-Dawla (al-Hasan) in the Jibal province (Rayy, Hamadan, and Isfahan), and 'Imad al-Dawla (Ali) in Fars (Shiraz). The early period of Buyid rule was characterized by the solidarity of these brothers, and reached its apogee in the reign of 'Adud al-Dawla (r. 975–983), son of Rukn al-Dawla. The Buyids built a royal palace (Dar al-Mamlaka) in Baghdad just north of the caliphal palace (Dar al-Khilafa) in a separation of powers that would continue later under the Seljuks, and the caliph's power eroded further; he no longer had a vizir, and became a puppet of the Buyids. The latter assigned him a daily salary, and could have him replaced by another Abbasid family member at will. This in fact happened to al-Mustakfi early on, when the Buyids suspected him of trying to reach out to the Hamdanids in Mosul, and as a result had him ejected, and replaced with his son, who assumed the title al-Muti' ("the obedient" – ostensibly to God, but in reality implying obedience

to the Buyid kings). A fleeting attempt was made for a counter-claim to
the caliphate in 349/960 by a grandson of al-Muktafi, who assumed the
title al-Mustajir bi'llah and tried to rally support in Armenia, but his
movement ended in failure.[93]

But even as the Buyids removed the title Commander of the Faithful
from the coinage of the Abbasids, leaving only the caliphs' names, they
kept the Baghdad-based caliphal institution in place. Why they did not
abolish the caliphate is a question that medieval observers reflected on at
length, arguing that, in fact, the new Iranian dynasty preferred to have an
Abbasid in the position of caliph rather than bring an Alid Imam into the
office of leadership. One advisor for the Buyid Mu'izz al-Dawla provided the rationale for this when he reportedly told the Buyid ruler that
none of his troops accepted the Abbasid right to leadership, and as such
the caliph was a marginalized figure; "but," he added, "if you install an
Alid in the caliphate, there is bound to be some who consider him
superior to you in everything, and if he ordered your slaying, they
would obey [the Imam] without question."[94] The examples of what al-
Mansur did to Abu Muslim, and what the Fatimid Ubaydallah al-Mahdi
did to Abu Abdallah al-Shi'i, provided a vivid illustration of how things
could go terribly wrong for supporters of the Alid cause.

Modern historians have read the Buyid desire to maintain the caliphal
institution somewhat differently, as a means to placate public opinion in
the Sunni-majority society in Baghdad and the Islamic world.[95] In spite
of its rapid loss of military authority, the caliphate was a symbolic legacy
of Islamic history, and a source of legitimation for various provincial
states. To abolish it risked creating a vacuum of political legitimacy and
protocol, and stirring up a conflict with the public and provincial
powers. Perhaps more critically, the Buyids themselves benefited from
keeping a caliphate that could serve as a foil to the Fatimid and Umayyad
caliphates in Egypt and al-Andalus. And they went farther, trying to join
the Abbasid and Buyid families in matrimony. The marriage of the caliph
al-Ta'i' to 'Adud al-Dawla's daughter in 369/979 would, the Buyids
hoped, yield an offspring who could later make both caliphal and
monarchical claims to leadership. But this plan floundered because the
caliph avoided conjugal relations with his Buyid bride.[96]

[93] Ibn al-Athir, *al-Kamil*, 8:529–530.   [94] Ibn al-Athir, *al-Kamil*, 8:452.
[95] Arnold, *The Caliphate*, 67.
[96] Joel Kraemer, *Humanism in the Renaissance of Islam: The Cultural Revival
      during the Buyid Period* (Leiden, 1992), 275.

In spite of their political dominance, the Buyids suffered greatly from a lack of confidence in their social and political credentials. Their humble background, as former fishermen and mountain-dwellers, and belonging to the Daylamites, who – along with the Turks – were considered in the worldview of Perso-Arab society of the time as the most uncivilized, always stood in stark contrast to the pedigree of former Persian elite families such as the Barmakids, Tahirids, and Samanids. In order to address this deficit of dignity, the Buyids became obsessed with the acquisition of grand titles, courtly ceremonial, and publicity, for which they needed the Abbasids. They spent lavishly on the construction of their palace by the Tigris, included their name alongside that of the caliph in the invocation of the Friday prayer (*khutba*) and on the coinage (*sikka*), and even etched their names in rock carvings in the area of Persepolis, which included ancient Achaemenid royal inscriptions. ʿAdud al-Dawla inscribed his name over the palace of Darius in Persepolis in 344/955–956, next to an inscription dating to Shapur II in 311 CE, and ʿAdud al-Dawla's son, Bahaʾ al-Dawla, added Shiʿi invocations in Persepolis in 373/974 that honored the Twelve Imams, and blended the image of his reign as *shahanshah* with that of ancient Iranian monarchs.[97]

Although militarily powerless, the Abbasid caliph remained crucial to the Buyids because he was theoretically the source of legitimacy in Islamic society. He could issue formal diplomas of investiture to new rulers, grant honorific titles, provide emblems of sovereignty and banners to the Buyids, ratify their peace treaties, and even be present on their military campaigns.[98] Both caliph and Buyid ruler made public appearances at court, during which the Buyids treated the caliph with great outward deference. In a notable account of such linkages of legitimacy, the historian Ibn al-Jawzi describes a ceremony at the caliph's court in 369/979, when the Buyid ʿAdud al-Dawla was to be invested with a new title, Taj al-Milla ("crown of the faith"), which he had requested. Al-Taʾiʿ appeared on the throne on that occasion, wearing the mantle of the Prophet and wielding the staff (*al-qadib*). He was girded with the sword of the Prophet, and in front of him was the Qurʾan that had belonged to the third caliph, Uthman, which was venerated as the one Uthman was reading when he was assassinated.

[97] Kraemer, *Humanism*, 280.
[98] Donohue, *The Buwayhid Dynasty*, 265–266, 276, 348.

Al-Ta'i' was surrounded by his armed guards and retinue, and sat
behind a curtain that 'Adud al-Dawla had asked to be lifted only
when he stood directly within sight of the caliph. Once all officials
and troops stood at their assigned positions in the assembly, and the
curtain was lifted, 'Adud al-Dawla bowed and prostrated himself
before the caliph. The latter then crowned and invested him with
precious cloaks. After all the protocols had been exhausted, the caliph
proclaimed in his edict: "I have resolved on delegating to you what God
has entrusted me with, in matters of managing the affairs of my subjects
in the east and west of the world, excepting my personal court and
immediate retinue. Therefore take charge of these duties with God's
guidance."[99] 'Adud al-Dawla then repeated his prostrations nine times,
as he advanced toward the caliph. With the envoy of the newly declared
Fatimid caliphate in Cairo present at the assembly, the Buyid message
was deliberately clear: they had now reached a peak of legitimacy
through their association with the Abbasid caliph.

Much of this political spectacle of Buyid privilege was crafted in light
of the pressure they put on the caliphate. The Buyids sought to give
a semblance of continuity in Sunni authority, but in reality the new rulers
were becoming more active in their support for the Shi'a. The Shi'i
segment of Islamic society was already long established in Baghdad,
from early Abbasid times, mostly in the al-Karkh market area on the
west side of Baghdad and around the Kazimayn Mosque, which housed
the tombs of the seventh Alid Imam of Twelver Shi'ism, Musa al-Kazim
(d. 186/802), and his grandson, Muhammad b. Ali b. Musa (d. 219/
834). The Buyids now went several steps further: Mu'izz al-Dawla (d.
356/967) and 'Izz al-Dawla Bakhtiyar (d. 367/978) encouraged aggressive public affirmations of Shi'i culture in and around the Baghdad area.
This began in 353/964 with the commemoration of two key occasions in
Shi'i history: 'Ashura, 10 Muharram on the Islamic calendar, which
marks the martyrdom of the Prophet's grandson, al-Husayn, in 61/
680; and Ghadir Khumm, on 18 Dhu'l-Hijja, which commemorates
the Prophet's blessing of Ali, viewed by the Shi'a as a designation for
the caliphate. These events were sometimes accompanied by public
expressions of cursing of the first two caliphs, Abu Bakr and Umar,
who were viewed by Sunnis as sacred figures but by the Shi'a as usurpers

---

[99] Ibn al-Jawzi, al-Muntazam fi Tarikh al-Muluk wa'l-Umam, ed. Muhammad
'Ata (Beirut, 1992), 14:269; Sabi', Rusum, 80–85.

of the caliphate, and in such a climate it was not long before the two communities came to blows.

In retaliation, Sunnis invented two new festivals and parked them close to the Shi'i holidays on the calendar: the Day of Mus'ab (on 18 Muharram), referring to Mus'ab b. al-Zubayr, the son of a Companion of the Prophet who also heroically stood up against the Umayyads and fell in battle, in 72/691, near where al-Husayn had earlier challenged the Umayyads in Iraq; and the Day of the Cave (on 26 Dhu'l-Hijja), marking the day when the first caliph, Abu Bakr, is thought to have stopped with the Prophet at a cave during their *hijra* from Mecca to Medina in 622. Over time, the Buyids found that their encouragement of Shi'i festivals was becoming a source of sectarian violence and increasing instability, affecting their rule. Both Sunnis and Shi'a would set out on parades across Baghdad and in the surrounding areas on these days, and quickly turn against one another. It was only later, when 'Adud al-Dawla (r. 975–983) took over power in 367/978 after a bloody coup against his cousin, the inept 'Izz al-Dawla Bakhtiyar, that the Buyids tried to curtail these provocative celebrations, and banned inflammatory rhetoric. 'Adud al-Dawla stands out in this period as a paragon of sound administration and competent rule. He took various measures to improve the welfare of his subjects, such as the construction of an irrigation network and canals in the Sawad region, and his rebuilding programs in western Baghdad, which included a hospital (al-Bimaristan al-'Adudi), on the former location of the Khuld Palace of the early Abbasids.[100] But the competent government of 'Adud al-Dawla was an exception in the Buyid period, and the older problems of military feudalism were about to return.

In spite of its political turmoil, the tenth century was unusual for being a time of great cultural flowering. The courts of the Hamdanids in Aleppo and the Buyids in Baghdad and Shiraz, along with those of the Samanids in Bukhara and later the Ghaznavids at Ghazna (in Afghanistan), became magnets for some of the most famous names in Arabic literature and Islamic science, such as al-Mutanabbi, Ibn Sina, and al-Farabi. The Tulunids, Samanids, and Buyids all shared with the Abbasids an exuberance for commerce and a high esthetic for artisanal skills. Great mosques, libraries, caravanserais, and hospitals became necessary ingredients of emerging urban centers, and both the lay and the learned moved across

[100] Coke, *Baghdad*, 110.

Iran, Syria, and Egypt without barrier or hindrance. With politics and military power removed from the free flow of economic activity across North Africa, the Middle East, and Central Asia, certain rhythms of life – originally shaped in the first century of Abbasid rule – now came to be shared in the provinces and proliferated across the Islamic world. Geographers, such as al-Muqaddasi and Ibn Hawqal, coined a new term for the Islamic world – *mamlakat al-Islam* (the kingdom of Islam) – to indicate this wide zone of shared language and culture that a modern historian has termed the "Islamic commonwealth."[101] People traveled in search of knowledge (especially hadith), and of new products and new patrons. Even after Baghdad lost its political power, people still looked to it the way people in the Christian world looked to Constantinople – a city of culture and commerce, a focus of historical identity, and the home of an institution dating back to ancient times. An empowered caliphate could still find revival under the right historical circumstances.

Cracks in the Buyid edifice of power started to emerge early. From its beginning, the Buyid system of government constituted a loose federation, which allowed autonomy, but also room for interference amongst the three founding brothers. While the founding generation was cooperative, it did not leave behind a clear system of inheritance and independence, and so squabbles began to happen after the death of Mu'izz al-Dawla in 356/967 and Rukn al-Dawla in 366/977. Buyid power was shaken by an internal Daylamite rebellion led by a disgruntled commander, Ruzbahan, in 345/956, while the famed military strength of the Daylamites as an infantry force was always limited by the lack of cavalry and archers. The Turks and Kurds quickly became instrumental in filling this gap, but they also leveraged their military participation into political influence, and before long Buyid authority became patchy on the ground, on top of the picture of rising discord amongst the younger generation of Buyid princes.

The excessive Buyid focus on the Iranian regions and neglect of the affairs of Syria, the Jazira, and Asia Minor provided yet another test for the dynasty's political credibility. The successful Byzantine push on the Islamic frontier in northern Syria and eastern Asia Minor suddenly accelerated in the mid-tenth century. The trend had already started soon after the overthrow of al-Muqtadir, during the reign of the Byzantine emperor

---

[101] Kennedy, *The Prophet and the Age of the Caliphates.*

Constantine VII (r. 912–959). After the on-and-off war with the Bulgar qaghanate (roughly located in the vicinity of modern Bulgaria, and to be distinguished from the Volga Bulgars), which began in 894, subsided with the death of its king, Symeon, in 927, the Byzantines turned their attention to expansion in the east in a sustained way, and in 322/934 captured the key town of Malatya – the hinge between the caliphate and the Armenian highlands to the northeast – and Edessa in 331/944. But the greatest Byzantine territorial gains were made in the reigns of the next two Byzantine soldier-emperors, Nicephorus Phocas (r. 963–969) and John Tzimisces (r. 969–976), who were emboldened by the discord among the Abbasids, Buyids, and Hamdanids, and pushed deep inside Asia Minor and Syria.[102] The Hamdanids, who put up the only serious resistance to this expansion, had limited military resources during this thirty-year struggle to save the frontier. The Hamdanid prince Sayf al-Dawla of Aleppo, who missed opportunities for diplomacy and often resisted the better advice of his counselors, seems to have been unaware of the renewed vigor of Byzantium. Muslim chronicles describe how the Byzantines increasingly fielded larger armies, heavily armored cavalry, and the appearance of foreign fighters on the Byzantine side: Rus, Khazar, and Bulgar.[103]

The cities on the frontier were gradually captured after some local attempts at defense. Antioch, which had been under Islamic rule for over three centuries, fell in 358/969 after a long siege, as did other important towns such as Mayyafariqin, Marʿash, Samosata, and Nisibin, and briefly Aleppo (in 351/962). The island of Crete was captured in 961, and Cyprus was annexed in 965, changing its neutral Arab-Byzantine condominium status, in effect since 688. These set-backs made headlines as far away as Khurasan. News of population expulsions, demolished mosques, and Qurʾan burnings brought bands of Iranian volunteer fighters from the east in 353/964 and 355/966, who clashed with the Buyids on the way to gain passage to Hamdanid territory.[104] The fall of Tarsus, which had a commanding view of the key road leading through the Taurus mountains, known as the Cilician Gates, in 354/965, was strategically and psychologically significant on both sides. The Byzantines were so elated that they carted off the city

[102] On this expansion, see Whittow, *The Making of Byzantium*, 319–327.
[103] Shepard, "Equilibrium to Expansion," 517.
[104] C. E. Bosworth, "The City of Tarsus and the Arab–Byzantine Frontiers in Early and Middle Abbasid Times," *Oriens* 33 (1992), 278 (no. 48), 284.

gates (along with those of the town of Massisa) to Constantinople as a trophy, while the local Muslim preacher, al-Husayn b. Muhammad al-Khawwas, gave a final sermon (*khutba*) on the last Friday before the city's surrender, on 10 Sha'ban/10 August, in which he invoked the name of the Abbasid caliph al-Mu'tadid, as if to suggest that the latter was the last caliph truly worthy of the name.[105] Tarsus would not be reconquered until 1275, by the Mamluk sultan al-Mansur Qalawun.

The Muslim populace of all the affected towns and regions in Asia Minor and Jazira were pushed out, and they descended as refugees on Baghdad, demanding that the caliph do something. Since the caliph lacked power, and the Buyid *amir*, 'Izz al-Dawla, cared little about confronting the Byzantines, the angry refugee population increasingly grew into a factor of agitation in Iraq, exacerbating Sunni–Shi'i tensions.[106] When a flippant message from the Buyid ruler to the caliph asked the latter to contribute money for a military campaign against the Byzantines, the destitute caliph wrote back with barely restrained rage:

The Sacred War would be incumbent on me if the world were in my hands, and if I had the management of money and troops. As things are, when all I have is a pittance insufficient for my wants, and the world is in your hands and those of the provincial rulers, neither the Sacred War, nor the Pilgrimage, nor any other matter requiring the attention of the Imam is a concern of mine. All you can claim from me is the name which is uttered in the prayer from your pulpits as a means of pacifying your subjects; and if you desire me to renounce that privilege also, I am prepared to do so and leave everything to you.[107]

The Abbasid clash with the Buyids over the Byzantine invasion of Syria signaled a new inclination on the part of the caliphs to find ways to reassert themselves, and the next caliph, al-Qadir, would explore a variety of religious tools to do this. Although robbed of all political authority, by the end of the tenth century the caliphs discovered that they still retained some decisions in the religious sphere, which could be leveraged and enriched into renewed power in later times. Specifically,

---

[105] Wheatley, *The Places Where Men Pray Together*, 418, no.185. According to al-Tarsusi's *Siyar*, al-Khawwas gave the farewell speech regarding Tarsus, but the *khutba* was given by another person: *Shadharat min Kutub Mafquda*, ed. Ihsan Abbas (Beirut, 1988), 455.

[106] Donohue, *The Buwayhid Dynasty*, 269.

[107] Donohue, *The Buwayhid Dynasty*, 269.

the caliphs had retained the prerogative to appoint key religious officials, such as mosque preachers (*khatib*s), judges, and muftis. In fact, the very profile of a mosque in Baghdad depended on the charter of privileges caliphs extended to it. Unlike the modern period, where any mosque can serve as place of worship for the Friday prayers, there was a distinction made in medieval Baghdad between a congregational mosque (*jami*'), where Friday prayers could be held, and a basic mosque (*masjid*), which served as a place for the other daily prayers. Baghdad in the tenth and eleventh centuries had only six congregational mosques, but hundreds of other *masjid*s. The caliph's authorization was needed to designate a mosque as a congregational mosque, after which it would be outfitted with a pulpit (*minbar*) and upgraded with an official cadre of preachers and caretakers.[108]

The key congregational mosques of the city of Baghdad, according to Khatib al-Baghdadi, were the Mosque of al-Mansur in the Round City, on the west side, and the Mosque of al-Mahdi in the Rusafa on the east side – the only two mosques for Friday prayer in Baghdad for a century and a half after the city's founding – later followed in the tenth century by the addition of the Baratha Mosque, a center of Shi'i teaching and agitation; the Mosque of the Caliphal Palace (Jami' al-Qasr); the Mosque of the fief of Umm Ja'far; and the Mosque of the Harbiyya quarter.[109] With the fragmented environment of religious education before the establishment of the madrasa in the eleventh century, the congregational mosque also served as the base for the format of education in a *halqa* (study-circle) session. The designation of teachers to *halqa*s was also something decided between the caliph and various circles of religious scholars. There were *halqa*s for various fields, such as hadith, jurisprudence (*fiqh*), grammar, and literature, and the professors of each of these study circles were appointed and paid by the caliph.[110] Students attended sessions based on the popularity of a professor, and highly accomplished writers, such as Khatib al-Baghdadi, had it as his lifetime wish to teach hadith at the famous congregational mosque of al-Mansur.

---

[108] George Makdisi, *The Rise of the Colleges: Institutions of Learning in Islam and the West* (Edinburgh, 1981), 13–14.

[109] Khatib al-Baghdadi, *Tarikh Baghdad*, 1:107–111; Makdisi, *The Rise of the Colleges*, 14.

[110] Makdisi, *The Rise of the Colleges*, 17, 19, 21.

1 Dirham, al-Mansur, 146/763, Baghdad; 2 Dirham, al-Mahdi, 159/776, Baghdad; 3 Dirham, Harun al-Rashid (*al-khalifa al-Rashid*), 171/787, Haruniyya; 4 Dirham, al-Maʾmun/Ali al-Rida/Dhuʾl-Riyasatayn, 203/818, al-Mashriq/Samarqand; 5 Dinar, Dhuʾl-Riyasatayn, 199/814, Iraq; 6 Dirham, al-Muʿtasim, 219/834, Fars

7 Dirham, al-Wathiq, 228/843, Isfahan; 8 Dinar, al-Nasir, 606/1209, Baghdad; 9 Dinar, al-Mustansir, 624/1227, Baghdad; 10 Dinar, al-Mustaʿsim, 645/1247, Baghdad; 11 (Mamluk) al-Sultan al-Malik al-Ashraf Khalil (r. 1290–1293), Muhyi al-Dawla al-Abbasiyya ("reviver of the Abbasid state"), Egypt

12 View of Samarra's Great Mosque and Spiral Minaret (Science Source Images)

13 Aerial view of Samarra (Ashmolean Museum, Oxford)

14 Herzfeld's drawing of Jawsaq al-Khaqani entrance at Samarra (reconstruction of portal and stairs to lake, D1101. Original drawing. Ernst Herzfeld Papers. Freer Gallery of Art and Arthur M. Sackler Gallery Archives, Smithsonian Institution, Washington, DC)

15 Herzfeld's drawing of Jawsaq al-Khaqani/Dar al-Khilafa (D1101. Original drawing. Ernst Herzfeld Papers. Freer Gallery of Art and Arthur M. Sackler Gallery Archives, Smithsonian Institution, Washington, DC)

16 Creswell's photo of portal to Jawsaq al-Khaqani (Ashmolean Museum, Oxford)

17 The mosque of Kazimayn and shrine of Shi'i imams in Baghdad, ca. 1925 (Heritage Images/akg-images)

18 View of Baghdad, early twentieth century (A. Kerim/Heritage Images/akg-images)

19 The Talsim Tower, Baghdad (A. Kerim/Heritage Images/akg-images)

20 Inscription above doorway of Rum Seljuk sultan ʿAla al-Din Kayqubad Mosque (Konya, 1220) invokes support for the caliph with the title "Proof of the Commander of the Faithful" (De Agostini Pictures Library/akg-images)

21 The Ghurid Minaret of Jam (Afghanistan, ca. 1174) invokes support for the caliph (Pictures from History/akg-images)

22 The renovated Mustansiriyya madrasa (Baghdad, 1234) (Gerard DeGeorge/akg-images)

23 Geometric (*girih*) design at the Mustansiriyya (Gerard DeGeorge/akg-images)

5 | *The Caliphate as a Religious Authority (990–1225)*

al-Qadir and the 'Ulama

The caliph's activities in the religious sphere maintained a level of importance for the Abbasids as an anchor of the religious institutions of society. The Buyids did not seem to interfere much with this, and focused their efforts mainly on the openly political issues. But with rumblings and attitude beginning to show from al-Ta'i', they decided to remove him in favor of al-Qadir, whom they brought from another branch of al-Muqtadir's descendants and thought would be a pliant figure. At forty-five, al-Qadir (r. 991–1031), the oldest Abbasid to assume the throne, may have seemed subdued with age, but he proved to be of a tenacious spirit. He realized from the outset the reduced powers of his caliphal office, and set out to endow it with a new religious assertiveness. Whereas in earlier times some caliphs, such as al-Mu'tasim and al-Mutawakkil, had resorted to courtly displays and ostentation to project authority, al-Qadir took an opposite approach, with a simplicity of lifestyle that had one writer refer to him as "the monk of the Abbasids" (*rahib bani al-'Abbas*).[1] Although previous caliphs, such as al-Muhtadi, had tried to appeal to religious sensibilities, al-Qadir was able to go farther in promoting a pious image because he had studied hadith, could teach this subject, and was sufficiently learned in *fiqh* for al-Subki (d. 771/1370) to include him in the ranks of Shafi'i religious scholars when he compiled his famous biographical dictionary of this group. Such perceptions made al-Qadir's claim of authority something based on more than just the argument of honorific descent from the family of the Prophet – he was in essence a professional fellow of the class of the *'ulama*.

---

[1] Abu Shuja' al-Rudhrawari, *Dhayl Tajarib al-Umam* (Beirut, 2004), 126.

Al-Qadir was also aided by the fact that he reigned for a long time, was probably of greater financial means than his immediate predecessors, and was contemporary with important writers on Sunni Islam, who, in retrospect, constituted what amounted to a "second founders" generation of sorts in the field of Sunni theology and law. This included Ibn Batta (d. 387/997), a quiet but influential Hanbali scholar, who encouraged the call to "command right and forbid wrong"; Abu Hamid al-Isfara'ini (d. 406/1015), a firebrand Shafi'i scholar and mentor of al-Mawardi who also once served as the caliph's envoy to Mahmud of Ghazna;[2] al-Baqillani (d. 403/1013), a Maliki/Ash'ari jurist who penned a book on the merits of the Rashidun at the caliph's behest; and Abu Abdallah al-Damghani (d. 478/1085), a Hanafi who was chief judge in Baghdad for thirty years and was important enough to be compared with Abu Yusuf, and later was buried next to Abu Hanifa.[3] These were partly the intellectual offspring of the new argumentative trend that began with Abu'l-Hasan al-Ash'ari (d. 324/935), and they all represented the ideologues of Sunni Islam, of which the caliphate was now its beleaguered political symbol under Buyid domination.

These religious scholars were also emblematic of a crucial moment, around 1000 CE, in the maturity of their social class that Islamic society would later formally identify as the *'ulama*. Although previously aloof from the Abbasid court in the ninth and tenth centuries, from the reign of al-Qadir the *'ulama* – and especially the Shafi'is – became regular visitors to the Abbasid court, and they gradually emerged as a lobby that garnered public support on behalf of the caliph. They acted as court advisors, undertook diplomatic missions on behalf of the caliph to foreign leaders, as al-Mawardi did in his journeys to Buyid and Seljuk leaders, and they attended caliphal investitures, as with Abu Ishaq al-Shirazi (d. 476/1083), who played the key role in selecting the nineteen-year-old al-Muqtadi as successor to al-Qa'im.[4] Later, al-Ghazali, al-Shashi, and Ibn 'Aqil would all be present at the investiture of al-Mustazhir. In its reshaped role, the Abbasid caliphate became the defender of a Sunni theology and patron of an official narrative of early Islam that centered on honoring Companions

---

[2] Ibn Taghribirdi, *al-Nujum al-Zahira*, 4:239.

[3] Al-Damghani's family would dominate the chief judgeship in Baghdad for most of the period between 447/1055 and 611/1214.

[4] al-Yafi'i, *Mira'at* (Beirut, 1997), 89, 107.

of the Prophet, such as Abu Bakr, Umar, Uthman, and Mu'awiya against contrary views of the Mu'tazila, and more importantly against those of the Shi'a. A seemingly scholastic debate carried out in the Mosque of al-Mansur was about to have reverberations across the Islamic world. The overall effect of al-Qadir's new policy revived the credibility of the caliphal office in a new way, described thus by Ibn al-Athir: "In his days (al-Qadir) respect for the Abbasid state was restored, and it gradually became strengthened and flourishing."[5]

One of the first opportunities that allowed al-Qadir to express his religious assertiveness came in 398/1006 when agitation by Shi'i scholars, including al-Mufid (d. 413/1022), put forward a copy of the Qur'an said to belong to the Prophet's Companion Abdallah b. Mas'ud, which was at variance with the widely used version of the Qur'an – and presumably supported Shi'i views. Abu Hamid al-Isfara'ini stood up against this action, and in a public rally of Sunnis in the capital burned copies of the Ibn Mas'ud Qur'an. Al-Qadir backed this measure and called for an end to the arguments, and in 400/1010 made a public appearance wearing the *burda* of the Prophet and, accompanied by al-Isfara'ini, he appeared at the Friday prayers where a reading was made from the canonical Uthman codex of the Qur'an.[6] The caliph was in essence affirming in a "King James Bible" kind of way that the Uthman codex would remain the only official text, and that this position was backed by the caliphate.[7]

Through such official backing of Sunni religious positions, the caliph was expanding his leadership profile, and competing with the Buyids by creating for himself a platform as defender of the faith against religious innovations (*bid'a*) of various sorts (Shi'a, Kharijite, or Mu'tazila). Although it may have seemed that, given his ardent Sunnism, al-Qadir was doomed to continue fighting with the Shi'a of Baghdad, he cleverly manipulated matters so that his main fight was with the Isma'ili Fatimids in Egypt, who were increasingly becoming a political and economic threat to the Buyids in Iraq, and a big ideological threat to Twelver Shi'ism in general. The Fatimids were not content to rule only over Egypt, North Africa, and Syria, but laid claim

---

[5] Ibn al-Athir, *al-Kamil*, 9:415.
[6] Ibn Kathir, *al-Bidaya wa'l-Nihaya* (Beirut, 1985), 6, pt. 11:362.
[7] It is worth noting here Egypt's first printing of the official Qur'an text in 1924 at a moment when King Fuad aspired to claim the title of caliph in competition with the Hashimite sharifs of Mecca and Yemen.

to the caliphate and to the leadership of the entire Muslim world, bankrolling this vision of conquest in the east with their newfound wealth from Mediterranean trade. In this environment of shared danger, prominent Twelver Shiʻi figures such as al-Sharif al-Radi (d. 406/ 1015) and al-Murtada (d. 436/1044) sided with al-Qadir when he directed his polemic against the Fatimids, while the Buyids found it useful to let the caliph express himself more fully. In 402/1011 he issued a caliphal proclamation (that was also signed by both Twelver Shiʻi and Sunni scholars) that debunked the Fatimid dynasty's genealogical claim of descent from Fatima as a myth, and attributed Fatimid origins to a follower of the Khurramiyya heresy.[8]

The culmination of al-Qadir's various official religious pronouncements came in 409/1018 when he put forward an official Abbasid exposition of "orthodox" religious doctrine that came to be known as *al-ʻaqida al-qadiriyya* (the Qadiri Creed). It called for the suspension of all debate on thorny theological questions, such as defining the attributes of God, repudiated the Muʻtazili views on the createdness of the Qurʼan, and stressed the equality of all the Companions of the Prophet. This last point was perhaps the one that used to polarize passions in the Baghdad streets the most. Al-Qadir's document, in simple language that smacks of a school-textbook instructional tone, helped fix an official historical narrative that enjoined respecting the merits of all the Companions, established a ranking of precedence for Abu Bakr, Umar, Uthman, and Ali according to their order of caliphal succession, made it anathema to denigrate the historical figures of Aisha, Muʻawiya, or other Companions, and discouraged investigating, or taking sides in, the matters over which they were in dispute.

The Qadiri Creed document, which was read in mosques and widely publicized, was a condensed summary of ideas anchored in the writings of significant Sunni scholars such as al-Baqillani (d. 403/1013), al-Isfaraʼini (d. 406/1015), and Abu Mansur al-Baghdadi (d. 429/1037), and drew a clear boundary between "correct belief" and heresy. In addition to curtailing speculative debate on theology, and laying the foundation of an official historical narrative of the Companions of the Prophet, the Qadiri Creed tried to streamline the definition of religious

---

[8] Shainool Jiwa, "The Baghdad Manifesto (402/1011): A Re-Examination of Fatimid-Abbasid Rivalry," in *The Fatimid Caliphate: Diversity of Traditions*, ed. Farhad Daftary and Shainool Jiwa (London, 2018).

faith, strengthen a sense of collectivity, and curb tendencies of intolerance and zealotry. Al-Qadir's document declares:

One should know that Faith is speech, action, and thought ... Faith may become greater or smaller – greater by obedience, smaller by refractoriness. It has different stages and divisions. The highest is the confession: "There is no god but God," and its most minimal reflection is when someone clears an obstacle from a busy road. Modesty is a branch of the faith, and self-control is part of the faith. Man knoweth not what is recorded about [him] with God and what is sealed there with Him [for the future] ... He should honestly carry out all laws and directions and do acts [that bring him closer to God], for all these are part of the faith ... We should declare no one an unbeliever for omitting to fulfill any of the legal ordinances except the prescribed prayer ... The neglect of other injunctions does not make one an unbeliever even if one is so criminal as not to admit the duty. Such are the doctrines of the Sunna and the community. He who stands by them stands in the clear light of truth, is under right guidance and on the true path ... Someone asked the Prophet: "towards whom one should be of goodwill?" He replied: "all the faithful, high and low." May God make us thankful for His favors and mindful of His mercies. Let Him make us defenders of pious practices and let Him forgive us and all the faithful.[9]

The caliph's success in imposing this creed projected a type of religious authority that previous caliphs such as al-Maʾmun and al-Muʿtasim could only have dreamt of. A tract that al-Qadir penned on the merits of the Companions and in refutation of the Muʿtazili creed on the createdness was also read every Friday in the Mosque of al-Mahdi in hadith study-circles.[10] Al-Qadir had garnered a new, authoritative profile by coming forward as the official spokesman of Sunnism, and his words became influential in the Islamic world even without his ruling over any territory. The Qadiri Creed was publicized again in 420/1029 – the year the Ghaznavids took Rayy from the Buyids – and re-announced and confirmed at an official assembly at the caliphal court in the reign of his successor, al-Qaʾim, in 433/1040.

Al-Mawardi (d. 450/1058), who has gained lasting fame for composing the government treatise *al-Ahkam al-Sultaniyya*, which became the

---

[9] Ibn al-Jawzi, *al-Muntazam*, 5:279–281; Mez, *The Renaissance of Islam*, 208–209 (slightly modified); George Makdisi, *Ibn ʿAqil: Religion and Culture in Classical Islam* (Edinburgh, 1997), 8–16.

[10] Mez, *The Renaissance of Islam*, 12; al-Dhahabi, *Siyar Aʿlam al-Nubalaʾ*, ed. Shuʿayb al-Arnaʾut (Beirut, 1981–1993), 15:128.

benchmark of the Sunni juristic theory of government, represented the culmination of this tide of Sunni revivalism and reaffirmations about the past. Although al-Mawardi was more a contemporary of al-Qadir's successor, al-Qaʾim, his work articulated and synthesized views previously put forward by the cadre of religious scholars who had supported al-Qadir. Unlike the carefully argued religious treatises of predecessors such as al-Baqillani and Abu Mansur al-Baghdadi, *al-Ahkam* reads more like a political manifesto in defense of the caliphate, best encapsulated in his opening statement: "The Imamate is established to succeed the position of prophecy in order to protect the faith and manage worldly affairs. And the conferring of the caliphate on someone who will undertake its tasks is a religious duty according to the consensus [of the scholars]."[11] This book, which H. A. R. Gibb suggests was written at the behest of the Abbasid caliph, makes no digression to political exemplars from the Sasanid period or the secular moral philosophy of Ibn al-Muqaffaʿ.[12] Al-Mawardi was out to defend the legitimacy of the caliph, and he did it in a way that borrowed a key term from Shiʿism – "Imam." Imam, for al-Mawardi, was not the gnostically inspired Imam of Shiʿism but the defender of Islamic rituals and the sharia, the necessary historical symbol of the community, and someone who decided matters in coordination with the *ʿulama* (*ahl al-hall waʾl-ʿaqd*). Al-Mawardi went further in recognizing the political rule of newly risen potentates in the outlying provinces, such as the Ghaznavids, whom he said could be recognized as *amir*s and sultans after gaining proper caliphal sanction. In his lucid exposition, al-Mawardi unabashedly "Sunnified" the term imam and created a partnership between the Imam/caliph and sultan, in a way that prefigured the coming alliance between the Abbasids and the Seljuks. That al-Qadir's successor was given the title al-Qaʾim – a regnal name laden with messianic connotations and once assumed by the second Fatimid caliph – shows determined effort by the Abbasids and the *ʿulama* to copy and coopt the ideological thrust of their Shiʿi rivals in North Africa.

Later, in his *Kitab al-Mustazhiri*, al-Ghazali would build on al-Mawardi's work by anchoring the caliph's legitimacy in *fiqh* (jurisprudence), and defining his necessary qualifications as *ʿilm* (religious

[11] al-Mawardi, *al-Ahkam al-Sultaniyya* (Beirut, 1985), 5.
[12] H. A. R. Gibb, "al-Mawardi's Theory of the Caliphate," in *Studies on the Civilization of Islam*, 152.

expertise), *ijtihad* (the ability to adduce sound opinions), and *waraʿ* (piety). In light of these arguments, a split clarified the divide between the spheres of authority of caliph and sultan.[13] It was not long after al-Mawardi's writings that the Abbasid caliphs increasingly started to use the term "Imam" to refer to themselves, which, along with Commander of the Faithful, became the standard titles of the Abbasids on Islamic coinage. The term "caliph," common on early Abbasid coinage, apparently was seen as insufficient to convey the pretensions of the office or to provide an answer to the sophisticated claims of rivals from Shiʿi Islam. In fact, around this time the Abbasid court secretaries introduced a new formula in the chancery referring to the caliph – "the most sacred, prophetic presence" – which became henceforth one of the most common ways the caliph was addressed in official correspondence until the end of the Abbasid caliphate.[14]

Resisting pressure from individual Sunni sects to exclude rivals, al-Qadir followed an ecumenical approach, including both Hanbalis and Hanafis in his circle of support, and tried to rise above their polemical disputes. He also improved his chances for success as he provided a role for the Shiʿa in his new vision of Abbasid leadership. Having narrowed his sectarian dispute down to Ismaʿilism, he reached out to representative leaders of Twelver Shiʿism, such as al-Sharif al-Radi and al-Murtada, whom he appointed on occasion as court judges for public grievances (*mazalim*), as leaders of the pilgrimage caravan to Mecca, and as envoys to the Fatimid and Ghaznavid courts.[15] A Shiʿi voice supportive of the caliph probably contrived a story that showed the fourth caliph, Ali, prophesying al-Qadir's accession to the caliphate. According to this account, when the Buyids were about to remove al-Taʾiʿ from the caliphal office, al-Qadir had a dream of seeing Ali across a bridge over a river as wide as the Tigris. Ali reportedly then asked al-Qadir if he would like to accede to the caliphate. When the latter said yes, Ali's hand stretched across the bridge to help al-Qadir cross over, after which Ali told him to be kind to his descendants (i.e. the Alids) when he became caliph.[16] According to al-Qadir, it was almost

[13] E. I. J. Rosenthal, *Political Thought in Medieval Islam* (Cambridge, 1968), 39–40.

[14] Mez, *The Renaissance of Islam*, 87.

[15] Teresa Bernheimer, *The Alids: The First Family of Islam, 750–1200* (Edinburgh, 2013), 53.

[16] Ibn al-Athir, *al-Kamil*, 9:81.

immediately after this vision that he received news of being selected for the caliphate.

In a world with few options for the caliphate, al-Qadir was probably also helped to gain support by the increasing reports about the eccentric behavior of the Fatimid caliph al-Hakim (r. 996–1021), which no doubt made al-Qadir's bookishness seem a preferable alternative. But the Abbasids were helped above all by the meteoric rise of a geographically distant ally in the form of the Ghaznavid dynasty (r. 366–582/977–1187), who were frantically searching for political legitimacy. Former Turkic soldiers in the service of the Samanids, the Ghaznavids supplanted their former masters, took over the region of Khurasan, and established their capital at Ghazna, a strategically located town some 80 miles south of Kabul on the road leading to Qandahar. Ghazna grew into a military base and a magnet for art and culture that provided patronage to the renowned al-Biruni (d. 440/1048) and Firdawsi (d. 411/1025).

The Ghaznavids copied the Samanids in being ardent Sunnis and in showing loyalty to the caliphate in Baghdad, but went beyond using the title *amir* to claim that of sultan, and aggressively initiated wars in India. In a deliberate effort to contrast with the Buyids, who had conspicuously failed to defend the Islamic frontier in Asia Minor, the Ghaznavids postured as the revivers of jihad campaigns, once considered the prerogative of the caliph. News of their sudden expansion into India, starting in 392/1002, and their professing the official Sunni ideology espoused by the caliph in Baghdad, resonated in Iraq as reviving the previous empire of the caliphs. Ghaznavid rule took over Samanid lands in Khurasan (with Bukhara and Samarqand captured in 389/999), and stretched west, severely weakening the Buyids with the conquest of Rayy in 420/1029. Indirectly taunting the Buyids, al-Qadir had the letters of Mahmud of Ghazna (r. 388–421/998–1030), which announced his conquests in India, read out publicly in the Baghdad mosques, and he bestowed on him titles such as Yamin al-Dawla wa Amin al-Milla ("right hand of the state and trustee of the faith") and Nasir Amir al-Mu'minin ("helper of the Commander of the Faithful"). An embassy sent from Baghdad arrived in Balkh, where it presented items that all future aspirants to the sultanate would seek: new honorific title (*laqab*), a special vestment (*khil'a*), and, above all, a diploma of investiture, proclaiming the prince's relationship to the caliph in a highly visible setting to all the administrative and military officials.

After the ceremony, members of the ruler's staff would themselves receive new ranks and honors in light of the rise in the position of their Ghaznavid sovereign.[17] This formula of Abbasid embassy and ceremonial coronation would be repeated with a myriad of dynasties, including the Seljuks, Zangids, Ayyubids, Ghurids, and the Delhi sultans.

The Seljuks

In this fast-changing environment of the eleventh century, yet another new source of support for the caliph was about to emerge, with the coming of the Seljuks from the Transoxanian frontier. Whereas the Ghazanvid Turks were army officers who rebelled against their Persian and Samanid paymasters, the Seljuks were a nomadic wave of Oghuz Turkmen who were being pushed west by environmental factors – a climate change in Central Asia, recently referred to as "the Big Chill" by Richard Bulliet – that set them searching for better pasture lands for their herds.[18] Iraq had been on the receiving end of other nomadic migrations before, mainly Arab and Kurdish tribal groupings in the late tenth century, such as with the movement of the Banu Khafaja to the area of Kufa, Asad to Hilla, 'Uqayl to Wasit, and Marwanids to Diyarbakir, but the arrival of the Seljuk Turks was an entirely new phenomenon. The Arabian tribal upsurges in Syria and Iraq between 950 and 1050 succeeded at best in forming local statelets that espoused Shi'i sympathies to varying degrees, and some of these, such as the Mirdasids, Marwanids, Numayrids, and Shaddadids, often served as clients to the Byzantines in the early eleventh century.[19] The Turkic migrations, in contrast, consisted of a new ethnic group which arrived in the Middle East as a massive wave that fanned out across the Iranian

---

[17] Gavin Hambly, "From Baghdad to Bukhara, from Ghazna to Delhi: The khil'a Ceremony in the Transmission of Kingly Pomp and Circumstance," in *Robes and Honor: The Medieval World of Investiture*, ed. Stewart Gordon (New York, 2001), 200–201.

[18] R. W. Bulliet, *Cotton, Climate, and Camels in Early Islamic Iran: A Moment in World History* (New York, 2009). Bulliet's findings have been amplified in Ronnie Ellenblum's book, *The Collapse of the Eastern Mediterranean: Climate Change and the Decline of the East* (Cambridge, 2013), 34–37, 64–65.

[19] Kennedy, *The Prophet and the Age of the Caliphates*, 250–308; Warren Treadgold, *A History of the Byzantine State and Society* (Stanford, 1997), 585, 587, 594.

world until it reached northern Iraq and Asia Minor. The new migrants brought an aspiration to build a wider kingdom, and, in spite of their nomadic Central Asian roots, were ready to acculturate to the urban Iranian lifestyle, and systems of administration. The cities of Marw, Nishapur, Rayy, Isfahan, and Hamadan provided them with different bases where this process of Turkic–Iranian synthesis unfolded.

Among the family and clan federations of the Turkmen communities being pushed west were the Seljuks, who, especially those led by Tughril and Chaghri, edged out rival contenders. The Ghaznavids, perhaps like the Khwarazm shahs who later took the brunt of the Mongol invasions, were caught by surprise by the size and military skill of the Seljuk invaders, and were quickly defeated in 431/1040 at the battle of Dandanqan, named after a fortress located some 30 miles south of Marw. Why and when the Turkmen converted to Islam remains unclear, but they seem to have done so en masse and to the Sunni branch of Islam, perhaps to facilitate their takeover of Khurasan. The Buyids, who had always seemed too big for their shoes, found their authority rapidly dwindling to the Fars region, and they crumbled in the face of the Seljuk challenge. In an ironic twist, the Abbasid al-Qa'im had to use his leverage as caliph to try and gain guarantees from the Seljuks for the safety of the last Buyid, al-Malik al-Rahim (r. 1048–1055).[20]

Unlike the Buyids, the Seljuks entered the fray of Islamic politics on a platform of defending Sunni Islam and the legitimacy of the Abbasid caliph. They took on the Ghaznavid model of rule, adopting the title of sultan, but unlike the Ghaznavids directed their war effort against the Fatimids, pledging to conquer Syria and Egypt, with Tughril declaring an intention to go on pilgrimage to Mecca, which meant that he wanted to take it from Fatimid control. Clearly the propaganda of al-Qadir had recruited an important follower in the anti-Isma'ili campaign. In those initial years of expansion in western Iran, Tughril's military roamed as far as Asia Minor in 1051 and 1054, and he had enough leverage with the Byzantines to make the emperor Constantine IX refurbish a mosque that had fallen into ruin in Constantinople, and allow the pronouncement of the Friday *khutba* in this mosque in favor of the Abbasid rather than the Fatimid caliph.[21]

[20] al-Subki, *Tabaqat al-Shafi'iyya al-Kubra*, ed. A. M. al-Hilw (Cairo, 1966), 5:249.
[21] Romilly Jenkins, *Byzantium: The Imperial Centuries, AD 610–1071* (London, 1966), 371; Ibn Muyassar, *al-Muntaqa min Akhbar Misr*, ed. Ayman Fu'ad

The transition from the caliphate of al-Qadir to al-Qaʾim around this time happened with little fanfare. Al-Qaʾim, who was thirty years old when he acceded to the caliphate, shows a seamless continuity with the policies of his father. Between them they reigned for eighty years, which lent stability to the image of the caliphal office. In an added step of assertiveness, al-Qaʾim appointed his own vizir, which had not been done since the caliphate came to be dominated by the Buyids,[22] and took another, less high-profile, economic step. In 427/1036 he forbade financial transactions that used the Fatimid dinar, and ordered the jurists to observe this ban in all contracts.[23] This must have stung the Fatimids, who waited for an opportunity to strike back. As Seljuk ambitions grew, Tughril wrote to Baghdad asking for its endorsement of his conquests in Iran, which he pledged to rule according to Islamic law. Al-Qaʾim interacted warmly with this rising figure, to whom he granted titles such as Malik al-Dawla ("king of the state") and Rukn al-Din ("pillar of the faith"), and sent the famous jurist al-Mawardi as an envoy to him on several occasions. At Jurjan in 435/1042–1043 Tughril reportedly went a distance of 4 farsakhs (12 miles) outside the city to receive al-Mawardi in honor of the letter he was carrying from the caliph,[24] and it was soon after, in 1045, that Tughril began to refer to himself on his coinage with the title sultan. Word of this Abbasid–Seljuk affinity and the revival of the Abbasid name probably encouraged the Zirid prince al-Muʿizz b. Badis in North Africa (Tunis) to switch his allegiance from the Fatimids to the Abbasids. In return, the Abbasid caliph sent to the Zirids of Qayrawan black banners in 435/1042–1043, along with an edict of investiture, which were conveyed via Constantinople to avoid Fatimid interception. The allegiance was later more strongly reaffirmed in 441/1049.[25]

Al-Qaʾim may have been happy to see the revival of Abbasid prestige and the acceptance by new powers of his religious authority within the frame of the sharia. But it was not lost on him that the recently converted Turks brought with them additional notions, rooted in Central Asian heritage and culture, that gave a heavenly mandate for the office of supreme leadership going beyond traditional Islamic views

Sayyid (Cairo, 1981), 14; Ibn Khallikan, *Wafayat al-Aʿyan*, ed. Ihsan ʿAbbas (Beirut, 1978), 5:66.

[22] Kennedy, *The Prophet and the Age of the Caliphates*, 243.
[23] Ibn al-Athir, *al-Kamil*, 9:452.   [24] Ibn al-Athir, *al-Kamil*, 9:522.
[25] Ibn al-Athir, *al-Kamil*, 9:522.

of the office of caliph.[26] Al-Qaʾim undoubtedly benefited from this mixing of Islamic and Turkic perceptions of leadership, but, as in Kipling's *The Man Who Would be King*, he let the strident gestures of reverence for his person grow and build up. The trend toward the mystical and the mythical in political construction would continue under later Abbasid caliphs, such as al-Nasir, who expanded the definition of Abbasid authority to encompass a new Sufi foundation.

When the Seljuks first arrived in Baghdad in 1055, their interest in Iraq was still tentative, as they remained focused on the Iranian regions. The nomadic Turkic tribes preferred the region of Iran and Azerbayjan as suitable pasture lands for grazing their herds to the cramped conditions in Iraq.[27] But in another way, the loose confederative nature of power among the various branches and clans of the Seljuk family motivated Tughril to seek a closer association with the Abbasid caliphate in order to consolidate power under his leadership. For this purpose he went a step further, requesting a betrothal between the caliph and his niece, Arslan Khatun Khadija, which helped strengthen ties and increased the prospect that Seljuk leadership would be consolidated in Tughril's family branch. The fears that pushed Tughril toward taking this step were soon justified when he faced a challenge from his brother, Ibrahim Yinal, who put forward a claim to Seljuk leadership. Tughril was forced to withdraw his army from Baghdad to put down this challenge, while the Fatimids seized on the opportunity offered by the power vacuum in Baghdad, and incited a coup by al-Basasiri. The latter was a former Turkic general in Abbasid service who had grown disgruntled at the arrival of the Seljuks as a rival military power – an enterprise that he blamed on encouragement and planning by the caliph's chief minister, Ibn al-Muslima.[28] Having relocated to Mosul, al-Basasiri bided his time, and the opportunity came when the Fatimids encouraged him to use his political ties to seize power in Baghdad and have the Abbasid caliph kidnapped and taken to Cairo. The Fatimids were so optimistic that they had already chosen the palace where they were going to keep the Abbasid under house arrest.[29]

[26] Osman Turan, "The Ideal of World Domination among the Medieval Turks," *Studia Islamica* 4 (1960).

[27] A. C. S. Peacock, *The Great Seljuk Empire* (Edinburgh, 2015), 50–51, 224.

[28] Claude Cahen, "Ibn al-Muslima," *EI²*, 891.

[29] Marius Canard, "al-Basasiri," *EI²*, 1074.

This daredevil plan progressed very far, as both the caliph and his minister were in fact captured, with the caliph being sequestered in Haditha/Ana in the upper reaches of the Euphrates, and the minister handed over for a brutal execution by al-Basasiri. This Abbasid absence dragged on for the whole of 1058, as al-Basasiri declared the *khutba* in Baghdad for the Fatimid caliph, and controlled the reins of power in coordination with the 'Uqaylid tribal forces of Mosul. As this situation continued, however, and for unclear reasons – whether because of a change of heart or in light of a strong secret warning from Tughril[30] – al-Qa'im's 'Uqaylid jailers refused to hand him over to the Fatimids. It seems that initially everyone had expected Tughril to lose the fight against Ibrahim Yinal, but the intervention of Tughril's nephew, Alp Arslan, on his side – coming with fresh troops in just ten days from Sistan to Hamadan across arid lands and trackless desert – saved the day.[31] The fortunes of both sultan and caliph now changed, and the folly of taking hostage a caliph who had just been joined in matrimony to the Seljuk family became apparent, as Tughril came back resolved to reclaim Iraq and defend the caliph.

The episode was a close call that nearly finished off the Abbasid caliphate, but al-Qa'im made it back, and Seljuk troops spread out across Iraq and the northern Syria region to capture the person whom Tughril, according to Ibn al-Athir, called "that dog al-Basasiri" – probably frustration vented in light of the latter's reported encouragement of the Ibrahim Yinal revolt in the first place. Al-Basasiri was hunted down and killed, while the caliph was restored to his position in Baghdad, with no less a figure than Tughril himself holding the bridle of the caliph's mule as the latter rode back to the caliphal palace.[32] On this second visit by Tughril to Baghdad in 451/1059, the full scale of the Seljuk–Abbasid alliance became clearer. Holding a formal ceremony for the restoration of the caliphate to Baghdad, al-Qa'im welcomed Tughril, who for added flair arrived at the caliph's reception in a flotilla of boats up the Tigris, then disembarked and rode on horseback to where the caliph was seated on an elevated platform. There, in front of the assembled men of the state, Tughril bowed and kissed the hand of the caliph, and sat listening to an official read the caliph's address to

---

[30] Khatib al-Baghdadi, *Tarikh Baghdad*, 9:403.
[31] al-Husayni, *Zubdat al-Tawarikh, Akhbar al-Umara' wa'l-Muluk al-Saljuqiyya*, ed. Muhammad Nur al-Din (Beirut, 1986), 60–61.
[32] Ibn al-Athir, *al-Kamil*, 9:647–648; Khatib al-Baghdadi, *Tarikh Baghdad*, 9:400.

him and the assembly. "The Commander of the Faithful is thankful for your efforts, and is comforted by your presence," al-Qaʾim's official announced. "It is his command that you govern all the regions that God has bestowed on him, and that you take charge of managing the affairs of his subjects in accordance with the guidance of God. [The caliph] wishes that you appreciate the bounty bestowed on you, and that you spread justice and welfare among the subject population, and avoid transgression."[33] After this proclamation was read, Tughril was invested with two crowns, signifying sovereignty over both the Arabs and the ʿAjam (non-Arabs), robed with seven special vestments, girded with a sword, and awarded the titles Rukn al-Dawla ("pillar of the state") and King of the East and the West. And in an ironic footnote to these events, we learn from the miscellaneous news for 462/1069 that the Fatimid caliph al-Mustansir, who had tried to take al-Qaʾim to Cairo, sent his family to Baghdad to escape the widespread famine in Egypt.[34] The amount of money that the Fatimids had put into their attempt to overthrow the Abbasids was said to have been so great that it spelled the beginning of the decline of the Fatimid state.[35]

Al-Qaʾim's religious aura grew beyond that of al-Qadir because his rescue from capture by the Fatimids was viewed as near miraculous. In an age when Sufism was on the rise, al-Qaʾim's image also took on an ascetic dimension among biographers, who described him abandoning the comforts of life, sleeping on his prayer mat, refusing even a pillow, and vowing to avoid the use of violence. Chroniclers noted that while Baghdad had suffered a drought for months, when al-Qaʾim returned to Baghdad it rained for thirty consecutive days, with the public attributing this bounty to the caliph's return.[36] Another boost for al-Qaʾim came on the battlefield when the next Seljuk sultan, Alp Arslan (r. 1063–1072), decisively defeated the Byzantines in 463/1071 at the battle of Manzikert and had the emperor, Romanus Diogenes, taken prisoner. This opened the way for the Seljuks to expand farther west, as one of their commanders, Atsiz, wrested control of Jerusalem from the Fatimids in the same year, and restored mention of the Abbasid caliph's name to the pulpits of the mosques of Jerusalem. Alp Arslan was an intrepid warrior who never had an opportunity to visit Baghdad, but it was during the reign of his son, Malikshah (r. 1072–1092), that the

---

[33] Ibn al-Athir, *al-Kamil*, 9:634.   [34] Ibn Khallikan, *Wafayat al-Aʿyan*, 5:230.
[35] Ibn al-Muyassar, *al-Muntaqa*, 21.   [36] Ibn al-Athir, *al-Kamil*, 9:648.

Seljuk state became more formally organized, with its main capital established at Isfahan, with Baghdad becoming the winter capital. Seljuk rule also expanded further under Malikshah, reaching the regions of the Hijaz and Yemen, which he seized from the Fatimids. The economic fallout from the Seljuk expansion west, especially with their takeover of Syria, dealt a serious blow to the Fatimids, who suffered a loss of important tax revenues as well as a disruption in their trade routes.[37]

The main architect of Seljuk political stability in this period was the famous Iranian vizir Nizam al-Mulk, who had served Alp Arslan before, but whose skills shone brightest in Malikshah's reign. Nizam al-Mulk, the first real organizer of the Seljuk state, loomed almost large as the Barmakids at the court of Harun al-Rashid, especially with his policy of encouraging mercantile and agricultural prosperity and extensive building projects for caravanserais. The vizir strongly advocated a policy of alliance between the Seljuk state and the *'ulama*, and consistently fought the lethal branch of Isma'ili Shi'ism known as the Nizaris, or Assassins. Ancient principles of the Persian monarchy were revived in Nizam al-Mulk's famous mirror for princes, *Siyasatnameh*. But perhaps his greatest single achievement with implications for the caliphate was the invention of the educational institution known as the madrasa.[38]

The madrasa, or Nizamiyya, as it came to be known in honor of the vizir, was a college of higher education in various fields related to Islamic learning, including *fiqh*, hadith, exegesis, and linguistics. It propagated what Nizam al-Mulk and a certain circle of scholars considered orthodox and correct doctrine (Sunni, and mainly Shafi'i), and as such the institution was a vehicle for responding to challenges from other sects, most notably the Isma'ili Shi'i ideology of the Fatimids propagated from the al-Azhar Mosque in Cairo. The madrasa was a residential college with staff and students on the payroll of the Seljuk state, and it graduated students with a training that qualified

---

[37] Amina Elbendary, "The Worst of Times: Crisis Management and *Al-Shidda Al-Uzma*," in *Money, Land and Trade: An Economic History of the Muslim Mediterranean*, ed. Nelly Hanna (London, 2002).

[38] For opposing takes on Nizam al-Mulk, cf. Neguin Yavari, *The Future of Iran's Past: Nizam al-Mulk Remembered* (Oxford, 2018) against a less sanguine view of the minister in Durand-Guédy, "What does the History of Isfahan tell us about Iranian Society?" and Carole Hillenbrand, "Nizam al-Mulk: A Maverick Vizier?" in *The Age of the Seljuqs*, ed. Herzig and Stewart.

them to continue in religious study, but more importantly groomed them to be the next class of civil servants and state officials in different corners of the empire. Branches of the Nizamiyya were founded in Mosul, Basra, Balkh, Marw, Herat, Isfahan, and Amul (near Jurjan), but the concentration of these colleges in eastern Iran (Khurasan) is particularly conspicuous and underscores the longstanding prominence of this region as a citadel of Sunni culture, especially when contrasted with western Iran (Azerbayjan), where heterodox beliefs were more common.[39]

Leading scholars of the time were invited to teach and direct various madrasas. Nizam al-Mulk invited Abu Ishaq al-Shirazi to teach in the most famous of these madrasa branches, the Nizamiyya of Baghdad, founded in 457/1065 (later followed in 484/1091 by a thirty-one-year-old al-Ghazali), while in Nishapur the vizir appointed the famous Abu'l-Maʿali al-Juwayni, al-Ghazali's teacher. In parallel to administrative centralization, the madrasa helped establish conformity in religious doctrine, and loyalty to religious officials. One gets a sense of this from the comment that Abu Ishaq al-Shirazi once made: "I travelled from Baghdad to Khurasan and I found in every town or village on my way the position of *qadi*, *mufti*, or *khatib* held by a former pupil of mine or by one of my followers."[40] It was on this journey to Nishapur in 475/1083, which Abu Ishaq undertook as envoy of the caliph al-Muqtadi to the Seljuk sultan Malikshah – to arrange the betrothal of the caliph to the sultan's daughter – that people reportedly came out to greet him along the way and touched his stirrup to gain his blessing.[41] Since Abu Ishaq was the caliph's envoy, such actions easily mixed reverence for him as a scholar with reverence for the caliph.

By far the most prestigious of these madrasas was the Nizamiyya of Baghdad. Appointment to the faculty of this school was considered a momentous event, and required confirmation by the caliph.[42] Ibn Jubayr, who visited Baghdad in 580/1185, attended prayers at the Baghdad Nizamiyya, and considered it the most splendid of the

---

[39] C. E. Bosworth, "The Political and Dynastic History of the Iranian World (AD 1000–1217)," in *CHIran*, vol. 5: *The Saljuq and Mongol Periods*, ed. J. A. Boyle (Cambridge, 1968), 72.

[40] A. L. Tibawi, "Origin and Character of the Madrasa," *BSOAS* 25 (1962), 236 (citing Subki, *Tabaqat al-Shafiʿiyya*, 3:89); al-Asnawi, *Tabaqat al-Shafiʿiyya* (Beirut, 2001), 2:7.

[41] Ibn al-Athir, *al-Kamil*, 10:125; Bosworth, "Political and Dynastic History," 75.

[42] Mackensen, "Four Great Libraries," 294.

thirty-odd colleges of east Baghdad.[43] Its library harbored a great collection of books donated by patrons such as Nizam al-Mulk himself, and later by scholars such as Ibn al-Najjar (d. 643/1245), who followed a common trend of professors who willed their books to a madrasa library. The Baghdad Nizamiyya remained a powerhouse of learning for generations, and graduated many students who flourished in later life, such as al-ʿImad al-Isfahani, Saladin's biographer; Ibn ʿAsakir, the historian of Damascus; Ibn al-ʿArabi, the jurist of Seville; Muhammad b. Abdallah (the future guide of the Almohads in North Africa known as al-Mahdi b. Tumart); and the Iranian poet Saʿdi of Shiraz. The college continued to thrive even after the more modern al-Mustansiriyya was built nearby.

While it is not clear whether the Abbasid caliph was involved in Nizam al-Mulk's general plan of the madrasa system, there can be no doubt that the vizir's vision was built on the ideological foundations established by al-Qadir and al-Qaʾim, and translated these initial caliphal attempts at standardization of Sunni beliefs into a blueprint for an empire-wide process of centralization, thereby ensuring the loyalty of the empire's subjects. Alongside his introduction of the madrasa system, Nizam al-Mulk was consistent about trying to maintain harmonious relations between the Seljuk sultan and the caliph, earning for himself the title Radiy Amir al-Muʾminin ("succor of the Commander of the Faithful"). The celebrated vizir cautioned Malikshah against any negative treatment of the Abbasid caliph, but it was also clear from the way Nizam al-Mulk took the initiative in religious affairs that he was working on transferring more authority from the caliph to the sultan. Al-Ghazali maintained a separation between the two offices, caliph and sultan, in his writings, and merely described facts on the ground when he stated: "We consider that the function of the caliphate is contractually assumed by that person of the Abbasid house, who is entrusted with it, and that the function of government in the various lands is carried out by means of sultans, who owe allegiance to the caliphate."[44] This view, mellowed by Ghazali's long residence in Baghdad, was still compatible with al-Mawardi's separation between the offices of Imam and *amir*, but al-Juwayni (d. 499/1105), who resided in distant Nishapur, was more hardline in the

---

[43] Ibn Jubayr, *Rihlat Ibn Jubayr* (Beirut, 1964), 296.
[44] Quoted in H. A. R. Gibb, "Some Considerations on the Sunni Theory of the Caliphate," in *Studies on the Civilization of Islam*, 142–143.

way he dismissed even the need for the office of caliph in light of the existence of that of sultan.[45] Since he upheld the sharia and waged war on behalf of the faith, al-Juwayni viewed the tasks of the caliph as fulfilled by the sultan. Reflecting the confidence of the *'ulama* class, he completely ignored the traditional view regarding the special blessings the Prophet once gave the Abbasids or the well-known assumption that the caliph must come from the Prophet's wider clan of Quraysh. While al-Juwayni's radical view remained on the fringe compared to al-Ghazali's, it was a signal of things to come with the Ilkhanids and the Ottomans, who ruled confidently as sultans without any attempt to revive a separate caliphate.

With its wider geographic realm, the Seljuk sultanate exceeded previous successor states to the Abbasids in the east, such as the Tahirids, Buyids, and Ghaznavids, but it also transformed Islamic culture and the region of the Middle East in a more fundamental way. The legacy of their sultanate as an ally and eventually heir to the caliphate and as defender of Sunni law would form the bedrock of later empires, such as the Ottomans, and the Seljuk imprint on the Islamic state would only come to an end in the modern period with World War I.[46]

The Conflict between Caliph and Sultan

The organizing vision of Nizam al-Mulk brought stability to both the Seljuk and Abbasid states. The Abbasids benefited from his ideological promotion of Sunnism, while the Seljuks adapted to the newly revived Persian principles of administration and government. The Abbasids did not rule politically in the shadow of Seljuk tutelage any more than they had under Buyid control, but the relation of caliph to sultan became vastly improved under the early Seljuks. As early as Tughril's reign, the Seljuks tried to establish close ties to the Abbasid dynasty through marriage links. The first came when al-Qa'im married Tughril's niece Arslan Khatun Khadija in 448/1056. Tughril himself asked to wed the caliph's daughter in 454/1062, and this caused tension because it went against the custom of refusing to marry an Abbasid princess to a foreigner, but the crisis was defused when Tughril died soon after

---

[45] Wael Hallaq, "Caliphs, Jurists, and Saljuqs in the Political Thought of al-Juwayni," *The Muslim World* 74 (1984); al-Juwayni, *al-Ghiyathi: Ghiyath al-Umam* (Jeddah, 2011), 415–436, 466–471.

[46] Frye, *The Golden Age of Persia*, 224.

drafting the marriage contract, and Alp Arslan returned the Abbasid princess to Baghdad. Al-Qaʾim then offered his son and successor, al-Muqtadi, in marriage to Sifri Khatun, daughter of Alp Arslan, in 464/ 1071.[47]

Al-Muqtadi's reign provides a sketch of the typical ups and downs in relations between caliph and sultan. When Malikshah acceded to power he extended Seljuk authority over Aleppo, Jazira, and much of Syria with a clear interest in regaining Abbasid territories formerly lost to the Fatimids. Malikshah entered Baghdad in 479/1086, accompanied by Nizam al-Mulk, and affirmed his piety by visiting the tombs of Abu Hanifa, Ahmad b. Hanbal, Maʿruf al-Karkhi, and the Alid Imam Musa al-Kazim. The next year al-Muqtadi married the daughter of Malikshah, to the great satisfaction of the bride's mother, the ambitious Turkan Khatun.[48] This wedding between the thirty-two-year-old caliph and the Seljuk princess took place when Seljuk power was at its peak, and generated a lot of interest. Ibn al-Athir provides a description of the journey of the bride from her father's palace to the Abbasid one in Baghdad that highlights the huge expense involved in the preparations and the sense of anticipation by those monitoring it:

In Muharram [8 April–7 May 1087] the dowry of Sultan Malikshah's daughter was transferred to the Caliphal Palace on 130 camels, magnificently clothed with Byzantine brocades. Most of the loads consisted of gold and silver and three howdahs. The dowry was also borne on 72 mules, draped in various sorts of regal brocades, whose bells and harness were of gold and silver. On six of them were twelve silver chests, containing jewels and finery that were beyond price. Preceding the mules were 33 horses of excellent stock, whose stirrups were of gold encrusted with various gems. There was also a large cradle, much of it gold.

Before the dowry rode Saʿd al-Dawla Goharaʾin, the amir Bursuq and others, over whom the inhabitants of the Muʾalla Canal scattered dinars and fabrics. The sultan had gone from Baghdad to hunt. Later the Caliph sent the Vizier Abu Shujaʿ to the Lady Turkan, the sultan's wife, preceded by about 300 processional candles and the like number of flambeaux. In the Harem there was not a single shop that did not light up a lantern or two, or even more. With Zafar, his eunuch servant, the caliph sent a litter, the most beautiful that had ever been seen. The vizier said to the Lady Turkan, "Our lord and master, the Commander of the Faithful says, 'God commands you to consign what you hold in trust to its worthy recipient.'" He has granted

[47] Ibn al-Athir, *al-Kamil*, 9:70–71. [48] Ibn al-Athir, *al-Kamil*, 9:160–161.

permission for the transfer of your treasure to his palace." She replied, "To hear is to obey." Nizam al-Mulk and the notables ranked below him in the sultan's state came, each of them with many candles and flambeaux. The wives of the great emirs and of those of lower rank came, each one of them separately with her entourage and her show of pomp, preceded by processional candles and flambeaux, all of which were carried by mounted men.

Then behind all came the princess, the sultan's daughter in a covered litter, all gold and gems. Two hundred Turkish maid servants encircled the litter, wonderfully mounted. Thus she proceeded to the Caliphal Palace. It was a sight to be remembered, the like of which had never been seen in Baghdad.

On the next day, the caliph invited the sultan's emirs to a banquet, which he ordered to be prepared. It is reported that 40,000 *mann*s of sugar were used. The caliph gave robes of honour to all of them and to all of any note in the army. He sent robes to the Lady wife of the sultan and to all the royal ladies. After that the sultan returned from his hunting.[49]

Relations between the Abbasids and the Seljuks seemed at their best here, and the next year the Seljuk princess gave birth to a male child, who was named Abu'l-Fadl Ja'far. This event awakened a new dimension of ambition in Malikshah, who now hoped to see this child designated as the future successor to the caliphate in place of an older son of al-Muqtadi, the future al-Mustazhir, who was already slated for the succession. Nizam al-Mulk had always advised that the caliph must be kept content, but now, with the new baby, he got more than he had bargained for in terms of harmony between the Abbasid and Seljuk houses. There was clearly no stopping Malikshah from changing all the rules of the game, and especially with added incitement by Turkan Khatun.

In broad daylight, and while surrounded by his entourage, Nizam al-Mulk was assassinated in 495/1092 by an agent of the Nizari Isma'ili sect of the Assassins. This was their signature style of attack, showing a daring meant to intimidate their political opponents, but in this particular case it appeared that the planning may have been done with some inside help. Aside from those jealous of his achievements and power, Nizam al-Mulk had built up a list of enemies for himself at court, including Turkan, and possibly Malikshah himself, who wanted a freer hand in doing what he wanted. Malikshah now found himself

---

[49] Ibn al-Athir, *al-Kamil*, trans. D. S. Richards as *Annals of the Saljuq Turks: Selections from al-Kamil fi'l-Ta'rikh of 'Izz al-Din Ibn al-Athir* (London, 2002), 232–233. A *mann* equaled roughly 2 pounds.

free to act with impunity against the caliph, and pressed to have the four-year-old Abu'l-Fadl put in place of the fourteen-year-old al-Mustazhir as heir apparent. As the pressure grew, Malikshah gave the caliph an ultimatum to leave Baghdad permanently for either Mecca or Medina. The caliph tried to delay for a month at first, but the sultan refused to grant him more than ten days. As fate would have it, the sultan died during the ten-day grace period. This increased the aura of good fortune (*karama*) around a caliph already respected for his religious image, but the event only delayed a coming confrontation. For the time being turmoil was averted, but looking forward the Abbasids were going to face difficulties not just with one Seljuk state in the absolute but with a myriad of its princes and potential successors.

Although the Seljuk state benefited from the ideological cohesion that Islam provided, and its bureaucratic institutions functioned well according to the guidance of Persian governing principles, it suffered from a key flaw – its lack of a clear line of dynastic succession. Turkic society did not seem to have a binding system in this regard, and agreements on succession were rarely durable in the face of energetic contenders for power. When Malikshah died, the field was opened for rivalry amongst his four young children, each of whom attracted a different faction of court and military supporters, and civil war raged for the next twelve years. The caliphs did not know whom to back amongst the Seljuks, and just tried to support whoever was closest to Baghdad – with a rare instance occurring in 498/1104 when two contending Seljuk claimants arrived in Baghdad at the same time, and while the *khutba* was made for Muhammad b. Malikshah on the west side, it was made for the infant Malikshah b. Barqyaruq on the east side, and with the preacher of the al-Mansur Mosque standing neutral and simply making the Friday blessings general, stating, "We ask God to improve the government of the world!"[50] Al-Mustazhir's reign encapsulates this tense balance. As usual, and in order to strengthen ties, the caliph tended to offer new titles of honor. Muhammad Tapar b. Malikshah was given the title Ghiyath al-Dunya wa'l-Din ("helper of the people and the faith")[51] in 492/1098, and fortunately for the caliph the latter eventually came out the victor in a struggle with Barqyaruq, and reunified the realm in 1105. Muhammad Tapar held the title al-Sultan al-Mu'azzam ("the great sultan"), while his brother Sanjar

---

[50] Ibn al-Athir, *al-Kamil*, 10:386.   [51] Ibn al-Athir, *al-Kamil*, 10:288–289.

governed in Khurasan with the lesser title Malik al-Mashriq ("king of the east").[52] The caliph al-Mustazhir cultivated cordial ties with the new Seljuk sultan, who receives a favorable representation in the sources, and al-Mustazhir married Turkan Khatun II, Muhammad's sister, in 504/1110. On a later visit in 510/1116 the sultan stayed all year in Baghdad, and on his departure the caliph gave him a Qur'an (*mushaf*), a banner, and – by his own request – some vestments that the caliph had once worn. In those years al-Mustazhir seems also to have acted for a while as a mediator between warring Seljuk princes. The caliph, who was only sixteen years old when he acceded to power, carefully managed his position under various pressures.

Anxiety about the outcome of the Seljuk succession notwithstanding, the social climate of Baghdad seems to have been prosperous in al-Mustazhir's reign. His wedding is described as a period of elaborate festivity in Baghdad,[53] and some narrators state that the days of this caliph's reign were like "days of joyous holiday."[54] This is perhaps best reflected by al-Mustazhir's order of the construction of a wall around the palace in 488/1095; the occasion quickly turned into a carnival, where professionals from different neighborhoods and craftsmen flaunted their own flags, animal emblems, and musical instruments and tunes.[55] It almost seems ironically prescient that while Islamic society was building a wall around its historic center in Baghdad, in the same year but only weeks apart, a world away in the Latin West, the Crusades were brewing. The pious were gathering to heed the call of Pope Urban II at the Council of Clermont to mount the First Crusade against the Islamic East and "enter upon the road to the Holy Sepulchre," to "wrest that land ... that floweth with milk and honey."[56]

Relations between Sunnis and Shi'a in al-Mustazhir's reign are generally described as peaceful, and even friendly,[57] and a Jewish traveler from Spain, Benjamin of Tudela, who visited the city in 565/1169, also commented on the prosperity of non-Muslims. Although Baghdad had lost much of its glitter by that time, Benjamin paints a picture of a city of splendor and cosmopolitan

[52] Bosworth, "Political and Dynastic History," 135.
[53] Ibn al-Jawzi, *al-Muntazam*, 9:155–166.   [54] Ibn al-Athir, *al-Kamil*, 10:535.
[55] Ibn al-Jawzi, *al-Muntazam*, 17:16.
[56] Edward Peters, *The First Crusade* (Philadelphia, 1970), 3.
[57] Ibn al-Athir, *al-Kamil*, 10:469–470.

life. He describes the caliph's palace in some detail, and the caliph's strong ties with the exilarch, the Babylonian head of the Jewish diaspora, known in Arabic as *ra's al-jalut* (Heb. *rosh ha-golah*), believed to be descended from the biblical King David, and adding that the caliph was well versed in the Torah and even knew how to read and write Hebrew:

> Baghdad is the great city and the royal residence of the Caliph Emir al-Muminin al-Abbasi of the family of Mohammed. He is at the head of the Mohammedan religion, and all the kings of Islam obey him; he occupies a position similar to the Pope over the Christians. He has a palace in Baghdad three miles in extent, wherein is a great park with all varieties of trees, fruit bearing and otherwise, and all manner of animals. The whole is surrounded by a wall, and in the park there is a lake whose water is fed by the river.
>
> In Baghdad there are about 40,000 Jews, and they dwell in security, prosperity and honor under the great Caliph; and among them are the great sages, the heads of Academies engaged in the study of the law. In this city there are ten Academies. [Benjamin then lists the names of rabbis in charge of these academies, and mentions the existence of twenty-eight synagogues]. And at the head of them all is Daniel, the son of Hisdai ... The Jews call him, "Our Lord, Head of the Captivity [of all Israel]" ... And every fifth day when he goes to pay a visit to the great Caliph, horsemen, Gentiles as well as Jews, escort him, and heralds proclaim in advance, "Make way before our Lord, the son of David, as is due unto him."
>
> The city of Baghdad is twenty miles in circumference, situated in a land of palms, gardens, and plantations. People come thither with merchandise from all lands. Wise men live there, philosophers who know all manner of wisdom, and magicians expert in all manner of witchcraft.[58]

It seems unlikely that Benjamin would have gained access to the Abbasid palace to provide such a detailed description, but he made it seem as if he did. His tendency to veer toward legend is evident when he claims that the caliph "only leaves his palace once a year." According to a recent analyst of his account, Benjamin deliberately sought to glorify Baghdad as the world's metropolis as a backdrop to describing the orderly and privileged situation of the Jewish population in Iraq. The

---

[58] Benjamin of Tudela, *The Itinerary of Benjamin of Tudela: Travels in the Middle Ages*, trans. A. Asher et al. (New York, 1983), 95–102.

overall purpose was to employ "Abbasid Iraq as a foil of crusader Palestine," where the situation of Judaism was bleak.[59]

Still, Benjamin of Tudela's depiction of Baghdad's society underscores a world of pious connectivity across cultures. It reached outside Baghdad to shared places of pilgrimage, such as a shrine located 20 miles south of Hilla, attributed to a prophet mentioned in the Qur'an (Dhu'l-Kifl), which remains a site of reverence. Jews identified the location as the shrine of the prophet Ezekiel, and competed with Muslims for the honorific task of caring for the shrine. While Islam was influenced by Judaism in this latter case, it happened in the other direction as well. Judaism's increasing attention to the elaboration of a genealogy attributed to the exilarch showing descent from King David, for example, has recently been shown as having developed, starting in the tenth century, under the influence of the Islamic definition of the *niqaba* (leadership) in the Hashimite family. The process emulated the elaboration of the office of *naqib al-ashraf* (marshal) for the Alid and Abbasid branches of the family.[60]

Beyond the frame of the twelfth century, it may be worth also drawing attention to the fact that Judaism underwent its major moments of intellectual and cultural formation, prior to the modern period, under Abbasid rule. Although the foggy pre-Abbasid period already knew the institution of the rabbinic academy and the discussions of the oral law that went along with it, Islamic society in general – and Baghdad in particular – opened new horizons of urbanization and cosmopolitanism that transformed Jewish society during what has been termed a "bourgeois revolution."[61] After a slow beginning in the ninth century, when Nestorian Christians dominated elite positions as translators, courtiers, bankers, and physicians, from the tenth century onward Jews gradually participated in the pace of international trade, which further strengthened the centrality of the rabbinic academies of Iraq as the reference point for religious interpretation.[62] The Abbasids recognized two leaderships in Jewish culture, that of the aforementioned

[59] Martin Jacobs, *Reorienting the East: Jewish Travelers to the Medieval Muslim World* (Philadelphia, 2014), 124–132.

[60] Bernheimer, *The Alids*, 89; Arnold Franklin, *This Noble House: Jewish Descendants in the Islamic East* (Philadelphia, 2012).

[61] S. D. Goitein, *Jews and Arabs: Their Contacts through the Ages* (New York, 1974), 144.

[62] M. Ben-Sasson, "Inter-Communal Relations in the Geonic Period," in *The Jews of Medieval Islam*, ed. Daniel Frank (Leiden, 1992), 26.

exilarch and the rabbinic (Geonim), which provided expert legal opinion. A third stream, that of the Karaites (those who emphasize the Bible to the exclusion of the oral commentaries of the rabbis), however, soon developed under the influence of the Islamic thought of the Muʿtazila, and entered into a deep feud with rabbinic circles. Although Judaism had lived under Hellenistic rule in ancient times, it was only in the Islamic period that "Greek science and Greek methods of thinking," according to S. D. Goitein, "made their entrance into Jewish life through the gates of Arab-Muslim literature."[63] The influence of the Abbasid translation movement therefore found important disciples among Karaite thinkers, such as the tenth-century Yaʿqub al-Qirqisani (d. ca. 318/930) and the eleventh-century Yusuf al-Basir (*fl.* 428/1036), both of whom were based in Iraq. These were preceded by Dawud b. Marwan of Raqqa (known as al-Muqammis, d. ca. 900), who was the earliest known medieval Jewish philosopher.[64]

On the opposite side of the fence, Saʿid b. Yusuf al-Fayyumi, also known as Saadya Gaon (d. 331/942), became a leading voice in responding to the Karaites. Originally from Egypt, but settled in Baghdad, Fayyumi's contributions included a translation of the Pentateuch into Arabic and the argumentative treatise *The Book of Beliefs and Opinions*, in which he tried to reconcile reason and revelation. His use of *kalam* methods to defend Rabbanite traditionalism evokes a parallel with his contemporary, Abu'l-Hasan al-Ashʿari, who also tried to rationalize the views of Sunni orthodoxy through *kalam*. Saadya's book became a model for later Jewish philosophers, and was not superseded until the emergence of Maimonides (d. 1204), who took the refutation of the arguments of speculative theology to a new level.[65] Maimonides' *Guide of the Perplexed* was, like Saadya's work, written in Arabic, and shows Islamic influences from philosophers such as al-Farabi, Ibn Sina, and al-Ghazali's *Tahafut al-Falasifa*.[66] The highpoint in the acculturation of Jews with Islamic society was probably reached in the twelfth century, when it became relatively common to encounter

---

[63] Goitein, *Jews and Arabs*, 141.

[64] H. Ben-Shammai, "Jewish Thought in Iraq in the 10th Century," in *Judaeo-Arabic Studies*, ed. Norman Golb (Amsterdam, 1995); and H. A. Wolfson, *Repercussions of the Kalam in Jewish Philosophy* (Cambridge, MA, 1979).

[65] P. B. Fenton, "Saʿadya ben Yosef," *EI²*, 661–662.

[66] G. Vajda, "Ibn Maymun," *EI²*, 876–878. Even the title *Guide of the Perplexed* was apparently borrowed from an earlier usage in al-Ghazali's *Ihyaʾ ʿUlum al-Din*: Sarah Stroumsa, *Maimonides in His World* (Princeton, 2009), 25.

cases of Jewish converts to Islam, who maintained elements of their former heritage, and were still accepted in both worlds. The most prominent of these was the philosopher Abu'l-Barakat Hibat-allah al-Baghdadi (d. after 560/1165), who was physician to various caliphs and sultans.[67]

al-Mustarshid: The Martyr Caliph

In spite of Seljuk hegemony, the Abbasid caliphate continued to represent a focal point in the Islamic world. From far-off Maghreb, an emissary of the Almoravid Ali b. Yusuf b. Tashfin came to Baghdad in 498/1104 declaring allegiance to the Abbasids, announcing the adoption of the official Abbasid black for banners, and received the title Amir al-Muslimin wa Nasir Amir al-Mu'minin ("prince of the Muslims and helper of the Commander of the Faithful").[68] Almoravid coins struck in Seville in 503/1109 show allegiance to the "Commander of the Faithful," with a reference to "al-ʿAbbasi" (the Abbasid), lest there be any confusion regarding which caliph the Almoravids were rooting for, the Abbasid or Fatimid.[69] The caliph could confer political honors, but he could offer little tangible support to an embassy from Ibn ʿAmmar, the ruler of Tripoli, who came in 501/1107 pleading for help against the onslaught of the Crusades. The exhortations of the caliph to the sultan to do something regarding the Crusades did not entirely go unheeded, but whatever help Muhammad provided was undermined by the machinations of local Turkic chiefs and Atabegs (Tughtigin in Damascus, Ridwan of Aleppo, and Ilghazi of Mardin), who took advantage of the disorder to defend their local turfs and privileges.[70]

The relatively stable period of rule by Malikshah and his son, Muhammad, quickly unraveled after the latter's death in 1118. Sanjar b. Malikshah (d. 552/1157), the overlord of the Seljuk princes, was now recognized as the most senior Seljuk, but he remained based in

---

[67] S. Pines, "Hibat-allah al-Baghdadi," *EI²*, 111–112; Sarah Stroumsa, "On Jewish Intellectuals who Converted in the Early Middle Ages," in Frank, ed., *The Jews of Medieval Islam*.

[68] Ibn Taghribirdi, *al-Nujum al-Zahira*, 5:191.

[69] Heather Ecker, *Caliphs and Kings: The Art and Influence of Islamic Spain* (Washington, DC, 2004), 166.

[70] Carole Hillenbrand, *The Crusades: Islamic Perspectives* (Edinburgh, 2000), 78–79, 104–110.

the east at Marw (contrary to previous protocols that recognized the sultan as based in Iraq), from which he ruled for sixty years. Iraq was created as a Seljuk subkingdom in 513/1119, and almost immediately became an object of contention among Seljuk princes, who were all children of Muhammad b. Malikshah: Mahmud, Tughril, Saljuq shah and Mas'ud. Around the same time, the Seljuks increased the pace of granting fiefdoms, as they created the Atabeg system, in which they assigned certain cities and regions to trusted lieutenants, who were nominally tied to a Seljuk prince; in reality, however, the Atabegs themselves were the real power in the region. This added a new class of political actors as auxiliaries to the mosaic of rivalries. Mosul and Jazira were assigned to 'Imad al-Din Zangi, and Mardin and Mayyafariqin to Ilghazi b. Artuq in 515/1121. Each of these figures had once served the Seljuks in Baghdad in the position of *shihna* (the military prefect of the city), and their regional fiefs eventually evolved into independent states when Seljuk control weakened: the Zangids in Mosul, Aleppo and neighboring environs (1127–1251), and the Artuqids in Mardin (1102–1409).[71]

Sanjar tried to stay above the fray in the contention among Seljuk princes for control of Iraq. He had supported Mahmud and later Tughril, but he grudgingly agreed to let the assertive Mas'ud (r. 1134–1152) take over after them. Ironically, it was al-Mustarshid who had encouraged Mas'ud to put forward a bid for leadership in western Iran against Tughril after the death of Mahmud, but their relations quickly soured. The coming conflict between caliph and sultan was not inevitable, but with the rise of an assertive caliph and the ambitions of Mas'ud, it was only a matter of time before the two would clash. Al-Mustarshid made the mistake of getting entangled in the rivalries of the Seljuk princes, and misread them as permanent animosities, only to find them healing, and turning many of the Seljuk princes against him. Competition in the Seljuk system was common on the occasions of political succession, and it was almost a sport to figure out who had the toughest mettle to rally the support of princes and clans around him.[72] The new caliph had probably mistakenly compared the rivalries among the children of Muhammad b. Malikshah to those he

---

[71] Other Atabeg states included the Eldiguzids in Tabriz (1145–1225), the Salghurids in Shiraz (1148–1242), and the Ahmadilis in Maragheh (1122–1220).

[72] Peacock, *The Great Seljuk Empire*, 131.

had once witnessed in al-Mustazhir's reign between Malikshah's sons Barqyaruq and Muhammad, but the stakes of that earlier conflict were far higher than those among the children of Muhammad b. Malikshah, who in the end always deferred to Sanjar.

An additional problem for the caliph lay in the rogue politics of the Mazyadid tribal chieftain Dubays b. Sadaqa in the Shi'i area of Hilla, some 60 miles south of Baghdad. Al-Mustazhir had tried to coopt Dubays's father, Sadaqa, by granting him the title Malik al-'Arab ("king of the Arabs"). This, however, only emboldened the Mazyadids into seeking to expand their power at the expense of the caliph, and to open direct relations with the Seljuks in order to exercise greater political influence over central Iraq. Mazyadid loyalty to the caliph was always ambiguous, and they switched sides between caliph and sultan depending on their interests. During the attempted Fatimid coup against the caliph al-Qa'im in the 1050s, the Mazyadids had joined al-Basasiri in his plot against the caliph and the Seljuks. But to a greater extent in al-Mustarshid's reign, the chronicles represent the travails of the caliph with the Seljuks as a product of intrigue by Dubays b. Sadaqa, who first encouraged Tughril to defy the Seljuk Mahmud and lay a claim to suzerainty over Iraq, and later switched sides from Tughril to Mas'ud. Dubays even joined the Crusaders in their failed siege of Aleppo in 1123, which opened the way for Aleppo's acceptance of domination by Mosul's Zangi in exchange for protection.

With various pressures around him, including the Seljuks, Mazyadids, and an emerging Zangi in Mosul, al-Mustarshid found it imperative to shore up his security, and look for new supporters. He became the first among the later Abbasid caliphs to show interest in matters of defense, rebuilding walls around Baghdad in 517/1123, raising an army, and venturing outside the capital on campaigns. An eloquent speaker, he could rally the public, and, saber in hand, waged battle against enemies, trying to patch together Abbasid political and military rule over Iraq. He became the symbol of a resurgent caliphate that did not just react to events dictated by the Seljuks, but shaped politics on the ground, and he began a process of military deterrence.[73] His first success came in 517/ 1123 when he led a campaign against Hilla and subdued Dubays b. Sadaqa but opted to pardon him in an act of pious amnesty.

---

[73] Eric Hanne, *Putting the Caliph in His Place: Power, Authority, and the Late Abbasid Caliphate* (Madison, NJ, 2007), 177–178.

Al-Mustarshid then ventured north against Zangi and, with Kurdish support, besieged his stronghold of Mosul in 527/1133, but failed to take the city after a three-month siege, and returned to Baghdad. It was in the course of this small war between the caliph and Zangi that the latter on one occasion found himself stranded on the wrong side of the Tigris with the caliph's army closing in on him; a pair of little-known freebooters who hailed from a small town near Akhlat and Tiflis, Najm al-Din Ayyub and his brother Asad al-Din Shirkuh, helped provide the boats that ferried Zangi across the river, and established the first bond of friendship between the Zangid and Ayyubid families.[74]

In 521/1127 the caliph's attention turned to a rising conflict with the Seljuk Mahmud, who came to assert control over Baghdad. It was only after a stalemate in a siege of the city that the two sides established an understanding, and Mahmud's sudden death soon after opened the way for new contenders to assert their claims for the Seljuk sultanate in Iraq, with Mas'ud emerging as the new leader. Al-Mustarshid found it difficult to reach an understanding with this upcoming leader, who had an army that reportedly numbered 15,000 troops, and in 529/1135 the caliph decided to stand up to the Seljuks. An opportunity seemed to present itself when a group of Turkic princes allegedly defected from Mas'ud's army, and came to Baghdad promising support to the caliph in a campaign against Mas'ud.

Under normal circumstances these overtures should have been trustworthy, but not necessarily in the twelfth-century world. Its track record was that of a Middle East of easily shifting alliances, long-distance and covert interferences, and inexplicable sudden deaths of major political actors – starting with Tughril, the founder of the Seljuk dynasty. Adding to the complication was the fact that the cities and districts of western Iran frequently shifted alliances amongst the Seljuk princes and the Abbasid caliph. Western Iran was like a giant jigsaw puzzle whose pieces could be combined in different ways, and there were many adventurous generals and potentates eager to play the game. Al-Mustarshid's simplistic worldview of either Abbasid or Seljuk domination in that region was to bring home a harsh lesson in the politics of the age.

Stretching himself thin, al-Mustarshid ambitiously set out on campaign, hoping to find support in areas of western Iran that the Abbasids

---

[74] Ibn Wasil, *Mufarrij*, 1:8.

had not controlled directly for over two centuries. The movement of his army was slow – no doubt in light of the massive caravan of cash, treasures, and supplies that he brought along to reward those who joined his side. Although initially successful, when the hour of battle came near the mountain of Bisitun, just outside the town of Hamadan, the loyalty of the caliph's Turkic troops faltered. The left wing of the caliph's army defected to Mas'ud, while the right wing feigned some combat against the Seljuks and then stopped.[75] The caliph found himself having to surrender together with his massive train of supplies – some 4 million dinars carried by 70 mules, and other supplies carried by 5,000 camels. All this material that he had planned to use to pay supporters now ended up in enemy hands. His campaign plan was sheer folly from the start, since it mixed the aims of conquest and ceremonial presentation.

As Mas'ud then moved around Azerbayjan to subdue his last remaining rival, Dawud b. Mahmud b. Muhammad, who had offered refuge to the caliph during the campaign, he took the caliph along as captive. The official Seljuk story of what happened next provides a mix of an apologetic and a cover-up. When word reached Sanjar about the caliph's defeat, he reportedly sent a strongly worded letter to Mas'ud ordering him to release al-Mustarshid immediately and treat him with full honor. "Even the cosmic order and the forces of nature would turn against us, if we fight with the Abbasids," he wrote. Mas'ud reportedly showed compliance with these commands, but the story goes that he left al-Mustarshid's elaborate tent compound in the area of Maragheh near Tabriz with hardly any guards. And it was in this setting of lax security that a group of assassins, said to belong to the Nizari Isma'ili sect of the Assassins, broke into the caliph's tent. Completely defenseless and focused on his devotional prayers, al-Mustarshid was killed "Thomas Becket" style, with multiple swords plunging into him.

This event sent shock waves back to Baghdad, where the public, long adjusted to a respected if not powerful caliphate, was outraged. The immediate execution of the gang of assassins suggests an effort to silence as much as to punish them. Mas'ud went a step further in damage control by having Dubays b. Sadaqa assassinated, ostensibly in vengeance for the caliph. The historian Ibn al-Athir does not seem to

[75] Ibn Wasil, *Mufarrij*, 1:16.

have believed this official version of events, and has left hints of a wider conspiracy against the caliph. A modern assessment of the events by Carole Hillenbrand builds on this by arguing that the caliph was duped into setting out on campaign against Mas'ud by a group of duplicitous commanders who were actually in Mas'ud's service.[76] Al-Mustarshid walked into a carefully organized trap, and, far from being a neutral bystander, Sanjar was the one who ordered the assassination.[77] In general, al-Mustarshid had grown too powerful for Seljuk interests, and they found it necessary to stop him before he became a magnet for more political loyalty.

Although certain previous Abbasid caliphs had been murdered (and were later followed by al-Musta'sim), none of them receives the empathy that al-Mustarshid does in the chronicles. The regicide of al-Amin in the ninth century is treated in moral and elliptical terms in complex and artful narratives centered on the concept of fate, while that of al-Musta'sim in the thirteenth is presented as the tragedy of a naïve and non-military sovereign coming up against an "Attila-type" invader who brought carnage to everyone who stood in his path. But al-Mustarshid's tragedy was unique, that of an energetic and organized sovereign who deserved better. He had tried to assert a political will that was his legitimate right, and went about this task without resorting to treachery, instead putting himself in the front line of battle. This created in historical writing a memory of a caliph who was reviving the model not just of the early Abbasids but of the idealized early Islamic caliphs, such as the Prophet's cousin and fourth caliph, Ali. An aura of hagiography was soon added to his sacrosanct image. One account compared the saga of al-Mustarshid setting out on his fateful journey to that of al-Husayn heading toward Karbala, while another suggested the sanctification of the caliph after death.[78] When the corpses of the assassins of al-Mustarshid were set alight on a pyre, the chronicler Ibn al-Kazaruni states, a hand of one the perpetrators apparently remained unaffected by the fire. On close examination, the clenched fist enclosed locks of al-Mustarshid's hair, torn out when he struggled to fend off his attackers. Those on the scene opined that the

---

[76] Carole Hillenbrand, "al-Mustarshid," *EI²*, 733–735.
[77] Ibn Wasil, *Mufarrij*, 1:61.   [78] Ibn Wasil, *Mufarrij*, 1:59.

locks of hair had protected the hand from the fire, and when they were removed, the hand was burnt to ashes.[79]

The next caliph, al-Rashid, quickly found himself in a highly tricky situation. In addition to the fact that he felt a duty to avenge his father's death, he received the insulting demand from Mas'ud – who had just seized the campaign treasury of al-Mustarshid – that he pay the sum of 400,000 dinars that Mas'ud claimed was previously owed him by al-Mustarshid. The young and inexperienced al-Rashid desperately took up arms and ventured outside the capital again to rally support against Mas'ud. Although al-Rashid could count Dawud b. Mahmud and the Atabeg Zangi among his allies, this was militarily insufficient. In addition, Zangi was a mercurial figure, and his policies were far from fixed. He could fight the Crusaders one day, battle rivals in Asia Minor on another, and still express an interest in Baghdad if an opportunity presented itself. In fact, Zangi tested the waters of al-Rashid's situation by setting out on the Khurasan Road to rally support. But when he came back to Baghdad, he suddenly opted to return to Mosul, probably sensing insurmountable odds.[80] Al-Rashid was ill-equipped to understand the shrewd calculations of Zangi, and on reaching Mosul he found himself having to leave again, probably in light of threats from Sanjar to Zangi if he continued to host the caliph. Al-Rashid's decision to relocate to Mosul for a while had been a bad one, for it made him lose touch with his only remaining base of supporters in Baghdad. However weakened the Abbasids were in those years, they could always still muster the support of the Baghdad public when everything else failed, and could argue their continued political relevance in coordination with the *'ulama*. With these factors removed, Mas'ud took advantage of the caliphal absence from Baghdad to invade the city, where he convened a meeting of religious scholars and pressured them to have the caliph deposed on trumped-up charges of wine drinking and sedition. Having lost his home ground in Baghdad and his second haven in Mosul, al-Rashid set out on the Khurasan Road toward Rayy with unclear objectives, whether to meet with Sanjar or to connect with old allies in Qazwin and Isfahan. The caliph wandered from

[79] Ibn al-Kazaruni, *Mukhtasar al-Tarikh*, ed. Mustafa Jawad (Baghdad, 1969), 222.

[80] Ibn Wasil, *Mufarrij*, 1:63, 65.

Hamadan to Isfahan, where he died as the victim of a robbery. He was buried in the mosque of Shahristan just outside Isfahan.[81]

The Revival of the Abbasids: al-Muqtafi–al-Mustadiʾ

Back in Baghdad, the Seljuk Masʿud had al-Muqtafi proclaimed caliph. It was all a replay of the Buyid scenario of deposing one caliph in place of another (al-Qadir), whom they thought would be a pliant figure. Why al-Muqtafi was chosen as caliph has a lot to do with the fact that he was a son-in-law of the vizir, Ali b. Tarrad al-Zaynabi. The latter was an ambitious former *naqib* (marshal) of the Hashimite family who had been trying to exert dominance over the caliphate. Al-Zaynabi was formerly in the service of al-Mustarshid, and went with him to the fateful battle near Hamadan, which the caliph lost. It is not unlikely that this minister had been privy to the conspiracy of the Turkic lieutenants who defected to Masʿud's side. At least one author of a medieval chronicle, Ibn al-ʿImrani, even states that while Masʿud envisaged some form of reconciliation with al-Rashid, al-Zaynabi prevented this, and rushed to have al-Rashid deposed with a fatwa from the religious scholars.[82]

Whatever the real details of the transition, on the accession of al-Muqtafi, Masʿud stipulated that the caliph should not have any troops and should confine himself to religious matters only. The palace was stripped of all wealth, and the stables emptied of horses. As a consolation perhaps, in 535/1140 Sanjar returned to the new caliph the insignia that had been taken from al-Mustarshid, the *burda* and the staff.[83] The caliphate seemed at its weakest. A key international development, however, was about to radically change the world for both caliph and sultan. And as always in Islamic history, the powerful winds of change began in Transoxiana, where the emergence of a new wave of Turkic migration from Central Asia brought the Qara Khitay invaders who clashed with, and defeated, Sanjar at the battle of Qatwan near Samarqand in 536/1141. The Qara Khitay were a migrant nomadic people, like the Ghuzz Turks before, who were coming under environmental pressure in their original homeland, and their victory was a product of their desperation,

[81]   Ibn Wasil, *Mufarrij*, 1:70.
[82]   Ibn al-ʿImrani, *al-Inbaʾ fi Tarikh al-Khulafaʾ*, ed. Qasim al-Samarrai (Leiden, 1973), 222.
[83]   Ibn al-Athir, *al-Kamil*, 11:79.

but they did not anticipate the repercussions of their success across various regions.

In neighboring Khwarazm, a vassal of the Seljuks but with the grand title of shah, Atsiz (governor 521–551/1127–1156), demanded his independence in 538/1143, while the Atabegs in the Fertile Crescent region began to assert themselves more freely. The Zangids, who were previously aloof and hostile to the Abbasids, took the opportunity to assert their power in Mosul on the ideological platform of fighting the Crusades, and sought to find common ground with the caliph in order to strengthen their political legitimacy. ʿImad al-Din Zangi (r. 1126–1146) and his son Nur al-Din (r. 1146–1174) slowly emerged as local rulers, and built up a base of Kurdish military support that would one day spawn the Ayyubid Saladin, providing an alternative center of gravity to Seljuk rule.

Zangi's political importance had already started rising after he successfully protected Aleppo from the Crusaders in 522/1128, but he became a star figure of jihad after he captured the Crusader kingdom of Edessa (al-Ruha/Turkish Urfa) in 539/1144, and his military chiefdom became the leading one in the Fertile Crescent region when his son, Nur al-Din, consolidated power over Damascus in 1154. These efforts brought the Zangids religious recognition from the Abbasid caliph al-Muqtafi, who officially bestowed on Nur al-Din Zangi the title al-Malik al-ʿAdil in 550/1155 and entrusted to him the mission (al-ʿahd) of leading the campaign to expand Islamic power in Syria and Egypt, which included the tasks of overthrowing the Fatimids in Egypt and of fighting the Crusades. The rise of the Zangids changed the geopolitics of the region as Mosul and Aleppo started replacing Hamadan and Isfahan as focal points for caliphal concern.

Al-Muqtafi was careful not to overplay his hand from the outset of his reign, but after Masʿud's death in 547/1152 and as the Qara Khitay dealt another blow to Sanjar in 548/1153, capturing him in battle, it was clear that the Seljuks were going downhill. The caliph began raising troops again – this time Greeks and Armenians, since the Turks had proved unreliable against the Seljuks – and he successfully warded off an invasion and a three-month siege of Baghdad by the Seljuk sultan Muhammad b. Mahmud in 551/1157.[84] The Baghdad

---

[84] Bosworth, "Political and Dynastic History," 128. Dhahabi, *Duwal*, 2:51. Ibn al-Athir, *al-Kamil*, 11:212–215.

populace showed great solidarity behind the caliph in defending their city, but circumstances also helped: in the absence of the sultan from Hamadan, other princes of the Seljuk family in Arran tried to seize it, forcing the sultan to rush back to defend his city. Unlike his immediate predecessors, however, al-Muqtafi did not venture outside the capital, and left it for his capable minister 'Awn al-Din Yahya b. Hubayra (d. 560/1165), and the latter's son 'Izz al-Din b. 'Awn (d. 562/1167), to extend territorial control over Basra, Kufa, Wasit, and Hilla. A man of wide learning and political skill, Ibn Hubayra remained in office for sixteen years, and he is compared in the accounts of this period to the Barmakids for having revitalized caliphal authority.[85]

Seljuk claimants to control over Iraq were humbled by Ibn Hubayra, who once received one of them, Sulayman shah, while riding a horse, a sign of dominance, while the Seljuk remained on foot; and when Malikshah III in Isfahan tried to have his name included in the *khutba* in Iraq in 555/1160, Ibn Hubayra devised a scheme to have him poisoned.[86] The position of the *shihna*, long the military strongman in Baghdad appointed by the Seljuks, was abolished by Ibn Hubayra, who was rewarded with the title Sultan al-Iraq.[87] Around the same time, the name of the Seljuk sultan was removed from Abbasid coinage after the death of Mas'ud.[88] For his part, the caliph went after potential threats to his rule. Al-Muqtafi never forgot the tragedies of al-Mustarshid and al-Rashid, and even many years after he had acceded to power, he tracked down all those who had signed the edict of deposition depriving al-Rashid of the caliphate, and had them sacked from their official posts in the judiciary or other government departments, while the Hashimite *naqib* and minister Ali b. Tarrad al-Zaynabi was not just sacked but had all his wealth confiscated as well. If these officials-turned-conspirators

[85] See Herbert Mason, *Two Statesmen of Medieval Islam: Ibn Hubayrah (499–560 AH/1105–1165 AD) and the Caliph al-Nasir (553–622 AH/1158–1225 AD)* (The Hague/Paris, 1972).

[86] Ibn al-Athir, *al-Kamil*, 11:206, 263.

[87] Edmund Bosworth, "The Steppe Peoples in the Islamic World," in *NCHI*, vol. 3: *The Eastern Islamic World: Eleventh to Eighteenth Centuries*, ed. David O. Morgan and Anthony Reid (Cambridge, 2010), 64, 71.

[88] Husayni, *Zubdat al-Tawarikh*; trans. C. E. Bosworth as *The History of the Seljuq State: A Translation with Commentary of the Akhbar al-Dawla al-Saljuqiyya* (London, 2011), 159.

could turn against al-Rashid, the caliph feared they might do the same to him.[89]

Al-Muqtafi's reign therefore marks a turning point in Abbasid history, as he transferred caliphal authority from the religious to the temporal sphere. Ibn al-Athir describes al-Muqtafi as a man of great intelligence, foresight, and military courage, and says that "he was the first caliph to get sole power over Iraq, to the exclusion of the Sultan ... and to have firm control over the Caliphate and over his troops,"[90] while al-Suyuti adds that al-Muqtafi "paved the road for a credible office of the Imamate, renewed the authority features of the caliphate, and handled important matters in person."[91] These descriptions comprise virtues that would have probably been familiar to a wider audience in the world of the twelfth century. Prowess, generosity, and personal attentiveness to government were also becoming stock items of the chivalric ideal to a Western Latin audience, who lionized figures such as the knightly William Marshall and Louis IX in medieval Europe for exhibiting these features.[92]

The reassertion of caliphal authority over Iraq continued smoothly during the reign of al-Muqtafi's successor, al-Mustanjid, who followed a lenient policy regarding taxation that gained him further favor. Al-Mustanjid felt sufficiently independent that in 561/1165 he dropped mention of the Seljuks from the coinage of Baghdad.[93] The new caliph, however, was a withdrawn figure, more famous for his interest in poetry and skill in using the astrolabe, an astronomical instrument. He selected palace officials badly, and was eventually the victim of an assassination led by the Turkic chamberlain Qaymaz and a coterie of officials, who sought to protect their privileges. The new caliph, al-Mustadi᾽, entered a world reminiscent of Samarran military bullying, and of easily made and unmade caliphs. Al-Mustadi᾽ took a gamble from the outset by appealing directly to the public, rallying its support against his palace officials; this strategy paid off, as the public heeded his call with great enthusiasm, helping him carry out a purge of all the domineering elements in the palace.[94]

The new international situation that had toppled Sanjar in the east and empowered al-Muqtafi was about to produce equally dramatic

[89]   Ibn Taghribirdi, *al-Nujum al-Zahira*, 5:260.
[90]   Ibn al-Athir, *al-Kamil*, 11:256.   [91]   Suyuti, *Tarikh al-Khulafa᾽*, 505.
[92]   Daniel, *The Arabs and Medieval Europe*, 179, 184–191.
[93]   Peacock, *The Great Seljuk Empire*, 153.   [94]   Mason, *Two Statesmen*, 79.

changes in the west that would benefit al-Mustadi˒ even further. The new caliph's reign coincided with the final demise of the Fatimid caliphate in 1171. Saladin, who was sent by Nur al-Din Zangi to take over Egypt, established the name of al-Mustadi˒ in the Friday *khutba*, and presided over the extension of Sunni political dominance in Egypt. This event was greatly celebrated in Baghdad, and the caliph sent special titles and robes of honor (*tashrif*) to both Nur al-Din (who was in Damascus for the ceremony) and Saladin (who was in Egypt), together with banners for all the mosques of Cairo and official Abbasid cloaks for all the mosque preachers (*khatibs*).[95] The event not only enhanced al-Mustadi˒'s role as the only remaining caliph in the Islamic world, it also allowed him to preside over the consecration of a region officially switching from Isma῾ili Shi῾ism to Sunnism. Saladin came to be represented in the literature of the time as the third – after Abu Muslim and Tughril – to bring revival to the Abbasid *da῾wa*, and the caliphate was increasingly referred to as "the guiding state" (*al-dawla al-hadiya*).[96] When he finally achieved his famous triumph over the Crusader armies in 1187, Saladin sent the caliph a trophy – the True Cross, which was captured at the battle of Hittin – making the caliph appear as the Islamic counterpart to the Pope in Christianity.[97] Throughout this period, Saladin kept up a vigorous correspondence with Baghdad, informing the caliph in a steady stream of letters of all progress in the battles against the Crusaders, and presented himself as a loyal soldier of the Abbasids. This political humility prepared the way for a later and larger request, when he asked for the caliph's sanction for him to claim title to all the territories formerly held by Nur al-Din.[98] "Syria," as Saladin explained in one of his letters to the caliph in almost political science terms, "always requires outside intervention in order to be stable (*al-sham la tantazimu umurahu bi-man fihi*)."[99]

At the same time that Saladin was scoring his successes against the Crusaders, the caliph found a second ally in the rising figure of Qilij Arslan II (r. 1156–1192), sultan of the Rum Seljuks, who achieved a resounding victory over the Byzantine emperor Manuel Comnenos at

[95] Ibn Wasil, *Mufarrij*, 1:219.
[96] Ibn Wasil, *Mufarrij*, 1:110–112; Suyuti, *Tarikh al-Khulafa˒*, 516.
[97] Le Strange, *Baghdad during the Abbasid Caliphate*, 274.
[98] Ibn Wasil, *Mufarrij*, 2:25, 28–29, 84, 92, 202–205, 226, 314.
[99] Abu Shama, *Kitab al-Rawdatayn fi Akhbar al-Dawlatayn*, ed. Ibrahim Shams al-Din (Beirut, 2002), 1:239.

the battle of Myriocephalon in 1176. This event gave the Rum Seljuks greater political confidence, which was reflected in 573/1178, when Qilij Arslan issued new dinars on which he referred to himself for the first time as "sultan," and included mention of the Abbasid caliph's name, "al-Mustadi'."[100] Investiture with the title sultan meant that the Seljuk leader must have acquired this honorific, as did Saladin, through a formal diploma of investiture from the Abbasid caliph. The cases of these two newly minted sultans, the Rum Seljuk and the Ayyubid, shows the continued importance of the Abbasids in lending legitimacy to newly rising monarchs; and to these two one can add a third, the Ghurid Mu'izz al-Din Muhammad (r. 1173–1206), based in Ghur (in modern Afghanistan), who was recognized by the Abbasids for establishing Muslim control over Delhi, and later built Delhi's famous Quwwat al-Islam Mosque in 587/1191.[101]

The reign of al-Mustadi' therefore offers what seems to be a culmination of the Sunni ideological policy that began with the reign of al-Qadir. The prolific scholar Ibn al-Jawzi played a similar role to that of al-Mawardi before, acting as advisor to the caliph, and championing his cause to the extent that he penned a mirror for princes entitled *al-Misbah al-Mudi' fi Khilafat al-Mustadi'* (*The Luminous Lamp on the Caliphate of al-Mustadi'*). Unlike previous such works, such as Nizam al-Mulk's *Siyasatnameh*, which emphasized Persian kingship, Ibn al-Jawzi shifted the exempla from Persian monarchs to the earlier caliphs and Companions of the Prophet. Ibn al-Jawzi was a madrasa teacher, but apparently also something of a rock star at mosques and public squares, where he gave eloquent and moving sermons to mesmerized audiences. The Andalusian traveler Ibn Jubayr devoted four pages just to describing Ibn al-Jawzi's lectures, and noted his "splendid triumphs of eloquence and learning, controlling the reins of verse and of rhymed prose" as the listeners were hypnotized and showed great outpourings of penitence. "Had we ridden over the high seas and strayed through the waterless desert,"

---

[100] Mecit, "Kingship and Ideology," 68.
[101] André Wink, "The Early Expansion of Islam in India," in *NCHI*, vol. 3, 99. The Ghurid mosque still includes an inscription that honors the Abbasid caliph, referring to the sultan as "helper of the Commander of the Faithful": W. E. Begley, *Monumental Islamic Calligraphy from India* (Villa Park, IL, 1985), 26.

Ibn Jubayr says, "only to attend the sermon of this man, it would have been a gainful bargain and a successful and prosperous journey."[102]

Al-Mustadi''s reign is noted in general for its extensive building activities. He is said to have rebuilt al-Taj Palace in Baghdad, which was first constructed by al-Muktafi in the early tenth century, and there were great construction projects for mosques, schools, and religious endowments in his reign. His two wives, al-Sayyida Banafsha and Zumurrud Khatun, were especially prolific in these efforts. Banafsha, follower of the Hanbalite school, ordered the construction of a bridge in Baghdad in 570/1174 that was named after her,[103] and a mosque in western Baghdad. She also converted a home that she owned into a madrasa for the Hanbalis in 570/1174, and entrusted Ibn al-Jawzi with its management – the very location where Ibn Jubayr later described a teaching session by Ibn al-Jawzi in 580/1184. Going further in her generous activities, Banafsha reportedly also hosted the wedding of Ibn al-Jawzi's daughter, Sibt Ibn al-Jawzi's mother, in one of her mansions. Less is known about Zumurrud Khatun, mother of the future caliph al-Nasir. Zumurrud was a follower of the Shafi'i school, and she ordered the construction of a Shafi'i madrasa in 580/1184, a cemetery near the tomb of Ma'ruf al-Karkhi, and the Khaffafin Mosque. The minaret of the mosque and the tower over her tomb remain as landmarks from that period in Baghdad today.

Banafsha and Zumurrud were not exceptions in that period in terms of women assuming the role of patronage for public buildings. Whereas in the ninth and tenth centuries, women at the Abbasid court mainly occupied the roles of singers and poetesses with names such as 'Arib ("Ardent") (al-Ma'mun), Mahbuba ("Beloved") (Mutawakkil), and Khamra ("Wine") (al-Muqtadir), in the Seljuk period one finds women at the Abbasid court in the eleventh and twelfth centuries playing a very different role, which complemented the political work of the caliphs and kings. While some of these women were princesses, such as al-Nasir's wife Saljuqi Khatun (d. 584/1188), daughter of Qilij Arslan II of the Rum Seljuks, others were of slave origin, such as al-Nasir's mother, Zumurrud, but they all shared a great say at the caliphal court, and partook in setting up endowments (*waqf*s) of public

---

[102] Ibn Jubayr, *Rihlat Ibn Jubayr*, trans. R. C. Broadhurst as *The Travels of Ibn Jubayr* (London, 1952), 230–231.
[103] Ibn al-Jawzi, *al-Muntazam*, 17–18:211.

projects, such as schools, mosques, libraries, and water fountains, and funded charities for the poor. In this, they echo the generous giving of Zubayda, wife of Harun al-Rashid, in the early Abbasid period. But it would be interesting to speculate how much the experience of these elite women as former slaves – and not just the obligation of religious tasks – may have colored their desire to improve the lot of the disadvantaged in general with these charitable projects. Zumurrud, who went on pilgrimage, for example, reportedly expressed her satisfaction at having shared the hardships of the poor in making the arduous journey to Mecca.

Ibn al-Saʿi provides a range of flattering representations of these elite women: ʿIsma Khatun, daughter of Malikshah and wife of al-Mustazhir, is described as "a highly intelligent woman, and among those who are firmest and having the soundest opinions," while Banafsha is described as "a woman of authority and real power, who was also pious, did all manner of good works, looked after the poor and destitute, and performed many righteous acts of charity";[104] and Shahan, daughter of the commander Sunqur al-Nasiri and wife of al-Mustansir, is described as someone who "[held] her own independent court and had a fiscal office, agents, functionaries, servants, and a splendid retinue. She spent liberally from her funds just as she pleased, and her authority on all manners was unquestioned."[105] The designation by al-Mustadiʾ of his son al-Nasir as his successor was even done under the influence of Banafsha, who suggested and lobbied for the idea, against the initial plans of the caliph.[106]

al-Nasir and the New Caliphal State

With the accession of al-Nasir to the caliphate, the Abbasid state had made firm progress toward reestablishing a considerable measure of political assertiveness, and looking back, relations between the Abbasids and Seljuks had greatly transformed. The era of Seljuk

---

[104] Ibn al-Saʿi, *Nisaʾ al-Khulafaʾ*, ed. Mustafa Jawad (Cairo, 1968); ed. and trans. Shawkat Toorawa as *Consorts of the Caliphs: Women and the Court of Baghdad* (New York, 2015), 110–111.

[105] Ibn al-Saʿi, *Nisaʾ al-Khulafaʾ*, trans. Toorawa, 121; al-Ghassani, *al-ʿAsjad al-Masbuk waʾl-Jawhar al-Mahkuk fi Tabaqat al-Khulafaʾ waʾl-Muluk*, ed. Shakir Mahmud Abd al-Munʿim (Baghdad, 1975), 599.

[106] Sibt Ibn al-Jawzi, *Mirʾat al-Zaman*, 14:501–502.

suzerainty over Baghdad had created a rough division between the political power of the sultans and the religious authority of the caliphs, symbolized in official terms by the presence of Dar al-Mamlaka of the Seljuk sultans and Dar al-Khilafa of the Abbasid caliph on the east bank of the Tigris. The Seljuks needed the Abbasid caliphs to project the religious legitimacy of the sultanate, and the caliphs had the ability to grant titles of honor (*laqab*) for both sultans and viziers. The Abbasid and Seljuk families intermarried frequently, but they engaged in a dance of political leverage and brinkmanship. Both dynasties were Sunni, but this did not prevent the Seljuks from keeping the Shi'i Mazyadid potentates in Hilla – even after defeating them during Muhammad b. Malikshah's reign – as a force of bullies, to keep a check on ambitious Abbasid caliphs. For their part, the Abbasids were often helped more through serendipity than through their own actions, such as Tughril's mysterious sudden death soon after his unwelcome betrothal to al-Qa'im's daughter; and the same happened to Malikshah after he ordered al-Muqtadi to abandon Baghdad within ten days.

Religion remained the main grounds for defining the foundation of their rule for both Abbasids and Seljuks. From the reign of al-Qadir to that of al-Mustadi' there was a steady growth in the definition of caliphal authority on the basis of Sunni ideology, and the caliphs were greatly helped by the articulate efforts of a highly skilled chancery that included such figures as Ibn Hamdun and Ibn al-Musilaya, and Muhammad b. Abd al-Karim al-Anbari – the latter having served as scribe for five caliphs.[107] Abbasid ambitions, however, did not cease with the attainment of religious authority, and they kept trying to exercise a measure of territorial control both in Iraq and outside it. Al-Mustarshid was the first to try and assert this ambition by raising an army and challenging the Seljuks, and al-Muqtafi succeeded in carving out a caliphal state in the region stretching from just south of Mosul to Basra. But the great leap forward in this direction came with the caliphate of al-Nasir. Al-Nasir stands out in the late Abbasid period for reviving Abbasid authority to a degree not known since the reign of al-Mu'tadid in the late ninth century. Biographical accounts give a description of this young man, who acceded to the caliphate at the

---

[107] al-'Imad al-Isfahani, *Kharidat al-Qasr wa Jaridat al-'Asr*, ed. Muhammad Bahjat al-Athari (Baghdad, 1955), 1:140–141, 184.

age of twenty-two, as a highly shrewd and tenacious politician, who kept tabs on his officials and on the leaders of foreign powers alike.[108] He benefited from an Abbasid espionage network, which at one point employed no less a distinguished literary figure than al-Hariri, author of the *Maqamat* stories, as an informant (*sahib al-khabar*) in Basra.[109]

Over the course of his reign, al-Nasir used various religious strands to strengthen his authority. He utilized public spectacle in Baghdad to increase the profile of the caliphate as an ancient monarchical institution surrounded by the trappings of tradition, and he devised new ways of projecting the sanctity of the Abbasid caliphal office. The political language of the Abbasid chancery in al-Nasir's reign increasingly referred to commands issued from the court as "prophetic decrees," the chancery issuing these as "the prophetic abode" (*al-diwan al-nabawi*), and the Abbasid ruling institution as "the guiding state" (*al-dawla al-hadiya*). The caliph built new palaces for himself that were intended to invite public admiration and curiosity, and one of these palaces, Qasr al-Misnat, was especially organized in such a way as to be kept distant from the public eye, as if it were a "forbidden city," to which even approach was prevented.[110]

Al-Nasir gradually built up his grip on power in a way that echoes Harun al-Rashid, with the sacking of the powerful minister Ibn al-Attar soon after the caliph's accession. In the area of diplomacy, al-Nasir's policies showed a greater preoccupation with the territories of the Iranian east than with those of Syria and Egypt. This was reflected particularly in the way the caliph showed strong interest in securing control over the Zagros highlands overlooking eastern Iraq. The opportunity for this came when the Seljuk ruler Tughril III (r. 1176–1194), based in Hamadan and Isfahan, tried to shore up his authority in this region by demanding the inclusion of his name in the *khutba* in Baghdad. Al-Nasir responded by ordering the demolition of the Seljuk Dar al-Mamlaka Palace in Baghdad in 583/1187, and encouraging the Khwarazm shahs, former governors for the Seljuks

---

[108] Dhahabi, *Siyar*, 22:192–243.

[109] The post reportedly continued among Hariri's descendants: Isfahani, *Kharidat al-Qasr*, 2:601. It is not unlikely that this official task shaped Hariri's imagination of the Abu Zayd character in the *Maqamat*, who often assumed various garbs and disguises in different settings as if reflecting the image of the spy.

[110] al-Ayyubi, *Midmar al-Haqa'iq wa Sirr al-Khala'iq*, ed. Hasan Habshi (Cairo, 1968), 88.

in Khwarazm, to fight the Seljuks.[111] The region of Khwarazm, more famous in the sixteenth century as the Khanate of Khiva (the town is now inside Uzbekistan, on its border with Turkmenistan), was long known for its rich agriculture and potential for trade. Like the Samanids of the ninth century, the Khwarazm shahs built up their power in this region, and harnessed Turkic nomadic migrations to build up an extensive army. Although initially vassals to the Seljuks, over time they sought to break free from their tutelage, and eventually took over their sultanate. By the end of the twelfth century the Khwarazm shahs were very eager to expand west toward Rayy, and they defeated and finished off the last of the Seljuks in 590/1194. Who was going to control the former lands of the Seljuks in western Iran, however, was a question that now put the newly rising power of the Khwarazm shah at odds with al-Nasir. The caliph started to assert his own authority over Khuzistan and Shiraz in 591/1195, and tried to expand his rule over Hamadan, Rayy, Qazwin, and Isfahan – the al-Jibal region that came be known in the Seljuk period as Iraq al-ʿAjam. Khuzistan was a famously rich province in the eastern Islamic world due to its intensive cultivation of sugarcane, and as such would have provided an important source of revenue for the caliphate.

Al-Nasir's success in expanding his rule was largely a result of the energetic policies of his vizir, Muʾayyad al-Din b. al-Qassab, who was originally from Shiraz, wielded wide influence in Khuzistan, and showed an ability to raise and lead an army. Ibn al-Qassab marched across western Persia in coordination with the Eldiguzids, the former Atabegs of Tughril III in Azerbayjan, and reached as far as Rayy in 592/1196, but the vizir died soon after. The Khwarazm shah, Tekish (r. 1172–1200), however, considered himself the rightful heir to Seljuk territories, and promptly invaded the area of Rayy and Jibal, took control of it, and demanded the inclusion of his name and that of his son in the Friday *khutba* in Baghdad. However, no sooner had Tekish died in 1200 than the population of the region he had occupied threw off the rule of the Khwarazm shahs with a vengeance, and the caliph together with the Eldiguzids proceeded to divide these former Seljuk territories between them. The caliph took control of Isfahan, Hamadan, Qazwin, and Zanjan, while the Eldiguzids came into possession of Rayy, Saveh, Qumm, and Kashan.[112]

[111] Ibn al-Athir, *al-Kamil*, 11:562.
[112] A. Bausani, "Religion in the Saljuq Period," in *CHIran*, vol. 5, 294.

For a while the caliph had placated Tekish by granting him the title of sultan and including his name in the *khutba*, but, typical of his international maneuvers, al-Nasir at the same time turned for help to another rising power in the east – the Ghurids in Firuzkuh (famous for its Jam Minaret), in an isolated province of rugged mountains called Ghur in the southern part of modern Afghanistan that had long defied neighboring dynasties. Geographical accounts, written from the comfort of Bukhara, reflected Khurasan's inability to dominate that region by describing Ghur's people as "bad-tempered, unruly, and ignorant."[113]

The Ghurids, eager to gain legitimacy through association with the caliph, fought against the Khwarazm shahs, ostensibly in his defense. Both the Khwarazm shahs and the Ghurids were implacable and resilient foes, one with authority rooted in Khurasan and in alliance with the Chinese Qara Khitay, and the other based in the south with power stretching into northern India. Just sitting in Baghdad, al-Nasir was able to unleash a war of great powers in the east that was looking for more auxiliaries. The Ghurids were initially successful, taking much of Khurasan in 594/1198, but, under 'Ala al-Din Muhammad b. Tekish, the Khwarazm shahs pushed back the Ghurids from all territories except Herat in 601/1204. These battles were fought to exhaustion on both sides. The Khwarazm shah's alliance with the non-Muslim Qara Khitay was deeply resented in Khurasan and Transoxiana, and his championing of a Shi'i Imam in place of the Abbasid caliph was also viewed as gratuitous in the Sunni Iranian circles, turning them toward the side of the caliph.

Fanning sectarian strife did not immediately translate into political mobilization, as it might have done in an earlier period under the Buyids and the Fatimids. The increased preoccupation with the Crusades was one factor; but the Abbasids had also over time devised ways of accommodating the Shi'i voice through new political measures, such as appointing a Shi'i vizir. Both al-Mustazhir and al-Mustarshid had Shi'i vizirs,[114] as did al-Mustansir and al-Musta'sim later on,[115] and one vizir, Ahmad b. al-Naqid, was milk brother of the future caliph al-Zahir.[116] The caliphs continued to maintain the official role of the *naqib* (marshal) of the Alid family, and various caliphs

---

[113] Levi and Sela, eds., *Islamic Central Asia*, 33.
[114] Bausani, "Religion in the Saljuq Period," 292.
[115] Carole Hillenbrand, "al-Mustansir," *EI*², 727.
[116] Dhahabi, *Siyar*, 23:108.

showed reverence to Shiʿi shrines as well as to Sunni ones, such as when al-Mustaʿsim visited the tombs of Musa al-Kazim and Ibn Hanbal soon after his accession in 640/1242.[117] The rising role of Sufism at the Abbasid court may have also played a role in reshaping the sectarian map of Islam in view of Sufism's special reverence for the fourth caliph, Ali. Unlike his staunchly Sunni predecessors, al-Nasir showed a strong interest in Shiʿism, so much so that some medieval writers referred to him as Shiʿi. His success in reconciling the two sects in Baghdad famously extended even to the Ismaʿilis, when in 608/1211 he finally obtained the submission of the Grand Master of the Assassins, Hasan III b. Muhammad al-Sabah, who agreed to the reintroduction of the sharia and Islamic rituals in his domains, publicly repudiated the idea of the "Expected Imam," and proclaimed his adherence to Sunni Islam.[118] It has been suggested that an image al-Nasir had carved over Bab al-Talsim, the Talisman Gate of Baghdad, in 618/1221, showing a seated figure holding two dragons at bay with his out-stretched hands, was meant as symbolic of the caliph's success in subordinating the Ismaʿili Grand Master and the Khwarazm shah.[119] The image remained there up until World War I, when the gate was blown up by the retreating Ottoman troops in 1917.

Al-Nasir's experiment with unity was part of his new ideological program of moral invigoration based on Sufism. Whereas in al-Mustadiʾ's reign it was the Hanbali hadith scholar Ibn al-Jawzi who dominated the court, in al-Nasir's it was the Sufi scholar Shihab al-Din Umar b. Muhammad al-Suhrawardi (d. 630/1234), who was a student of Abd al-Qadir al-Jilani (d. 561/1166), and interacted with leading Sufis of the time, such as Muʿin al-Din al-Chishti (d. 633/1236), Ibn al-Farid (d. 632/1235), and students of Najm al-Din Kubra (d. 618/1221). Iraq had a long history of ascetic and Sufi figures, including Rabiʿa of Basra, Maʿruf al-Karkhi, Bishr al-Hafi, al-Hallaj, Junayd, and al-Ghazali, but it was in the twelfth century that it became increasingly a homeland for Sufi movements including the Rifaʿiyya in Basra, named after its founder, al-Ahmad al-Rifaʿi (d. 578/1182). For al-Nasir, however, it was the Suhrawardiyya that mattered the most. The writings of Suhrawardi compared the relationship between a Sufi

---

[117] Ghassani, ʿAsjad, 512; on al-Mustansir's equal distribution of charities to Sunnis and Shiʿis, see 470.
[118] Bosworth, "The Steppe Peoples," 72.
[119] Bosworth, "Political and Dynastic History," 168–169.

master and his students to that of the caliph and his subjects. His book
'Awarif al-Ma'arif has remained into the modern period as
a foundational text for Sufi novices seeking to set themselves on the
path (*tariqa*), but the majority of his references to the caliphate are to be
found in some of his other epistles that remain in manuscript.[120]
Suhrawardi himself served as the caliph's religious advisor, and on
several occasions as his official emissary to Ayyubid princes in Syria
and Egypt (604/1207), the Khwarazm shah 'Ala al-Din Muhammad
(614/1217), and the Seljuk sultan of Rum, 'Ala al-Din Kayqubad (618/
1221).[121]

The caliph also took an active interest in *futuwwa* ("manliness,"
"chivalry") as a vehicle for social and political devotion to his rule. His
interest began in 578/1182 when, at a ceremony in a park outside the
Abbasid palace, he was initiated by a Sufi shaykh, Abd al-Jabbar
b. Yusuf b. Salih (d. 583/1187), into the Rahhasiyya order. In 1207 al-
Nasir developed a movement based on *futuwwa*, making himself its
focus. The Futuwwa became a club of supporters who recognized the
caliph in a "grand master" position of sorts. Although *futuwwa* was
a familiar idea in Sufism, it was al-Nasir who made it mainstream and
legitimate in orthodox terms.[122] The thirteenth-century Ibn Wasil
describes an invitation sent out by al-Nasir in 607/1210 to various
rulers asking them to drink the cup (*ka's*) of *futuwwa* for him.[123] Ibn
al-Mi'mar (d. 642/1244), author of *Kitab al-Futuwwa*, which he says
he composed for al-Nasir, lays out the principles of the concept, and
describes how the drinking of this water (almost akin to the sacred
water of Zamzam in Mecca) represents a symbol of a pact of loyalty.[124]

---

[120]   Erik Ohlander, *Sufism in an Age of Transition: 'Umar al-Suhrawardi and the
        Beginnings of Islamic Mystical Brotherhoods* (Leiden, 2008), 250, 255.
[121]   Ohlander, *Sufism in an Age of Transition*, 275–278; Rachel Goshgarian,
        "*Futuwwa* in Thirteenth-Century Rum and Armenia: Reform Movements and
        the Managing of Multiple Allegiances on the Seljuk Periphery," in *The Seljuks
        of Anatolia: Court and Society in the Medieval Middle East*, ed.
        A. C. S. Peacock and Sara Nur Yildiz (London, 2013), 231; Mason, *Two
        Statesmen*, 122–123.
[122]   Goshgarian, "*Futuwwa* in Thirteenth-Century Rum and Armenia," 229, 247.
[123]   Ibn Wasil, *Mufarrij*, 3:206–207.
[124]   Ibn al-Mi'mar, *Kitab al-Futuwwa*, ed. Mustafa Jawad (Beirut, 2012),
        115–117, 229–232. Qamar-ul Huda, "The Prince of Diplomacy: Shaykh Umar
        al-Suhrawardi's Revolution for Sufism, Futuwwa Groups and Politics under
        the Caliph al-Nasir," *Journal of the History of Sufism* 3 (2001), 267–268.

The Futuwwa became a chivalric order that enjoined its members to refrain from harming others, give generously, abstain from complaint, and hold particular reverence for Ali, the Prophet's cousin, as a model of noble values.[125] Its members were initiated in a special ceremony at which they were assigned a rank, took an oath, and dressed in specific garments (special trousers and belt); on at least one occasion, Ibn al-Mi'mar's book was presented as a gift, during the initiation ceremony of a new princely member, 'Izz al-Din Kay Kawus (r. 1211–1219).[126] To what extent the Futuwwa movement was influenced by the Western Christian orders of knighthood rather than the Shi'i orders is an open question, but the caliph seemed intent on making it a way to rally support for his leadership from different Islamic sects, and a tool to strengthen solidarity and loyalty to the caliphate at various levels of society.

At the highest levels, various sultans and princes, including the Ayyubids, Ghurids, and Seljuks of Rum, joined the Futuwwa, forming a kind of caliphal club, and at a later date even the Khwarazm shah Jalal al-Din joined it during the caliphate of al-Mustansir. In his efforts to establish religious unity around his caliphal office and to use Sufi networks to expand his temporal authority, al-Nasir is sometimes compared to Pope Gregory VII (1073–1085) and the latter's use of the monastic orders to strengthen his powers.[127] Whereas al-Qadir had devised an organizing program based on curtailing theological debate, and a canonical view of the Islamic past, in his *al-'aqida al-qadiriyya*, al-Nasir took ideology to another level, blending the sharia with Sufism. In 612/1215 yet another ideological embassy was dispatched from Baghdad to various dynasts, bearing a book of hadith entitled *Ruh al-'Arifin (The Spirit of Gnosis)*, which the caliph had reportedly compiled.[128] The book probably related hadiths that touched on mystical and ethical ideas espoused by al-Nasir, and it became a kind of second manifesto of official caliphal guidance (after the Qadiri Creed of the eleventh century) for Islamic society in general, and Islamic rulers in particular. A wide range of *'ulama* came to frequent

---

[125] Qamar-ul Huda, "The Prince of Diplomacy," 264, 267–268.
[126] Sara Nur Yildiz and Hasim Sahin, "In the Proximity of Sultans: Majd al-Din Ishaq, Ibn 'Arabi and the Seljuk Court," in Peacock and Yildiz, eds., *The Seljuks of Anatolia*, 182.
[127] Julian Baldick, *Mystical Islam* (New York, 1989), 74.
[128] Ibn Wasil, *Mufarrij*, 3:228.

the court of al-Nasir during this period, which strengthened the links amongst Anatolian, Syrian, and Iraqi towns, and these 'ulama, in turn, were instrumental in bringing to the fore a new cadre of spiritual masters, such as Ibn Arabi (d. 638/1240).[129]

Within the Iraq region, the caliph's policies fostered stability for his rule, but when one looks to his relations with the east, the situation remained perilous. Both the caliph and the Khwarazm shah had unrealistic claims to territorial expansion and power, and both had prickly personalities. A poorly worded letter from one to the other could trigger conflict, and send them into a stubborn mode of belligerence. In the case of the Khwarazm shah this was more dangerous because he built up so much confidence that when one aspiring leader, Genghis Khan, wrote what he thought was a carefully worded, friendly letter, flattering the shah as "king of the west" as he (i.e. Genghis) was "king of the east," and referring to Khwarazm shah 'Ala al-Din Muhammad as "dear to him like a son of his," the shah was offended by the patronizing tone and grew suspicious of Mongol overtures for closer trade relations.[130] A mission of merchants sent by the Mongols to Transoxiana in 1218 was famously suspected of spying by the local Khwarazm governor of the town of Utrar, and he had them all put to death. Although sundry reports about Mongol strength were shared with the Khwarazm shah, he seems to have underestimated the potential danger. 'Ala al-Din's domination of former Seljuk territories, stretching from the Oxus to the Persian Gulf and into the Indus river region, made him contemptuous of other powers.

On his western front, the Khwarazm shah kept up his belligerence to the caliph. Having discovered a cache of secret correspondence between the caliph and the Ghurids in Ghazna, which he captured in 612/1215, the Khwarazm shah resolved on marching on Baghdad in person. The correspondence described the close alliance between Baghdad and the Ghurids, and showed the caliph's encouragement of hostilities to the Khwarazm shah. In 614/1217 the Khwarazm shah undertook an ambitious campaign to the west, hoping to capture Baghdad and repeat former models of Buyid and Seljuk domination

---

[129] Ibn Arabi benefited around this time from much networking with the Baghdad 'ulama and caliphal envoys, such as Awhad al-Din al-Kirmani: Yildiz and Sahin, "In the Proximity of Sultans," 186, 197–198 no. 36.

[130] J. A. Boyle, "Dynastic and Political History of the Il-khans," in *CHIran*, vol. 5, 303–304; Bartold, *Turkestan*, 397.

of the caliphate. At Hamadan, however, a ferocious blizzard decimated the ranks of his army, and forced him to retire back east. In a society that read in forces of nature signs of good or bad fortune, this was taken as a sign of divine support for the caliphate.[131] But, as if nothing had happened, the Khwarazm shah started to pick a fight with the Mongols, and he was officially at war with all his neighbors. In 617/1220 the Mongols began a vengeful invasion of the Khwarazm state. Nearly all the major cities of Transoxiana and Khurasan were destroyed, while ʿAla al-Din fled before this scourge. And when he died on an island in the Caspian, his son Jalal al-Din (d. 628/1231) took up the desperate fight, gathering the remnants of his troops and holding on to areas not fully dominated by the Mongols. Although he scored a few military successes, he was generally on the run, but with ingenuity and speed that baffled the Mongols, once crossing the Indus, after a military defeat, in full view of Genghis Khan. After eluding the Khan in India for three years, he made it back to Iran, swashbuckling his way with a contingent of devoted followers, reaching west into Azerbayjan, Georgia, and Armenia in 1226. The Abbasids were mainly spectators in this great war, but they would have watched with anxiety the movement of the Mongol troops west. Although the Mongols were active in western Iran in the Hamadan region, and even raided further west, as far as the town of Irbil, they seem to have avoided a direct clash with the Abbasid caliphate at this stage.

Whether Baghdad, which al-Nasir had fortified with a new wall in 618/1221, presented a challenge is not clear. Some medieval chroniclers suspected that the caliph had been in secret touch with the Mongols, and that he had encouraged them to invade the domains of the Khwarazm shah. Ibn al-Athir, the earliest source for these rumors, was generally hostile to al-Nasir, and his views have been repeated by some modern historians.[132] Others have found this charge unfounded and based mostly on impressions from al-Nasir's previous record of encouragement for the Ghurids against the Khwarazm shahs.[133] More recently, Bosworth has agreed with this latter view, adding that ultimately "the policies of provocation pursued by ʿAlaʾ al-Din Muhammad [b. Tekish] brought down on his head the Mongols in 1217, with

---

[131] Ibn al-Athir, *al-Kamil*, 12:318.
[132] Ibn al-Athir, *al-Kamil*, 12:440; Angelika Hartmann, "al-Nasir," *EI²*.
[133] Bartold, *Turkestan*, 400.

fateful consequences ... for the Islamic lands in Asia as a whole."[134] The medieval chronicles describe a jittery mood in Baghdad as the Mongols approached Iraq, and al-Nasir scrambling for troops, writing to the Ayyubid princes in Syria and Egypt for military support.[135] The year this distress call was sent out, 618/1221, Egypt was coming under threat from a Crusade that landed in Damietta, and the Ayyubid al-Kamil expressed regret at not being able to help Baghdad. In the event, however, the Mongols had decided not to press further with their invasion.

Al-Nasir died in 1225, after a long reign of stern rule over Baghdad. Biographers are divided on his personality, with some viewing him as beneficial to his people, and others as a conniving collector of revenues. He was said to have hoarded two cisterns' worth of gold coins, but he was also known to be a benefactor. When in 589/1193 he ordered an expansion of the Nizamiyya library, he donated to it his palace book collection, which Ibn Khaldun says surpassed the library of al-Hakam II of al-Andalus (r. 961–976), which comprised 400,000 books.[136] Writing under the patronage of the rival prince of Mosul, Ibn al-Athir painted a negative image of al-Nasir as a fickle ruler who coveted other people's wealth and undermined the prosperity of the Iraq region. Another medieval author has countered this by noting how al-Nasir showed restraint by holding back from confiscating the assets of his minister al-Qummi after sacking the latter from office, and still another source points to generous donations by al-Nasir to individuals, and his bequests for the reconstruction of the shrine of Musa al-Kazim in Baghdad, and for another shrine in Samarra.[137]

Like Harun al-Rashid, al-Nasir was said to have made a habit of frequently going around Baghdad in disguise, experimenting with a range of outfits: once he was dressed like a *faqih*, another time resembling a Turk, and another a Persian merchant.[138] This made him, according to some, the original model for the *Thousand and One Nights*, especially in light of the fact that most extant versions of

---

[134] Bosworth, "The Steppe Peoples," 75; and Timothy May, *The Mongol Empire* (Edinburgh, 2018), 60–61.

[135] Ibn al-Athir, *al-Kamil*, 12:378–379; Ibn Wasil, *Mufarrij*, 4:50; Ibn Kathir, *al-Bidaya*, 7:13, 102.

[136] Mackensen, "Four Great Libraries," 297.

[137] Ghassani, *'Asjad*, 322; Ayyubi, *Midmar*, 85, 178.

[138] Ayyubi, *Midmar*, 119.

the *Nights* date to the late medieval period.[139] The thirteenth-century caliph reportedly took his covert activities to a more complex level, trying to influence diplomatic relations. One of his master tricks was to forge a letter in the name of one leader and send it to another, resulting in friendship or enmity between the two. His crafty behavior, combined with his interest in mysticism, gave rise to rumor that he dabbled in the occult and black magic, and that he was helped by supernatural powers – genies who expedited his commands in far-off lands. The reality was probably more prosaic, since the caliph's rule never expanded much beyond central and southern Iraq. His personality is difficult to read, but he seemed to have exhibited extreme expressions of emotion, such as in the year-long mourning period he ordered in 599/1202 for the death of his mother, Zumurrud Khatun. Her funeral was a highly public daytime event, in which all Baghdad joined in mourning, no doubt on account of her many charitable activities, with the caliph leading the cortège on a lengthy journey from south to north and across the Tigris to the cemetery she had endowed near the tomb of Ma'ruf al-Karkhi on the west side of Baghdad. According to Sibt b. al-Jawzi even the dutiful vizir, Nasir al-Din Nasir b. Mahdi al-'Alawi, was overcome by the blistering heat and had to sit down more than thirty times during the procession.[140] A long period of mourning then followed, in which all state officials were obliged to wear white for a whole year. No drum was sounded or sword allowed out of its scabbard for months after the funeral, and the caliph ordered the donation of all of Zumurrud's vast estate to charity.[141]

We gain a glimpse of al-Nasir and of Baghdad during his time from the words of the Andalusian traveler Ibn Jubayr, who once chanced on the caliph's "motorcade" passing through the city from west to east, with the caliph "preceded and followed by officers of the army, Turkish, Persian and others, and surrounded by around fifty drawn swords in the hands of the men about him." Ibn Jubayr describes those times in Baghdad as follows:

[139] Josef Horovitz, "The Origins of the Arabian Nights," *Islamic Culture* 1 (1927), 47.
[140] Sibt Ibn al-Jawzi, *Mir'at al-Zaman*, 14:504–505.
[141] Ibn Abi Udhayba, *Insan al-Uyun fi Mashahir Sadis al-Qurun*, ed. Ihsan al-Thamiri et al. (Amman, 2007), 228; al-Safadi, *al-Wafi bi'l-Wafayat* (Beirut, 1962–2010), 14:213.

This city has two parts, an eastern and a western, and the Tigris passes between them ... the people, men and women, who night and day continuously cross [the river] in recreation are numberless. Ordinarily, and because of the many people, the river had two bridges, one near the palaces of the Caliph, and the other above it.

The baths in the city cannot be counted, but one of the sheikhs told us that, in the eastern and western parts together, there are about two thousand ... The colleges are about thirty, and all in the eastern part; and there is not one of them that does not outdo the finest palace. The greatest and most famous is the Nizamiyya, which was built by Nizam al-Mulk, and restored in 504/ 1110. These colleges have large endowments and tied properties that give sustenance to the faqihs who teach in them, and are dispensed on the scholars. A great honor and an everlasting glory to the land are these colleges and hospitals.

In the western part of the city are the orchards and walled-in gardens whence are brought fruits to the eastern part ... The eastern part of the city has magnificent markets, is arranged on the grand scale and enfolds a population that none could count save God Most High. The eastern part has four gates: first that on the high part of the bank, the Bab al-Sultan; then Bab al-Safariya; then the Bab al-Halba; and then Bab al-Basaliya. These are the gates in the walls that surround the city from the high to the low parts of the bank and wind round it in a long semi circle. Inside, in the markets, are many gates. To be short the state of this city is greater than can be described.

The Caliph's palaces lie at its periphery (i.e. of the eastern side) and comprise a quarter or more of it ... A large part of these palaces is used by the Caliph, and he has taken the high belvederes, the splendid halls, and the delightful gardens.

The Caliph would sometimes be seen in boats on the Tigris, and sometimes he would go into the desert to hunt. He goes forth in modest circumstance in order to conceal his state from the people, but despite this concealment his fame only increases. Nevertheless, he likes to appear before the people, and show affection for them. They deem themselves fortunate in his character, for in his time they have obtained ease, justice, and good living, and great and small they bless him. We saw this Caliph Abu'l-'Abbas Ahmad al-Nasir ... in the western part in front of his belvedere there. He had come down from it and went up the river in a boat to his palace high on the east bank. He is a youth in years, with a fair beard that is short but full ... is of fair skin, medium stature, and comely aspect. He is about five and twenty years of age. He wore a white garment (*qaba'*) embroidered with gold, and on his head was a gilded cap encircled with black fur of the costly and precious kind used for (royal) clothes, such as that of the marten or even better. His purpose was concealment of his state, but the sun cannot be hidden even if veiled.[142]

Al-Nasir's successor to the caliphate was his eldest son, Abu Nasr Muhammad, who took the title al-Zahir. Although initially designated as successor in 585/1189, al-Zahir's Sunni piety seems to have alarmed the caliph's Shi'i vizir, al-Qummi, who convinced the caliph to change the succession to his other son, Ali. Since the latter did not survive his father, however, al-Nasir was forced to return al-Zahir for the succession in 612/1215. After the nearly forty-seven-year reign of al-Nasir, al-Zahir reigned for a mere nine months. Aged fifty-two at his accession, he was older than previous Abbasid caliphs acceding to the caliphate, but his short reign does raise questions about courtly mischief and ministerial intrigue working to the caliphate's detriment in its final years. Historians generally leave a favorable record of al-Zahir's policies, particularly for the way he put an end to his father's intrusive espionage on people and unjust taxation. He released many political prisoners, and returned much confiscated property to its rightful owners, and became renowned for charitable giving. Ibn al-Athir gives a favorable image of al-Zahir, comparing him to Umar b. Abd al-Aziz, the short-reigned ascetic caliph of the Umayyad dynasty, who corrected many wrongs of his predecessors.

---

[142] Ibn Jubayr, *Rihlat Ibn Jubayr*, trans. Broadhurst, 234–239.

6 | *The Twilight of the Abbasid Caliphate (1225–1258)*

al-Mustansir: The Last Abbasid Renaissance

With the accession of al-Zahir's son, al-Mustansir, the Abbasid state finally attained a renewed stability after years of perilous contention with the Seljuks and Khwarazm shahs, and the stress experienced under al-Nasir's overbearing rule. From childhood, al-Mustansir had caught the attention of observers with his penchant for learning, leading his grandfather al-Nasir to nickname him *al-qadi* (the judicious one). Al-Mustansir built on al-Nasir's vision of revitalizing the caliphate as an independent state and focal point of universal Islamic allegiance, and he projected political attentiveness from the beginning of his reign. Suspecting that the long-time minister, Muhammad al-Qummi, who had constructed a belvedere for reviewing troops from his *diwan*, was up to something, al-Mustansir had him arrested by the courtiers Ibn al-'Alqami and Ibn al-Naqid in 629/1231, ending his twenty-five year tenure in office. Al-Mustansir's program for resurgence, however, was happening too late, at a moment when the conventional system of kingdoms and states in the Islamic world was being uprooted by the Mongol storm.

In the years coinciding with al-Mustansir's reign, there was still some ambiguity as to the intentions of the Mongols, whose viceroy in western Asia, Chormaghun, was based in Azerbayjan, and had focused his attention on gaining the submission of Armenia (1236), the Georgian kingdom (1238), and various Islamic towns in Asia Minor and western Iran (Isfahan being taken in 1235). Baiju, who succeeded Chormaghun as supreme commander, continued to pound Asia Minor, scoring a victory over the Rum Seljuks at the battle of Kosedag, near Sivas, in 1243, and gaining the submission of Akhlat, Mayyafariqin, Harran, Edessa, and Mardin in 1243–1244. The pressure in the eastern Anatolian region made the Abbasids increasingly apprehensive of whether the Mongols would turn around and zero in on Iraq. Al-Mustansir kept up a steady interest in matters of defense, refortifying the city walls and raising a sizable army, albeit nothing close to the exaggerated figure of 100,000 troops given in some sources. And to rev up the national Abbasid spirit, al-Mustansir added a new inscription in 636/1239 on his coinage, that read "*nasr min allah wa fath qarib*" (victory is forthcoming soon from God: Qur'an 61:13) that encouraged steadfast defense in expectation of final success – a situation perhaps reminiscent of the repeated inscription "*wa la ghalib illa allah*" (there is no victor but God) on the walls of the Alhambra Palace at Granada, which was crafted as ornament but also as talisman during the years of Christian pressure on the last Islamic stronghold in al-Andalus. Both inscriptions reflected a similar spirit of defense and foreboding about danger from a neighboring enemy.

In 629/1232 the Mongols made an attempt to take the town of Irbil in northern Iraq from its local leader, Muzaffar al-Din Kokbari, the long-reigning brother-in-law of Saladin, but the caliph sent a force that helped repel the invaders. Just before he died in 630/1233, Muzaffar al-Din (r. 1190–1232), who lacked a male successor, bequeathed Irbil to the caliph, and al-Mustansir found himself burdened with a wider responsibility, a task made all the more difficult in light of the collusion in coming years between Badr al-Din Lu'lu' (r. 1222–1259), the ruler of Mosul, and the Mongols.[1] Irbil was about 250 miles north of Baghdad, but only 50 miles east of Mosul, the den of collaboration with the Mongols. The Mongols raided Irbil once more in 634/1237, but its citadel held out until a relief force arrived from Baghdad.[2] They came knocking again in 635/1238, and this time in a two-pronged attack on Irbil and Khanaqin (just inside the modern eastern border of Iraq, some 100 miles east of Baghdad), clearly using the former as a decoy. In addition to making a general call to arms in the city and the outlying bedouin districts, al-Mustansir received contingents of support on this occasion from the Ayyubid rulers of Ba'albek and Damascus. In a battle outside Baghdad, some 7,000 Abbasid troops, led by the capable Iqbal al-Sharabi, faced a 15,000-strong Mongol force, and although in the beginning the Abbasid army pushed back on the right and left flanks, the Mongol center held, and, using their famed tactic of feigned retreat, the Mongol army counterattacked, badly mauling the caliph's army. Such pitched battles were not usually

---

[1] Ibn Kathir, *al-Bidaya*, 7:13, 156; Dhahabi, *Siyar*, 23:157.
[2] Peter Jackson, *The Mongols and the Islamic World* (New Haven, 2017), 83.

the favored context for military confrontation by the Mongols. According to a recent assessment, they preferred warfare that involved besieging towns and then slowly weakening them into submission.[3]

The heavy fighting in 635/1238, however, seems to have deterred both sides, and the next year witnessed some brisk diplomacy as the caliph sent envoys to Qazwin in 637/1239, where they met the Mongol Chormaghun. The two parties seem to have reached a temporary understanding then, since the Mongols did not appear again until 643/1245, when the Abbasids, once again under Iqbal al-Sharabi, had to deal with the threat. In the meantime, the Abbasids did not let down their guard, and as early as 634/1237 the caliph took the extraordinary step of asking the *'ulama* to issue a fatwa for the priority of jihad over pilgrimage to Mecca in those times of threat. The measure helped the caliph recruit more citizens for his army to fend off the Mongols, but it also served as an austerity measure that eliminated the expenditure and ostentation that usually accompanied the preparation of the official pilgrimage caravan to Mecca.

In his internal governing policy, al-Mustansir built on the approach of his immediate predecessors, involving both Sunni and Shi'i voices in his rule, and employing key Shi'i figures as high court officials, such as Ahmad b. al-Naqid (d. 642/1244), and Mu'ayyad al-Din b. al-'Alqami (d. 656/1258). He maintained equal attention to the well-being of both sects, and just as he invested in the upkeep of Sunni mosques, building the Qumriyya Mosque on Baghdad's west side in 626/1228, he undertook repairs to the main mosque in the Shi'i neighborhood of al-Karkh, also on Baghdad's west side, in 1230, and rebuilt the two shrines of the Alid imams in Samarra, Ali al-Hadi and al-Hasan al-'Askari.[4] He also extended financial patronage to Shi'i scholars, such as Ibn Abi'l-Hadid (d. 656/1258), who became a leading scribe in the chancery and director of Baghdad libraries, and Radi al-Din b. Tawus (d. 663/1266), to whom the caliph gifted a house on the east side of Baghdad on Badri Street, a neighborhood of exclusive residences for Baghdad's elite, including Iqbal al-Sharabi. It was probably in this very house that Ibn Tawus was able to sit out the carnage in the city when the Mongols invaded in 1258.[5] This reaching out by al-Mustansir to both Sunnis

---

[3] Jackson, *The Mongols and the Islamic World*, 87–88.
[4] Ibn Kathir, *al-Bidaya*, 7:170.
[5] L. Veccia Vaglieri, "Ibn Abi'l-Hadid," *EI²*; Etan Kohlberg, *A Medieval Muslim Scholar at Work: Ibn Tawus and His Library* (Leiden, 1992), 5, 10.

and Shi'is no doubt helped weld a sense of national unity around the caliphate in Iraq, and enhanced its profile as a magnet for political loyalty across the region.

Ibn al-Tiqtaqa, who was a devout Shi'i, could not but give a favorable depiction of the caliph, saying:

> al-Mustansir was energetic, most lavish, rivaling the wind in generosity and charity. His gifts were too well known to need mention, and too great be reckoned. If it were said that there were none among the Abbasid Caliphs like him, the sayer would be speaking truly. His are noble monuments, the greatest of which is the Mustansiriyya, which is too great to be described, and too well known to need description . . . and other mosques, monasteries, and rest houses.[6]

Another mention of the caliph's generous charitable giving is provided toward the beginning of Ibn al-Tiqtaqa's mirror for princes, *al-Fakhri*, where he pairs him with the Mongol Ogedei Khan (r. 1229–1241), who is touted as the most generous giver, exceeding al-Mustansir; but then the author adds the important remark: "but alas, where would the caliph have had the access to the riches available for Uqtay (Ogedei)," as if finally making al-Mustansir superior within the frame of his means.[7]

Like al-Nasir before him, al-Mustansir continued to receive declarations of loyalty from rising regional powers. The former Turkmen vassal of the Ayyubids in Yemen, Nur al-Din Umar b. Ali b. Rasul (r. 1229–1249), who started the Rasulid dynasty (1229–1454), sought legitimacy from Baghdad by sending an embassy in 637/1240 asking for the title of sultan and a diploma of investiture from the caliph.[8] And from India came a similar request from Iltutmish (r. 1210–1236), a former slave-lieutenant and son-in-law of the last Ghurid ruler, who took power in 1211, and founded the Delhi sultanate. Ruling an area that eventually stretched from Lahore to the Ganges delta, Iltutmish turned Delhi from a minor fortress to an imperial capital, and wrote to Baghdad requesting legal sanction for his authority. Iltutmish had once spent time in Baghdad, as well as other cities such as Bukhara and Ghazna, and so understood the world of distant courts and religious legitimacy. He cultivated ties with the *'ulama*, and sent one such emissary, Rashid al-Din Abu Bakr Habash, bearing gifts and a request for caliphal recognition. Juzjani, court

---

[6] Ibn al-Tiqtaqa, *al-Fakhri*; trans. Whitting, 317.
[7] In al-Tiqtaqa, *al-Fakhri*, 23.   [8] Suyuti, *Tarikh al-Khulafa'*, 529.

historian to later Delhi sultans, mentions that the Abbasid caliph al-Nasir sent Iltutmish a diploma of investiture in 626/1229,[9] that granted him the title Nasir Amir al-Mu'minin ("helper of the Commander of the Faithful").[10] The Abbasid embassy was received amid great fanfare and ceremony in Delhi, after which the caliph's name and the newly granted title were included on Delhi's coinage. A later embassy was also sent by al-Mustansir, and in fact mention of the Abbasid caliph continued to appear on the coinage of the Delhi sultans during the reigns of the next three rulers – Mahmud Shah Nasir al-Din (r. 644–664/1246–1266), Ghiyath al-Din Balban (r. 664–685/1266–1287), and Mu'izz al-Din Kaykubad (r. 685–689/1287–1290) – long after the caliphate in Baghdad had fallen to the Mongols in 1258.[11]

Not all those who pledged allegiance to Baghdad were as durable as the Rasulids or the sultans of Delhi. A knightly envoy from al-Andalus arrived in 629/1231 – escorted by a messenger from Egypt's Ayyubid sultan al-Kamil – seeking political recognition for his prince, Muhammad b. Yusuf (Ibn Hud, r. 1228–1238), who ruled over the towns of Murcia and Seville.[12] The latter was a descendant of the once-famous Taifa kingdom in Saragossa, and now in the thirteenth century was trying to defy the authority of the Almohads who claimed the title of caliph. In response, al-Mustansir sent a delegation the following year (631/1234), led by a Kurdish religious scholar bearing the emblems of investiture (the banners, the robes of honor, and the edict). This recognition brought Ibn Hud the loyalty of a newly emergent prince, also named Muhammad b. Yusuf (Ibn al-Ahmar), who founded the Muslim kingdom of Granada (1232–1492), and even hosted the Abbasid embassy and investiture ceremony of Ibn Hud in Granada.[13] It was an ephemeral statement of grandness, however, since Ibn Hud would be overwhelmed in the next few years by the Christian kingdoms of Spain, while Granada will be left to chart its own path of political

[9] Peter Jackson, *The Delhi Sultanate* (Cambridge, 1999), 37–38; Blain Auer, *Symbols of Authority in Medieval Islam: History, Religion and Muslim Legitimacy in the Delhi Sultanate* (London, 2012), 114.

[10] P. Hardy, "Dihli Sultanate," *EI²*, 267; A. S. Bazmee Ansari, "Iltutmish," *EI²*, 1155; Auer, *Symbols*, 108, 116.

[11] Arnold, *The Caliphate*, 86–87; Peter Jackson, "Muslim India: The Delhi Sultanate," in *NCHI*, vol. 3.

[12] Ibn al-Fuwati (attrib.), *Kitab al-Hawadith al-Jami'a*, ed. B. A. Ma'ruf (Beirut, 1997), 33; Ghassani, *'Asjad*, 442.

[13] Ibn Khaldun, *Tarikh Ibn Khaldun* (Beirut, 1992), 4:203–204.

survival for the next two-and-a-half centuries. What is perhaps striking about these missions west is not the caliber of the aspiring ruler involved, but that the caliph took it sufficiently seriously to dispatch an embassy on an arduous and dangerous journey to al-Andalus. The envoy's ship would have had to survive a Mediterranean world teeming with enemies: the Almohads, Normans, Crusader knights of various stripes, and a plethora of Spanish and Italian navies.

In the area of religious culture, al-Mustansir was tutored by the mystic Shihab al-Din Umar al-Suhrawardi, but he does not seem to have been exuberant about Sufism the way al-Nasir was. *Futuwwa* probably remained integral to his policy as he tried to rally the support of regional political leaders, but al-Mustansir seems to have switched back to Nizam al-Mulk's model of trying to attract the jurist and hadith *'ulama* to court and to expand the madrasa system as a basis for elite and popular support. And toward this effort he undertook the most ambitious building project yet for a madrasa when he ordered the construction of al-Mustansiriyya madrasa, begun in 625/1228 and completed in 631/1234.

Caliphs before al-Mustansir had mostly funded the building of mosques, Sufi lodges, and mausoleums, but this was the first time a caliph funded the creation of a madrasa. In a refinement of this policy, however, he now reached out to all four schools of Sunni jurisprudence, rather than just one, as was customary, stipulating in the school's foundation charter the inclusion of all four sects (Hanafi, Shafi'i, Hanbali, and Maliki), thereby indicating a new measure of ecumenicism. The objective was not only academic but also political, as the caliph tried to reduce sectarian tensions. Throughout much of the twelfth century partisanship among theological sects had led to civil strife in Iranian cities – such as in Nishapur, Rayy, Shiraz, Isfahan, and Qazwin – between Hanafis and Shafi'is (among other disputes involving the Mu'tazila, Twelvers, and Isma'ilis), and in the early thirteenth century the historian al-Rawandi urged the Rum Seljuk sultan to try and mitigate this atmosphere of sectarian discord; but it was the Abbasid caliph who answered this call.[14] His project stood out as

---

[14] Bausani, "Religion in the Saljuq Period," 285. For a classic study on the sectarian rivalry and strife in Nishapur, see Richard Bulliet, *The Patricians of Nishapur* (Cambridge, MA, 1972). Also al-Rawandi, *Rahat al-Sudur wa Ayat al-Surur*, Arabic trans. Ibrahim al-Shawaribi, Abd al-Nu'aym Hasanyn and Fu'ad al-Sayyad (Cairo, 1960), 140.

a logical extension of al-Nasir's attempt to attain a more universal pan-Islamic unity under caliphal leadership.[15]

Medieval observers concurred that the new madrasa was an architectural and artistic wonder of its day. Although the building structure survived the Mongol invasion, it has lost all its original artwork and former splendor, and we can only speculate on what it may have looked like by extrapolating from the better-preserved contemporary monuments in the neighboring regions of Iran, Turkey, and Syria. The actual structure of the school was in the typical rectangular design of the age built of brick, the most common building material in Persia, and deployed patterns of vaulting and muqarnas that were widely used in areas adjacent to Iraq. The Mustansiriyya's main decorative style seems to have been somber, calligraphic, and geometric, resembling that in some Rum Seljuk structures, such as the Ulu Cami in Malatya (ca.1224) and the Cifte madrasa of Kayseri in Asia Minor (1205). The madrasa's walls may well have been covered with similar colorful tiles of turquoise, white, and manganese purple.[16] In particular, the new madrasa seems to have perfected a geometric design known as *girih* (from the Persian word for knot), where star and polygon shapes blend to evoke quasi-crystalline and harmonious networks of interlacing and interlocking geometrical shapes – and all apparently according to an underlying mathematical system.[17]

In a city that already included over thirty madrasas, al-Mustansiriyya was intended as an elite college comprising 248 students (62 in each of the 4 legal schools), who received instruction in law, Qur'an study, hadith, and various aspects of Arabic including calligraphy. This template of learning was the quintessential curriculum that prepared students to serve in the civil service and as functionaries of the Abbasid caliphate. The madrasa also provided some instruction in mathematics, medicine, and the natural sciences. The resources available for students were probably state of the art for the time, and so probably was the meal plan sketched out in the school charter. The Mustansiriyya library housed over 80,000 rare books, and included a system for borrowing books, with paper and pens provided by the college for copying material,

---

[15] Hillenbrand, "al-Mustansir," 728.
[16] Richard Ettinghausen and Oleg Grabar, *Islamic Art and Architecture, 650–1250* (New Haven, 2001), 215–218, 231.
[17] John Noble Wilford, "In Medieval Architecture Signs of Advanced Math," *New York Times* (27 February 2007).

along with lamps to light the way for tasks.[18] The famous historian Ibn al-Saʿi (d. 674/1274), whose many books on Abbasid history were lost in the Mongol invasion, was its first librarian. The school also included a bath house, a hospital, a pharmacy, storage systems for cooling water, and a kitchen that served both teachers and students. The endowment of the school was funded by revenue-generating properties (*waqf*) in the neighboring markets that yielded 70,000 dinars a year. The names of miscellaneous scholars who taught at al-Mustansiriyya are mentioned in some sources, along with the name of its clock engineer, Nur al-Din Ali b. Taghlib al-Saʿati, and its master physician, Ibn al-Sabbagh, both of whom are reported as having died in 683/1284 and lived till over one hundred years of age.[19]

Although the Abbasids were famous for their rapid construction of buildings, with the benchmark set by the Nizamiyya of Nizam al-Mulk, which was built in two years, al-Mustansiriyya took six years to complete. A lot of effort was expended on its architectural style and esthetic innovation, and one can find linkages in the muqarnas detail of its artwork and its calligraphic style of Arabic inscriptions with monuments as far away as al-Andalus and Delhi. A new perspective on Islamic art history has recently argued that in fact certain calligraphic, ornamental, and architectural devices that flourished in Baghdad and the east in the twelfth and thirteenth centuries, such as the arabesques, geometrical designs (the aforementioned *girih*), and muqarnas vaulting were hallmarks of a wave of Sunni revival long promoted by the Abbasid caliphs. In their totality and diffusion across various architectural structures in different parts of the Islamic world, these artistic styles represented, according to the art historian Gülru Necipoğlu, trademarks of loyalty to the Abbasid center, and a "new visual order projecting a shared ethos around the religious authority of the Abbasid caliphate."[20]

[18] Mackensen, "Four Great Libraries," 299.

[19] Ibn al-Fuwati, *Hawadith*, 179, 480; al-Sulami, *Taʾrikh ʿUlamaʾ Baghdad al-Musamma Muntakhab al-Mukhtar*, ed. Abbas al-Azzawi (Baghdad, 1938), 163.

[20] Gülru Necipoğlu, *The Topkapi Scroll: Geometry and Ornament in Islamic Architecture* (Santa Monica, 1995), 107, 109. Tabbaa argues that the public display in the Iranian east of new forms of Arabic calligraphy, which were developed in Abbasid Baghdad, was meant to reflect "the spiritual reign of the caliphate": Yasser Tabbaa, *The Transformation of Islamic Art during the Sunni Revival* (London, 2001), 76–77; and on the similar use of arabesques and muqarnas, 122–124.

Located right on the Tigris and just to the north of the caliphal palace, al-Mustansiriyya was clearly planned with attention to river and green park vistas that also made use of easy water transport to the school. Equally central was the perspective of the traffic moving through the Tigris. The morning and evening commuters on the river could behold the building in its highly visible "Westminister" style of propaganda that signified the ruler's authority.[21] The extant ruins of al-Mustansiriyya preserve its original riverside entrance together with a massive stucco panel that announces the name of the caliph as the patron of the project. Written in highly ornamental *thuluth* Arabic calligraphy and taking up ten lines, the engraved panel provides a mirror of political and religious messages from the time. The dedication reads:

In the name of God, the Compassionate, the Merciful. This school was built for God who does not overlook the efforts of those who do good deeds, and who rewards the believers and doers of charity with paradise. He (i.e. the caliph) commanded that it (i.e. the structure) be established as a madrasa for jurists of all four rites. Our lord and master (*sayyiduna wa mawlana*) the imam of Muslims and the caliph of the Lord of the heavens (*khalifat rabb al-ʿalamin*), Abu Jaʿfar al-Mansur al-Mustansir bi-llah, Commander of the Faithful. May God enhance the foundations of the faith through the everlasting strength of his (the caliph's) rule, and may He revive the minds of the seekers of knowledge (*qulub ahl al-ʿilm*) with [the caliph's] increasing bounty and support. In the year 630 (AH), may God's benedictions and blessings be upon the Prophet Muhammad and his family.[22]

The inauguration of the school (*daʿwa*) in 631/1234 involved a great festivity to which all the leading scholars of the day were invited. The caliph himself arrived in a lavish parade and presided in person over the opening ceremony.

It took another two years, however, to complete the great assembly hall (*iwan*) across from the madrasa, a building that captured the attention of contemporaries with its famous mechanical clock. This

---

[21] It was not random that in 1905 Britain chose as the location for its diplomatic mission – the British Residency – a site just across from al-Mustansiriyya on the west bank of the Tigris. The massive size of the Residency made a similar statement of visibility, but with the added touch of a gunboat moored on the water to send a message about the military power of the British Empire: Coke, *Baghdad*, 297.

[22] al-Aʿzami, *al-Madrasa al-Mustansiriyya fi Baghdad* (Baghdad, 1981), 36–38.

clock, situated high up on a wall inside the hall – in a "New York Grand Central Station" style – and set against the background of a celestial map featuring the constellations, may have adhered to Ibn al-Jazri's engineering principles preserved in his famous *Book of Knowledge of Ingenious Mechanical Devices*, which includes a chapter on the working of a clock. The chroniclers describe the clock of al-Mustansiriyya as having small windows with golden doors (indicating sunlight) that, one by one, rotated every hour to become silver doors as the time elapsed. Every hour a ball would roll out from the beaks of two falcon-shaped sculptures, and this would trigger a rotation of one of the windows, in addition to movement of discs, gold or silver, like the sun or moon (for a.m. or p.m.) against the blue background of the celestial map. A disc of the moon waxed and waned, depending on the time elapsed, and something similar happened to the sun disc, one increasing and the other decreasing. This mechanical clock, a form of water clock or clepsydra, caught the attention of observers at the time, and poets composed verses in its honor.[23] While such a clock served as a reminder at the madrasa for the beginnings of the five times of prayer, with its artwork and robotics it served to reflect the grandeur of al-Mustansir's patronage, and the advancements of the age – in a way akin to the introduction of clock towers to city squares as emblems of modernity in the nineteenth century.

Baghdad in the early thirteenth century continued to witness great leaps in scientific interest. Islamic art during this period also underwent a florescence in the areas of illustration and painting in book manuscripts, which now, and in color, vividly narrated various topics, covering botany, medicine, pharmacy, automatons, and dramatic stories, such as Ibn al-Muqaffa''s fables in *Kalila wa Dimna*, and Hariri's *Maqamat*. Yahya b. Mahmud al-Wasiti led the illustration movement that has been termed "the Baghdad school of art."[24] Al-Wasiti left to posterity illustrations that became iconic: a scene with heralds on camels announcing the end of the Ramadan fast with trumpets, with fluttering banners in the background bearing verses from the Qur'an; the departure of a pilgrimage caravan for Mecca; a scene of quiet study in a library with books piled up in uneven ways in several stacks;

[23] Ibn al-Fuwati, *Hawadith*, 111–112; Ghassani, *'Asjad*, 471–472; al-Irbili, *Khulasat al-Dhahab al-Masbuk Mukhtasar min Siyar al-Muluk* (Baghdad, 1964), 287–288.

[24] Wiet, *Baghdad*, 159.

a village scene with the locals peering at visitors entering town on
a camel, and depictions of Sinbad-like voyages on the Indian Ocean.
Gaston Wiet observes that al-Wasiti was a "true master of composition
and grouping, [and] does everything possible to develop both synthesis
and detail,"[25] while Richard Ettinghausen has commented on the
"freedom and realism" that characterize the Baghdad school of painting, where "the figures are placed logically in their context, whether it
consists of landscapes, sometimes treated with real concern for description, or architecture."[26] Wasiti's paintings provide a vivid range of
colors, depict an assortment of activities, and explore the psychological
through a contrasting variety of expressions assigned to the characters
depicted.

The paintings dating to this period also provide a new source of
historical information on Islamic society of the late Abbasid period. "In
their realism," Ettinghausen argues, "these paintings reveal many features of medieval life otherwise unknown."[27] The sudden burst of
creativity in the area of manuscript illustration around this time also
raises questions about the reasons for the newfound acceptance in
Islam, traditionally iconoclastic, of human and figural depiction. The
unconventional openness of al-Nasir to different ideas could have
inspired confidence for artistic experiment. But the phenomenon
could have also represented the culmination of existing trends centered
on learning and patronage of high culture. The culture of the madrasa
in medieval Baghdad probably stimulated a refinement in the arts of the
book, whereby a rising merchant class that was interested in book
collecting demanded a new, more artistic, trend in book production.[28]

At the turn of the thirteenth century the art of Islamic calligraphy
also underwent new esthetic turns, as great calligraphers of the age
infused the Qur'ans of the period with motifs of sinuous clouds and
Chinese-inspired ornamental designs that surrounded the Arabic text.
It was out of the academic environment of the Nizamiyya and
Mustansiriyya and their pressure for excellence that the famed calligrapher Yaqut al-Musta'simi (d. 698/1298) emerged, flourished, and set
the rules for the greatest refinement in Qur'anic calligraphy. Yaqut was
the third great master calligrapher of Islam after Ibn Muqla and Ibn

---

[25] Wiet, *Baghdad*, 161.   [26] See Wiet, 162.
[27] Richard Ettinghausen, *Arab Painting* (New York, 1977), 104.
[28] Ettinghausen, *Arab Painting*, 81.

al-Bawwab, and in fact his tomb is to be found in Baghdad alongside those of Ibn al-Bawwab and Ahmad b. Hanbal.[29] He devised a new way of trimming the reed-pen, which opened up new horizons in calligraphic art (particularly for the styles of *naskh*, *rayhani*, and *muhaqqaq*), and he trained or directly inspired a group known as the "six students" spanning the late thirteenth and fourteenth centuries. Yaqut's influence was strongly felt by the Timurid calligrapher Shams al-Baysunghuri in the first half of the fifteenth century, who followed his Abbasid predecessor in every aspect from the shaping of letters to the spacing of lines on a page.[30] Yaqut would cast a long shadow over the Ottoman period, whose calligraphers would refer to him as the "center for scribes" ("the *qibla* of the *kuttab*" [with *qibla* referring to the direction of prayer to Mecca]).

The caliph took a personal interest in the proper functioning of the school he built, and frequently stopped by for inspections. He had his own belvedere from which he could look on classes in session, and listen in on lectures and the debates of students. The school sometimes also served as a convention center where the caliph hosted meetings with princely dignitaries such as the Zangid Arslan Shah of Sharazur and Isma'il b. Badr al-Din Lu'lu' of Mosul. And it was also there that the caliph mediated reconciliation in 633/1235 between squabbling Ayyubid princes: al-Nasir Dawud and his uncles, al-Kamil and al-Ashraf. The Mustansiriyya was one of the few structures of Abbasid history to survive the various invasions. The Mongols seem to have admired it, and allowed Nasir al-Din al-Tusi (d. 672/1273), an astronomer formerly in the service of the Grandmaster of the Assassins and later of Hulegu, to cart off al-Mustansiriyya's prized book collection to a new library in Maragheh, the Mongol base near Tabriz.

In various ways al-Mustansir's reign represents a new peak in the Abbasid caliphate, with his ability to weld a spirit of cooperation within Iraq among its diverse sects, and in continuing al-Nasir's policy of making the caliphate a focal point of allegiance in the Muslim world. In 634/1237, a letter from al-Mustansir to 'Ala al-Din Kayqubad, who was besieging an Ayyubid force in the town of Amid (modern Diyarbakir), carried enough weight to have the leader of the Rum Seljuks call off the siege, and honor the caliph's diplomatic

---

[29] Sheila Blair, *Islamic Calligraphy* (Edinburgh, 2006), 242.
[30] Roxburgh, *Writing the Word of God*, 42.

intervention.[31] The Abbasid leader was certainly someone taken seriously by his contemporaries for his charisma, if not for his military capabilities. In personal terms, al-Mustansir comes across as a firm political leader, but also as an introspective figure, genuinely devout and inclined to humility and openness to the public. It was not uncommon, when he set out with his entourage in a formal procession to the Friday prayer, for this caliph of medium build and blondish looks, to dismount from his steed and continue to the mosque on foot, with hardly any of his guards and wearing nothing but a white tunic, to the astonishment of shopkeepers and onlookers.[32]

The Mongols and the Last of the Abbasids

When al-Mustansir died unexpectedly, possibly due to medical foul play, he was succeeded by one of his sons, who lacked both the energy and experience of his father. Abu Ahmad al-Mustaʿsim was not the first choice of the court officials, but he seemed a pliant type, preferable to the caliph's brother, whose bellicose rhetoric threatened an escalation with the Mongols. After a stealthy nighttime succession, arranged by Ibn al-ʿAlqami, a public ceremony was held the next day where various officials were brought to offer the *bayʿa* at the palace. The announcement was then made in the various Friday mosques, and, as the new caliph's name was mentioned, a designated official scattered the sums of 1,000 dinars and 1,000 dirhams on the assembled congregation.[33]

Since al-Mustaʿsim was the last caliph before the fall of the caliphate, it is natural that historians would find faults in him, and so it is difficult to shine a clear light on him. Although a literate person, al-Mustaʿsim is described as parsimonious, distracted by his great interest in music – on which he expended a lot of money, inviting singers from far-off lands to his court – and for having withdrawn into a haughty seclusion. There are no edifying stories of his interaction with the public, as with al-Nasir and al-Mustansir, and little that reflects his individual opinions and policy vision.[34] A minor incident, when he visited al-Mustansiriyya, shows him

---

[31]　Ibn al-Fuwati, *Hawadith*, 120.
[32]　Ibn Taghribirdi, *al-Nujum al-Zahira*, 6:345; Dhahabi, *Siyar*, 23:156; Ibn Kathir, *al-Bidaya*, 7:123.
[33]　Ibn al-Fuwati, *Hawadith*, 193.
[34]　For some nuance in reading the image of al-Mustaʿsim, see Kritzeck, "Ibn-al-Tiqtaqa and the Fall of Baghdad," 173.

rebuking a librarian when he saw a scattered pile of books, but the only major statement of direct speech attributed to him (outside the correspondence with Hulegu) comes from 648/1250, when the Ayyubid dynasty in Egypt faced a power vacuum on the death of the sultan al-Salih Ayyub b. al-Kamil. During a scramble in Cairo to defend Egypt against the Crusade of Louis IX, the Mamluk soldiery pledged allegiance to Shajarat al-Durr, the former concubine and widow of al-Salih. Given the novelty of a situation where a woman was about to lead an Islamic kingdom, al-Mustaʿsim reportedly sent the Mamluk commanders a letter in which he rebuked them: "If there is not a man left among you, tell us and we will send you one!"[35] Although Shajarat al-Durr had already begun to mint her name and title on Egypt's coinage as *malikat al-muslimin* ("queen of the Muslims"), the expression of dissatisfaction from Baghdad played no small part in pushing her to marry one of the Mamluk commanders who eventually took over power after her eighty-day reign.

Within Baghdad, al-Mustaʿsim displayed little ingenuity in handling political matters. He kept on the officials who had served his father, and was content to leave important decisions to his court chancellor (*dawatdar*), Aybak, and his vizir, Ibn al-ʿAlqami, who quickly became bitter rivals. In a reversal of his father's policy, and almost immediately after his accession, the new caliph lifted the ban on making the pilgrimage from Iraq to Mecca,[36] in a clear attempt to gain popularity and create a festive atmosphere. He followed this up with an even more fateful step when he decided to reduce the size of the army, probably in reaction to requests from the troops for pay increases,[37] and he apparently continued to do so, and for no clear reason, as late as 650/1252 and 655/1257, even with the looming Mongol danger.[38] Many of these experienced troops are said to have gone over to Syria, where they probably served under the Ayyubids and the Mamluks later on.

---

[35] Ibn Iyas, *Badaʾiʿ al-Zuhur fi Waqaʾiʿ al-Duhur*, ed. Muhammad Mustafa (Beirut, 2010), 1:287. Dunlop hypothesizes that Shajarat al-Durr's title al-Mustaʿsimiyya al-Salihiyya, Malikat al-Muslimin reflects a conciliatory gesture of political affinity to Baghdad, after her accession, especially since al-Salih had willed his domains to the caliph to decide on its future leader: Dunlop, *Arab Civilization*, 263–264. The background of Shajarat al-Durr prior to her appearance beside Egypt's al-Malik al-Salih, however, remains a mystery.
[36] Ibn al-Fuwati, *Hawadith*, 202.   [37] Ibn al-Fuwati, *Hawadith*, 304.
[38] Ibn al-Fuwati, *Hawadith*, 350.

The adversity of al-Musta'sim's caliphate was such that, even before he had to deal with the Mongol danger, Baghdad was ridden by Sunni–Shi'a tensions. An incident of religious provocation in 653/1255 quickly led to polarization and a febrile atmosphere in which Sunni zealots inflicted violence on the Shi'a. With the caliph's failure to interfere in order to pacify the city, a Shi'i grudge spread across Iraq, waiting for an opportunity to retaliate, and it was against this background that the Shi'i vizir, Ibn al-'Alqami probably grew hostile and started hatching plots against the caliph. And as if the revival of endemic sectarianism was not enough, the natural elements also conspired against the city. Baghdad suffered heavy torrential rains in those years, causing a rise in the level of the Tigris and the inundation of the western side of Baghdad in 1248. In 653/1255, however, the Tigris and the Euphrates flooded both sides of Baghdad, culminating in 654/1256 with the destruction of a great number of buildings, and damage to the ramparts and towers of the city.[39] These events were probably only partly caused by weather conditions, and probably exacerbated by the collapse of dykes and reservoirs upstream in both rivers. The inundation no doubt undermined the defenses of the city and created a displacement of the population. News of a volcanic eruption in the Hijaz in 654/1256 whose flowing lava reached the city of Medina would have further colored the psychology of a society seething with images of the end of times. Rumors in 654/1256 that the *dawatdar* Aybak was plotting to depose the caliph in favor of another candidate were hotly denied by Aybak, but they are likely to have a grain of truth, showing frustration with the negligence of the caliph.

The most cataclysmic of challenges for the Abbasids was still on the way with the invasion of the Mongols under Hulegu in 1258. After the initial conquests of Genghis Khan in 616/1219 and for some time after his death in 1227 it seemed for a while that Mongol interest in the Islamic world was waning, with the withdrawal of the Mongol troops in 1225 and a lull of about six years. The death of the last Khwarazm shah, Jalal al-Din, in 628/1231 seemed to remove the Mongols' key adversary from the region. What had changed, in fact, was that the new Khan, Ogedei (r. 1229–1241), Genghis Khan's son, had redirected the thrust of the Mongol offensive. In the Far East, armies were sent against Korea and northern China in 1234, while in the west the campaign was

---

[39] Wiet, *Baghdad*, 158.

directed toward Russia and eastern Europe as Mongol armies penetrated Poland and Hungary in 1241 and reached the outskirts of Vienna.

The westward Mongol thrust north of the Black Sea gave rise to the subsidiary khanate of the Golden Horde, under the leadership of Batu, a son of Jochi, the eldest son of Genghis Khan. Coming from this senior line, and confident in the safety of his very distant appanage, away from the Mongol capital, Karakorum, Batu quickly developed a political mind of his own. He had tolerated working with Ogedei, but when the latter died, and his son Guyuk (r. 1246–1248) was proclaimed Great Khan after a period of regency led by Guyuk's mother, the enmity came out into the open. Guyuk's efforts became concentrated on trying to bring Batu to submission, which brought all foreign campaigns to a halt. When Guyuk died after a short reign, Batu seized the opportunity to bring Mongke, a grandson of Genghis through his youngest son, Tolui, to power as Great Khan. While the Toluids were therefore indebted to the Golden Horde for the succession, and had a common enemy in the line of Ogedei, they would soon ironically find themselves at odds with the Jochids.

To understand Mongol policy at that seemingly quiet juncture therefore is to enter a world of rivalries within the Mongol ruling house, and the struggle between Genghis Khan's children and grandchildren over succession to the Great Khanate. This polarization only increased when Berke Khan (r. 1257–1266), a grandson of Genghis Khan through his eldest son, Jochi, later converted to Islam, reportedly at the hands of a Sufi master of the Kubrawiyya order in Bukhara. A brewing rivalry between the Muslim Berke and the Shamanist Hulegu would, in addition to religion, have a more thorny aspect over the question of who should control the territory of Azerbayjan and western Iran, which the Jochids considered theirs by testament from the days of Genghis Khan.

The proclamation of Tolui's son, Mongke, as Great Khan (r. 1251–1260), after being sidelined for a long time by Ogedei's family, was marked in the Mongol heartland with great celebration, and a pledge of new grand campaigns. This time, however, these were to be directed against the Middle East, with the campaign to be led by Mongke's brother, Hulegu; and against China, under the command of Mongke's other brother, Qubilai. Ironically, Hulegu's campaign was originally intended to undo the damage done by the campaigns of Genghis Khan, and to try and reincorporate the Iranian region in the

Mongol empire, and bring a new measure of security and economic repair. The key target of Hulegu's campaign was the order of the Assassins, whose hit-and-run tactics and invincibility in their fabled stronghold at Alamut in the Elburz mountains in northern Iran had defied invaders for generations. The Assassins had gone a step further, provoking the Mongols by sending a hit squad to try and assassinate Mongke Khan in Karakorum.[40] In previous decades they had successfully intimidated leaders such as the Ayyubid Saladin (d. 589/1193) and the Seljuk Sanjar (d. 552/1157) with threatening notes planted inside their tents and bedchambers – Saladin, in fact, survived an actual assassination attempt in 571/1176, involving no less than four assassins who attacked him one after the other. Similar tactics this time produced massive outrage from the Mongols, who resolved on finishing off the Assassins' holdouts once and for all. With regard to Baghdad, the Mongol objective was more nuanced – in essence, to acquire the allegiance of the caliph, but to wage war on him only if he resisted.

The campaign of Hulegu set out in 1252, reaching Samarqand only in 653/1255. The size of the invading force can be gauged from the description that it took a full month for the main army to cross the Oxus in Dhu'l-Hijja 653/January 1256. In Baghdad that year, the people were witnessing the inauguration of a new madrasa named al-Madrasa al-Bashiriyya, endowed by the caliph's wife. As with al-Mustansiriyya, the opening of this school took place amid great fanfare, and was an occasion attended by all the officials, scholars, teachers, and citizenry. The reception included great amounts of food and sweets (the latter alone requiring 27,000 *ratl*s of sugar for preparation), most of which was left over in such excess that it later was distributed in various neighborhoods of Baghdad.[41]

As the Mongol army arrived in western Iran, everyone in the region probably hoped for the onset of a winter like the one that once turned back the campaign of the Khwarazm shah, Muhammad b. Tekish, against the Abbasid caliph al-Nasir. The winter of 654/1256, however, was unusually mild, and the attempts of the Grand Master, Rukn al-Din Khurshah, to procrastinate through correspondence and embassies failed. Eventually he came out in person to meet Hulegu, and the latter

---

[40] David Morgan, *The Mongols* (London, 2007), 130.
[41] Ghassani, *'Asjad*, 609. A *ratl* roughly equaled 1 pound.

ordered him to command the forces in various castles to cease resistance and open the gates of their holdouts. The Assassins' castles were then taken over one after the other, dismantled stone by stone, and their treasures plundered and carted off to the Mongol hideout on Shahi island in a lake in northwest Iran. The Isma'ili Grand Master was then allowed to travel to meet Mongke Khan, but was killed along the way, one of many broken promises of safety by the Mongols to those agreeing to surrender.

After he established his base in Hamadan, in March 1257, Hulegu began a cycle of brisk correspondence with the caliph, which began with a rebuke. "When the Heretics' (i.e. the Assassins) fortresses were conquered we sent emissaries to request assistance from you. In reply you said that you were in submission, but you did not send troops. Now, a token of submissiveness and allegiance is that you assist us with troops when we ride against foes. You have not done so, and you send excuses ... "

Although the Abbasids had previously cooperated with foreign leaders, Hulegu's situation was very different because he was a non-Muslim leader. Pledging alliance, much less allegiance, would have constituted a religious and moral challenge to a caliphate that prided itself on being a religious symbol in Islam. From the Mongol point of view, religious difference need not have formed an obstacle, since they prided themselves on running an empire that included various belief systems, and had already obtained the allegiance of many Muslim princes.[42] Genghis Khan had relied on Muslim officials, and Ogedei in particular was known as an admirer of Muslim scholars, scientists, and administrators.[43] But even so, Baghdad still considered itself the focal center of Islamic allegiance, and there was great pride in the long stability of the ruling house. Al-Musta'sim's personality may have been lackluster, but medieval chroniclers came to admire the fact that he was the ninth consecutive ruler in a series of father-to-son successions, a feature that was noted by chroniclers with pride. There was none of the turmoil of the tenth and eleventh centuries, when shifts to siblings or other family branches in the succession indicated great instability.

[42] Jackson, *The Mongols and the Islamic World*, 89–92.
[43] Johan Elverskog, *Buddhism and Islam on the Silk Road* (Philadelphia, 2010), 138–139, 43–44. The favorable Muslim view of Ogedei is especially evident in Juzjani's *Tabaqat-i Nasiri*: May, *The Mongol Empire*, 120.

Hulegu no doubt recognized his relatively recent pedigree of descent from Genghis Khan, compared with that of the caliph, but this differential only made him more determined to assert his importance emphatically. He chided the caliph:

No matter how ancient and grand your family may be, and no matter how fortunate your dynasty has been, is the brightness of the moon such that it can eclipse the brilliance of the sun? Talk of what the Mongol army has done to the world and those in it from the time of Genghis Khan until today may have reached your hearing from common and elite, and you may have heard how, through God's strength, they have brought low the dynasties of the Khwarazmians, the Seljuks, the Daylamite kings, the Atabegs, and others, all of whom were families of might and majesty.

The general thrust in Hulegu's letter was therefore demanding submission rather than an end to the caliphate, and in this he may well have considered his entry to Baghdad justified in light of previous similar incursions such as those of the Buyids and the Seljuks, to whom he refers in his next statement: "The gates of Baghdad were not closed to any of those groups, and they kept thrones there. With the might and power we possess, how shall they be closed to us?" The letter was therefore at great pains to show that the Mongols were holders of the greater kingdom, successors to the Buyids, Seljuks, and Khwarazm shahs, and a lot in the letter hinged on holding up this honor. The Mongol leader was eager to play the role of sultan, coexisting with the caliph, but in a dominant role.

Hulegu concluded by giving the caliph another opportunity, although in effect it was an ultimatum:

Previously we have given you advice, but now we say you should avoid our wrath and vengeance … The past is over. Destroy your ramparts, fill in your moats, turn the kingdom over to your son, and come to us. If you do not wish to come, send all three, the vizier, Sulayman shah, and the Dawatdar, that they may convey our message word for word. If our command is obeyed, it will not be necessary for us to wreak vengeance, and you may retain your lands, army, and subjects. If you do not heed our advice and dispute with us, line up your soldiers and get ready for the field of battle.[44]

[44] Morris Rossabi, *The Mongols and Global History: A Norton Documents Reader* (New York, 2011), 106–107.

The caliph's diplomatic policy in handling this situation was in deep disarray. He may well have tried to send the high-level delegation that the Mongols demanded, but the *dawatdar* and Sulayman shah refused to go.[45] Sending a lower-ranking embassy bearing a monetary gift and some treasures probably did more damage in terms of offending Mongol pride than if he had not sent anything. Baghdad in those years was hardly in any state to put up a fight against the Mongol invasion. The death of the commander Iqbal al-Sharabi in 653/1255, probably poisoned, removed the most experienced military figure on the Abbasid side for handling such a crisis. But for their part, the Mongols were almost clueless about the complete vulnerability of Baghdad. Throughout those months of negotiation there was a widespread belief in the Mongol high command that the army of the caliph was enormous.[46] The glorified reputation of Baghdad as a huge population center and metropolis of trade added to Mongol trepidation. This situation probably only began to change after al-Musta'sim's chief minister, Ibn al-'Alqami, went about his famous duplicity, writing to Hulegu in private about the actual weaknesses of the Abbasid capital and promising his loyalty.[47]

The movement of the Mongols from Hamadan to Baghdad was not entirely smooth. They encountered resistance at Kermanshah, which was probably aligned with the caliph, and as a result the town was destroyed.[48] The Abbasid army, although small, was still efficient and loyal to the caliph, as it ventured outside Baghdad to take up defensive positions. When the Mongols tried to buy off the leader of its advance guard, Kara Sonqur, thinking that his Kipchak Turkic background would put him closer to some troops in their camp, he scoffed at the offer and told the invaders that they should seek clemency from the caliph. The *dawatdar* led the mission to repel the Mongols on the outskirts of the city, but, inexperienced in their tactics of feigned retreats, and too stubborn to accept advice to withdraw, he found many of his troops trapped as they tried to pursue some fleeing Mongol troops. His army was practically annihilated, and the Mongols then wreaked havoc on the area, destroying dykes and canals, flooding a vast landscape that turned a battlefield into a swamp, with

[45] Jackson, *The Mongols and the Islamic World*, 128.
[46] Jackson, *The Mongols and the Islamic World*, 83, 128.
[47] Wiet, *Baghdad*, 165.
[48] Boyle, "Dynastic and Political History of the Il-khans," 347.

the *dawatdar* barely escaping with some of his troops back to Baghdad. It had been four centuries since the environment around the Abbasid capital had last been used as a weapon, and the Mongol lesson would later be adapted on land by the Mamluks who applied a scorched-earth policy to the pastures that the Mongols needed for their horses and for advancing through Syria.[49]

The Mongols finally arrived at Baghdad on 22 Muharram 656/ 29 January 1258, and ranged their troops on different sides of the city. Baiju, who commanded the Mongol army in Asia Minor, descended upon Baghdad, accompanied by aid from Mosul's Machiavellian Badr al-Din Lu'lu', and took up positions on the city's western side. Ketbuqa, who had led another Mongol army through southern Iran, took up his position to the south of the city, while outside its eastern walls Hulegu commanded the main army. The heavy weaponry was ranged around the city: mechanical double and triple crossbows that could fire multiple massive naphtha-bearing arrows, each 3 meters in length, and giant mangonels that needed managing by thousands of Chinese engineers who were brought especially for such tasks. Special wagons even ferried the loads of boulders, from the Iranian highlands, to be used in the catapults, since the Baghdad area lacked a supply of rocks. The siege of Beijing in 1215 had taught the Mongols about a range of projectiles with a wider range and accuracy, and incendiary concoctions which, although they fall short of being labeled "gunpowder weapons," could cause a wide perimeter of devastation.[50] The bombardment began on 4 February, pounding the weakest tower in the city's walls, Burj al-'Ajami, located between the Talisman and Kalwadha Gates. It is rumoured that Baiju may have tried to make secret contact with the caliph during the hostilities,[51] but his purpose is unclear – whether to secure better terms of surrender, or even the safety of the caliph. In the years before the arrival of Hulegu, Baiju had been deeply invested in the conquest of the Islamic kingdoms of Asia Minor and more aligned with the Golden Horde Mongols of Russia. Hulegu suspected some duplicity, and, as

[49] Timothy May, *The Mongol Conquests in World History* (London, 2012), 138–141.
[50] John Man, *The Mongols: Genghis Khan, His Heirs and the Founding of Modern China* (London, 2014), 222–223.
[51] Ibn Wasil, *Mufarrij*, 6:216.

a result, it was around this juncture that Baiju suddenly disappeared from the scene.

On 10 February, a week after the bombardment began, the caliph agreed to lead a delegation to meet with Hulegu, going to the Mongol camp with his children and a delegation of scholars, along with Sulayman shah and Aybak (the commander and court chancellor). The two adversaries had finally come face to face: they seem to have been of similar build, not very tall, and quite close in age (both died aged forty-nine), but al-Musta'sim had a darker complexion. At the meeting, Hulegu reportedly showed courtesy, but asked the caliph to call on the population to lay down their weapons, and come out of the city in exchange for safety. This ploy, which had been used by the Mongols with the chief of the Assassins, worked again. As the caliph made this proclamation, and the population began to stream out, the Mongols proceeded to slaughter them systematically. The city was sacked on 13 February, and the caliph was forced to accompany the Mongol leader and Nasir al-Din al-Tusi into the city and disclose where he hoarded Abbasid treasures and wealth.

The circumstances that finally led to the caliph's death on 16 February 1258 are not clear. Western sources based on Marco Polo's account reflect on the Mongol chief's rebuke of the caliph for hoarding wealth rather than using it to build an army to defend the city. They follow up by saying that the Mongol khan imprisoned the caliph with his wealth, where he died of starvation. This account is probably fictional with its moralizing lesson about the transience of wealth and the need for attentive political rule. Islamic sources describe greater hesitance in deciding the fate of the caliph, showing the Mongol leader mired with superstitious anxieties about what could happen if he killed the last caliph in a dynasty that had been around for over five centuries. Rumor had it that such a regicide could trigger an upset in the order of the natural world, with such results as the sun not rising, and the pastures enduring droughts.

An astrologer named Husam al-Din, who was sent directly by Mongke Khan but apparently had his own personal sympathies for the caliph, tried to save the Abbasid ruler from execution by stoking such fears. His rival, the astrologer Nasir al-Din al-Tusi (d. 672/1273), dismissed these views, putting forward other arguments. Tusi had earlier in his career tried hard to enter al-Musta'sim's service, but found his way to advancement blocked by a clique of court advisors and officials, which probably included resistance from Ibn al-'Alqami.

This was payback time. In light of the Mongol rule against shedding the blood of royals except in battle, the decision was finally taken to have the caliph rolled up in a carpet and stampeded to death by moving horses. Mongol historians soon after found it awkward to justify this event. In his *History of the World Conqueror*, Juvaini (d. 682/1283) skipped over it, and tried instead to emphasize the Mongol conquest of the Nizari Isma'ili fortress of Alamut, claiming it as the bigger contribution of the Mongol conquests to Islam.[52]

The curtain finally fell on Abbasid rule with the death of al-Musta'sim, and Baghdad was abandoned to pillage and destruction, which Hulegu later confirmed in a letter to his distant Western ally, Louis IX, in 1262.[53] Observers lamented the fading of the great city, most famously in a poem by Sa'di of Shiraz.[54] Only the Shi'i and Christian areas, including churches, were spared in this wave of violence, mainly in deference to the religious sympathies of Hulegu's two Nestorian Christian wives as well as his commander Ketbuqa. Armenian and Georgian troops, and the Crusader force led by Bohemund VI of Antioch, eagerly joined in the carnage, as they would again at Aleppo.[55] The rapid shift in Hulegu's position toward a violent conquest of Baghdad after the initial phase of negotiation while he was in Hamadan raises questions about what motivated his heightened belligerence. It is possible that the continued defiance of Baghdad risked emboldening more resistance to the Mongol invasion, which was still expected to conquer Syria and Mamluk Egypt. The role played by al-Musta'sim's chief minister, Ibn al-'Aqlami, was also crucial in encouraging a harder stance, as the latter played a double game between caliph and khan, providing the latter with valuable information on Abbasid weaknesses, while misleading the caliph about the prospects of the negotiations.[56]

---

[52] Levi and Sela, eds., *Islamic Central Asia*, 143.

[53] The Baghdad casualties are put at 2 million dead in Hulegu's letter, according to David Morgan's revised reading of the texts: Morgan, *The Mongols*, 133, 196. Apparently the figure of 200,000 that Morgan gave in the earlier edition of his book was a misreading, but one must still account for exaggeration. The Persian chronicler Mustawfi gives a figure of 800,000.

[54] *Sa'di al-Shirazi: Ash'aruhu al-'Arabiyya*, ed. Ja'far al-Shirazi (Beirut, 1980), 34–41. Another neglected poem on the fall of Baghdad is by Taqi al-Din Isma'il b. Abi'l-Yusr: Joseph De Somogyi, "Adh-Dhahabi's *"Ta'rikh al-islam"* as an Authority on the Mongol Invasion of the Caliphate," *JRAS* 68 (1936), 602.

[55] Thomas T. Allsen, *Mongol Imperialism: The Policies of the Grand Qan Mongke in China, Russia, and the Islamic Lands, 1251–1259* (Berkeley, 1987), 83–85.

[56] Morgan, *The Mongols*, 132; Ghassani, *'Asjad*, 641.

But Hulegu's growing boldness in bringing down the caliph was also in no small measure a product of his growing ambition to garner an achievement that would enhance his profile among the descendants of Genghis Khan. Although Hulegu had completed the conquest of the Assassins and of Baghdad, and received the title "Il-Khan" (vassal of the Khan), his move to assert his control over Azerbayjan put him on a collision course with Berke Khan and the Golden Horde in Russia, who claimed it as part of their appanage. The brewing polarization between Berke and Hulegu grew worse, as Berke increasingly allied himself with the Mamluks, while Hulegu aligned himself with the Crusaders. Hulegu's attempt to rush back from the Middle East to Karakorum after hearing of the death of the Great Khan Mongke clearly illustrates his ambition for a higher leadership role. He was too late, however, since his brother, Qubilai, at greater proximity to the Mongol capital while based in China, was quickly chosen as Great Khan.

When Mongke Khan originally sent Hulegu to the Middle East, China and the Islamic world represented the two dominant and ancient cultural orbits of Asia and civilization in general. By asserting his control over Baghdad, Hulegu was attempting to project his new reputation as the conqueror of a caliphate that had been in existence since the beginning of Islam – an achievement that would have been useful in the event of his candidacy for succession to the supreme rulership of the Mongol empire. Unfortunately for him, this chance came while he was deeply immersed in the Islamic campaign. And far from weakening the resolve of neighboring regional leaders, his heavy-handed dealing with Baghdad awakened a desire for renewed resistance. The town of Mayyafariqin held out for twenty months before falling to Hulegu's army, making the Mongols lose precious time for a planned attack on Egypt. The Mamluks were able to harness various factors within a short time to strategic advantage, as they set about organizing a calculated risk in taking on the Mongol army in Syria, and scoring a victory at Ayn Jalut on 3 September 1260. This event emboldened Berke Khan of the Golden Horde to open hostilities against Hulegu in Azerbayjan, and with distractions on different fronts the Mongols from then on lost their momentum for expansion.[57]

---

[57] Morris Rossabi, *Khubilai Khan* (Berkeley, 1988), 55.

The Abbasids in Egypt (1260–1517)

In the years leading up to Ayn Jalut, Egypt was still reeling from a rough dynastic transition from the Ayyubids to the Mamluks, the latter having seized power through coups by a series of military commanders: Aybak, Qutuz, and then Baybars. The Mamluks were not a unified group, and were hesitant about leading Egypt without an Ayyubid figurehead who could legitimize their role. The death of al-Salih Ayyub on the eve of the Crusade of Louis IX, which landed in Egypt at Damietta, created a power vacuum that was temporarily filled by al-Salih's widow, Shajarat al-Durr – in essence the first of the Mamluks to assume political power. The subsequent violent and chaotic shuffling of power and the aforementioned Mamluks made the vacuum of political legitimacy glaring in the absence of the Ayyubids, who were consumed by their internecine squabbles in Syria. With the Ayyubids swept away by the Mongol invasion of Syria, the Mamluks had to organize the fight for Egypt's survival on their own. The Mongols had provided a stimulant for political and religious mobilization, which helped to unite the Mamluks behind one of their own leaders – first Qutuz, who led the Mamluks at the battle of Ayn Jalut, and, more critically later, Baybars, who deployed various strategies to block the Mongol advance in Syria.

In their search for greater political legitimacy, the Mamluks benefited after the fall of Baghdad from the arrival of refugee members of the Abbasid family, one of whom, a brother of al-Mustansir, was welcomed by Baybars and encouraged to reassume the position of caliph in Cairo, also with the regnal name al-Mustansir. Three years after the office of the caliphate became vacant, Egypt made preparations to reinstall a new line of Abbasid caliphs. The ceremony for this occasion, held in Rajab 659/June 1260, was intended to be a grand one, since in a sense it was a double investiture of caliph and sultan, al-Mustansir and Baybars. The caliph's procession began at the citadel, located on a summit just outside the city, to Cairo, which functioned as the fortress and palace of the Mamluks. Both caliph and sultan entered Cairo through its Gate of Victory (Bab al-Nasr), to an area where all the princes, commanders, and the *'ulama* were assembled. The caliph's full genealogy was then publicly recited, and the authenticity of his belonging to the Abbasid family affirmed. Then the chief judge, Taj al-Din, rose to give the oath of allegiance to the caliph, followed by the sultan Baybars, and the high-profile al-'Izz b. 'Abd al-Salam (d. 660/

1262), a jurist and mystic, who was said to have been invested with the Sufi *khirqa* (a cloth of blessing) directly from al-Suhrawardi of Baghdad.[58] The new al-Mustansir then officially bestowed the title of sultan on Baybars, cloaked him with a black mantle, and granted him sovereignty over Syria, Egypt, and all lands that he would conquer in the future. The chief judge, military commanders, and various ministers next rose to give the oath of allegiance to the Mamluk sultan.[59]

Baybars had stage-managed the spectacle in an effort to whip up public support for his rule in Cairo. The day following the ceremony, Baybars minted the name of the new caliph on Mamluk coins alongside his own as sultan, now assuming the title Qasim Amir al-Mu'minin ("partner of the Commander of the Faithful"), and ordered the revival of the *khutba* of the Friday prayer in the formerly abandoned al-Azhar Mosque – neglected since the fall of the Fatimids – where the names of both caliph and sultan were proclaimed. The overall picture greatly resembled the investiture of the early Seljuks by the Abbasid caliph in Baghdad, but perhaps with the added benefit to Baybars of leveraging the symbolic religious authority of the caliph to provide a counterbalance against the hegemonic institution of the *'ulama*. The event was a watershed moment, not just in political history, but in cultural terms as well, since, according to Ibn Iyas, this repositioning of the caliphate in Cairo enhanced the prestige of Egypt over other regions of the Islamic world, and attracted high-profile religious scholars to settle in Cairo, making this city the heir to "the City of Peace."[60]

Soon after, al-Mustansir was encouraged by Baybars to try, with the help of a small army, to regain control of Baghdad. Whether he counted on Arab tribal support in the Syrian desert is not clear, but after a failed military engagement with the Mongols when he entered Iraq, al-Mustansir simply vanished from history, with no information on what happened to him. Back in Cairo, Baybars sought out another Abbasid in 1262, whom he styled as caliph with the title al-Hakim, but this time with much less fanfare attached to the investiture ceremony, perhaps since the major goal of solidifying Mamluk monarchical legitimacy had already been accomplished with al-Mustansir.[61] For

---

[58] Ibn Iyas, *Bada'i' al-Zuhur*, 1:318.
[59] Ibn Iyas, *Bada'i' al-Zuhur*, 1:313–316.
[60] Ibn Iyas, *Bada'i' al-Zuhur*, 1:321.
[61] P. M. Holt, "Some Observations on the Abbasid Caliphate in Cairo," *BSOAS* 47 (1984).

Baybars, who was allied with Berke Khan of the Mongol Golden Horde in the Black Sea region through diplomatic and trade ties, including a betrothal to Berke's daughter, the caliph served another purpose. Just as al-Mustansir had helped Baybars rise in political rank and religious importance through a formal investiture ceremony, al-Hakim was able to provide similar honors to Berke's envoy to Cairo, which strengthened the Baybars–Berke alliance against Hulegu. When war broke out between Berke and Hulegu, Baybars could now count on Berke's support in light of the trappings of honor delivered on behalf of the Abbasid caliph to Berke at his capital, Saray.[62] This may well have been the most important task the new caliph was expected to accomplish, since the Abbasid was increasingly in the shadows during Baybars' reign.

Al-Hakim held the position of caliph for forty years and saw several Mamluk leaders come and go, including Baybars (r. 1260–1277), Qalawun (r. 1279–1290), al-Ashraf Khalil (r. 1290–1293), and Muhammad b. Qalawun (reigned three times between 1293 and 1341). Popular perception has often dismissed the caliphate in Cairo as a feeble institution that played no significant role in politics. This minimalist view, however, has been exaggerated, and recent assessments of Mamluk history have shown the Abbasid caliphate as a vital institution for Mamluk political legitimization. Although the Mamluks took great advantage of the honorific role they played in securing pilgrimage routes to Mecca, refurbishing the mosque of the Ka'ba, and investing heavily in building religious structures, they also cultivated an image as warriors of the faith involved in jihad campaigns against the Mongols and the Crusader kingdoms, thereby reenacting the role that the caliphs once had. The Mongol threat to take Syria still loomed large throughout al-Hakim's caliphate, and the Mamluks fought to deter this in battles in 675/1277 and 680/1281, while they also mounted sieges that reconquered the last Crusader holdouts, including Antioch, Tripoli, Acre, and other fortresses.

Throughout these, the caliph supported the Mamluks, with his name and prestige, as warriors of the faith. His black banners appeared alongside the Mamluk yellow ones in battle, and his name was always used in the last-minute exchanges of letters of threat before war with the Ilkhanids. The latters' arrogant claims to superiority due to their

---

[62] Holt, "Some Observations," 503.

descent from Genghis Khan, especially when they taunted the Mamluks as being of slave origin, could only be responded to by the Mamluk claim to be hosting the Abbasid caliphate, to which all Muslims owed obedience.[63] Al-Ashraf Khalil b. Qalawun even enhanced the symbolic importance of the Abbasids by including on his coins the inscription "Reviver of the Abbasid State" (*muhyi al-dawla al-abbasiyya*), and, fresh from his conquest of the last Crusader base at Acre, even contemplated the re-conquest of Iraq.[64] The Abbasid sanctioning of Mamluk rule allowed the sultans to posture as the central leaders of the Islamic world.[65] The conversion of the Ilkhanid khan Ghazan (r. 1295–1304) to Islam in 694/1295 could make a dent in the Mamluk Islamic ideology but not override it because of the position of the caliphate in Cairo. This may even explain why the Ilkhanid Uljaitu experimented with converting to Shi'ism in his search for a cohesive ideology that could be Islamic while countering the Sunni foundation of Mamluk rule.

The presence of the Abbasids in Cairo was significant to a range of other dynasts during the Mamluk period. The Jalayrid sultan Ahmad in Iraq (r. 1382–1410) proclaimed himself allied to the caliph when he declared his title on coins as Helper of the Commander of the Faithful (*mughith amir al-mu'minin*), and Muhammad b. Muzaffar (r. 1313–1357), the founder of the Muzaffarid dynasty, which ruled in Isfahan, Shiraz, and Kerman between 1313 and 1393, declared his allegiance to the caliph al-Mu'tadid after capturing Tabriz in 1357, as did his son, Shah Shuja' (r. 1357–1384) in 1369 to the caliph al-Mutawakkil.[66] The Ottomans, who were active in conquests in the Balkans and found themselves in competition with other Turkic principalities in Asia Minor, also sought Abbasid caliphal support. The Ottoman Bayazid (r. 1389–1402), who famously scored a victory in 1396 against a Crusader army at the battle of Nicopolis, sought in 1394 to acquire a diploma of investiture from the Abbasid caliph, and, indirectly, an alliance with the Mamluk sultan Barquq (r. 1382–1389 and 1390–1399). Bayazid obtained from the Abbasid al-Mutawakkil II

---

[63] Anne Broadbridge, *Kingship and Ideology in the Islamic and Mongol Worlds* (Cambridge, 2008), 14–15, 84, 149–150.

[64] Broadbridge, *Kingship*, 45–49.

[65] Cihan Yüksel Muslu, *The Ottomans and the Mamluks: Imperial Diplomacy and Warfare in the Islamic World* (London, 2014), 9–10.

[66] Arnold, *The Caliphate*, 102–103.

the title Sultan al-Rum, and came to be viewed as the official heir of the Seljuks.[67]

In India, the name of the Abbasid caliph also resonated with importance, and perhaps for longer. Initial ties were established between Baghdad and the Delhi sultanate as far back as 617/1220 when the caliph al-Nasir sent out an envoy, Radi al-Din Abu'l-Fada'il al-Saghani (d. 650/1253), to Iltutmish (r. 1210–1236). The ideological message of al-Nasir seems to have taken deep root in India, where the envoy stayed for seven years before returning to Baghdad to find a new caliph, al-Mustansir.[68] Delhi was not a place people left quickly in those days. The city had grown tremendously with refugees from the Mongol invasions of Khurasan, including scholars, merchants, and artisans, and it afforded great opportunities for wealth, networking, and adventure.

After receiving the caliph's diploma of investiture, the Delhi sultans styled themselves with the new title Nasir Amir al-Mu'minin ("helper of the Commander of the Faithful") on their coins, and mention of the caliph continued until 695/1296 with the reign of the Khalji sultan, Rukn al-Din Ibrahim.[69] When Ibn Battuta visited India in 735/1333, he mentioned the existence of a neighborhood of Delhi that was named "the Abode of the Caliphate," said to have been given by the Delhi sultan to a grandson of al-Mustansir when he visited, possibly after the fall of Baghdad.[70] Relations between the Mamluks and Delhi were established in the fourteenth century when the caliph was allowed to play the role of granting a diploma of investiture, such as in the embassy sent by al-Mu'tadid in 754/1353 to Firuz Shah (r. 1351–1388) with a mandate (*manshur*) conferring on him the title Sayf al-Khilafa ("sword of the caliphate") and Qasim Amir al-Mu'minin ("partner of the Commander of the Faithful"). Another Abbasid embassy arrived the next year bearing a new title, Sayyid al-Salatin ("lord of the sultans"), from the new caliph, al-Mutawakkil.

[67] Broadbridge, *Kingship*, 150, 175; Muslu, *The Ottomans and the Mamluks*, 79, 141.
[68] Jackson, *The Delhi Sultanate*, 37, 44–45.
[69] Jackson, *The Delhi Sultanate*, 45.
[70] *Ibn Battuta: Travels in Asia and Africa, 1325–1354*, trans. H. A. R. Gibb (London, 1929), 194. A great-grandson of the same al-Mustansir, named Abdallah b. Muhammad al-Abbasi (d. 808/1406), reportedly settled on the island of Sumatra, where he was a revered figure: Giancarlo Casale, "Tordesillas and the Ottoman Caliphate: Early Modern Frontiers and the Renaissance of an Ancient Islamic Institution," *Journal of Early Modern History* 19 (2015), 503.

The caliph's aim from the mission was to send the message to the princes of the Indian subcontinent that Firuz Shah was their sovereign, and that to obey the sultan was to obey the caliph himself.[71]

The importance of the Abbasid caliphal office therefore continued well into the fourteenth century as a factor of dynastic legitimization, political mobilization, and as a catalyst for establishing diplomatic ties among geographically distant and politically diverse states. For a brief period in 815/1412 the Mamluks even contemplated designating the Abbasid caliph as their sultan, when al-Musta'in reigned for six months until the Mamluk power struggle was resolved with the rise of the sultan al-Mu'ayyad Shaykh.[72] What changed this international order in the Islamic world was the invasion of the Middle East by Tamerlane (r. 1369–1404), and specifically his capture of Syria from the Mamluks in 803/1401. Although Egypt was spared from conquest, this came at the high price of Mamluk political acquiescence to a new Mongol leadership, and their toning down of the importance of Abbasid caliphal legitimization.[73] During the tussle with the Mamluks, Tamerlane did not envision abolishing the caliphate, but threatened to appoint the caliph himself if he took over Egypt, and referred to himself as the "refuge of the caliphate" (*maladh al-khilafa*).[74]

The Abbasid caliphate stayed on in Cairo as a politically reduced entity throughout the fifteenth century. During this period, the position of the caliph had become mainly one of social dignity comparable to that of a notable or religious functionary, such as the *qadi*, *mufti*, or *naqib al-ashraf*. The caliph would join with this group to visit the Mamluk sultan on religious holidays to wish him well on the occasion of Ramadan or the great feasts, but the caliphate was otherwise reduced as a political symbol. It remained in this situation until the Ottomans conquered Syria and Egypt and finished off the Mamluk state in 922/1516–1517. After Selim I defeated the Mamluks at the battle of Marj Rahit near Aleppo in 1516, he reportedly held

---

[71] Jackson, *The Delhi Sultanate*, 296–298. Auer, *Symbols*, 115. As late as 1474, an embassy from Delhi arrived in Egypt, seeking a diploma of investiture from the caliph: Carl Petry, "The Military Institution and Innovation in the Late Mamluk Period," in *The Cambridge History of Egypt*, vol. 1: *Islamic Egypt, 640–1517*, ed. Carl Petry (Cambridge, 1998), 464.

[72] Jean-Claude Garcin, "The Regime of the Circassian Mamluks," in Petry, ed., *The Cambridge History of Egypt*, vol. 1, 292.

[73] Broadbridge, *Kingship*, 189, 192–194.   [74] Arnold, *The Caliphate*, 117.

a ceremony in the great mosque of Aleppo where he met with the
Abbasid caliph al-Mutawakkil III (d. 945/1543) and was proclaimed
as "Servant of Mecca and Medina."[75] Legend has it that it was at this
meeting that the caliph handed the sultan the famous insignia of the
caliphate – especially the mantle (*burda*) of the Prophet and some
relics – before both caliph and sultan entered Damascus together
during the Ottoman march on Egypt. The purported insignia were
then reportedly sent to Constantinople, where they were stored in the
Eyüp Mosque – named after Abu Ayyub al-Ansari, a Companion of the
Prophet, who died in one of the early Islamic sieges of the city and was
buried at the walls of the city.[76] It remained famous as the place where
the sultans were routinely invested with the symbols of sovereignty
upon their accession to rule.[77] The Abbasid caliph was then brought
out to Constantinople, where he resided for a while, but was later
allowed to return to Egypt. The political role of the Abbasids ended
here, and the term "caliphate" entered a realm of ambiguous meaning
that varied between theories expounded by the religious scholars and
attempts by some dynasts to revive it for their own political purposes.

---

[75] Halil İnalcik, *The Ottoman Empire: The Classical Age 1300–1600* (London,
1973), 33; Michael Winter, "The Ottoman Occupation," in Petry, ed., *The
Cambridge History of Egypt*, vol. 1, 499.
[76] Arnold, *The Caliphate*, 140–142.
[77] Colin Imber, *The Ottoman Empire, 1300–1650* (New York, 2009), 102, 105,
106.

7 | Conclusion

The Abbasid caliphate always stands at the center of any analysis of the enigmatic Islamic conception of the caliphate, and the shaping of Islamic beliefs in general. The notion of Islam as a universal religion and the office of the caliph as supreme leader was fully clarified only in the Abbasid period, as Thomas Arnold argued in his study *The Caliphate*, published in in 1924, the year that the institution of the caliphate was abolished. Historians today research the intellectual history of Islam, and its origins, according to sources composed mostly in the Abbasid period, and debate questions on the caliphate according to definitions that emanated from debates that thrived under the Abbasids. Their history yields the lesson that monarchical dynasties are not necessarily important only at moments of imperial coercion, but also as a source of influence on shaping culture and ideology long after they have lost their political power.

As an empire, the Abbasid state held wide political and military sway only in its first century, but its loss of this power in the east and in North Africa calls for a pause of reflection. For better or for worse, the Abbasids had to rule over an exceptional variety of geographical terrains and climatic zones, and in fact no previous state had ruled over such a diverse region for such a long period. The Roman empire had the Mediterranean Sea in its midst, and could transport troops from one end of it to another in twenty days of clear sailing.[1] And, barring the tenacious exception of Trajan, the Romans generally floundered when they had to press deep inland, as with their Mesopotamian campaigns in the third century against the Parthians and Sasanids. The Abbasids did not have the possibility of water transport in ruling their eastern empire, and had to deal daily with complex terrain and inhospitable pockets of dissidence.[2] As one observer of military history has commented on the striking continuity of strategic military challenges in the mountainous

---

[1] Brown, *The World of Late Antiquity*, 13.
[2] Chris Wickham, *The Inheritance of Rome* (New York, 2009), 333–335.

region of modern-day Afghanistan: "The difficulties that Alexander the Great faced in fighting the mountain tribes of the Kunar Valley in the fourth century BC were not that much different from those faced by the Americans in the twenty first century."[3]

The caliphs faced the same challenges on the borders of China and India, and also had to balance their priorities with attention to various corners of the empire: North Africa, Asia Minor, the Fertile Crescent, and the Arabian Peninsula. The Abbasids, unlike the Umayyads, understood the cost of military expansion in terms of social dissidence – especially since they had grown out of one such movement – and they tried to curtail the tide of jihad. Modern views of the Middle Ages as a period colored by religious zealotry and Crusades can often exaggerate the role of holy war. In reality, the Abbasids – and even the Byzantines – were more eager to establish boundaries on territoriality, such as in the way Harun al-Rashid (r. 786–809) and the Byzantine Basil II (r. 975–1025) showed restraint in expansion, the first in Asia Minor and the second in Syria, even when they had the opportunity to make more conquests and were at the height of their power. And as late as the thirteenth century, the Abbasids would be taunted for this by upstarts such as the Khwarazm shah Muhammad b. Tekish (r. 1200–1220), who wrote to the caliph al-Nasir, saying: "The Abbasid Caliphs had been backward in undertaking holy wars in the way of God Almighty and though possessing the means thereto, had failed to defend the frontiers, to extirpate the heterodox and the heretical and to call the infidel to the True Faith."[4]

A more realistic view of how far central power can reach also guided Abbasid internal policy. The caliphs favored a policy of consolidation within the empire and stable tax collection, and even there they showed some flexibility when the revenues did not reflect the full capabilities of the provinces. A register of such revenue collection provided by the tenth-century al-Jahshiyari shows, for the reign of Harun al-Rashid, Iraq's tax yield totaling 164 million dirhams, Egypt's at 42 million, and Khurasan at 28 million. The empire was clearly being run mostly on the agricultural and financial wealth of the home province, Iraq.[5] In provincial government, the caliphs favored striking better arrangements in

---

[3] Thomas Barfield, *Afghanistan: A Cultural and Political History* (New York, 2010), 69.

[4] George Lane, *The Mongols* (London, 2018), 57.

[5] Jahshiyari, *Kitab al-Wuzara'*, 281–288. Hugh Kennedy, "The Decline and Fall of the First Muslim Empire," *Der Islam* 81 (2004), 11–12; Saleh Ahmed el-Ali,

which they tried to coopt the loyalty of diverse groups of regional elite, such as in the cases of Tabaristan, Ushrusuna, Khwarazm, and even Khurasan. Although the caliphs of the ninth century did not easily give up on the idea of an Abbasid imperium, they were willing to leave a lighter footprint in distant provinces, such as North Africa, and prepared to accept compromise: they could entertain the idea of a Saffarid in place of the Tahirids in charge of Khurasan, if he could cooperate with them, and a perennial Tulunid in Egypt if he would pay a credible share of the province's revenue. But even after they had done this, and scuttled some provinces, like weights from a nineteenth-century air balloon, they still found it difficult to take off.

Over time it became evident that the problem was not so much that Baghdad was eager to rule far-off peoples, but that people from far-off lands wanted to rule Baghdad. Even before the discovery of oil, Iraq was the much-sought-after prize of the alluvial plain of the Tigris and the Euphrates, and the inevitable road for invading armies. It was not the Egypt of the Nile region, where it took determined effort – even obsession – by the likes of Alexander to digress in order to invade it; Iraq simply stood as the inevitable bridge for invaders. Maintaining agricultural stability in the Tigris–Euphrates region was already a tough job to accomplish in peaceful times in light of issues such as river flooding and desalination. To add to these, military threat made it close to impossible. The mosaic ethnic, religious, and cultural nature of Iraq also added another precarious layer that could be aggravated by foreign threat and worsen an internal situation of jockeying for power. Political and military turmoil in Iraq sometimes also left international ripple effects. The diversion of trade routes, during the period of the Zanj revolt and Qaramita raids on Iraqi towns in the ninth and tenth centuries, from the Persian Gulf toward the Red Sea region, perhaps did not just empower Fatimid Egypt but helped other Mediterranean towns farther afield, such as Pisa, Amalfi, and Genoa, to take off as city-states at the expense of Constantinople and its traditional trade ties with the east.[6]

At the outset of its founding in 750, Baghdad may have seemed a starry-eyed choice for a capital when the borders of the Islamic empire

"A New Version of Ibn al-Mutarrif's List of Revenues in the Early Times of Harun al-Rashid," *JESHO* 14 (1971).

[6] Armand Citarella, "The Relations of Amalfi with the Arab World before the Crusades," *Speculum* 42 (1967).

were distant and secure, but there was no telling how this city could be defended if it came under threat. Unlike Constantinople, which was mostly surrounded by water and defended by fabled stone walls, Baghdad was a sitting duck with walls of at best sun-dried and baked brick to defend it. Astrologers had overlooked these constraints when Baghdad was first founded, and they saw Jupiter sitting in Sagittarius, but the caliphs later had to deal with down-to-earth consequences. Baghdad residents in later centuries were going to discover an added environmental hazard to their city. From the mid-tenth century there is increasing evidence of harsher winters that not only caused flooding – most notably in 328–353/944–964, 466/1072, 554/1159, and the years just before the Mongol sack of Baghdad – but probably also degraded the city's defenses, hence the frequent references to caliphs, such as al-Qaʾim, al-Mustazhir, al-Mustarshid, al-Muqtafi, al-Nasir, and al-Mustansir, building – or more often just "rebuilding" – the city's walls, probably after being shaken by torrential rains and flooding.

Still, we do a disservice to the Abbasid caliphate to judge it as an empire; it may be more pertinent to view it as an Islamic political institution. And here one finds the more interesting long-term trends in Abbasid history. For too long the history of the caliphate after its initial golden age in the eighth and ninth centuries has been marginalized, and "viewed," according to Eric Hanne, "as some sort of constant throughout Islamic history," diverging from or falling short of an expected standard. But, as Hanne adds, "the *Caliphate*, much like *Islamic history* and the *Middle East*, is a difficult term to define."[7] The scholarly attention often heaped on surveying theoretical definitions of the "imamate" or "caliphate" by intellectuals, such as al-Mawardi and al-Ghazali (in the classical period) and Muhammad Abduh and Ali Abd al-Raziq (in the modern period), and even by modern orientalists, such as Ann Lambton and E. I. J. Rosenthal, does not answer how this definition "played itself out" in relation to events on the ground and with respect to religious, social, political, and military developments.[8]

The unique and consistent feature of the Abbasid caliphate over the centuries was its adaptability to changing times: from its first years as

---

[7] Hanne, *Putting the Caliph in His Place*, 26–27.
[8] Hanne, *Putting the Caliph in His Place*, 27; against the minimizing views of Arnold, *The Caliphate*, 68, 193; Lambton, *State and Government in Medieval Islam*, 138.

a messianic revolution that toppled the Umayyad Arab kingdom and put in its place a trend of Perso-Arab integration; to a later period when the caliphate actively shaped the process of codification of Islamic texts and engaged intellectual currents such as those of the Mu'tazila; to the period beyond when the caliph al-Qadir energetically redefined the position of caliph as "imam," whose power rested on coordination with the authority of the religious scholars; and finally to the twelfth–thirteenth-century period of al-Nasir and al-Mustansir, when the caliph tried to incorporate new dimensions of Sufism and *futuwwa* in defining loyalty to the state and established an alliance with the Sufi master al-Suhrawardi. In each phase Abbasid plans were slowed down or undermined by some factor: rivalry from the Alids, resistance from traditionalist *'ulama* (such as Ahmad b. Hanbal), resistance from provincial *'ulama* (such as al-Juwayni), and, in the case of Sufism, having to deal with the short attention span of Sufis who could quickly move on and coalesce around another spiritual Grand Master, as they did after the death of al-Suhrawardi. Nevertheless, the Abbasids were resilient survivors, and tried different strategies to strengthen their authority; it is one of history's great ifs to ask what new idea they would have adapted to next had they been spared destruction by the Mongols.

Baghdad under Abbasid rule grew into a magnet for the greatest talents in every field, and provided a model for provincial dynasties and emerging cities, such as Nishapur, Bukhara, Shiraz, Aleppo, Mosul, and Cairo, but none captured the special magic of Baghdad's name, with its roots stretching to early Islamic history and memory of its great caliphs and their achievements. The continuity of the Abbasid caliphate for five centuries gave it an aura of antiquity and indispensable custom dating back to the time of the Prophet. The Abbasid capital represented more than anything the bridge that connected the Mediterranean world with the Iranian east, and stimulated constant movement of scholars, artisans, and merchants between east and west, and personified the Perso-Arab hybridity of culture. In the twilight of the thirteenth century, Sharaf al-Din Muhammad b. Abdallah al-Sulami (570–655/1175–1257), a scholar from al-Andalus, could still travel from his hometown of Murcia – the town of the more famous Ibn Arabi – to study hadith and poetry at al-Mustansiriyya with Ibn al-Najjar, continue to Nishapur, Herat, and Marw to study with other scholars, then return to Baghdad, and visit

Mecca after stopping in Damascus.[9] However, after the Mongol conquest of Baghdad such movement was disrupted. The pre-Islamic boundary between the Roman and Sasanid worlds along the Euphrates river returned, albeit in the form of a hard border between the Mamluk and Ilkhanid empires.

Although the Abbasid caliphate did not receive the support it needed against the Mongols in 1258, its downfall resonated with attempts to fill the vacuum. In Egypt, the Mamluk Baybars welcomed a refugee of the Abbasid family, and installed him as a ceremonial caliph, using the event to bolster the religious legitimacy of the emerging Mamluk sultanate. In India, the Delhi sultans continued to include the Abbasid caliph's name on coinage well into the early fourteenth century. The Mongols themselves tried to do some damage control by including a Qur'an verse on their coinage that described the transience of political power: "O God, Master of the Kingdom, Thou Givest the Kingdom to whom Thou wilt."[10] Then when the Ilkhanids converted to Islam they sought to fill the vacuum by including on their coinage the names of the first four caliphs of early Islam – the Rashidun caliphs. By making the Rashidun figures who are perceived by Muslims as the saintly figures of early Islam, points of cultural reference, the Ilkhanids eliminated the potential for Abbasid caliphal revival, and ironically made the definition of the office of the caliphate impossibly hagiographic – or "fundamentalist," to borrow a term from the modern period. This nevertheless coincided well with the interests of the class of the 'ulama across the Muslim world who viewed a Hashimite caliph doubly with apprehension: as a potential rival source of religious authority to the texts of the sharia, which the 'ulama considered their area of specialization; and as a figure whose claim to leadership on the basis of kinship to the Prophet sounded like the original basis of the Shi'i criterion for legitimate political succession.[11] Therefore, while the forces that originally brought down the caliph were Mongol, those that made sure the caliphate was not resurrected were the 'ulama. The price

[9] Naji Ma'ruf, *Tarikh 'Ulama al-Mustansiriyya* (Baghdad, 1965), 2: 209.
[10] Qur'an 3:26.
[11] In December 1915, when the British sounded out Ibn Saud about his reaction to a possible Hashimite caliph in Mecca, the answer overlapped with this. Sir Percy Cox reported the reaction to London, saying: "[Ibn Saud] reminded me that the Wahhabis did not recognize any *Caliph* after the first four": John Townsend, *Proconsul to the Middle East: Sir Percy Cox and the End of Empire* (London, 2010), 75.

of the vacuum left by the caliphate as a mediating institution in Islamic society has not been sufficiently recognized.[12]

The Abbasid caliphate included in its history the reigns of thirty-seven caliphs, and, while in Cairo as a shadow caliphate, the ceremonial reigns of seventeen. In the event of a revival of the caliphate, the fourteenth-century Qalqashandi provides thirty-seven additional titles that future caliphs can adopt.[13] There never was a revival of the Abbasid caliphate, but the title "caliph" was embraced in one form or another by various dynasts. The Hafsids of Tunisia sized up the situation in the 1250s and were early-bird claimants to the title. The Mamluk sultan Baybars referred to himself as "partner of the Commander of the Faithful," while the Ottoman sultan Selim, after the battle of Chaldiran, was praised as "king of the throne of the caliphate."[14] In fact, the Ottomans and Safavids, who were archenemies, each placed a claim. Suleyman the Magnificent referred to himself as the "inheritor of the Grand Caliphate,"[15] and inscribed the word "caliph" among his many titles that he listed over the portal to his famous Süleymaniye Mosque,[16] while the founder of the Persian Safavid empire, Shah Isma'il (r. 1501–1524), according to Khwandamir (d. 942/1525), wore "the crown of the caliphate and world conquest on his head."[17] In India, the Mughals also tapped into the caliphal title. In 937/1530 the famed city of Agra, home to the Taj Mahal, was called the "seat of the caliphate," and a little later the Mughal Akbar (r. 1556–1605) directly proclaimed himself on his coinage "the great sultan, the exalted khalifa"; and the title remained in use among the Mughals till 1760.[18] None of these dynasties

---

[12] A recent author, scanning the range of modernizing steps taken by the Ottoman empire and Egypt in the nineteenth century, intersects with this on the question he raises: "If Islam engaged so successfully with modernity until the First World War, why since then has reactionary revivalism been able to impose itself on ever wider swathes of the Muslim world?": de Bellaigue, *The Islamic Enlightenment*, xxiii.

[13] Qalqashandi, *Ma'athir*, 470. [14] Arnold, *The Caliphate*, 132.

[15] Turfan Buzpinar, "Opposition to the Ottoman Caliphate in the Early Years of Abdulhamid II: 1877–1882," reprinted in *The Caliphate and Islamic Statehood*, ed. Carool Kersten (Berlin, 2015), 3:7.

[16] Caroline Finkel, *Osman's Dream: The Story of the Ottoman Empire, 1300–1923* (London, 2005), 115, 145.

[17] Sussan Babaie, "Persia: The Safavids 1501–1722," in *The Great Empires of Asia*, ed. Jim Masselos (London, 2010), 139; see also 216 in the same volume.

[18] D. S. Margoliouth, "The Caliphate Historically Considered," *The Moslem World*, 11 (1921), 338; D. Sourdel et al., "Khalifa," *EI²*, 946.

claimed the title of caliph by virtue of kinship to the Prophet, but only as holders of a symbolic religious authority.

After the subsiding of the classical period, the late nineteenth and early twentieth centuries witnessed diverse attempts by various political parties to revive the caliphate as a political office and to use it to their advantage. The Ottomans did that in the years leading up to World War I to strengthen their authority as sultans and caliphs, while the British tried during the war to counter the Ottomans with a push for an Arab caliphate based in Mecca, led by a member of the Hashimite family. In the postwar period the idea of caliphate continued to resonate, as it combined with quests for liberation from Western colonial rule. In India, between 1919 and 1924, the Khilafat Movement, of which Gandhi was a member, called for nation building and independence from the British empire and Western domination. These latter evocations of the term "caliphate" were not at the time anchored in a formal picture of "Islamic" statehood, but rather were used loosely for political mobilization, and by way of nostalgia for better times – along the lines of leftist utopian movements of the nineteenth century, imagining a past and trying to reinterpret it to provide solutions for the present.[19] The evocations of a "golden age" in Abbasid times also paralleled the rise of a nostalgic wave of medievalism in the West, which looked back on the Middle Ages as a time of chivalry, cohesion, spirituality, and "moral grandeur."[20]

Today, the term "caliphate" has come to denote in journalistic use a form of political and religious tyranny, a fanatical version of the application of Islamic law, and general intolerance toward other faiths – another reinterpretation, albeit a distorted one, at the beginning of the twenty-first century. It may be useful to recall that such radical perceptions of the term float mostly in the realm of media coverage and are far removed from the actual historical reality of achievements when a caliphate existed in the medieval period. If we take a longer view of the influence of the office of the caliphate on

---

[19] See the editors' introduction to Madawi Al-Rasheed, Carool Kersten, and Marat Shterin, eds., *Demystifying the Caliphate: Historical Memory and Contemporary Contexts* (New York, 2013).

[20] The phenomenon is examined especially for the cases of France and England in David Lowenthal, *The Past Is a Foreign Country, Revisited* (Cambridge, 2015), 45, 173, 175; Norman Cantor, *Inventing the Middle Ages* (New York, 1991), 42–43.

changes in Islamic society, it may be worth noting that most of the dramatic social and legal reforms instituted by, for instance, the Ottomans in the nineteenth century were only feasible because of the ability of a sultan to posture as caliph. The Gülhane Reform of 1839 which established the equality of all subjects of the empire before the law, the reforms of 1856 which eliminated social distinctions based on religion, the abolition of slavery in 1857, and the suspension of the traditional penalties of Islamic law (*hudud*) in 1858[21] would all have been inconceivable without the clout that the umbrella of the caliphate afforded to the office of the reforming monarch.

The Abbasids may seem far removed from these developments in modern history, but what makes them relevant is the theme of adaptability to change. The Abbasids had begun the trend of patronizing the Hanafi branch of Islamic law, which allowed for rational flexibility, and this legalistic current, which became the official basis of Islamic law under the Ottomans, would later allow the opening of the door for various reforming steps in the modern period. With al-Ma'mun we find a caliph who not only encouraged scientific thinking but also sought to curb the militant preaching that goes with the slogan of "preventing vice and promoting virtue" – today famously associated with the Wahhabi branch of Islam. And in their later history the Abbasids continued to encourage policies that seemed ecumenical in spirit or accepting of new trends. This was reflected in the way al-Nasir incorporated Sufism and *futuwwa* in the Abbasid system as mainstream ideas and followed policies that were inclusive of both Sunni and Shi'i Muslims, and in the way his successor, al-Mustansir, patronized the building of religious schools that included more than one branch of Islamic legal practice. The many examples of Muslims and non-Muslims serving together in the Abbasid bureaucracy provided a model that later Islamic empires could refer to as a precedent. Historians of the modern Middle East often limit their purview of stimulus to change as coming from the West or from a modern background, but looking at the broad sweep of Abbasid history, it may be just as useful to explore echoes of progressive steps toward change from the Islamic past itself.

---

[21] Coulson, *A History of Islamic Law*, 151.

Appendix: The Abbasid Caliphs

In Iraq
al-Saffah (132–136/750–754)
al-Mansur (136–158/754–775)
al-Mahdi (158–169/775–785)
al-Hadi (160–170/785–786)
Harun al-Rashid (170–193/786–809)
al-Amin (193–198/809–813)
al-Ma'mun (198–218/813–833)
al-Mu'tasim (218–227/833–842)
al-Wathiq (227–232/842–847)
al-Mutawakkil Ja'far (232–247/847–861)
al-Muntasir Muhammad (247–248/861–862)
al-Musta'in Ahmad (248–252/862–866)
al-Mu'tazz Muhammad (252–255/866–869)
al-Muhtadi Muhammad (255–256/869–870)
al-Mu'tamid Ahmad (256–279/870–892)
al-Mu'tadid Ahmad (279–289/892–902)
al-Muktafi Ali (289–295/902–908)
al-Muqtadir Ja'far (295–320/908–932)
al-Qahir Muhammad (320–322/932–934)
al-Radi Muhammad (322–329/934–940)
al-Muttaqi Ibrahim (329–333/940–944)
al-Mustakfi Abdallah (333–334/944–946)
al-Muti' Fadl (334–363/946–974)
al-Ta'i' Abd al-Karim (363–381/974–991)
al-Qadir Ahmad (381–422/991–1031)
al-Qa'im Abdallah (422–467/1031–1075)
al-Muqtadi Abdallah (467–487/1075–1094)
al-Mustazhir Ahmad (487–512/1094–1118)
al-Mustarshid al-Fadl (512–529/1118–1135)

al-Rashid Mansur (529–530/1135–1136)
al-Muqtafi Muhammad (530–555/1136–1160)
al-Mustanjid Yusuf (555–566/1160–1170)
al-Mustadiʾ Hasan (566–575/1170–1180)
al-Nasir Ahmad (575–622/1180–1225)
al-Zahir Muhammad (622/1225–1226)
al-Mustansir Muhammad (623–640/1226–1242)
al-Mustaʿsim Abdallah (640–656/1242–1258)

In Egypt
al-Mustansir b. al-Zahir (659/1261)
al-Hakim I (660–701/1261–1302)
al-Mustakfi b. al-Hakim (701–740/1302–1340)
al-Wathiq I b. Ahmad b. al-Hakim (740–741/1340–1341)
al-Hakim II b. al-Mustakfi (741–753/1341–1352)
al-Muʿtadid I b. al-Mustakfi (753–763/1352–1362)
al-Mutawakkil I b. al-Muʿtadid (763–779/1362–1377), first time
al-Muʿtasim b. Mutawakkil (779/1377), first time
al-Mutawakkil (779–785/1377–1383), second time
al-Wathiq II (785–788/1383–1386)
al-Muʿtasim (788–791/1386–1389), second time
al-Mutawakkil (791–808/1389–1406), third time
al-Mustaʿin b. Mutawakkil (808–816/1406–1414)
al-Muʿtadid II b. al-Mutawakkil (816–845/1414–1441)
al-Mustakfi II b. al-Mutawakkil (845–855/1441–1452)
al-Qaʾim b. al-Mutawakkil (855–859/1451–1455)
al-Mustanjid b. al-Mutawakkil (859–884/1455–1479)
al-Mutawakkil II b. al-Mustaʿin (884–903/1479–1497)
al-Mustamsik b. al-Mutawakkil II (903–914/1497–1508), first time
al-Mutawakkil III (914–922/1508–1516), first time
al-Mustamsik (922–923/1516–1517), second time
al-Mutawakkil III (923/1517), second time

Glossary

Abna' (lit. "the sons"): used metaphorically with reference to commanders in the early Abbasid period as "loyalists to the Abbasid state and revolution."

ahl al-hadith religious scholars who based their views on hadith texts rather than mostly on rational opinion.

ahl al-ra'y religious scholars whose legal judgments were based on rational opinion (*ra'y*) in addition to hadith.

amir al-umara' Chief Prince, a position created in 324/936 by the Abbasids to handle security matters in Iraq.

amir al-mu'minin Commander of the Faithful; another title for the caliph, more frequently used on Abbasid coinage.

Atabeg: tutor or guardian to a Seljuk prince.

bay'a the oath of allegiance.

"createdness creed": a doctrine of speculative theology espoused by the Mu'tazila that referred to the Qur'an as the "created" word of God.

da'i (pl. *du'at*): propoagandist, usually of a Shi'i religious movement.

da'wa call or propaganda, such as for the Abbasid revolution.

dawla (lit. "the state"): the term had a millennial connotation when first used by the Abbasids.

diwan: government department.

faqih (pl. *fuqaha'*): jurist.

farsakh: a medieval measurement of distance; 3 miles/6 kilometers.

fiqh: Islamic jurisprudence.

fitna (lit. "temptation"): a religious term of reference for discord and civil strife within the Muslim community.

futuwwa (lit. "manliness," "chivalry"): solidarity group of young men, pledging loyalty to a religious master, along Sufi lines; initiation through special ceremonies; gained momentum after the twelfth century.

ghulam (pl. *ghilman*): military slave; equivalent to "mamluk" in the later medieval period.

hadith: the sayings of the Prophet Muhammad.

Hanafi: a school of jurisprudence attributed to Abu Hanifa, and espousing the emphasis of rational method (*ra'y*).

Hanbali: a school of jurisprudence named after Ahmad b. Hanbal; strictly based on hadith.

hijra the Prophet's migration from Mecca to Medina in 622.

ijma' consensus on a religious opinion.

Imam: leader of prayer, but increasingly of a religious movement; often Shi'i in character.

iqta' system of land grants; akin to feudalism but with differences.

Isma'ilism: A branch of Shi'ism that recognizes Isma'il, the son of the Sixth Imam, Ja'far al-Sadiq, as a messianic figure. The Fatimid dynasty espoused Isma'ili beliefs, as did other splinter groups (the Nizari Assassins in Persia and Syria). The sect is represented today through the adherents of the Agha Khan.

isnad chain of transmitters of a hadith report.

jama'a the community of believers.

kalam scholastic and speculative discussion of theological questions.

katib (pl. *kuttab*): a government bureaucrat; the class of ministers.

khalifa (pl. *khulafa*): caliph.

Kharijites (lit. "schismatics"): a group that broke with Ali's caliphate in the 650s and made piety the only criterion for caliphal qualifications.

khutba the sermon preceding the Friday prayer.

madrasa: a college specializing in Islamic religious sciences; the institution was invented by the Seljuk vizir Nizam al-Mulk in the eleventh century.

Maliki: a school of jurisprudence that was dominant in North Africa and al-Andalus, and privileged hadith and traditional custom as sources for Islamic law.

mawla (pl. *mawali*): "client" or "slave"; also in an opposite sense "master."

Mihna: lit. "trial," generally in reference to al-Ma'mun's trial of religious scholars over the question of the "createdness creed" of the Qur'an.

minbar: mosque pulpit.

Mu'tazila: an Islamic movement of speculative theology (*kalam*) that flourished in the reigns of al-Ma'mun, al-Mu'tasim, and al-Wathiq; overlaps with Shi'ism on some theological interpretations.

niqaba: leadership of the Abbasid, Alid, or the Hashimite family; the *naqib* as "marshal" or representative of the family to the government.

qadi judge.

Qadiri Creed: the official Sunni doctrine propagated by the caliph al-Qadir in 409/1018; ended feud with the Mu'tazila, and refuted the Isma'ili Shi'i views of the Fatimids.

Rashidun caliphs: the "rightly guided caliphs." The Islamic term of reference to the reigns of the first four successors to the Prophet (Abu Bakr, Umar, Uthman, and Ali).

Shafi'i: a school of jurisprudence named after al-Shafi'i; holds a middle ground between Hanafis and Hanbalis. It flourished with Nizam al-Mulk's madrasas.

sharia: Islamic law.

Shi'a: partisanship for Ali's caliphate; the movement later championed rule by his descendants, growing into various sects (Isma'ili, Twelver, Zaydis, and others).

shihna: office of military prefect (usually in Baghdad) representing the authority of the Seljuk sultan.

shura (lit. "consultation"): referring to the process by which the third caliph, Uthman, was said to have been selected.

sikka the minting of coinage; official inscriptions on coins.

Sira: the story of the Prophet Muhammad; compiled by Ibn Ishaq and redacted by Ibn Hisham.

Sufism: mysticism.

sunna: the practices of the Prophet Muhammad.

tiraz: the government-controlled textile factories; they produced textiles bearing caliphal titles.

Thughur: the frontier fortresses; usually in reference to the Abbasid–Byzantine border provinces in Asia Minor.

Twelvers: The dominant branch of Shiʻi Islam (also known as Imami). The sect differs from Ismaʻilism by recognizing descendants of Ali as Imams through the line of Jaʻfar al-Sadiq's son Musa al-Kazim, and continuing down to the Twelfth Imam. The Twelfth Imam is believed to have gone into occultation, and will return as the messianic Mahdi. Twelvers recognize the field of esoteric meanings of religious texts, and the special knowledge of the Imam at exegesis (*taʾwil*), and his binding authority to appoint a successor through testament (*nass*).

ʻulama (sing. ʻalim): religious scholars, clerics.

vizir: chief minister.

Zaydiyya: a Shiʻi sect named after Zayd, grandson of al-Husayn. It eschews Twelver and Ismaʻili ideas such as occult explanations of the Qurʾan, a "hidden" Imam, and dissimulation, and differs from Sunnism only in insisting on an Imam figure from the family of Ali who should lead the state. Historically, Zaydiyya was mostly dominant in Yemen.

Dynasties Contemporary with the Abbasids

The Aghlabids (800–909)

Descended from al-Aghlab, a military leader in the army of the caliph al-Mansur, this family of governors of Tunisia (known as the province of Ifriqiyya) gained autonomy with the governor, Ibrahim b. al-Aghlab (800–812), in the reign of Harun al-Rashid in return for a fixed sum of tax revenues. The Aghlabids championed Sunni doctrines within the Maliki sect of jurisprudence, and waged vigorous conquests in the Mediterranean. They conquered Sicily in 827–832 (Syracuse in 876), parts of southern Italy in 840–842, and raided Rome in 846. The Aghlabids were mainly a naval power; their attempt to take Egypt in 896 ended in failure, and they eventually succumbed to the Fatimid conquest of Qayrawan in 909.

The Tahirids (821–873)

The first provincial dynasty that gained autonomy from the Abbasids in the eastern regions. It was named after Tahir b. al-Husayn, who led al-Ma'mun's army during the succession crisis against al-Amin. It was based at Nishapur, and reached its greatest success during the tenure of Abdallah b. Tahir (828–845), who improved the agricultural system, and was a patron of Arabic literature and Islamic (Sunni) religious sciences. The Tahirids did not claim full independence, maintained their titles as *amir*s, and may have contributed some tax revenues to Baghdad. A branch of the family also held the task of military prefect in Baghdad (*sahib al-shurta*) till the late ninth century.

The Saffarids (867–911)

An Iranian military family, formerly lieutenants in the Abbasid army, with a working-class background (al-Saffar, "the coppersmith"). They challenged Abbasid control of Sistan (Sijistan) after a Kharijite movement there, and successfully expanded at the expense of the Tahirids of Khurasan. Saffarid ambition to dominate the wealthier Samanid region of Transoxiana brought an end to their relatively short run.

The Samanids (874–999)

A Sunni Iranian dynasty of aristocratic background that first emerged as governors in al-Ma'mun's reign in 819 in Bukhara and Samarqand, eventually ruling independently over Transoxiana, and becoming a hub of trade with Central Asia, the Volga river, and the Baltic Sea, and a magnet of patronage for Persian literary culture and Sunni learning. It was later dominated by the Turkic Qarakhanids and the Ghaznavids.

The Tulunids (868–905)

Named after Ahmad b. Tulun, a former officer in the Abbasid Turkic army at Samarra, this dynasty grew out of its service as governors in Egypt during the period of political chaos at Samarra after the murder of al-Mutawakkil. Ibn Tulun expanded his rule to Syria, and tried to shape caliphal politics, encouraging al-Mu'tamid to come to Egypt, and to shake off the military hegemony of his more powerful brother, al-Muwaffaq. Eventually, al-Muwaffaq's son and future caliph, al-Muʿtadid, subdued the Tulunids into cooperation through a matrimonial tie, and the end of the last significant leader of the Tulunids, Khumarawayh, soon followed.

The Umayyads in al-Andalus (756–1031)

Their emirate began in 756 under Abd al-Rahman I, and flourished in the tenth century under Abd al-Rahman III (r. 912–961) who declared himself caliph in 929. The Umayyad state devolved into petty kingdoms (Muluk al-Tawaif or "party kings") after 1031, and was later dominated by the Almoravids of North Africa, who checked the Christian advance in 1086, after the fall of Toledo in 1085.

The Hamdanids (929–1003)

An Arab dynasty with tribal and military roots, and of Shiʿi leanings, that ruled over northern Syria and Iraq with its centers of power in Aleppo and Mosul (Aleppo was taken from the Ikhshidids in 945). It became famous for patronage of scholars, poets, and philosophers such as al-Mutanabbi and al-Farabi, and for a series of military confrontations with the Byzantines in Asia Minor.

The Buyids (930–1030)

An Iranian dynasty that grew out of the Iranian Daylam, in the southwest of the Caspian Sea region, known for its originally humble mountain-dweller roots. The three children of Ahmad b. Buya eventually expanded their military hegemony over Fars, Rayy, and Iraq, reaching its apogee with ʿAdud al-Dawla (r. 949–975 [in Fars]; 975–983 [in Baghdad]). The religious views of the Buyids were Shiʿi, but ranged between Zaydi and Twelver Shiʿi affinities. The Buyids seized Baghdad in 945, but lost it to the Turkic Seljuks in 1055.

The Ikhshids (935–969)

A dynasty named after an aristocratic title *ikhshid* (of Transoxanian background) that the Abbasid caliphs gave to Muhammad b. Tughj, who became governor over Egypt, Syria, and the Hijaz (935–946).

The Fatimids (909–1171)

A dynasty of Ismaʿili Shiʿi background; originally led by Ubaydallah al-Mahdi (r. 910–934), who established its capital Mahdiyya in Tunisia in 921. The Fatimids later expanded east to Egypt, the eastern Mediterranean region, and the Hijaz. They founded Cairo as their capital in 969, declared themselves caliphs, and built the Azhar Mosque as a center of Ismaʿili missionary activity. The Fatimids successfully fomented a coup in Abbasid Baghdad led by al-Basasiri, who pledged allegiance to Fatimid Egypt in 1058–1059, but the event provoked the Seljuks to make a determined effort to reestablish their control over Baghdad, and to champion Sunni ideology. Tunisia, left under a Zirid governor in 973, became an autonomous Zirid emirate, loyal to the Abbasids, starting in 1048. The dynasty reached its apogee with the reigns of al-Muʿizz (953–975) and al-Aziz (975–996), took a troubled turn with al-Hakim (r. 1017–1021), and in 1171 succumbed to the Ayyubid Saladin (r. 1169–1193), who led an army originally dispatched by Nur al-Din Zangi of Aleppo.

The Ghaznavids (976–1118)

Named after the city of Ghazna, which this dynasty founded in Afghanistan as its capital and courtly center, the Ghazavids were originally military commanders in the service of the Samanids. This first in a wave of Turkic dynasties grew out of a frontier warrior ethos, dominated much of northern India under the rule of Mahmud of Ghazna (r. 998–1030), and seized power from the Samanids and Buyids in most of Iran. It patronized scholars such as Ibn Sina (Avicenna) and al-Biruni. It has left important ruins at Ghazna, Bust, and Lashkari Bazar in Afghanistan.

The Seljuk Sultanate (990–1194)

This Turkic dynasty originated from Central Asia, and was named after Saljuq, whose grandchildren (Tughril Beg and Chaghri Beg) expanded their military domination over the Iranian world between 1030 and 1040, supplanting the Ghaznavids. The Seljuks continued Samanid and Ghaznavid support for Sunnism, and sought legitimacy from the Abbasid caliph in Baghdad, eventually coming to save the Abbasids from a Fatimid threat in 1055–1059, and in the process dominated Iraq and Abbasid Baghdad. The dynasty reached its peak under the rule of Alp Arslan (r. 1063–1072) and his son, Malikshah (r. 1072–1092), whose vizir Nizam al-Mulk was famous for structuring institutions such as the madrasa educational network (Nizamiyyas), and patronizing scholars such as al-Ghazali. Seljuk defeat against the Qara Khitay in 1141 began the sultanate's decline.

The Khwarazm shahs (1150–1220)

A dynasty that ruled in northwest Transoxiana, originally as vassals for the Seljuks in Khwarazm (Khiva). The dynasty challenged the Seljuk sultan Sanjar, and eventually, under the leadership of ʿAla al-Din Tekish (r. 1172–1200), ended the Seljuk state in 1194. It also ended the Ghurid dynasty in 1215, and tried unsuccessfully to invade Baghdad and to dominate the Abbasid caliph al-Nasir. Its belligerent rejection in 1218 of Mongol interests in trade and political contacts in Transoxiana led to Genghis Khan's invasion of the region, and conquest of Iran in 1220.

The Ghurids (1149–1215)

A Sunni Turkic dynasty that grew out of its original base Firuzkuh (near Jam) in Afghanistan and expanded into India; its most famous ruler, Ghiyath al-Din Muhammad b. Sam (r. 1163–1203), was also a patron of architecture, such as structures at Herat, Jam, and Chisht.

The Ilkhanids (1256–1336)

"Il-khan" was the title by which the Mongol rulers in Persia were known, from Hulegu (r. 1256–1263) to Abu Said (r. 1316–1336). They were rivals from 1260 onward to the Mongol empire of the Golden Horde, which aligned itself with the Mamluks in Egypt and Syria. The dynasty first converted to Sunni Islam under Ghazan (r. 1295–1304), and shifted its capital from Tabriz to Sultaniyya in Azerbaijan in 1307.

The Zangids (1127–1173)

A dynasty founded in Mosul by a Seljuk military commander, ʿImad al-Din Zangi, and later flourishing in the reign of his son, Nur al-Din, who shifted its capital to Aleppo.

The Ayyubids (1169–1260)

A dynasty of Kurdish background; originally in the military service of the Zangid Nur al-Din of Aleppo. Its most famous ruler was Saladin, who was dispatched to conquer Egypt in 1169. Saladin's new base in Egypt helped him expand his challenges to the Crusader kingdoms, and eventually re-conquer Jerusalem in 1187. The dynasty retained a political cohesion in Egypt but fragmented into fiefdoms in Syria and Asia Minor in its last decades.

The Mamluks (1250–1517)

A dynasty of elite military troops, formerly slaves of the Ayyubids, which took over power during the military scramble to ward off the Seventh Crusade of Louis IX. Its hold on power was firmly established when the Mamluks defeated the Mongols in 1260 and invested heavily in building up their capital, Cairo, especially under al-Nasir Muhammad b. Qalawun and Qaytbay. The Mamluk state went through two phases: the Bahri Mamluks (1250–1382), and the Burji Mamluks (1382–1517), the former mainly Qipchak Turks (from the Volga-Dnieper steppes), the latter Circassian (from the Caucasus region). The Mamluks ended the Crusader kingdoms in the eastern Mediterranean, held the Mongols in check, and eventually succumbed to the Ottomans under Selim I.

Bibliography

Reference Works

Encyclopedia of Islam, 2nd ed., ed. H. A. R. Gibb et al., Leiden, 1960–2009.

The Cambridge History of Iran, vol. 4: *From the Arab Invasion to the Saljuqs*, ed. R. N. Frye, Cambridge, 1975; vol.5: *The Saljuq and Mongol Periods*, ed. J. A. Boyle, Cambridge, 1968.

The Cambridge History of Islam, vol. 2B: *Islamic Society and Civilization*, ed. P. M. Holt, Ann K. S. Lambton, and Bernard Lewis, Cambridge, 1970.

The New Cambridge History of Islam, vol. 1: *The Formation of the Islamic World, Sixth to Eleventh Centuries*, ed. Chase Robinson, Cambridge, 2010; vol. 3: *The Eastern Islamic World: Eleventh to Eighteenth Centuries*, ed. David O. Morgan and Anthony Reid, Cambridge, 2010.

Beckwith, Christopher, *Empires of the Silk Road*, Princeton, 2009.

   The Tibetan Empire in Central Asia, Princeton, 1987.

Begley, W. E., *Monumental Islamic Calligraphy from India*, Villa Park, IL, 1985.

Blair, Sheila, *Islamic Calligraphy*, Edinburgh, 2006.

Bosworth, C. E., *The Islamic Dynasties*, Edinburgh, 1967.

   Carolingian Chronicles: Royal Frankish Annals and Nithard's Histories, trans. Bernhard Walter Scholz, Ann Arbor, 1970.

Coulson, Noel, *A History of Islamic Law*, Edinburgh, 1964.

Creswell, K. A. C., *A Short Account of Early Muslim Architecture*, London, 1958.

Dunlop, D. M., *Arab Civilization to AD 1500*, London, 1971.

Grabar, Oleg, *The Formation of Islamic Art*, New Haven, 1973.

al-Hassani, Salim T. S., ed., *1001 Inventions: The Enduring Legacy of Muslim Civilization*, Washington, DC, 2012.

Hattstein, Markus, *Islam: Art and Architecture*, Potsdam, 2015.

Humphreys, R. Stephen, *Islamic History: A Framework for Inquiry*, Princeton, 1994.

Kennedy, Hugh, *The Prophet and the Age of the Caliphates: The Islamic Near East from the Sixth to the Eleventh Century*, London, 2004 [1986].

Lambton, Ann, *State and Government in Medieval Islam*, Oxford, 1981.

Lane Poole, Stanley, *Catalogue of the Collection of Arabic Coins Preserved in the Khedivial Library in Cairo*, Oxford, 1897.

Le Strange, Guy, *Baghdad during the Abbasid Caliphate*, London, 1900.

Lands of the Eastern Caliphate, London, 1905.

Levi, Scott and Ron Sela, *Islamic Central Asia: An Anthology of Historical Sources*, Bloomington, 2010.

Milwright, Marcus, *An Introduction to Islamic Archaeology*, Edinburgh, 2010.

Netton, Ian R., *Islamic and Middle Eastern Travellers and Geographers*, London, 2007.

Petry, Carl F., ed., *The Cambridge History of Egypt*, vol. 1: *Islamic Egypt, 640–1517*, Cambridge, 1998.

Rosenthal, E. I. J., *Political Thought in Medieval Islam*, Cambridge, 1968.

Young, M. J. L., J. D. Latham, and R. B. Serjeant, eds., *Religion, Learning, and Science in the Abbasid Period*, Cambridge, 1990.

Primary Sources in Translation

al-Andalusi, Saʿid b. Ahmad (d. 462/1070), *Tabaqat al-Umam*, translated by Semaʿan Salem et al. as *Science in the Medieval Islamic world*, Austin, 1991.

Baladhuri (d. 279/892), *Futuh al-Buldan*, ed. Salah al-Din al-Munajjid, 2 vols., Cairo, 1956–1957; trans. P. Hitti and F. Murgotten as *The Origins of the Islamic State*, 2 vols., New York, 1916–1924.

Bayhaqi, Abu'l-Fadl (d. 477/1070), *Tarikh-i Bayhaqi*, trans. C. E. Bosworth and rev. Mohsen Ashtiany as *The History of Beyhaqi (The History of Sultan Masʿud of Ghazna, 1030–1041) by Abu'l-Fazl Beyhaqi*, Boston, 2011.

Benjamin of Tudela (twelfth century), *The Itinerary of Benjamin of Tudela: Travels in the Middle Ages*, trans. and introd. A. Asher et al., New York, 2010 [1983].

Einhard (d. 840), *The Life of Charlemagne by Einhard*, foreword by Sidney Painter, Ann Arbor, 1960.

Gardizi, *Zayn al-Akhbar* (fifth/eleventh century), partially trans. C. E. Bosworth as *The Ornament of Histories: A History of the Eastern Islamic Lands AD 650–1041: The Persian text of Abu Saʿid b. Abd al-Hayy Gardizi*, London, 2011.

Hudud al Alam, "The Regions of the World": A Persian Geography, 372AH–982 AD, trans. V. Minorsky, Oxford, 1937.

al-Husayni, Sadr al-Din Abu'l-Hasan Ali b. Nasir (d. after 622/1225), *Zubdat al-Tawarikh, Akhbar al-Umaraʾ wa'l-Muluk al-Saljuqiyya*, ed. Muhammad Nur al-Din, Beirut, 1986; trans. C. E. Bosworth as *The History of the Seljuq State: A Translation with Commentary of the Akhbar al-Dawla al-Saljuqiyya*, London, 2011.

Ibn Abd Rabbih (d. 328/940), *al-ʿIqd al-Farid*, ed. Ahmad Amin et al., 8 vols., Cairo, 1940–1953; partial trans. Issa Boullata as *The Unique Necklace*, vols. 1–3, Reading, 2007–2011.

Ibn al-Athir, ʿIzz al-Din (d. 630/1232), *al-Kamil fi'l-Tarikh*, ed. C. J. Tornberg, 12 vols., repr., Beirut, 1965–1967; selections trans. D. S. Richards as *Annals of the Saljuq Turks: Selections from al-Kamil fi'l-Ta'rikh of ʿIzz al-Din Ibn al-Athir*, London, 2002.

Ibn Battuta (d. 779/1377), *Ibn Battuta: Travels in Asia and Africa, 1325–1354*, trans. H. A. R. Gibb, London, 1929.

Rihlat Ibn Battuta (Beirut, 1964); trans. H. A. R. Gibb as *The Travels of Ibn Battuta*, Cambridge, 1962.

Ibn Fadlan, *Ibn Fadlan and the Land of Darkness: Arab Travellers in the Far North*, trans. Paul Lunde and Caroline Stone, London, 2012.

Ibn Jubayr (d. 614/1217), *Rihlat Ibn Jubayr*, Beirut, 1964; trans. R. C. Broadhurst as *The Travels of Ibn Jubayr*, London, 1952.

Ibn al-Muqaffaʿ (d. 139/756), *Kalilah wa Dimnah: An English Version of Bidpai's Fables Based upon Ancient Arabic and Spanish Manuscripts*, trans. T. B. Irving, Newark, DE, 1980.

Ibn al-Nadim (d. 388/998), *al-Fihrist*, trans. Bayard Dodge as *The Fihrist of al-Nadim: a Tenth-Century Survey of Muslim Culture*, 2 vols., New York, 1970.

Ibn al-Saʿi (d. 674/1274), *Nisaʾ al-Khulafaʾ*, ed. Mustafa Jawad, Cairo, 1968; ed. and trans. Shawkat Toorawa as *Consorts of the Caliphs: Women and the Court of Baghdad*, New York, 2015.

Ibn al-Tiqtaqa (d. 709/1309), *al-Fakhri*, Beirut, 1966; trans. C. E. J. Whitting as *al-Fakhri: On the Systems of Government and the Moslem Dynasties*, London, 1947.

Juzjani (d. after 664/1265), *Tabakat-i Nasiri (A History of the Muhammedan Dynasties of Asia)*, 2 vols., trans. Major H. J. Raverty, London, 1881.

Khatib al-Baghdadi (d. 463/1071), *al-Tatfil*, Cairo, 1983; trans. Emily Selove as *Selections from the Art of Party-Crashing in Medieval Iraq*, Syracuse, 2012.

Liudprand of Cremona (d. 972), *The Embassy to Constantinople and Other Writings*, ed. John Julius Norwich, London, 1993.

al-Masʿudi (d. 345/956), *Muruj al-Dhahab*, ed. Charles Pellat, 7 vols., Beirut, 1965–1970; selection trans. Paul Lunde and Caroline Stone in *Meadows of Gold: The Abbasids*, London, 1989.

al-Mawardi (d. 450/1058), *al-Ahkam al-Sultaniyya*, Beirut, 1985; trans. Wafa' H. Wahba as *The Ordinances of Government*, Reading, 1996.

al-Muqaddasi (d. 381/991), *Ahsan al-Taqasim fi Marifat al-Aqalim*, Leiden, 1906; trans. Basil Collins as *The Best Divisions for Knowledge of the Regions*, Reading, 2001.

Nizam al-Mulk (d. 485/1092), *The Book of Government or Rules for Kings*, trans. Hubert Darke, New Haven, 1960.

al-Qadi al-Rashid, Ahmad b. al-Rashid (ca. fifth/eleventh century), *Kitab al-Dhakha'ir wa'l-Tuhaf*, ed. Muhammad Hamidullah, Kuwait, 1959; trans. Ghada al-Hijjawi al-Qaddumi as *Book of Gifts and Rarities*, Cambridge, MA, 1996.

al-Sabi', Hilal b. al-Muhassin (d. 448/1056), *Rusum Dar al-Khilafa*, edited by Mikhail Awwad, Baghdad, 1964; trans. Elie Salem as *The Rules and Regulations of the 'Abbasid Court*, Beirut, 1977.

al-Suyuti, Jalal al-Din (d. 911/1505), *Tarikh al-Khulafa'*, Beirut, 1994; trans. H. S. Jarett as *History of the Caliphs*, Amsterdam, 1881.

al-Tabari, Abu Ja'far (d. 310/923), *Tarikh al-Rusul wa'l-Muluk*, ed. M. J. de Goeje, Series I–III, Leiden, 1879–1901; trans. as *The History of al-Tabari*, gen. ed. Ihsan Yarshater, 39 vols., Albany, 1985–1998; and John Alden Williams as *al-Tabari: The Early 'Abbasi Empire*, 2 vols., Cambridge, 1989.

Tarikh-e Sistan, trans. Milton Gold, Rome, 1976.

al-Tha'alibi (d. 429/1038), *The Book of Curious and Entertaining Information, The Lata'if al-Ma'arif of al-Tha'alibi*, trans. C. E. Bosworth, with introd. and notes, Edinburgh,1968.

Theophilus of Edessa's Chronicle, ed. and trans. Robert Hoyland, Liverpool, 2011.

Two Arabic Travel Books: Account of China and India (Abu Zayd al-Sirafi) ed. and trans. Tim Mackintosh-Smith and *Mission to the Volga (Ahmad b. Fadlan)*, ed. and trans. James Montgomery, New York, 2014.

al-Ya'qubi (d. 282/897), *Kitab al-Buldan*, ed. M. J. de Goeje, Leiden, 1892; trans. Bernard Lewis in *Islam: From the Prophet Muhammad to the Capture of Constantinople*, 2 vols., vol. 2: *Religion and Society*, Oxford, 1987.

Mushakalat al-Nas li-Zamanihim, Beirut, 1962; trans. William G. Millward as "The Adaptation of Men to their Time: An Historical Essay by al-Yaqubi," *Journal of the American Oriental Society* 84 (1964), 329–344.

Tarikh, Beirut, 1970; trans. Matthew S. Gordon et al. as *The Works of Ibn Wadih al-Ya'qubi*, 3 vols., Leiden, 2018.

Primary Sources

al-Abbasi, al-Hasan b. Abdallah (eighth/fourteenth century), *Athar al-Uwal fi Tartib al-Duwal*, ed. Abd al-Rahman Umayra, Beirut, 1989.

Abu'l-Fida (d. 732/1331), *Taqwim al-Buldan*, ed. M. Reinaud, Paris, 1840.

Abu Nu'aym al-Isbahani (d. 430/1038), *Dhikr Akhbar Isbahan*, ed. Sven Dedering, 2 vols., Leiden, 1931–1934.

Abu Shama (d. 665/1267), *Kitab al-Rawdatayn fi Akhbar al-Dawlatayn*, ed. Ibrahim Shams al-Din, 3 vols., Beirut, 2002.

Abu Shuja' al-Rudhrawari (d. 498/1095), *Dhayl Tajarib al-Umam*, Beirut, 2004.

Akhbar al-Dawla al-'Abbasiyya (anonymous/ninth century) ed. 'Abd al-'Aziz al-Duri et al., Beirut, 1971.

Ali b. al-Jahm (third/ninth century), *Diwan*, Beirut, 2010.

al-Asnawi (d. 771/1370), *Tabaqat al-Shafi'iyya*, ed. Kamal al-Hout, 2 vols., Beirut, 2001.

al-Ayyubi, Muhammad b. Taqi al-Din Umar (d. 617/1220), *Midmar al-Haqa'iq wa Sirr al-Khala'iq*, ed. Hasan Habshi, Cairo, 1968.

al-Azdi (d. 334/945), *Tarikh al-Mawsil*, ed. Ahmad Mahmud, 2 vols., Beirut, 2006.

al-Azraqi (d. 222/837), *Akhbar Makka*, ed. F. Wustenfeld, Leipzig, 1858.

al-Baghdadi, Muhammad b. Habib (d. 246/860), *Kitab al-Muhabbar*, ed. Ilse Lichtenstadter, Hyderabad, 1942.

al-Baladhuri (d. 279/892), *Ansab al-Ashraf*, vol 3: *al-Abbas b. Abd al-Muttalib wa waladuhu*, ed. Abd al-Aziz al-Duri, Wiesbaden, 1978.

al-Biruni (d. 440/1048), *Kitab al-Athar al-Baqiya 'an al-Qurun al-Khaliya*, ed. E. Sachau, Leipzig, 1923.

al-Dhahabi, Shams al-Din (d. 748/1348), *Duwal al-Islam*, ed. Hasan Marwa, 2 vols., Beirut, 1999.

Siyar A'lam al-Nubala', ed. Shu'ayb al-Arna'ut, 23 vols., Beirut, 1981–1993.

al-Ghassani, al-Malik al-Ashraf (d. 803/1401), *al-'Asjad al-Masbuk wa'l-Jawhar al-Mahkuk fi Tabaqat al-Khulafa' wa'l-Muluk*, ed. Shakir Mahmud Abd al-Mun'im, Baghdad, 1975.

Ibn Abi Udhayba (d. 853/1449), *Insan al-Uyun fi Mashahir Sadis al-Qurun*, ed. Ihsan al-Thamiri et al., Amman, 2007.

Ibn Dihya (d. 633/1235), *al-Nibras fi Tarikh Bani al-Abbas*, Cairo, 2001.

Ibn al-Faqih al-Hamadani (d. 365/975), *Mukhtasar Kitab al-Buldan*, ed. M. J. de Goeje, Leiden, 1885.

Ibn al-Fuwati (attrib. [d. 723/1323]), *Kitab al-Hawadith al-Jami'a*, ed. B. A. Ma'ruf, Beirut, 1997.

Ibn Habib, Abd al-Malik (d. 238/853), *Kitab al-Tarikh*, ed. Jorge Aguade, Madrid, 1991.

Ibn al-'Imrani (d. 580/1185), *al-Inba' fi Tarikh al-Khulafa'*, ed. Qasim al-Samarrai, Leiden, 1973.

Ibn Iyas (d. 930/1423), *Bada'i' al-Zuhur fi Waqa'i' al-Duhur*, ed. Muhammad Mustafa, 6 vols., Beirut, 2010.

Ibn al-Jawzi, Abu'l-Faraj (d. 597/1202), *al-Muntazam fi Tarikh al-Muluk wa'l-Umam*, ed. Muhammad 'Ata, 18 vols. in 16, Beirut, 1992.

Ibn Kathir (d. 774/1373), *al-Bidaya wa'l-Nihaya*, 14 parts in 8 vols., Beirut, 1985.

Ibn al-Kazaruni (d. 697/1297), *Mukhtasar al-Tarikh*, ed. Mustafa Jawad, Baghdad, 1969.

Ibn Khaldun (d. 808/1406), *Tarikh Ibn Khaldun*, 7 vols., Beirut, 1992.

Ibn Khallikan (d. 681/1282), *Wafayat al-A'yan*, ed. Ihsan 'Abbas, Beirut, 8 vols., 1968–1972.

Ibn al-Mi'mar (d. 642/1244), *Kitab al-Futuwwa*, ed. Mustafa Jawad, Beirut, 2012.

Ibn Muyassar (d. 678/1278), *al-Muntaqa min Akhbar Misr*, ed. Ayman Fu'ad Sayyid, Cairo, 1981.

Ibn al-Qifti (d. 646/1248), *Ikhbar al-Ulama' bi-Akhbar al-Hukama'*, Beirut, n.d. [Cairo, 1908].

Ibn Qutayba (d. 276/889), *Kitab al-Ma'arif*, ed. Tharwat 'Ukasha, Cairo, 1969.

Ibn Shahin al-Zahiri (d. 873/1468), *Zubdat Kashf al-Mamalik*, ed. P. Ravaisse, Paris, 1894.

Ibn Taghribirdi, Abu'l-Mahasin Yusuf al-Atabiki (d. 874/1470), *al-Nujum al-Zahira fi Akhbar Misr wa'l-Qahira*, 16 vols., Cairo, 1963–1972.

Ibn Wasil (d. 697/1297), *Mufarrij al-Kurub fi Akhbar Bani Ayyub*, vols. 1–3 ed. Jamal al-Din al-Shayyal, Cairo, 1953–1960; vols. 4–5 ed. Sa'id 'Abd al-Fattah 'Ashur and Husayn Muhammad Rabi', Cairo, 1972–1977; vol. 6 ed. Umar Tadmuri, Beirut, 2004.

al-Irbili (d. 717/1317), *Khulasat al-Dhahab al-Masbuk Mukhtasar min Siyar al-Muluk*, Baghdad, 1964.

al-Isfahani, al-'Imad (d. 597/1201), *Kharidat al-Qasr wa Jaridat al-'Asr*, ed. Muhammad Bahjat al-Athari, Baghdad, 1955.

al-Jahiz (d. 255/869), *Rasa'il al-Jahiz*, ed. Abd al-Salam Muhammad Harun, 2 vols., Beirut, 1991.

al-Jahshiyari (d. 331/942), *Kitab al-Wuzara' wa'l-Kuttab*, ed. Mustafa al-Saqqa et al., Cairo, 1938.

al-Juwayni (d. 478/1085), *al-Ghiyathi: Ghiyath al-Umam*, Jeddah, 2011.

Khatib al-Baghdadi (d. 463/1071), *Tarikh Baghdad*, 14 vols., Cairo, 1931.

al-Kindi (d. 350/961), *Kitab al-Wulat wa'l-Qudat*, ed. R. Guest, Leiden, 1912.

al-Maqdisi, Mutahhar b. Tahir (fourth/tenth century), *Kitab al-Bad' wa'l-Tarikh*, ed. Clement Huart, 6 vols., Paris, 1899–1919.

Miskawayh (d. 421/1030), *Tajarib al-Umam*, ed. Sayyid Hasan, 6 vols., Beirut, 2012.

al-Mas'udi (d. 345/956), *Kitab al-Tanbih wa'l-Ishraf*, ed. M. J. de Goeje, Leiden, 1894.

al-Qalqashandi (d. 821/1418), *Ma'athir al-Inafa fi Ma'alim al-Khilafa*, ed. Abd al-Sattar Ahmad Farraj, Beirut, 2006.

Subh al-A'sha, ed. Nabil Khalid al-Khatib, Beirut, 2012.

al-Qazwini (d. 682/1283), *Athar al-Bilad wa Akhbar al-'Ibad*, Beirut, n.d.

al-Qazwini, Abd al-Karim b. Muhammad (d. 622/1226), *al-Tadwin fi Akhbar Qazwin*, ed. A. al-'Attaridi, 4 vols., Beirut, 1987.

Qudama b. Ja'far (d. 337/948), *Kitab al-Kharaj wa Sina'at al-Kitaba*, ed. Muhammad al-Zabidi, Baghdad, 1981.

al-Rawandi (sixth/twelfth century), *Rahat al-Sudur wa Ayat al-Surur*, Arabic trans. Ibrahim al-Shawaribi, Abd al-Nu'aym Hasanyn and Fu'ad al-Sayyad, Cairo, 1960.

al-Sabi', Ibrahim b. Hilal (d. 384/994), *al-Mukhtar min Rasa'il Abu Ishaq Ibrahim b. Hilal al-Sabi'*, ed. Shakib Arslan, Beirut, n.d.

al-Wuzara', ed. Hasan al-Zayn, Beirut, 1990.

Sa'di al-Shirazi: Ash'aruhu al-'Arabiyya, ed. Ja'far al-Shirazi with a foreword by Ihsan Abbas, Beirut, 1980.

al-Safadi, Khalil b. Aybak (d. 763/1363), *al-Wafi bi'l-Wafayat*, 32. vols., Beirut, 1962–2010.

al-Shabushti (d. 388/998), *Kitab al-Diyarat* ed. Gurgis Awwad, Beirut, 1966.

Sibt Ibn al-Jawzi (d. 654/1256), *Mir'at al-Zaman fi Tarikh al-A'yan*, ed. Kamil Salman Juburi, 23 vols. in 22, Beirut, 2013.

al-Subki (d. 771/1370), *Tabaqat al-Shafi'iyya al-Kubra*, ed. A. M. al-Hilw, 10 vols., Cairo, 1964–1976.

al-Sulami, Muhammad b. Rafi' (d. 412/1021), *Ta'rikh 'Ulama' Baghdad al-Musamma Muntakhab al-Mukhtar*, ed. Abbas al-Azzawi, Baghdad, 1938.

al-Suli (d. 335/946), *Kitab al-Awraq: Akhbar al-Radi*, ed. James Heyworth Dunne, 3 vols., Beirut, 1934–1936.

al-Tanukhi, Abu Ali al-Muhassin (d. 384/994), *Kitab al-Faraj ba'd al-Shidda*, ed. Abboud al-Shalji, 5 vols., Beirut, 1978.

Nishwar al-Muhadara wa Akhbar al-Mudhakara, ed. Abboud al-Shalji, 8 vols., Beirut, 1971–1973.

al-Tarsusi (d. ca. late fourth/tenth century), *Shadharat min Kutub Mafquda*, ed. Ihsan Abbas, Beirut, 1988.

Tayfur, Ahmad b. Abi Tahir (d. 380/993), *Kitab Baghdad*, Cairo, 1949.

al-Washsha' (d. ca. 325/936), *al-Muwashsha aw al-Zurf wa'l-Zarafa*, Beirut, 1965.

al-Yafi'i (d. 768/1367), *Mira'at al-Janan wa 'Ibrat al-Yaqzan fi Ma'rifat Hawadith al-Zaman*, ed. Khalil al-Mansur, 4 vols., Beirut, 1997.

Yaqut al-Hamawi (d. 626/1229), *Mu'jam al-Buldan*, 7 vols., Beirut, 2015.

Secondary Sources

Abbott, Nabia, *Two Queens of Baghdad*, Chicago, 1946.

Agha, Saleh Said, *The Revolution Which Toppled the Umayyads*, Leiden, 2003.

Ahsan, M. M., *Social Life under the Abbasids, 179–289 AH, 786–902 AD*, London, 1979.

el-Ali, Saleh Ahmed, "A New Version of Ibn al-Mutarrif's List of Revenues in the Early Times of Harun al-Rashid," *Journal of the Economic and Social History of the Orient* 14 (1971), 303–310.

Ali, Samer, *Arabic Literary Salons in the Islamic Middle Ages: Poetry, Public Performance, and the Presentation of the Past*, Notre Dame, IN, 2010.

Allsen, Thomas T., *Mongol Imperialism: The Policies of the Grand Qan Mongke in China, Russia, and the Islamic Lands, 1251–1259*, Berkeley, 1987.

Antrim, Zayde, *Routes and Realms: The Power of Place in the Early Islamic World*, Oxford, 2012.

Arberry, A. J., *The Koran Interpreted*, 2 vols. in 1, London, 1955.

Arnold, Thomas, *The Caliphate*, Oxford, 1924.

Ashtiany Bray, Julia et al., eds., *The Cambridge History of Arabic Literature*, vol. 2: *Abbasid Belles-Lettres*, Cambridge, 1990.

Auer, Blain, *Symbols of Authority in Medieval Islam: History, Religion, and Muslim Legitimacy in the Delhi Sultanate*, London, 2012.

al-Aʿzami, Khalid Khalil Hammudi, *al-Madrasa al-Mustansiriyya fi Baghdad*, Baghdad, 1981.

Babaie, Sussan, "Persia: The Safavids 1501–1722," in Masselos, ed., *The Great Empires of Asia*, 138–166.

Bacharach, Jere, "Laqab for a Future Caliph: The Case of the Abbasid al-Mahdi," *Journal of the American Oriental Society* 113 (1993), 271–274.

Baker, P. W., and I. D. Edge, "Islamic Legal Literature," in Young et al., eds., *Religion, Learning, and Science*, 139–154.

Baldick, Julian, *Mystical Islam*, New York, 1989.

Barfield, Thomas, *Afghanistan: A Cultural and Political History*, New York, 2010.

Bartold, W., *An Historical Geography of Iran*, ed. C. E. Bosworth, trans. Svat Soucek, Princeton, 1984.

Turkestan Down to the Mongol Invasion, London, 1928.

Bausani, A., "Religion in the Saljuq Period," in *CHIran*, vol. 5, 283–302.

Behrens-Abouseif, Doris, "The Citadel of Cairo: Stage for Mamluk Ceremonial," *Annales Islamologiques* 24 (1988), 25–79.

Bell, Gertrude, *Palace and Mosque at Ukhaidir*, Oxford, 1914.

Belting, Hans, *Florence and Baghdad: Renaissance Art and Arab Science*, trans. Deborah Lucas Schneider, Cambridge, MA, 2011.

Ben-Sasson, Menahem, "Inter-Communal Relations in the Geonic Period," in Frank, ed., *The Jews of Medieval Islam*, 17–31.

Ben-Shammai, H., "Jewish Thought in Iraq in the 10th Century," in *Judaeo-Arabic Studies*, ed. Norman Golb, Amsterdam, 1995, 15–32.

Bernheimer, Teresa, *The Alids: The First Family of Islam, 750–1200*, Edinburgh, 2013.

Bernstein, William, *A Splendid Exchange: How Trade Shaped the World*, New York, 2008.

Blankinship, Khalid Yahya, *The End of the Jihad State: The Reign of Hisham b. Abd al-Malik and the Collapse of the Umayyads*, Albany, 1994.

Bligh Abramski, I., "Umayyad Elements in the Abbasid Regime," 133/750–322/932," *Der Islam* 65 (1988), 226–243.

Bloom, Jonathan, and Sheila Blair, *Islamic Art*, London, 1997.

Bonner, Michael, "al-Khalifa al-Mardi: The Accession of Harun al-Rashid," *Journal of the American Oriental Society* 108 (1988), 79–91.

"The Naming of the Frontier: 'Awasim, Thughur, and the Arab Geographers," *Bulletin of the School of Oriental and African Studies* 57 (1994), 17–24.

Bosworth, C. E., "Administrative Literature," in Young et al., eds., *Religion, Learning and Science*, 155–167.

"The City of Tarsus and the Arab–Byzantine Frontiers in Early and Middle Abbasid Times," *Oriens* 33 (1992), 268–286.

The Ghaznavids: Their Empire in Afghanistan and Eastern Iran, *994–1040*, Beirut, 1973.

"The Ghurids in Khurasan," in *Medieval Central Asia and the Persianate World*, ed. D. G. Tor and A. C. S. Peacock, London, 2015, 210–221.

"The Interaction of Arabic and Persian Literature and Culture in the 10th and Early 11th Centuries," *al-Abhath* 27 (1978–1979), 59–75; repr. in *Medieval Arabic Culture and Administration*, London, 1982.

"The Persistent Older Heritage in the Medieval Iranian Lands," in *The Rise of Islam*, ed. Vesta Sarkhosh Curtis and Sarah Stewart, London, 2009, 30–43.

"The Political and Dynastic History of the Iranian World (AD 1000–1217)," in *CHIran*, vol. 5, 1–202.

"The Steppe Peoples in the Islamic World," in *NCHI*, vol. 3, 21–77.

"The Tahirids and Arabic Culture," *Journal of Semitic Studies* 14 (1969), 45–79.

Bowen, Harold, *The Life and Times of Ali b. Isa, the "Good Vizier"*, Cambridge, 1928.

Boyle, J. A., "Dynastic and Political History of the Il-Khans," in *CHIran*, vol. 5, 303–421.

Brett, Gerard, "The Automata in the Byzantine 'Throne of Solomon'," *Speculum* 29 (1954), 477–487.

Broadbridge, Anne, *Kingship and Ideology in the Islamic and Mongol Worlds*, Cambridge, 2008.

Brown, Peter, *The World of Late Antiquity*, London, 1971.

Buckler, F. W., *Harunu'l-Rashid and Charles the Great*, Cambridge, MA, 1931.

Bulliet, Richard W., *Conversion to Islam in the Medieval Period*, Cambridge, MA, 1979.

   Cotton, Climate, and Camels in Early Islamic Iran: A Moment in World History, New York, 2009.

   The Patricians of Nishapur, Cambridge, MA, 1972.

Buzpinar, Turfan, "Opposition to the Ottoman Caliphate in the Early Years of Abdulhamid II: 1877–1882," repr. in Kersten, ed., *The Caliphate and Islamic Statehood*, 6–27.

Cameron, Hamish, *Making Mesopotamia: Geography and Empire in a Romano-Iranian Borderland*, Leiden, 2019.

Canfield, Robert, ed., *Turko-Persia in Historical Perspective*, Cambridge, 1991.

Cantor, Norman, *Inventing the Middle Ages*, New York, 1991.

Casale, Giancarlo, "Tordesillas and the Ottoman Caliphate: Early Modern Frontiers and the Renaissance of an Ancient Islamic Institution," *Journal of Early Modern History* 19 (2015), 485–511.

Challis, Keith, et al., "Corona Remotely-Sensed Imagery in Dryland Archaeology: The Islamic City of al-Raqqa, Syria," *Journal of Field Archaeology* 29 (2002–2004), 139–153.

Christys, Ann, "The Queen of the Franks Offers Gifts to the Caliph al-Muktafi," in *The Languages of Gift in the Middle Ages*, ed. Wendy Davies and Paul Fouracre, Cambridge, 2013, 149–170.

Citarella, Armand, "The Relations of Amalfi with the Arab World before the Crusades," *Speculum* 42 (1967), 299–312.

Clot, André, *Harun al-Rashid and the World of the Thousand and One Nights*, trans. John Howe, London, 1989.

Cobb, Paul, *White Banners: Contention in Abbasid Syria, 750–880*, Albany, 2001.

Cohen, Mark, "What Was the Pact of 'Umar? A Literary-Historical Study," *Jerusalem Studies in Arabic and Islam* 23 (1999), 100–157.

Coke, Richard, *Baghdad: The City of Peace*, London, 1935 [1927].

Cook, William R. and Ronald B. Harzman, *The Medieval Worldview*, Oxford, 1983.

Cooper, Lisa, *In Search of Kings and Conquerors: Gertrude Bell and the Archaeology of the Middle East*, London, 2017.

Cooperson, Michael, "Baghdad in Rhetoric and Narrative," *Muqarnas*, ed. Gülru Necipoğlu, 13 (1996), 99–113.

Classical Arabic Biography: The Heirs of the Prophet in the Age of al-Ma'mun, Cambridge, 2000.

al-Ma'mun, Oxford, 2005.

Costa, P. M., "Early Islamic Painting: From Samarra to Northern Sicily," *New Arabian Studies* 3 (1993), 14–32.

Cowe, S. Peter, "Patterns of Armeno-Muslim Interchange on the Armenian Plateau in the Interstice between Byzantine and Ottoman Hegemony," in *Islam and Christianity in Medieval Anatolia*, ed. A. C. S. Peacock et al., Farnham, 2015, 77–106.

Crone, Patricia, "On the Meaning of the Abbasid Call to al-Rida," in *The Islamic World from Classical to Modern Times: Essays in Honor of Bernard Lewis*, ed. C. E. Bosworth, Charles Issawi, Roger Savory, and A. L. Udovitch, Princeton, 1989, 95–111.

Slaves on Horses: The Evolution of the Islamic Polity, Cambridge, 1986.

Crone, P. and M. Hinds, *God's Caliph: Religious Authority in the First Centuries of Islam*, Cambridge, 1986.

Cunliffe, Barry, *By Steppe, Desert, and Ocean: The Birth of Eurasia*, Oxford, 2015.

Curta, Florin, "Markets in Tenth-Century al-Andalus and Volga Bulgharia: Contrasting Views of Trade in Muslim Europe," *al-Masaq* 25 (2013), 305–330.

Daniel, Elton L., "The Anonymous History of the Abbasid Family and Its Place in Islamic Historiography," *International Journal of Middle East Studies* 14 (1982), 419–434.

The Arabs and Medieval Europe, London, 1974.

"The Islamic East," in *NCHI*, vol. 1, 448–505.

The Political and Social History of Khurasan under Abbasid Rule, 747–820, Minneapolis and Chicago, 1979.

Danner, Victor, "Arabic Literature in Iran," in *CHIran*, vol. 4, 566–594.

Daryaee, Touraj, *Sasanian Persia*, London, 2009.

de Bellaigue, Christopher, *The Islamic Enlightenment: The Struggle between Faith and Reason, 1798 to Modern Times*, New York, 2017.

de la Vaissiere, Étienne, *Samarcande et Samarra. Élites d'Asie centrale dans l'Empire abbaside*, Paris, 2007.

De Somogyi, Joseph, "Adh-Dhahabi's 'Ta'rikh al-islam' as an Authority on the Mongol Invasion of the Caliphate," *JRAS* 68 (1936), 595–604.

Donohue, John, *The Buwayhid Dynasty in Iraq 334 H/945 to 403 H/1012*, Leiden, 2003.

Dunlop, D. M., "Arab Relations with Tibet in the 8th and 9th Centuries AD," *Islam Tetkikleri Institusu Dergisi* 5 (1973), 301–318.

Durand-Guédy, David, *Iranian Elites and Turkish Rulers: A History of Isfahan in the Saljuq Period*, London, 2010.

"What Does the History of Isfahan Tell us about Iranian Society during the Seljuq Period?" in *The Age of the Seljuqs*, ed. Edmund Herzig and Sarah Stewart, London, 2015, 58–73.

Duri, Abd al-Aziz, *al- 'Asr al- 'Abbasi al-Awwal*, Beirut, 1945.

The Rise of Historical Writing among the Arabs, trans. Lawrence I. Conrad, Princeton, 1983.

Tarikh al-Iraq al-Iqtisadi fi al-Qarn al-Rabi' al-Hijri, Beirut, 1942.

Ecker, Heather, *Caliphs and Kings: The Art and Influence of Islamic Spain*, Washington, DC, 2004.

Eger, A. Asa, *The Islamic–Byzantine Frontier*, London, 2015.

Elad, Amikam, "Aspects of the Transition from the Umayyad to the Abbasid Caliphate," *Jerusalem Studies in Arabic and Islam* 19 (1995), 89–132.

The Rebellion of Muhammad al-Nafs al-Zakiyya in 145/762: Talibis and Early Abbasis in Conflict, Leiden, 2016.

Elbendary, Amina, "The Worst of Times: Crisis Management and Al-Shidda Al-Uzma," in *Money, Land and Trade: An Economic History of the Muslim Mediterranean*, ed. Nelly Hanna, London, 2002, 67–84.

El Cheikh, Nadia, *Byzantium Viewed by the Arabs*, Cambridge, MA, 2004.

"Caliphal Harems, Household Harems: Baghdad in the Fourth Century of the Islamic Era," in *Harem Histories: Envisioning Places and Living Spaces*, ed. Marilyn Booth, Durham, NC, 2010, 87–103.

"The 'Court' of al-Muqtadir: Its Space and Its Occupants," in *'Abbasid Studies II, Occasional Papers of the School of Abbasid Studies, 28 June–1 July 2004*, ed. J. Nawas, Leuven, 2010, 319–336.

Women, Islam, and Abbasid Identity, Cambridge, MA, 2015.

El-Hajji, A., "The Andalusian Diplomatic Relations with the Vikings during the Umayyad Period (AH 138–366/AD 755–976)," *Hesperis-Tamuda* 8 (1967), 67–110.

El-Hibri, Tayeb, "The Abbasids and the Relics of the Prophet," *Journal of Abbasid Studies* 4 (2017), 62–96.

"Coinage Reform under the Abbasid Caliph al-Ma'mun," *Journal of the Economic and Social History of the Orient* 36 (1993), 58–83.

"The Empire in Iraq, 763–861," in *NCHI*, vol. 1, 269–304.

"Harun al-Rashid and the Mecca Protocol of 802: A Plan for Division or Succession," *International Journal of Middle East Studies* 24 (1992), 461–480.

Parable and Politics in Early Islamic History: The Rashidun Caliphs, New York, 2010.

"The Redemption of Umayyad Memory by the Abbasids," *Journal of Near Eastern Studies* 61 (2002), 241–265.

Reinterpreting Islamic Historiography: Harun al-Rashid and the Narrative of the Abbasid Caliphate, Cambridge, 1999.

"Tabari's Biography of al-Muʿtasim: The Literary Use of a Military Career," *Der Islam* 86 (2009), 187–236.

"Umar b. al-Khattab and the Abbasids," *Journal of the American Oriental Society* 136 (2016), 1–21.

Ellenblum, R., *The Collapse of the Eastern Mediterranean: Climate Change and the Decline of the East*, Cambridge, 2013.

Elverskog, Johan, *Buddhism and Islam on the Silk Road*, Philadelphia, 2010.

Ertug, Ahmet, *The Seljuks*, Istanbul, 1991.

Esin, E., "Tarkhan Nizak or Tarkhan Tirek?" *Journal of the American Oriental Society* 97 (1977), 323–332.

Ettinghausen, Richard, *Arab Painting*, New York, 1977 [1962].

Ettinghausen, Richard and Oleg Grabar, *Islamic Art and Architecture, 650–1250*, New Haven, 2001.

Fehervari, G., "Art and Architecture," in *The Cambridge History of Islam*, vol. 2B, 702–740.

Finkel, Caroline, *Osman's Dream: The Story of the Ottoman Empire, 1300–1923*, London, 2005.

Fischer, Andreas and Ian Wood, eds., *Western Perspectives on the Mediterranean: Cultural Transfer in Late Antiquity and the Early Middle Ages, 400–800 AD*, London, 2014.

Foote, Rebecca and J. P. Oleson, "Humeima Excavation Project, 1995–96," *Fondation Max van Berchem Bulletin* 10 (1996), 1–4.

Fowden, Garth, *Empire to Commonwealth: Consequences of Monotheism in Late Antiquity*, Princeton, 1993.

Frank, Daniel H., ed., *The Jews of Medieval Islam*, Leiden, 1992.

Franklin, Arnold, *This Noble House: Jewish Descendants in the Islamic East*, Philadelphia, 2012.

Freely, John, *Light From the East: How the Science of Medieval Islam Helped to Shape the Western World*, London, 2011.

Freeman Fahid, Deborah, *Chess and Other Games: Pieces from Islamic Lands*, London, 2018.

Frye, Richard, *The Golden Age of Persia: The Arabs in the East*, London, 1975.

The Heritage of Central Asia: From Antiquity to the Turkish Expansion, Princeton, 1996.

Ibn Fadlan's Journey to Russia: A Tenth-Century Traveler from Baghdad to the Volga River, Princeton, 2005.

"The Samanids," in *CHIran*, vol. 4, 136–161.

Frye, Richard and Aydin Sayili, "The Turks in the Middle East before the Seljuks," *Journal of the American Oriental Society* 63 (1953), 194–207.

Garcin, Jean-Claude, "The Regime of the Circassian Mamluks," in Petry, ed., *The Cambridge History of Egypt*, vol. 1, 290–317.

George, Alain, "Direct Sea Trade between Early Islamic Iraq and Tang China: From the Exchange of Goods to the Transmission of Ideas," *Journal of the Royal Asiatic Society*, series 3, 25 (2015), 579–624.

Gibb, H. A. R., *The Arab Conquests in Central Asia*, London, 1923.

Arabic Literature, Oxford, 1963.

"An Interpretation of Islamic History," in *Studies on the Civilization of Islam*, 3–33.

"al-Mawardi's Theory of the Caliphate," in *Studies on the Civilization of Islam*, 151–165.

"Some Considerations on the Sunni Theory of the Caliphate," in *Studies on the Civilization of Islam*, 141–150.

Studies on the Civilization of Islam, ed. Stanford Shaw and William Polk, Princeton, 1962.

Gil, Moshe, "The Radhanite Merchants and the Land of Radhan," *Journal of the Economic and Social History of the Orient* 17 (1974), 299–328.

Glubb, John Bagot, *The Course of Empire*, London, 1965.

Goitein, S. D., "Attitudes towards Government in Islam and Judaism," repr. in *Studies in Islamic History and Institutions*, Leiden, 1966, 197–213.

Jews and Arabs: Their Contacts through the Ages, New York, 1974.

"The Rise of the Near Eastern Bourgeoisie," *Journal of World History* 3 (1956–1957), 583–604.

Goodman, L. E., "The Translation of Greek Materials into Arabic," in Young et al., eds., *Religion, Learning, and Science*, 477–497.

Goodwin, Jason, *Lords of the Horizons: A History of the Ottoman Empire*, London, 1998.

Gordon, Matthew, *The Breaking of a Thousand Swords: A History of the Turkish Community of Samarra (200–275/815–889 CE)*, Albany, 2001.

Gordon, Stewart, ed., *Robes and Honor: The Medieval World of Investiture*, New York, 2001.

Goshgarian, Rachel, "Futuwwa in Thirteenth-Century Rum and Armenia: Reform Movements and the Managing of Multiple Allegiances on the Seljuk Periphery," in Peacock and Yildiz, eds., *The Seljuks of Anatolia*, 227–263.

Grabar, Oleg, *The Shape of the Holy: Early Islamic Jerusalem*, Princeton, 1996.

"Upon Reading al-Azraqi," *Muqarnas* 3 (1982), 1–7.

Gruendler, Beatrice, "Modernity in the Ninth Century: The Controversy around Abu Tammam," *Studia Islamica* 112 (2017), 131–148.

Gruendler, Beatrice, and Louise Marlow, eds., *Writers and Rulers: Perspectives on Their Relationship from Abbasid to Safavid Times*, Wiesbaden, 2004.

Gutas, Dimitri, *Greek Thought, Arabic Culture: The Graeco-Arabic Translation Movement in Baghdad and Early Abbasid Society*, New York, 1998.

Hallaq, Wael, "Caliphs, Jurists, and Saljuqs in the Political Thought of al-Juwayni," *The Muslim World* 74 (1984), 26–41.

Hambly, Gavin, "From Baghdad to Bukhara, from Ghazna to Delhi: The khilʻa Ceremony in the Transmission of Kingly Pomp and Circumstance," in Gordon, ed., *Robes and Honor*, 193–224.

Hanne, Eric, *Putting the Caliph in His Place: Power, Authority, and the Late Abbasid Caliphate*, Madison, NJ, 2007.

   "Women, Power, and the Eleventh and Twelfth Century Abbasid Court," *Hawwa: Journal of Women of the Middle East and the Islamic World* 3 (2005), 80–110.

Hawting, G. R., *The First Dynasty of Islam: The Umayyad Caliphate, AD 661–750*, Carbondale, IL, 1986.

Heck, Paul, *The Construction of Knowledge in Islamic Civilization: Qudama b. Jaʻfar and his Kitab al-Kharaj wa Sinaʻat al-Kitaba*, Leiden, 2002.

Heidemann, Stefan, "Numismatics," in *NCHI*, vol. 1, 648–663.

Hillenbrand, Carole, *The Crusades: Islamic Perspectives*, Edinburgh, 2000.

   "Nizam al-Mulk: A Maverick Vizier?" in *The Age of the Seljuqs*, ed. Edmund Herzig and Sarah Stewart, London, 2015, 24–35.

Hoag, John, *Islamic Architecture*, New York, 1975.

Hodges, Richard and David Whitehouse, *Mohammed, Charlemagne, and the Origins of Europe: Archaeology and the Pirenne Thesis*, Ithaca, 1983.

Holt, P. M., "Some Observations on the Abbasid Caliphate in Cairo," *Bulletin of the School of Oriental and African Studies* 47 (1984), 501–507.

Horovitz, Josef, "The Origins of the Arabian Nights," *Islamic Culture* 1 (1927), 36–57.

Hoyland, Robert, *Seeing Islam as Others Saw it*, Princeton, 1997.

Humphreys, R. Stephen, *Islamic History: A Framework for Inquiry*, Princeton, 1991.

   From Saladin to the Mongols: The Ayyubids of Damascus, 1193–1260, Albany, 1977.

Huxley, Julian, *From an Antique Land*, London, 1954.

Imber, Colin, *The Ottoman Empire, 1300–1650*, New York, 2009.

Imhof, Agnes, "Traditio vel Aemulatio? The Singing Contest of Samarra, Expression of a Medieval Culture of Competition," *Der Islam* 90 (2013), 1–20.

İnalcik, Halil, *The Ottoman Empire: The Classical Age 1300–1600*, London, 1973.

Jackson, Peter, *The Delhi Sultanate*, Cambridge, 1999.

The Mongols and the Islamic World, New Haven, 2017.

"Muslim India: The Delhi Sultanate," in *NCHI*, vol. 3, 100–127.

Jacobs, Martin, *Reorienting the East: Jewish Travelers to the Medieval Muslim World*, Philadelphia, 2014.

Jenkins, Romilly, *Byzantium: The Imperial Centuries, AD 610–1071*, London, 1966.

Jiwa, Shainool, "The Baghdad Manifesto (402/1011): A Re-Examination of Fatimid–Abbasid Rivalry," in *The Fatimid Caliphate: Diversity of Traditions*, ed. Farhad Daftary and Shainool Jiwa, London, 2018, 22–79.

Jokisch, Benjamin, *Islamic Imperial Law: Harun-al-Rashid's Codification Project*, Berlin, 2007.

Kennedy, Hugh, *The Armies of the Caliphs*, London, 2001.

"The Decline and Fall of the First Muslim Empire," *Der Islam* 81 (2004), 3–30.

The Early Abbasid Caliphate: A Political History, London, 1981.

The Great Arab Conquests, New York, 2007.

"The Reign of al-Muqtadir (295–320/908–932): A History," in van Berkel et al., eds., *Crisis and Continuity at the Abbasid Court*, 11–47.

When Baghdad Ruled the Muslim World, Cambridge, MA, 2005; also published as *The Court of the Caliphs: The Rise and Fall of Islam's Greatest Dynasty*, London, 2004.

Kersten, Carool, ed., *The Caliphate and Islamic Statehood: Formation, Fragmentation and Modern Interpretation*, 3 vols., Berlin, 2015.

Keshani, Hussein, "The Abbasid Palace of Theophilus: Byzantine Taste for the Arts of Islam," *al-Masaq* 16 (2004), 76–91.

Khazanov, Anatoly and André Wink, eds., *Nomads in the Sedentary World*, Richmond, 2000.

Kilpatrick, Hilary, "Monasteries through Muslim Eyes: The Diyarat Books," in *Christians at the Heart of Islamic Rule: Church Life and Scholarship in Abbasid Iraq*, ed. David Thomas, Leiden, 2003, 19–38.

Kimber, Richard A., "The Early Abbasid Vizierate," *Journal of Semitic Studies* 37 (1992), 65–85.

King, Anya H., *Scent from the Garden of Paradise: Musk and the Medieval Islamic World*, Leiden, 2017.

Klat, Michel G., *Catalogue of the Post-Reform Dirhams: The Umayyad Dynasty*, London, 2002.

Kohlberg, Etan, *A Medieval Muslim Scholar at Work: Ibn Tawus and His Library*, Leiden, 1992.

König, Daniel G., *Arabic-Islamic Views of the Latin West: Tracing the Emergence of Medieval Europe*, Oxford, 2015.

Kraemer, Joel, *Humanism in the Renaissance of Islam: The Cultural Revival during the Buyid Period*, Leiden, 1992.

Krahl, Regina, John Guy, J. Keith Wilson, and Julian Raby, eds., *Shipwrecked: Tang Treasures and Monsoon Winds*, Washington, DC, 2010.

Kritzeck, James, "Ibn-al-Tiqtaqa and the Fall of Baghdad," in *The World of Islam: Studies in Honor of Philip Hitti*, ed. James Kritzeck and R. Bayly Winder, Princeton, 1959, 159–184.

Lane, George, *The Mongols*, London, 2018.

Lange, Christian and Songül Mecit, eds., *The Seljuqs: Politics, Society and Culture*, Edinburgh, 2011.

Lassner, Jacob, "The ʿAbbasid Dawla: An Essay on the Concept of Revolution in Early Islam," in *Tradition and Innovation in Late Antiquity*, ed. F. M. Clover and R. S. Humphreys, Madison, WI, 1989, 247–270.

 Islamic Revolution and Historical Memory, New Haven, 1986.

 The Shaping of Abbasid Rule, Princeton, 1980.

 The Topography of Baghdad in the Early Middle Ages, Detroit, 1970.

Latham, J. D., "Ibn al-Muqaffaʿ and Early Abbasid Prose," in Ashtiany et al., eds., *The Cambridge History of Arabic Literature*, vol. 2, 48–77.

Le Strange, Guy, *Palestine under the Moslems: A Description of Syria and the Holy Land from AD 650 to 1500*, London, 1890.

Levine, Neil, *The Urbanism of Frank Lloyd Wright*, Princeton, 2016.

Lewis, Bernard, "Egypt and Syria," in *The Cambridge History of Islam*, vol. 2B, 175–230.

 "Regnal Titles of the first Abbasid Caliphs," in *Dr. Zakir Husain Presentation Volume*, New Delhi, 1968, 13–22.

Liu, Xinru, *Silk and Religion: An Exploration of Material Life and the Thought of People, AD 600–1200*, Oxford, 1996.

 The Silk Road in World History, Oxford, 2010.

Lombard, Maurice, *The Golden Age of Islam*, trans. Joan Spencer, New York, 1975; repr. with introd. by Jane Hathaway, Princeton, 2004.

Lowenthal, David, *The Past Is a Foreign Country, Revisited*, Cambridge, 2015.

Lukitz, Liora, *A Quest in the Middle East: Gertrude Bell and the Making of Modern Iraq*, London, 2006.

Lyons, Jonathan, *The House of Wisdom: How the Arabs Transformed Western Civilization*, London, 2009.

Mackensen, Ruth, "Four Great Libraries of Medieval Baghdad," *Library Quarterly* 2 (1932), 279–299.

Madelung, Wilferd, "The Minor Dynasties of Northern Iran," in *CHIran*, vol. 4, 198–249.

"The Origins of the Controversy Concerning the Creation of the Koran," repr. in *Religious Schools and Sects in Medieval Islam*, London, 1985.

Makdisi, George, *Ibn 'Aqil: Religion and Culture in Classical Islam*, Edinburgh, 1997.

The Rise of the Colleges: Institutions of Learning in Islam and the West, Edinburgh, 1981.

Man, John, *The Mongols: Genghis Khan, His Heirs and the Founding of Modern China*, London, 2014.

Marefat, Mina, "Wright's Baghdad: Ziggurats and Green Visions," *DC Papers*, Barcelona, 2008.

Margoliouth, D. S., "The Caliphate Historically Considered," *The Moslem World* 11 (1921), 332–343.

Marsham, Andrew, *Rituals of Islamic Monarchy: Accession and Succession in the First Muslim Empire*, Edinburgh, 2009.

Ma'ruf, Naji, *Tarikh 'Ulama al-Mustansiriyya*, 2 vols., Baghdad, 1965.

Mason, Herbert, *Two Statesmen of Medieval Islam: Ibn Hubayrah (499–560 AH/1105–1165 AD) and the Caliph al-Nasir (553–622 AH/1158–1225 AD)*, The Hague/Paris, 1972.

Masselos, Jim, ed., *The Great Empires of Asia*, London, 2010.

May, Timothy, *The Mongol Conquests in World History*, London, 2012.

The Mongol Empire, Edinburgh, 2018.

McClary, Richard, *Architecture of the Rum Seljuqs*, Edinburgh, 2017.

McCormick, Michael, *Charlemagne's Survey of the Holy Land*, Washington, DC, 2011.

McNeil, William H., et al., eds., *The Islamic World*, Chicago, 1983.

Mecit, Songül, "Kingship and Ideology under the Rum Seljuqs," in *The Seljuqs: Politics, Society and Culture*, ed. Christian Lange and Songül Mecit, Edinburgh, 2011, 63–78.

Melchert, Christopher, "Religious Policies of the Caliphs from al-Mutawakkil to al-Muqtadir, AH 232–295/AD 847–908," *Islamic Law and Society* 3 (1996), 316–342.

Meserve, Margaret, *Empires of Islam in Renaissance Historical Thought*, Cambridge, MA, 2008.

Mez, Adam, *The Renaissance of Islam*, trans. Salahuddin Khuda Bukhsh and D. S. Margoliouth, London, 1937.

Miah, Shamsuddin, *The Reign of al-Mutawakkil*, Dacca, 1969.

Micheau, Francoise, "Baghdad in the Abbasid Era: A Cosmopolitan and Multi-Confessional Capital," in *The City in the Islamic World*, ed. Renata Holod et al., 2 vols., Leiden: Brill, 2008, vol. 1, 219–245.

Morgan, David, *The Mongols*, London, 2007 [1986].

Morony, Michael, *Iraq after the Muslim Conquest*, Princeton, 1984.

Muslu, Cihan Yüksel, *The Ottomans and the Mamluks: Imperial Diplomacy and Warfare in the Islamic World*, London, 2014.

Nabhan, Gary, *Cumin, Camels, and Caravans: A Spice Odyssey*, Berkeley, 2014.

Nasir, Sari, *The Arabs and the English*, London, 1976.

Nawas, John Abdallah, "A Reexamination of Three Current Explanations for al-Ma'mun's Introduction of the Mihna," *International Journal of Middle East Studies* 26 (1994), 615–629.

  al-Ma'mun, the Inquisition, and the Quest for Caliphal Authority, Atlanta, 2015.

Necipoğlu, Gülru, *The Topkapi Scroll: Geometry and Ornament in Islamic Architecture*, Santa Monica, 1995.

Nicholson, R. A., *A Literary History of the Arabs*, London, 1966.

Nissen, Hans and Peter Heine, *From Mesopotamia to Iraq*, Chicago, 2009.

Noonan, T. S., "Why Dirhams First Reached Russia: The Role of Arab–Khazar Relations in the Development of the Earliest Islamic Trade with Eastern Europe," *Archivum Eurasiae Medii Aevi* 4 (1984), 151–282.

Northedge, Alastair, *The Historical Topography of Samarra*, London, 2005.

Ohlander, Erik, *Sufism in an Age of Transition: 'Umar al-Suhrawardi and the Beginnings of Islamic Mystical Brotherhoods*, Leiden, 2008.

O'Leary, De Lacy, *Arabic Thought and Its Place in History*, New York, 1939.

Omar, Farouq, *The Abbasid Caliphate, 132/750–170/786*, Baghdad, 1969.

Osti, Letizia, "Abbasid Intrigues: Competing for Influence at the Caliph's Court," *al-Masaq* 20 (2008), 5–15.

Pancaroğlu, Oya, *Perpetual Glory: Medieval Islamic Ceramics from the Harvey B. Plotnick Collection*, Chicago and New Haven, 2007.

Patton, Douglas, *Badr al-Din Lu'lu', Atabeg of Mosul, 1211–1259*, Seattle, 1991.

Paul, Nicholas L., *To Follow in Their Footsteps: The Crusades and Family Memory in the High Middle Ages*, Ithaca, 2012.

Peacock, A. C .S., *The Great Seljuk Empire*, Edinburgh, 2015.

Peacock, A. C. S. and Sara Nur Yildiz, eds., *The Seljuks of Anatolia: Court and Society in the Medieval Middle East*, London, 2013.

Pellat, Charles, *The Life and Works of al-Jahiz: Translation of Selected Texts*, trans. D. M. Hawke, London, 1969.

Peters, Edward, *The First Crusade*, Philadelphia, 1970.

Petry, Carl F., "The Military Institution and Innovation in the Late Mamluk Period," in Petry, ed., *The Cambridge History of Egypt*, vol. 1, 462–489.

Picard, Christophe, *The Sea of the Caliphs: The Mediterranean in the Medieval Islamic World*, trans. Nicholas Elliott, Cambridge, MA, 2018.

Pinto, Olga, "The Libraries of the Arabs during the Time of the Abbassides," *Islamic Culture* 3 (1929), 210–243.

Qamar-ul Huda, "The Prince of Diplomacy: Shaykh Umar al-Suhrawardi's Revolution for Sufism, Futuwwa Groups and Politics under the Caliph al-Nasir," *Journal of the History of Sufism* 3 (2001), 257–278.

Al-Rasheed, Madawi, Carool Kersten, and Marat Shterin, eds., *Demystifying the Caliphate: Historical Memory and Contemporary Contexts*, New York, 2013.

Ricci, Alessandra, "The Road from Baghdad to Byzantium and the Case of the Bryas Palace in Istanbul," in *Byzantium in the Ninth Century: Dead or Alive?* ed. Leslie Brubaker, Ashgate, 1995, 131–149.

al-Rifa'i, Ahmad, *'Asr al-Ma'mun*, 3 vols., Cairo, 1927.

Robertson, John, *Iraq: A History*, London, 2015.

Robinson, Chase, *A Medieval Islamic City Reconsidered: An Interdisciplinary Approach to Samarra*, Oxford, 2001.

Rosen-Ayalon, Miriam, *Islamic Art and Archaeology in Palestine*, Walnut Creek, CA, 2006.

Rossabi, Morris, *Khubilai Khan*, Berkeley, 1988.
  The Mongols and Global History: A Norton Documents Reader, New York, 2011.

Roxburgh, David, *Writing the Word of God: Calligraphy and the Qur'an*, New Haven, 2007.

Ruggles, D. Fairchild, "The Mirador in Abbasid and Hispano-Umayyad Garden Typology," *Muqarnas* 7 (1990), 73–82.

Runciman, Steven, "Baghdad and Constantinople," *Sumer* 12 (1956), 43–50.
  "Charlemagne and Palestine," *English Historical Review* 50 (1935), 606–619.

Rustow, Marina, *The Lost Archive: Traces of a Caliphate in a Cairo Synagogue*, Princeton, 2020.

Satia, Priya, *Spies in Arabia: The Great War and the Cultural Foundations of Britain's Covert Empire in the Middle East*, Oxford, 2008.

Sawa, George, *Music Performance Practice in the Early Abbasid Era, 132–320 AH/750–932 AD*, Toronto, 1989.

Schafer, Edward, *The Golden Peaches of Samarkand*, Berkeley, 1963.

Scharfe, Patrick, "Portrayals of the Later Abbasid Caliphate: A Reappraisal of the Buyid-Era Caliphs in Arabic Chronicles, 334/945–447/1055," *Journal of Abbasid Studies* 1 (2014), 108–142.

Seymour, Michael, *Babylon: Legend, History and the Ancient City*, London, 2013.

Shaban, M. A., *The Abbasid Revolution*, Cambridge, 1970.
  Islamic History: A New Interpretation, 2 vols., Cambridge, 1971–1976.

Sharon, Moshe, *Black Banners from the East*, Jerusalem, 1983.

Shepard, Jonathan, "Equilibrium to Expansion, 886–1025," in *The Cambridge History of the Byzantine Empire c. 500–1492*, ed. Jonathan Shepard, Cambridge, 2008, 493–536.

Smith, Byron Porter, *Islam in English Literature*, London, 1967.

Sourdel, Dominique, *Le Vizirat 'abbasside de 740 a 936*, 2 vols., Damascus, 1959–1960.

Southern, R. W., *Western Views of Islam in the Middle Ages*, Cambridge, MA, 1962.

Spellberg, Denise, *Politics, Gender, and the Islamic Past: The Legacy of 'Aisha bint Abi Bakr*, New York, 1994.

Springborg, Patricia, *Western Republicanism and the Oriental Prince*, Austin, 1992.

Stroumsa, Sarah, "On Jewish Intellectuals who Converted in the Early Middle Ages," in Frank, ed., *The Jews of Medieval Islam*, 185–189. *Maimonides in His World*, Princeton, 2009.

Sypeck, Jeff, *Becoming Charlemagne: Europe, Baghdad, and the Empires of AD 800*, New York, 2006.

Sykes, Mark, *The Caliphs' Last Heritage*, London, 1915.

Tabbaa, Yasser, *The Transformation of Islamic Art During the Sunni Revival*, London, 2001.

Tibawi, A. L., "Origin and Character of the Madrasa," *Bulletin of the School of Oriental and African Studies* 25 (1962), 225–238.

Townsend, John, *Proconsul to the Middle East: Sir Percy Cox and the End of Empire*, London, 2010.

Treadgold, Warren, *A History of the Byzantine State and Society*, Stanford, 1997.

Turan, Osman, "The Ideal of World Domination among the Medieval Turks," *Studia Islamica* 4 (1960), 77–90.

Turner, John P., "al-Afshin: Heretic, Rebel or Rival," in *Abbasid Studies II: Occasional Papers of the School of Abbasid Studies, Leuven, 28 June–1 July 2004*, ed. John Nawas, Leuven, 2010, 119–142.

Inquisition in Early Islam: The Competition for Political and Religious Authority in the Abbasid Empire, London, 2013.

van Berkel, Maaike, "The Bureaucracy," in van Berkel et al., eds., *Crisis and Continuity at the Abbasid Court*, 87–109.

"The Young Caliph and His Wicked Advisors: Women and Power Politics under Caliph al-Muqtadir," *al-Masaq* 19 (2007), 3–15.

van Berkel, Maaike, Nadia El Cheikh, Hugh Kennedy, and Letizia Osti, eds., *Crisis and Continuity at the Abbasid Court: Formal and Informal Politics in the Caliphate of al-Muqtadir (295–320/908–932)*, Leiden, 2013.

van Bladel, Kevin, *The Arabic Hermes: From Pagan Sage to Prophet of Science*, Oxford, 2009.

Vasiliev, A. A., *A History of the Byzantine Empire*, 2 vols., Madison, 1952.
von Grunebaum, Gustave, *Classical Islam: A History, 600 AD–1258 AD*, New York, 1970.
   Islam: Essays in the Nature and Growth of a Cultural Tradition, Chicago, 1955.
Waines, David, "The Third Century Internal Crisis of the Abbasids," *Journal of the Economic and Social History of the Orient* 20 (1977), 282–306.
Walmsley, Alan, *Early Islamic Syria: An Archaeological Assessment*, London, 2007.
Wasserstrom, Steven, *Between Muslim and Jew*, Princeton, 1995.
Watson, Andrew M., *Agricultural Innovation in the Early Islamic World*, Cambridge, 1983.
   "Back to Gold – and Silver," *Economic History Review* 20 (1967), 1–34.
Weinberg, Steven, *To Explain the World: The Discovery of Modern Science*, New York, 2015.
Wellhausen, Julius, *The Arab Kingdom and Its Fall*, trans. M. G. Weir, Calcutta, 1927.
Wendell, C., "Baghdad: *Imago Mundi* and Other Foundation-Lore," *International Journal of Middle East Studies* 2 (1971), 99–128.
Wheatley, Paul, *The Places Where Men Pray Together: Cities in the Islamic Lands, Seventh to Tenth Centuries*, Chicago, 2000.
Whittow, Mark, *The Making of Byzantium*, Berkeley, 1996.
Wickham, Chris, *The Inheritance of Rome*, New York, 2009.
Wiet, Gaston, *Baghdad: Metropolis of the Abbasid Caliphate*, trans. Seymour Feiler, Norman, OK, 1971.
Wilford, John Noble, "In Medieval Architecture Signs of Advanced Math," *New York Times*, 27 February 2007.
Wink, André, "The Early Expansion of Islam in India," in *NCHI*, vol. 3, 78–99.
Winter, Michael, "The Ottoman Occupation," in Petry, ed., *The Cambridge History of Egypt*, vol. 1, 490–516.
Wolfson, H. A., *Repercussions of the Kalam in Jewish Philosophy*, Cambridge, MA, 1979.
Wood, Philip, "Christians in the Middle East, 600–1000: Conquest, Competition and Conversion," in *Islam and Christianity in Medieval Anatolia*, ed. A. C. S. Peacock et al., Farnham, 2015, 23–50.
Yavari, Neguin, *The Future of Iran's Past: Nizam al-Mulk Remembered*, Oxford, 2018.
Yildiz, Sara Nur and Hasim Sahin, "In the Proximity of Sultans: Majd al-Din Ishaq, Ibn 'Arabi and the Seljuk Court," in Peacock and Yildiz, eds., *The Seljuks of Anatolia*, 173–205.

Yücesoy, Hayrettin, *Messianic Beliefs and Imperial Politics in Medieval Islam: The Abbasid Caliphate in the Early Ninth Century*, Columbia, SC, 2009.

Zakeri, Mohsen, "From Futuwwa to Mystic Political Thought: The Caliph al-Nasir li-Din Allah and Abu Hafs al-Suhrawardi's Theory of Government," in *Islamic Alternatives: Non-Mainstream Religion in Persianate Societies*, ed. Shahrokh Raei, Berlin, 2017, 29–54.

Zaman, Muhammad Qasim, *Religion and Politics under the Early Abbasids*, Leiden, 1997.

Zaouli, Lilia, *Medieval Cuisine of the Islamic World*, trans. M. B. De Bevoise, Berkeley, 2007.

Index

.

Printed in Great Britain
by Amazon

42555588R00205